The Grill Bible • Traeger Grill & Smoker Cookbook

The Guide to Master Your Wood Pellet Grill With 500 Recipes for Beginners and Advanced Pitmasters

PETER DEVON

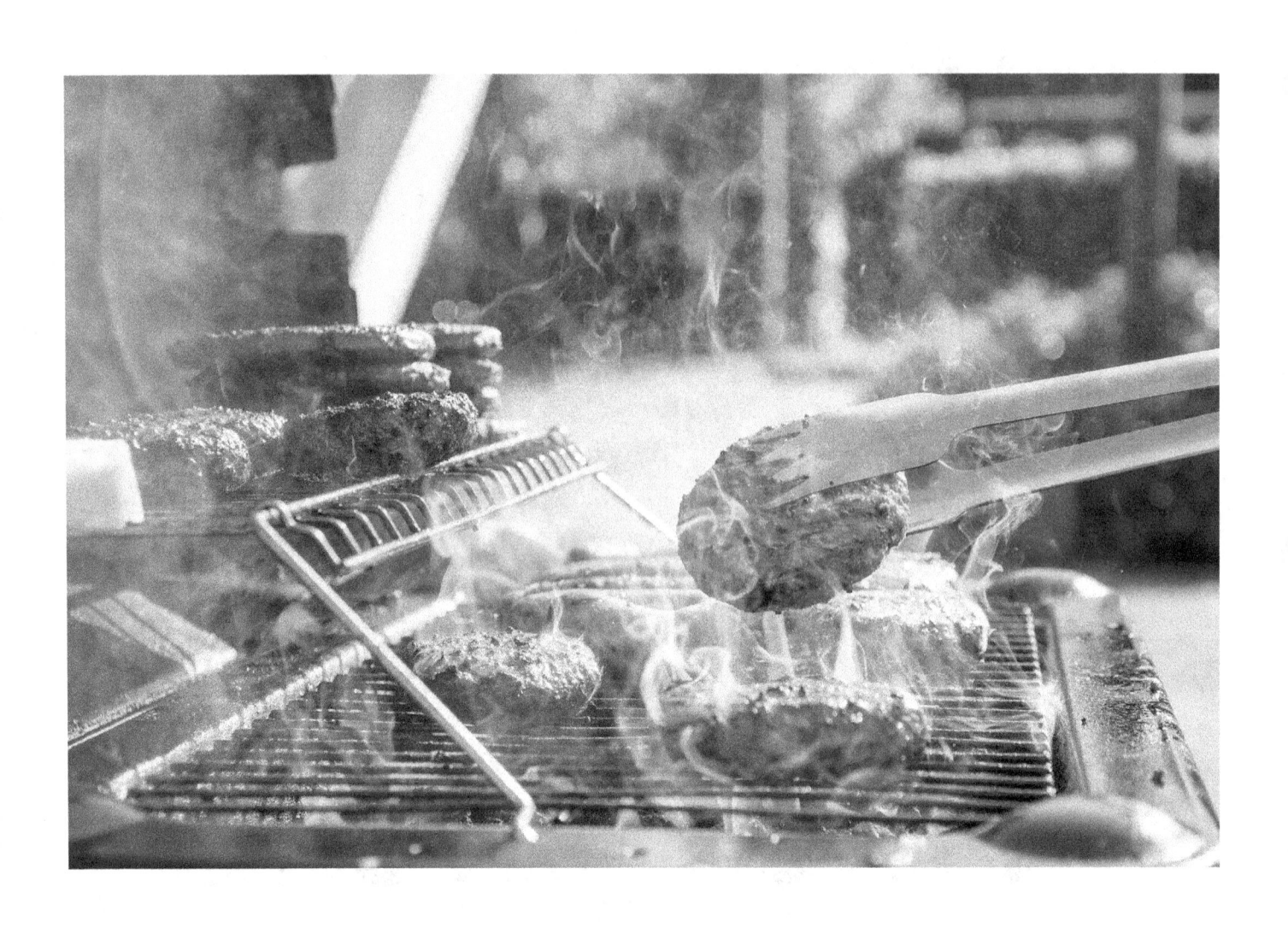

Contents

Wood Pellet Smoker and Grill Cookbook 20
INTRODUCTION 21
1.2 Why a Wood Pellet Smoker-Grill? 21
1.3 Temperature Control 21
1.4 History of Wood Pellet Smoker-Grills 22
CHAPTER 2: APPETIZERS AND SIDES 23
2.1 Atomic Buffalo Turds 23
2.2 Smashed Potato Casserole 24
2.3 Bacon-Wrapped Asparagus 24
2.4 Brisket Baked Beans 25
2.5 Garlic Parmesan Wedges 25
2.6 Roasted Vegetables 26
2.7 Twice-Baked Spaghetti Squash 27
2.8 Applewood-Smoked Cheese 27
2.9 Hickory-Smoked Moink Ball Skewers 27
2.10 Traeger Smoked Jalapeno Poppers 28
2.11 Smokey Meatball Appetizer 28
2.12 Cold Smoked Cheese Easy Brie Appetizer 29
2.13 Smoked Tomatoes on The Traeger Grill 29
2.14 Smoked Olives 30
2.15 Classic Banana Bread 30
2.16 Spaghetti Squash with Brown Butter and Parmesan 31
2.17 Double Smoked Ham on Pellet Grill 31
2.18 Grilled Peach Salsa 32
2.19 Pizza Bites 33
2.20 Spicy Shrimp Skewers 33
2.21 Traeger Jerk Shrimp 34
2.22 Hellfire Chicken Wings 34
2.23 Grilled Bison Sliders 35
2.24 Smoked Jalapeño Poppers 35

2.25 Easy Garlic Cheese Bombs 35

2.26 Traeger Baked Corn Dog Bites..36

2.27 Baked Heirloom Tomato Tart 37

2.28 Grilled Piña Colada 37

2.29 BBQ Chicken Nachos 37

2.30 Chinese BBQ Pork 38

2.31 Smoked Pickled Green Beans 39

2.32 Seared Lemon Garlic Scallops 39

2.33 Baked Asparagus Pancetta Cheese Tart 40

2.34 Smoked Deviled Eggs 40

2.35 Baked Soft Pretzel with Beer Cheese Sauce 41

2.36 Bacon Grilled Cheese Sandwich 42

2.37 Stuffed Avocados..43

2.38 Braised Backstrap Shredded Tacos 43

CHAPTER 3: BEEF RECIPES..44

3.1 Blackened Saskatchewan Tomahawk Steak 44

3.2 Traeger BBQ Brisket..44

3.3 Garlic, Lemon, And Goat Cheese Mashed Potatoes 44

3.4 Traeger Prime Rib Roast...45

3.5 Italian Beef Sandwich..45

3.6 Thai Beef Skewers 46

3.7 BBQ CHILI BURGER 46

3.8 Traeger Filet Mignon...47

3.9 Whiskey Bourbon BBQ Cheeseburger 47

3.10 Steak Taco Salad 48

3.11 Cowboy Cut Steak 49

3.12 Grilled Butter Basted Porterhouse Steak 49

3.13 Tin Foil Dinner 49

3.14 Roasted Hatch Chile Burger with Smoked Cheese Sauce...50

3.15 Grilled Tomahawk Steak 50

3.16 Smoked Chili Rib Eye Steaks 51

3.17 Smoked Bourbon Jerky 52

3.18 Slow Roasted Shawarma 52

3.19 Reverse Seared Rib Eye Caps 53

3.20 BBQ Beef Short Ribs 53

3.21 Grilled T-Bone Steaks with Bloody Mary Steak Sauce 53

3.22 Grilled Thai Beef Salad 54

3.23 Grilled Ribeye with Green Butter 54

3.24 Smoked Peppered Beef Tenderloin 55

3.25 BBQ Sweet Pepper Meatloaf 55

3.26 Traeger Pot Roast Sandwich 56

3.27 Grilled Steak Salad 57

3.28 Smoked Corned Beef & Cabbage 57

3.29 Traeger French Dip Sandwich 58

3.30 3-2-1 BBQ Beef Cheek 58

3.31 Grilled Wagyu Burgers 59

3.32 Braised Italian Meatballs 60

3.33 Grilled Piranha 60

3.34 Reverse Seared Porterhouse Steak 61

3.35 Reverse Seared Filet Mignon with Red Wine Reduction 61

3.36 Grilled Flank Steak with Peperomia 62

3.37 Grilled Cheesesteak Sandwich 63

3.38 Reverse Seared Ny Strip Steak 63

3.39 Traeger Ny Strip Steak 64

3.40 Grilled Peppercorn Steaks with Mushroom Cream Sauce 64

3.41 BBQ Brisket Grilled Chees 65

3.42 Smoked Pastrami Sandwich 65

3.43 Ultimate Loaded Nachos 66

3.44 Grilled London Broil with Blue Cheese Butter 67

3.45 Smoked Chili Con Queso 67

3.46 Smoked Italian Meatballs 68

3.47 Smoked Brisket Pot Pie 68

CHAPTER 4: LAMP RECIPES 70

4.1 Whole Rack of Lamb 70

4.2 Slow Roasted Shawarma 70

4.3 Roasted Leg of Lamb 71

4.4 Grilled Lamb Chops with Rosemary Sauce 71

4.5 Roasted Leg of Lamb with Red Wine Reduction 72

4.6 Grilled Lamb Burgers with Pickled Onions 73

4.7 Braised Lamb Shank 74

4.8 Greek Style Roast Leg of Lamb Recipe 74

4.9 Smoked Lamb Sausage 75

4.10 Lamb Lollipops with Mango Chutney 75

4.11 Pistachio Crusted Lamb with Vegetables 76

4.12 Smoked Lamb Leg with Salsa Verde 77

4.13 Armenian Style Lamb Shanks with Barley Risotto 78

4.14 BBQ Lamb Wraps 79

4.15 Slow Roasted BBQ Lamb Shoulder 79

4.16 Braised Lamb Shoulder Tacos 80

4.17 Ultimate Grilled Lamb Burger 81

4.18 Grilled Lamb Kabobs 81

4.19 Roasted Rack of Lamb 82

4.20 Grilled Butterflied Leg of Lamb 82

4.21 Braised Irish Lamb Stew 83

CHAPTER 5: CHICKEN RECIPES 84

5.1 Hellfire Chicken Wings 84

5.2 Buffalo Chicken Thighs 84

5.3 Beer Braised Chicken Tacos with Jalapeño Relish 85

5.4 Slow Roasted Shawarma 86

5.5 BBQ Chicken Nachos 86

5.6 Spicy BBQ Chicken 88

5.7 Traeger BBQ Half Chickens 88

5.8 Smoked Deviled Eggs 88

5.9 Pickled Brined Hot Chicken Sandwich 89

5.10 Baked Chicken Cordon Bleu 90

5.11 Roasted Teriyaki Wings 90

5.12 Smoked Korean Wings 91

5.13 Roasted Buffalo Wings 92

5.15 Roasted Tequila-Lime Wings 92

5.16 Smoked Chicken Tikka Masala 93

5.17 Roasted Rosemary Orange Chicken 94

5.18 Loaded Grilled Chicken Tacos 94

5.19 Grilled Thai Chicken Burgers with Papaya Slaw 96

5.20 Baked Buffalo Chicken Dip 96

5.21 Tomatillo Braised Chicken 97

5.22 Grilled Sticky Ginger Chicken Thighs 98

5.23 BBQ Game Day Chicken Wings and Thighs 98

5.24 Baked Garlic Parmesan Wings 98

5.25 Roasted Habanero Wings 99

5.26 Smoked Chicken Tikka Drumsticks 100

5.27 Lemon Rosemary Beer Can Chicken 100

5.28 Ultimate Traeger Thanksgiving Sandwich 101

5.29 Baked Thanksgiving Shepherd's Pie 101

5.30 Roasted Cornish Game Stuffed Hens 102

5.31 Baked Chicken Pot Pie 103

5.32 Grilled Chicken Fajitas 103

5.33 Smoked Chicken with Chimichurri 105

5.34 Grilled Sriracha Wings 105

5.35 Whole Smoked Chicken 106

5.36 Grilled Honey Garlic Wings 106

5.38 Competition BBQ Chicken Thighs 107

5.39 Roasted Sweet Thai Chili Wings 107

5.40 BBQ Chicken Thighs 108

5.41 Smoked Chicken Leg & Thigh Quarters 108

5.42 Smoked Wings 109

5.43 Chicken Parmesan Sliders with Pesto Mayonnaise 109

5.44 Chicken Picadillo Empanadas 110

5.45 Chicken Salad 110

CHAPTER 6: TURKEY RECIPES 112

6.1 Herb Roasted Turkey 112

6.2 Smoked Bourbon & Orange Brined Turkey 112

6.3 Traeger Leftover Turkey Soup 113

6.4 Smoked Turkey 113

6.5 Smoked Turkey Legs 114

6.6 Traditional Thanksgiving Turkey 114

6.7 Turkey Jalapeno Meatballs 115

6.8 Wild Turkey Southwest Egg Rolls 115

6.9 Smoked Wild Turkey Breast 116

6.10 Grilled Wild Turkey Orange Cashew Salad 116

6.11 Baked Cornbread Turkey Tamale Pie 117

6.12 BBQ Pulled Turkey Sandwiches 118

6.13 Roasted Spatchcock Turkey 118

6.14 Spatchcocked Maple Brined Turkey 119

6.15 Homemade Turkey Gravy 120

6.16 Roasted Honey Bourbon Glazed Turkey 120

6.17 Roasted Autumn Brined Turkey Breast 121

6.18 Ultimate Smoked Turkey 121

6.19 Smoked Wild Turkey Jerky 123

6.20 BBQ Chicken Breasts 123

6.21 Beer-Brined Turkey 123

6.22 Cooking A Full Turkey on A Wood Pellet Grill & Smoker 124

CHAPTER 7: PORK RECIPES 125

7.1 Smoked Traeger Pulled Pork 125

7.2 Smoked Pig Shots Recipe 125

7.3 Grilled German Sausage with A Smoky Traeger Twist 126

7.4 Texas Style Smoked Pulled Pork 126

7.5 Spice Rubbed Pork Tenderloin 127

7.6 Apple Cider Braised Smoked BBQ Pulled Pork 127

7.7 Bourbon Brown Sugar Smoked Pork Loin 128

CHAPTER 8: SEAFOOD RECIPES 130

8.1 Spicy Shrimp Skewers 130

8.2 Baja-Style Fish Tacos 130

8.3 Traeger Jerk Shrimp 131

8.4 Traeger Smoked Mussels 131

8.5 Grilled Lobster Tails 132

8.6 Garlic Salmon 133

8.7 Grilled Penang Curry Salmon 133

8.8 Seared Lemon Garlic Scallops 134

8.9 Whole Grilled Red Snapper 134

8.10 Roasted Halibut in Parchment 135

8.11 Grilled Lobster with Lemon Garlic Butter Recipe 135

8.12 BBQ Oysters 136

8.13 Maple Glazed Salmon 136

8.14 Lemon Garlic Smoked Salmon Recipe 137

8.15 Easy and Flavorful Smoked Tilapia 137

CHAPTER 9: DESSERTS RECIPES ... 138
9.1 Strawberry Shortbread ... 138
9.2 Leave No Trace Chocolate-Chunk Oatmeal Cookies ... 138
9.3 Double Chocolate Chip Brownie Pie ... 140

CHAPTER 10: SPECIALTIES ... 141
10.1 Baked Wood-Fired Pizza ... 141
10.2 Braised Rabbit Stew ... 141
10.3 Grilled Duck Breasts ... 142
10.4 Smoked Dry Rubbed Baby Back Ribs ... 142

CHAPTER 11: TRICKS, TIPS, TOOLS & COOKING TIME ... 144
11.1 Tools ... 144
11.2 Cooking Tips & Tricks ... 144
    11.2.1 Quality Meat and Seasonings ... 144
    11.2.2 FTC ... 144
    11.2.3 USDA Minimum Internal Temperatures ... 144
    11.2.4 Indirect and Direct Grill Setup ... 144
    11.2.5 Recommended Wood Pellet Flavors ... 144
    11.2.6 Prepping for The Grill ... 144
    11.2.7 Cooking Times ... 145
    11.2.8 Preheating ... 145
    11.2.9 Thawing Food ... 145
    11.2.10 Internal Temperature ... 145

The Ultimate Traeger Grill Smoker Cookbook ... 146

Chapter 1: Introduction ... 148

Purchasing Guide for a Traeger Grill ... 148

Tips for Maintaining Your Traeger Grill ... 149

Clean Your Traeger Grill ... 150

Chapter 2: Beef & Lamb Recipes ... 151

Flank Steak with Tomato Sauce Marinated ... 151

Grilled Steak with Marinated Wine ... 151

Beef Shoulder Tenders Marinated Chimichurri Sauce ... 152

Traeger Grill Beef Balsamic Steak ... 152

Beef Strip Steak with Ground Pepper ... 153

Indian Pot Chuck Roast ... 153

Traeger Grill Meatball Kebabs ... 154

Easy Traeger Grill Veal Chops	155
Traeger Grill Beef Quesadillas	155
Lime Salty Marinated Garlic Steaks	156
Traeger Grill Beef with Pepper Coat, Herb and Garlic	156
Beef with Chili Garlic Sauce	157
Beef Crackers Burgers	157
Traeger Grill Thai Beef Kebabs with Soya Sauce	158
Pineapple Lamb Kebabs	159
Beef Loin Steak	160
Thyme Rib Steak	160
Red Wine Beef Kebabs	161
Pearl Continental Barbecued Steak	161
Indian Rib Eye Steak	162
Garlic-Traeger Grill Flank Steak	162
Garlic and Oregano Traeger Grill Strip Steak	163
Beef Steak with Capers, Olives, and Red Bell Peppers	163
Traeger Grill Chipotle Steak	164
Skirt Steak with Garlic	164
Traeger Grill Potatoes with Blue Cheese Sauce	165
Traeger Grilled Onions Steaks	166
Grilled Chuck Roast	166
Buffalo Burgers with Cheese	167
Grilled Big Beef Burger with Cheese	168
Barbecued Steaks with Parsley	168
Traeger Grilled Beef Tenderloin	168
Traeger Grilled Smoked Beef T-Bones	169
Traeger Grilled Prime Rib with Cream	169
Traeger Grilled Brisket	170
Grilled Lamb Burgers	170
Flank Steak with Crouton Salad	171
Traeger Grilled Barbecued Brisket	172
Smoked Beef Brisket with Apricot Barbecue Sauce	172
Grilled Beef Jerky with Cup Soy Sauce	173
Traeger Prime Mignons	174
Style Mustard Steak	174

London Asada Marinade Broil	175
Barbecue Bourbon Whiskey Steak	175
Traeger Grilled Beef Roast in Olive Oil	176
Beef Ribs in Barbecue Sauce	176
Santa Maria-Style Tri-Tip with Garlic	176
Chili-Glazed Garlic Meat	177
Traeger Chili Beef Short Ribs	177
White Vinegar Barbecued Ribs	178
Lamb Chops with Raisin Sauce	178
Traeger Grill Lamb with Ground Cinnamon	179
Better Burgers with Barbecue Sauce	180
Traeger Grill Lamb Chops with Minced Garlic	180
Lamb Kofta Kebabs with chopped Parsley	181
Butterflied Leg Mushroom Soy Sauce	181
Ground Black Pepper Lamb Kebabs	182
Herb Marinated Soy Sauce Lamb Chops	183
Grilled Asian Lamb Chops	183
Chopped Cilantro Moroccan Leg of Lamb	184
Traeger Grilled Lamb and Apricot Sosa ties	184
Garlic Minced Lamb Chops	185
Traeger Grilled Beef Tenderloin	185
Traeger Grilled Rack of Lamb	187
Greek Yogurt Lamb Burgers	187
Lemon Oil Sliced Over Arugula with Garlic	188
Chapter 3: Pork Recipes	189
Barbecued Pork Steaks with Worcestershire Sauce	189
Traeger Grilled Pork Chops with Minced Garlic	189
Traeger Grilled Pork Chops	189
Traeger Grilled Barbecued Pork Ribs	190
Southern Pulled Pork with Ground Cumin	191
Traeger Grilled Pork Tenderloin with Pineapple	191
Teriyaki Kebabs with Cherry Tomatoes	192
Grilled Back Barbecued Ribs	193
Maple Garlic Pork Tenderloin Ground Black Pepper	193
Maple Glazed Ribs Cider Vinegar	194

Rubbed Pork Chops with Bourbon 194

Traeger Grilled Pork Tenderloin 195

Traeger Grilled Chorizo Quesadillas 195

Smoked Grilled Pork Ribs 196

Grilled Pork Ribs with Dark Brown Sugar 197

Boneless Glazed Pork Chops 197

Ham Steaks with Fresh Lime 198

Leaf Parsley Baby Back Ribs 198

Indian Pork Satay with Lemongrass 199

Pork Tenderloin in Olive Oil 200

Pork Kebabs with marinated Mushrooms 200

Chili-Rubbed Pork with Salsa 201

Pork Tenderloin in Ground Pepper 201

Spicy Asian Rubbed Pork Chops 202

Traeger Grilled Tomatoes and Green Onions 202

Grilled Cider Vinegar Pork Chops 203

Parisian Traeger Grilled Pork Chops 203

Chorizo Burgers and Traeger Grilled Red Onions 204

Grilled Sausage Hoagies with Bell Pepper 205

Yellow Mustard Baby Back Ribs 206

Chapter 4: Poultry Recipes 207

Shish Tao Traeger Grilled Chicken 207

Traeger Grilled Pizza with Barbecued Chicken with Cheddar Cheese 207

Traeger Grilled Butter Chicken 208

Maple Barbecued Chicken with Hot Chili Sauce 209

Traeger Grilled Chicken with Sweet Red Chili 209

Cornish Lemon and Thyme Game Hens 209

Barbecue Mustard Grilled Chicken Breasts 210

Traeger Grilled Chicken Koftas 211

Thai Traeger Grilled Chicken with White Pepper 211

Garlic-Traeger Tomato Grilled Chicken 212

Catalan Cinnamon Chicken Quarters 213

Thai Grilled Chicken Satay with Soy Sauce 213

Spicy Plum Chutney Grilled Chicken Thighs 214

Chicken Tikka Skewers with Cherry Tomatoes 215

Sweet & Spicy Grilled Chicken	216
Mustard Chicken Drumsticks	216
Grilled Chicken Tikka Kebabs	217
Grilled Chicken & Chorizo Kebabs	217
Barbecued Grilled Chicken Tikka Burgers	218
Rotisserie Melted Butter Chicken	219
Traeger Grilled Chicken Breasts Tikka	219
Chicken Breasts Tikka with Mustard Paste	220
Chicken Breasts with Pesto	220
Grilled Chicken Breasts Tikka Lemon-Marinated	221
Boneless Grilled Garlic Chicken	221
Salted Rubbed Chicken Breasts	222
Olive Oil Chicken Tenders Basted	222
Traeger Grilled Herb Chicken Burgers	223
Grilled-Glazed Chicken Leg Piece	223
Lemon Barbecue Chicken Tikka	224
Grilled Chicken Thighs with Olive Oil	224
Grilled Hens with Lemon Slices	225
Chicken Thighs with Smashed Traeger Grilled Potatoes	225
Grilled Chicken with Blood Orange Oil	226
Honey Grilled Chicken Wings with Mustard	227
Lime Grilled Chicken Kebabs	227
Asian Turkey Grilled Tikka Burgers	228
Salted Grilled Chicken Wings with Jalapeno	228
Spicy Chicken Tacos with Garlic	229
Roasted Shawarma with Tomatoes	230
Chicken Grilled Mayonnaise Salad	230
BBQ Chicken Mexican Blend	231
Chili Bonnet Chicken	232
Traeger Grilled Thai Chicken Burgers	232
Mayonnaise Chicken Cheese Dip	233
Smokey Chicken with Garlic	233
Grilled Honey Wings with Blue Cheese	234
Grilled Chicken Tikka with Beer Marinated	234
Buffalo March Masala Chicken BBQ	235

Traeger Grilled Lowing sodium BBQ Chicken	235
Salted and Black Pepper BBQ Chicken Thighs	236
Olive Chicken Leg with Spices	236
Grilled Chicken Wings with Chili Barbecue Sauce	237
Chicken Arugula Leaves with Mayonnaise	237
Indian Sweet and Spicy Chicken Wings	237
Chicken Bouillon with Vegetable Oil	238
Chapter 5: Seafood Recipes	239
Marinated Lemon Grilled Barbecued Swordfish	239
Barbecued Salmon with Vegetable Oil	239
Traeger Grilled Squid with Soy Sauce	240
Traeger Grilled Fillets in Butter	241
Traeger Grilled Thai Red Packets	241
Barbecued Lemon Halibut Steaks with Soy Sauce	242
Traeger Grilled Salty Trout with Parsley	242
Barbecued Olive Oil Teriyaki Tuna Steaks	243
Grilled Tuna with Honey Glaze	243
Grilled Blackened Fish in Melted Butter	244
Marinated Halibut Steak in Grapefruit Juice	244
Traeger Grilled Sea Bass with Butter	245
Grilled Swordfish with Sesame Oil	245
Traeger Grilled Catfish in Asian Style	246
Barbecued Sea Bass with Lemon Juice	247
Traeger Grilled Salted Trout	247
Traeger Grilled Tandoori with Ground Cumin	248
Traeger Grilled Bass with Rice Wine	248
Lime & Basil Tilapia	249
Sea Bass Kebabs with Dried Oregano	250
Moroccan Traeger Grilled Fish Kebabs	250
Traeger Grilled Fish Cakes	251
Grilled Tarragon Fish with Canola Oil	251
Indian Style Trout with Olive Oil	252
Perch with Sage with Zucchini	253
Traeger Grilled Jamaican Jerk Catfish	253
Sweet & Sour Halibut with Cider Vinegar	254

Grilled Halibut & Red Pepper Kebabs	254
Fish Grilled Roll Ups with Worcestershire Sauce	255
Traeger Grilled Catfish with Lemon Juice	255
Asian Jerk Red Snapper with Soy Sauce	256
Traeger Grilled Fresh Sardines	256
Marinated with Plum Tomatoes Monkfish	257
Grilled Shrimp and Pineapple Skewers	258
Traeger Grilled Red Snapper	259
Charred Courgettis Skewered Swordfish	259
Mango Salsa Marinated Scallop Brochettes	260
Dijon Mustard Salmon Burgers	261
Grilled Ground Cumin Fish Kebabs	261
Grilled Salmon with Lemon Marinated	262
Grilled Salmon with Fresh Herbs	263
Traeger Grilled Snapper with Soy Sauce	263
Traeger Grilled Shark with Ketchup	264
Grilled Lacquered Salmon with Lemon Juice	265
Traeger Grilled Salmon with Herbs	265
Asian Mahi Grilled Marks	266
Salmon Wrapped with Fresh Thyme	266
Traeger Grilled Halibut with Oregano	267
Halibut Marinated with Red Wine	268
Black Pepper Salmon with Orange Juice	268
Crusted Halibut Chile-and-Peanut	269
Salted Halibut with Chipotle Sauce and Mayonnaise	270
Tuna with a Black Tapenade Sauce	270
Spicy Tuna Steaks with Cayenne Pepper	271
Swordfish with Traeger Grilled Peppers and Olives	271
Grilled Shrimp with Soft Tacos and Salsa	272
Grilled Salted Shrimp with Olive Oil	273
Traeger Grilled Sliced Calamari	273
Large Grilled Shrimp Skewers	273
Tangy Shrimp with Garlic and Paprika	274
Traeger Grilled Oysters	275
Thai Spiced Prawns	275

Garlic Traeger Grilled Shrimps	276
Traeger Grilled Oysters	276
Traeger Grilled Crab with Minced Cilantro	277
Sesame Scallops with Vegetable Oil	277
Margarita Shrimps with Olive Oil	278
Scallops with An Oregano Leaves	278
Grilled Scallops & Tomato Kebabs	279
Traeger Grilled Lobster with Butter	279
Traeger Grilled Prawns & Garlic Chili Sauce	280
Traeger Grilled New England Seafood	280
Honey Traeger Grilled Shrimps	281
Grilled Scallops Wrapped in Prosciutto	282
Shrimp & Scallop Kebabs	282
Black Pepper Ginger Shrimp	283
Traeger Grilled Crab Legs	284
Grilled Shrimp & Broccoli Florets	284
Barbecued Oysters Served with Rice Vinegar	285
Black Pepper Scallops, Orange & Cucumber Kebabs	285
Prawns with Pictou Virgin Olive Oil	286
Grilled Black & White Pepper Shrimps	287
Traeger Grilled Prawns	287
Traeger Grilled Rock Lobster	288
Grilled Bacon Wrapped Shrimps	289
Chapter 6: Vegetables Recipes	290
Salted Asparagus Spears	290
Grilled Corn in the Husk	290
Grilled Walla Walla Sweet Onions	290
Traeger Grilled Roma Tomatoes	291
Traeger Grilled of Zucchini	291
Grilled Cherry Tomato Skewers	292
Grilled Choy with Sesame Oil	292
Salted Grilled Eggplant with Herbs	293
Asian Grilled Eggplant with Mayonnaise	293
Traeger Grilled Acorn Squash	293
Traeger Grilled Ratatouille	294

Grilled Eggplant Stacks with Fresh Mozzarella	295
Potatoes Tossed with Extra-Virgin Olive Oil	296
Traeger Grilled Yukon Gold Potatoes	296
Traeger Grilled Potatoes with Blue Cheese	296
Traeger Grilled Polenta with Onion Wedges	297
Traeger Grilled Tomatoes and Green Onions	298
Lemon Couscous with Apricots	298
Grilled Orzo Salad with Kalamata Olives and Feta	299
Traeger Grilled Sweet Corn	299
Grilled Noodle Salad with Black Sesame Seeds	300
Traeger Grilled with Walnut Vinaigrette	300
Grilled Bruschetta in Olive Oil	301
Israeli Couscous with Zucchini and Parsley	301
Grilled Carrot Salad	302
Grilled Eastern Chickpea Salad	302
Chapter 7: Starters, Salads & Appetizers Recipes	303
Salted Jalapeno Poppers	303
Traeger Grilled Baguette with Herbs	303
Traeger Grilled Spicy Trout	303
Teriyaki Wings with Soy Sauce	304
Antipasto Crostini with Basil Leaves	304
Traeger Barbecue Sausage	305
Smoked Grilled Salmon with Green Herbs	305
Chicken Quesadillas Tortillas	306
Barbecued Chicken Breasts	306
Pepperoni-Provolone Bread with Dried Parsley	307
Traeger Grilled Corn Salsa	307
Grilled Honey Wings	308
Grilled Potato Salad with Sour Cream	309
Greek Salad with Olive Oil	309
Grilled Michi Orzo Salad	310
Traeger Grilled Radicchio Salad	310
Traeger Grilled Shrimp Cocktail	311
Traeger Grilled Pineapple	311
Traeger Grilled Peaches	312

Chapter 8: Pizza Recipes	313
Grilled Margherita Pizza	313
Italian Sausage & Rapini Pizza	313
Meat and Treat Pepperoni Pizza	314
Spanish Supreme Mushroom Pizza	314
Crave Special Pizza	315
Sausages Pepper Pizza	316
Cheddar Cheese Pizza	316
Basil Base Pesto Pizza	317
Grilled Tomato & Cabranes Pizza	317
Grilled Squash-Palooza Pizza with Fontina Cheese	318
Special Vegetable Grilled Pizza	318
Forty Olive & Pimiento Pizza	319
Grilled Mushroom Pizza	320
Grilled Veggie Pizza	320
Asparagus with Pizza	321
Lobster & Corn Pizza	322
Bacon Casino Pizza	322
Black Pepper Salmon Pizza	323
American Style Puttanesca Pizza	324
Double Treat Corn Pizza	324
Grilled Crabmeat Pizza	325
Traeger Grilled Pineapple and Onion Pizza	325
Shrimp Pizza with Tabasco sauce	326

© Copyright 2020 by Peter Devon - All rights reserved.

This content is provided with the sole purpose of providing relevant information on a specific topic for which every reasonable effort has been made to ensure that it is both accurate and reasonable. Nevertheless, by purchasing this content you consent to the fact that the author, as well as the publisher, are in no way experts on the topics contained herein, regardless of any claims as such that may be made within. As such, any suggestions or recommendations that are made within are done so purely for entertainment value. It is recommended that you always consult a professional prior to undertaking any of the advice or techniques discussed within.

This is a legally binding declaration that is considered both valid and fair by both the Committee of Publishers Association and the American Bar Association and should be considered as legally binding within the United States.

The reproduction, transmission, and duplication of any of the content found herein, including any specific or extended information will be done as an illegal act regardless of the end form the information ultimately takes. This includes copied versions of the work both physical, digital and audio unless express consent of the Publisher is provided beforehand. Any additional rights reserved.

Furthermore, the information that can be found within the pages described forthwith shall be considered both accurate and truthful when it comes to the recounting of facts. As such, any use, correct or incorrect, of the provided information will render the Publisher free of responsibility as to the actions taken outside of their direct purview. Regardless, there are zero scenarios where the original author or the Publisher can be deemed liable in any fashion for any damages or hardships that may result from any of the information discussed herein.

Additionally, the information in the following pages is intended only for informational purposes and should thus be thought of as universal. As befitting its nature, it is presented without assurance regarding its prolonged validity or interim quality. Trademarks that are mentioned are done without written consent and can in no way be considered an endorsement from the trademark holder

Wood Pellet Smoker and Grill Cookbook

200 Delicious Recipes to Master the Barbeque and Enjoy it with Friends and Family

PETER DEVON

INTRODUCTION

The clinical definition of a wood pellet smoker-grill is a barbecue pit that uses compressed hardwood sawdust like apple, cherry, hickory, maple, mesquite, oak, and other wood pellets to smoke, grill, roast, and bake. The wood pellet smoker grill provides you with flavor profiles and moisture that only hardwood cooking can achieve. Depending on the manufacturer and model, grill temperatures range from 150°F to well over 600°F on many models. The days when people say you can't sear and grill on a wood pellet smoker-grill are gone! Wood pellet smoker-grills provide succulence, convenience, and safety unmatched by charcoal or gas grills. The smoke profile is milder than other smokers you might be used to. Because of their design, they produce the versatility and benefits of a convection oven. Wood pellet smoker-grills are safe and simple to operate.

The basic components of a wood pellet smoker-grill are:

HOPPER—The hopper is where the wood pellets are stored. Ensure that you maintain an ample number of pellets depending on the length of the cook, the temperature of the cook, and the hopper capacity.

AUGER—The pellets are then fed through the auger, the feed mechanism that delivers the pellets to the firepot.

FIREPOT—This is where the wood pellets that heat the grill are ignited and burn. The large hole in the firepot is for the pellet tube, which houses the auger; the lower center hole below it is for the igniter rod, and the other holes are for the fan airflow. It's a good practice to empty or vacuum out the ashes after every few cooks in order to allow the igniter to work more efficiently.

IGNITER ELEMENT/ROD—This rod ignites the wood pellets in the firepot. With the firepot removed you can see the igniter rod and the pellet feed tube that the auger uses to deliver pellets to the firepot.

FAN—The fan is very important as it maintains a variable and/or constant flow of air, keeping the pellets

HEAT DEFLECTOR—The heat deflector is a specially designed plate that covers the firepot. Its purpose is to absorb the heat and spread it out evenly below the grease/drip pan, effectively turning your wood pellet smoker-grill into a wood-fired convection oven. burning in the firepot and resulting in convection cooking.

GREASE/DRIP PAN—The grease pan is used for indirect cooking, smoking, roasting, and baking. It routes the grease produced during cooking to the grease bucket. Scrape off any caked-on residue from cooks as required. If using foil (highly recommended), replace the foil every few cooks.

FLAME ZONE PAN—For direct grilling at high temperatures. Used in conjunction with searing grates and griddle accessories.

GREASE BUCKET—The grease bucket collects runoff grease and fat from cooking sessions. Grease accumulation depends on how much you choose to trim fat caps and excess fat from meat and poultry. Lining your grease bucket with foil helps with cleanups. I like to use an old coffee can to store my runoff grease. It's safe to dispose full coffee cans in your garbage.

1.2 Why a Wood Pellet Smoker-Grill?
When looking for your next outdoor cooking device for your barbecue needs, your best option on the market today is a wood pellet smoker-grill. You've used the rest, now use the best! No more buying a new grill every few seasons or needing more than one grill. Wood pellet smoker-grills, allow you to smoke, cook low and slow, roast, bake, and grill, and like propane grills, they preheat in 10 to 15 minutes. With its indirect heat design there are no flare-ups, and you'll never have any of the harsh smoke flavors sometimes generated by charcoal or straight wood fires. A wood pellet smoker-grill not only produces the best moist foods you'll ever experience, but it is by far one of the easiest to operate and maintain. Everything is automated. Merely ensure that your hopper is full of wood pellets and that your unit is plugged into a power source. The only movable parts in a wood pellet smoker-grill are the auger and fan. The tricky part to other types of smoker-grills has always been the necessary monitoring of the units to keep the temperatures steady. This is not necessary with wood pellet smoker-grills because they are designed to maintain temperatures within set guidelines.

1.3 Temperature Control
It's all about control. To quote Ron Popeil on his Ronco rotisserie, "Set it, and forget it!" As we learned earlier, the controller adjusts the rate of pellet flow and the fan to maintain your set-point temperature. For the most part, most manufacturers choose a third-party controller or design their own. Obviously, not all controllers are created equal. Some are just better than others and should be a strong consideration when selecting your wood pellet smoker-grill. Look for a controller that provides pinpoint heat control. Basically, there are three types of controllers: analog, digital, and PID. Analog controllers are the most basic unit. They only provide three positions, known as LMH for low, medium, and high smoke. These controllers are mostly found on entry-level units. They typically do not have an RTD or thermocouple temperature probe to provide a feedback loop. This is the least desirable controller, and I would not recommend a unit with one of these. The temperature on these units wildly fluctuates and is unable to correct itself for ambient temperatures. The auger on and off durations for low, medium, and high is the only control you have and is usually set by the grill manufacturer.

Digital controllers use an RTD temperature probe to provide a feedback loop. Most digital controllers have a 25-degree Fahrenheit increment setting. With the installation of an RTD temperature probe, some digital controllers are a direct replacement for LMH controllers. Similar to the thermostat in your home, once you reach your preset temperature; the controller runs the auger for a certain number of seconds and then shuts off for a certain number of seconds and goes into an idle mode until the temperature deviates a preset amount. At that time the cycle is repeated. Some digital controllers allow you to adjust the idle mode to compensate for ambient temperatures.

1.4 History of Wood Pellet Smoker-Grills
Today there is a multitude of wood pellet smoker-grill manufacturers providing a wide range of excellent barbecue pits. These units cover a broad spectrum, from entry level to sophisticated pits priced from $300 to over $2,500. Just a few decades ago, this was not the case. Wood pellet smoker-grills were first introduced in the 1990s by a small company in Oregon called Traeger Grills. Years ago, I remember watching Traeger commercials featuring Terry Bradshaw, and ogling Traeger grills at my local Ace Hardware store. Those commercials made it look so simply, and I can now attest to the fact that they were right! The industry only grew by leaps and bounds once Traeger's original patent expired. More and more people became exposed to the fabulous, mouth-watering food from a wood pellet smoker-grill, but as recently as 2008 only two companies manufactured wood pellet smoker-grills: Traeger and its rival MAK, also based in Oregon. Today there are more than 20 brands of excellent wood pellet smoker-grill manufacturers carried by a wide range of outlets from local barbecue stores, butcher shops, feed stores, hardware stores, big box stores, online outlets, and direct from the manufacturer.

CHAPTER 2: APPETIZERS AND SIDES

2.1 Atomic Buffalo Turds
Ingredients:

- 10 medium jalapeño peppers
- 8 ounces regular cream cheese at room temperature ¾ cup shredded Monterey Jack and cheddar cheese blend (optional) 1 teaspoon smoked paprika
- 1 teaspoon garlic powder
- ½ teaspoon cayenne pepper
- ½ teaspoon red pepper flakes (optional)
- 20 Little Smokies sausages
- 10 thinly sliced bacon strips, cut in half

Instructions:

- Put your food service gloves on, if using. Wash and slice the jalapeño peppers lengthwise. Using a spoon or paring knife, carefully remove the seeds and veins and discard them. Place the jalapeños on a vegetable grilling tray and set aside.
- In a small bowl, mix the cream cheese, shredded cheese, if using, paprika, garlic powder, cayenne pepper, and red pepper flakes, if using, until fully incorporated.
- Fill the hollowed jalapeño pepper halves with the cream cheese mixture. Wrap half a slice of thin bacon around each jalapeño pepper half.
- Use a toothpick to secure the bacon to the sausage, making sure not to pierce the pepper. Place the ABTs on a grilling tray or pan.
- Configure your wood pellet smoker-grill for indirect cooking and preheat to 250°F using hickory pellets or a blend.
- Smoke the jalapeño peppers at 250°F for approximately 1½ to 2 hours, until the bacon is cooked and crispy.

2.2 Smashed Potato Casserole
Ingredients:

- 8 to 10 bacon slices
- ¼ cup (½ stick) salted butter or bacon grease
- 1 small red onion, sliced thinly
- 1 small green bell pepper, sliced thinly
- 1 small red bell pepper, sliced thinly
- 1 small yellow bell pepper, sliced thinly
- 3 cups mashed potatoes
- ¾ cup sour cream
- 1½ teaspoons Texas Barbecue Rub (page 171) 3 cups shredded sharp cheddar cheese, divided
- 4 cups frozen hash brown potatoes

Instructions:

- Cook the bacon in a large skillet over medium heat until crisp, about 5 minutes on each side. Set the bacon aside.
- Transfer the rendered bacon grease to a glass container.
- In the same large skillet, over medium heat, warm the butter or bacon grease and sauté the red onion and bell peppers until al dente. Set aside.
- Spray a 9 × 11-inch casserole dish with nonstick cooking spray, and spread the mashed potatoes in the bottom of the dish.
- Layer the sour cream over the mashed potatoes and season with Texas Barbecue Rub.
- Layer the sautéed vegetables on top of the potatoes, retaining the butter or bacon grease in the pan.
- Sprinkle with 1½ cups of the sharp cheddar cheese followed by the frozen hash brown potatoes.
- Spoon the remaining butter or bacon grease from the sautéed vegetables over the hash browns and top with crumbled bacon.
- Top with the remaining 1½ cups of sharp cheddar cheese and cover the casserole dish with a lid or aluminum foil.
- Configure your wood pellet smoker-grill for indirect cooking and preheat to 350°F using your pellets of choice.
- Bake the smashed potato casserole for 45 to 60 minutes, until the cheese is bubbling.
- Let rest for 10 minutes before serving.

2.3 Bacon-Wrapped Asparagus
Ingredients:

- 1-pound fresh thick asparagus (15 to 20 spears)
- extra-virgin olive oil
- 5 slices thinly sliced bacon
- 1 teaspoon Pete's Western Rub (page 169) or salt and pepper

Instructions:

- Snap off the woody ends of asparagus and trim so they are all about the same length.
- Divide the asparagus into bundles of 3 spears and spritz with olive oil. Wrap each bundle with 1 piece of bacon and then dust with the seasoning or salt and pepper to taste.
- Configure your wood pellet smoker-grill for indirect cooking, placing Teflon coated fiberglass mats on top of the grates (to prevent the asparagus from sticking to the grill grates). Preheat to 400°F using any type of pellets. The grill can be preheated while prepping the asparagus.
- Grill the bacon-wrapped asparagus for 25 to 30 minutes, until the asparagus is tender and the bacon is cooked and crispy.

2.4 Brisket Baked Beans
Ingredients:

- 2 tablespoons extra-virgin olive oil 1 large yellow onion, diced
- 1 medium green bell pepper, diced
- 1 medium red bell pepper, diced
- 2 to 6 jalapeño peppers, diced
- 3 cups chopped Texas-Style Brisket Flat (page 91) 1 (28-ounce) can baked beans, like Bush's Country Style Baked Beans 1 (28-ounce) can pork and beans
- 1 (14-ounce) can red kidney beans, rinsed and drained 1 cup barbecue sauce, like Sweet Baby Ray's Barbecue Sauce ½ cup packed brown sugar
- 3 garlic cloves, chopped
- 2 teaspoons ground mustard
- ½ teaspoon kosher salt
- ½ teaspoon black pepper

Instructions:

- In a skillet over medium heat, warm the olive oil and then add the diced onion, peppers, and jalapeños. Cook until the onions are translucent, about 8 to 10 minutes, stirring occasionally.
- In a 4-quart casserole dish, mix the chopped brisket, baked beans, pork and beans, kidney beans, cooked onion and peppers, barbecue sauce, brown sugar, garlic, ground mustard, salt, and black pepper.
- Configure your wood pellet smoker-grill for indirect cooking and preheat to 325°F using your pellets of choice. Cook the brisket baked beans uncovered for 1½ to 2 hours, until the beans are thick and bubbly. Allow to rest for 15 minutes before serving.

2.5 Garlic Parmesan Wedges
Ingredients:

- 3 large russet potatoes
- ¼ cup extra-virgin olive oil
- 1½ teaspoons salt
- ¾ teaspoon black pepper
- 2 teaspoons garlic powder
- ¾ cup grated Parmesan cheese
- 3 tablespoons chopped fresh cilantro or flat-leaf parsley (optional)
- ½ cup blue cheese or ranch dressing per serving, for dipping (optional)

Instructions:

- Gently scrub the potatoes with cold water using a vegetable brush and allow the potatoes to dry.
- Cut the potatoes lengthwise in half, then cut those halves into thirds.
- Use a paper towel to wipe away all the moisture that is released when you cut the potatoes. Moisture prevents the wedges from getting crispy.
- Place the potato wedges, olive oil, salt, pepper, and garlic powder in a large bowl, and toss lightly with your hands, making sure the oil and spices are distributed evenly.
- Arrange the wedges in a single layer on a nonstick grilling tray/pan/basket (about 15 × 12 inches).
- Configure your wood pellet smoker-grill for indirect cooking and preheat to 425°F using any type of wood pellets.
- Place the grilling tray in your preheated smoker-grill and roast the potato wedges for 15 minutes before turning. Roast the potato wedges for an additional 15 to 20 minutes until potatoes are fork tender on the inside and crispy golden brown on the outside.
- Sprinkle the potato wedges with Parmesan cheese and garnish with cilantro or parsley, if desired. Serve with blue cheese or ranch dressing for dipping, if desired.

2.6 Roasted Vegetables

Ingredients:

- 1 cup cauliflower florets
- 1 cup small mushrooms, halved
- 1 medium zucchini, sliced and halved
- 1 medium yellow squash, sliced and halved
- 1 medium red bell pepper, chopped into 1½ to 2-inch pieces 1 small red onion, chopped into 1½ to 2- inch pieces
- 6 ounces small baby carrots
- 6 medium stemmed asparagus spears, cut into 1-inch pieces
- 1 cup cherry or grape tomatoes
- ¼ cup roasted garlic–flavored extra-virgin olive oil
- 2 tablespoons balsamic vinegar
- 3 garlic cloves, minced
- 1 teaspoon dried thyme
- 1 teaspoon dried oregano
- 1 teaspoon garlic salt
- ½ teaspoon black pepper

Instructions:

- Place the cauliflower florets, mushrooms, zucchini, yellow squash, red bell pepper, red onion, carrots, asparagus, and tomatoes into a large bowl.
- Add olive oil, balsamic vinegar, garlic, thyme, oregano, garlic salt, and black pepper to the vegetables.
- Gently hand toss the vegetables until they are fully coated with olive oil, herbs, and spices.
- Evenly scatter the seasoned vegetables onto a nonstick grilling tray/pan/basket (about 15 × 12 inches).
- Configure your wood pellet smoker-grill for indirect cooking and preheat to 425°F using any type of wood pellets.
- Transfer the grilling tray to the preheated smoker-grill and roast the vegetables for 20 to 40 minutes, or until the vegetables are al dente. Serve immediately.

2.7 Twice-Baked Spaghetti Squash
Ingredients:

- 1 medium spaghetti squash
- 1 tablespoon extra-virgin olive oil
- 1 teaspoon salt
- ½ teaspoon pepper
- ½ cup shredded mozzarella cheese, divided
- ½ cup grated Parmesan cheese, divided

Instructions:

- Carefully cut the squash in half lengthwise using a large, sharp knife. Remove the seeds and pulp of each half using a spoon.
- Rub olive oil over the insides of the squash halves and sprinkle with salt and pepper.
- Configure your wood pellet smoker-grill for indirect cooking and preheat to 375°F using any type of wood pellets.
- Place the squash halves face-up directly on the hot grill grates.
- Bake the squash for approximately 45 minutes, until the internal temperature reaches 170°F. When done, the spaghetti squash will be soft and easily pierced with a fork.
- Transfer the squash to a cutting board and allow to cool for 10 minutes.
- Increase the wood pellet smoker-grill temperature to 425°F.
- Being careful to keep the shells intact, use a fork to rake back and forth across the squash to remove the flesh in strands. Note that the stands look like spaghetti.
- Transfer the strands to a large bowl. Add half the mozzarella and Parmesan cheeses, and stir to combine.
- Stuff the mixture back in the squash shell halves, and sprinkle the tops with the remaining mozzarella and Parmesan cheeses.
- Bake the stuffed spaghetti squash halves for another 15 minutes at 425°F, or until the cheese starts to brown.

2.8 Applewood-Smoked Cheese
Ingredients:

- 1 to 2½-pound block of the following suggested cheeses: Gouda
- sharp cheddar
- extra-sharp 3-year cheddar
- Monterey Jack
- pepper Jack
- Swiss

Instructions:

- Depending on the shape of the cheese blocks, cut the cheese blocks into manageable sizes (about 4 × 4-inch blocks) to enhance smoke penetration.
- Allow the cheese to rest uncovered on the counter for 1 hour to allow a very thin skin or crust to form that acts as a barrier to heat but allows the smoke to penetrate.
- Configure your wood pellet smoker-grill for indirect heat and prepare for cold-smoking by installing a cold-smoke box. Ensure smoker box louver vents are fully open to allow moisture to escape from the box.
- Preheat your wood pellet smoker-grill to 180°F, or use the smoke setting if you have one, using apple pellets for a milder smoke flavor.
- Place the cheese on Teflon-coated fiberglass nonstick grill mats, and cold smoke for 2 hours.
- Remove the smoked cheese and allow to cool for an hour on the counter using a cooling rack.
- Vacuum-seal and label your smoked cheeses before refrigerating for a minimum of 2 weeks to allow the smoke to penetrate and for the flavor of the cheese to mellow.

2.9 Hickory-Smoked Moink Ball Skewers
Ingredients:

- ½ pound ground beef (80% lean)
- ½ pound ground pork sausage
- 1 large egg
- ½ cup Italian bread crumbs
- ½ cup minced red onions

- ½ cup grated Parmesan cheese
- ¼ cup finely chopped parsley
- ¼ cup whole milk
- 2 garlic cloves, minced, or 1 teaspoon crushed garlic 1 teaspoon oregano
- ½ teaspoon kosher salt
- ½ teaspoon black pepper
- ¼ cup barbecue sauce, like Sweet Baby Ray's ½ pound thinly sliced bacon, cut in half PREPPING

Instructions:

- In a large bowl, combine the ground beef, ground pork sausage, egg, bread crumbs, onion, Parmesan cheese, parsley, milk, garlic, salt, oregano, and pepper. Do not overwork the meat.
- Form 1½-ounce meatballs, approximately 1½ inches in diameter, and place on a Teflon-coated fiberglass mat.
- Wrap each meatball with half a slice of thin bacon. Spear the Moink balls onto 6 skewers (3 balls per skewer).
- Configure your wood pellet smoker-grill for indirect cooking.
- Preheat your wood pellet smoker-grill to 225°F using hickory pellets.
- Smoke the Moink ball skewers for 30 minutes.
- Increase your pit temperature to 350°F until the meatballs' internal temperature reaches 175°F and the bacon is crispy (approximately 40 to 45 minutes).
- Brush the Moink balls with your favorite barbecue sauce during the last 5 minutes.
- Serve the Moink ball skewers while they're still hot.

2.10 Traeger Smoked Jalapeno Poppers
Ingredients:

- 12 jalapeño peppers
- 8-ounces cream cheese, room temperature
- 10 pieces of bacon

Instructions:

- Preheat your Traeger or another wood-pellet grill to 350°.
- Wash and cut the tops off of the peppers, and then slice them in half the long way. Scrape the seeds and the membranes out, and set aside.
- Spoon softened cream cheese into the popper, and wrap with bacon and secure with a toothpick.
- Place on wire racks that are non-stick or have been sprayed with non-stick spray, and grill for 20-25 minutes, or until the bacon is cooked.

2.11 Smokey Meatball Appetizer
Ingredients:

- 1 lb. lean ground hamburger
- 1/3 C panko bread crumbs
- ½ C finely grated parmesan
- ½ C shredded old cheddar or asiago cheese
- 1 Tbsp garlic powder
- 1 Tbsp onion powder
- 1 Tbsp brown sugar
- 1 tsp kosher salt
- ½ tsp smoked paprika
- ¼ tsp chili powder
- ¼ tsp chipotle powder
- 1/8 tsp cumin
- ½ C onion, finely diced
- 1 jalapeño, finely diced
- 1 large egg, lightly beaten
- 1/8 C Worcestershire

- ½ C BBQ sauce
- 1/3" cubes of aged cheddar or asiago cheese

Instructions:

- Pre-heat the Memphis Pellet Grill to 225 F.
- Mix all of the **Ingredients:** together, except for the cheese cubes and BBQ sauce, in the order given, until everything is evenly incorporated.
- Make 1 ½" meatballs by rolling a small portion of the mixture between the palms of your hands. You will have approximately 30 meatballs when done.
- Press one cheese cube down into the center of each meatball. Once again roll each of the meatballs around, between the palms of your hands, to seal the cube of cheese inside.
- Put the cheese filled meatballs on a flat pan lined with parchment paper. Place the pan on the bottom grate of the pre-heated Memphis Grill. Close the lid and smoke for a half-hour.
- Baste the meatballs with your favorite BBQ Sauce. Close the lid and continue smoking for another half-hour. Baste again then turn the Memphis up to 350 F and close the lid. Bake for another 20 – 25 minutes. The meatballs are done when the internal temperature reaches 160 F.

2.12 Cold Smoked Cheese Easy Brie Appetizer
Ingredients:

- 21 ounces Brie cheese wheel (brought to room temperature)

Instructions:

To Smoke:

- Fill your smoker container with your choice of pellets.
- Place inside your grill, and ignite. Close the lid for a few minutes to create some smoke.
- Place the room temperature cheese on the grill (not near the smoker container).
- Close the lid, and smoke until your desired level of flavor. We smoked ours for about 80 minutes. **NOTE** Be sure the internal temperature of your grill stays under 90°F...YOU DON'T WANT TO COOK/MELT THE CHEESE.
- When done, remove from grill.
- Place on a board, along with a cheese knife, crackers, meats, and toppings.

2.13 Smoked Tomatoes on The Traeger Grill
Ingredients:

- Tomatoes, cut in half
- Dried lovage (optional)
- Sea salt
- Black pepper
- Olive oil (enough to coat the tomatoes)

Instructions:

- Set your Traeger Grill to the Smoke setting.
- Slice tomatoes in half and coat with olive oil in a bowl large enough to hold them. Add a liberal pinch of sea salt, freshly cracked black pepper, and dried lovage to taste (if using). Use your hands and mix the tomatoes until evenly coated in the mixture.
- Place tomatoes on a baking sheet and then on the Traeger Grill.
- Increase temperature to about 180-200.
- Tomatoes will be done in approximately 45 minutes. The edges will begin to curl and insides to bubble.

2.14 Smoked Olives
Ingredients:

- 1 cup black olives such as Greek Kalamata or Atalante, drained lightly
- 1 cup green olives, drained lightly
- 2 tbs extra-virgin olive oil
- 2 tbs white wine - vermouth works great
- 2 garlic cloves minced
- 3/4 tsp dried rosemary We have also used oregano with some great success but the rosemary has a better all-around taste.
- fresh ground black pepper to taste
- Perfect Mix Pellets

Instructions:

- Set pellet grill at 220 with perfect mix pellets.
- Arrange the olives in a shallow piece of heavy-duty foil molded into a small tray.
- Add the remaining **Ingredients:**
- Place the olives in the smoker and cook until the olives absorb half of the liquid and take on a light but identifiable smoke flavor, 30-50 minutes. Time depends on your grill!! Taste test after about 15-20 minutes.
- The olives can be served immediately with some asiago grated cheese over them or can sit for several hours to develop the flavor further.
- Refrigerate any leftovers. Be sure to save the leftover olive oil for bread dipping.

2.15 Classic Banana Bread
Ingredients:

- 2 cups all-purpose flour
- 3/4 teaspoon baking soda
- 1/2 teaspoon salt
- 1 cup sugar
- 1/4 cup butter, softened
- 2 large eggs
- 1 1/2 cups mashed ripe banana (about 3 bananas)
- 1/3 cup plain low-fat yogurt
- 1 teaspoon vanilla extract Cooking spray

Instructions:

- Preheat oven to 350°.
- Lightly spoon flour into dry measuring cups; level with a knife. Combine the flour, baking soda, and salt, stirring with a whisk.
- Place sugar and butter in a large bowl, and beat with a mixer at medium speed until well blended (about 1 minute). Add the eggs, 1 at a time, beating well after each addition. Add banana, yogurt, and vanilla; beat until blended. Add flour mixture; beat at low speed just until moist. Spoon batter into an 8 1/2 x 4 1/2-inch loaf pan coated with cooking spray.
- Bake at 350° for 1 hour or until a wooden pick inserted in center comes out clean. Cool 10 minutes in pan on a wire rack; remove from pan. Cool completely on wire rack.

2.16 Spaghetti Squash with Brown Butter and Parmesan
Ingredients:

- 1 spaghetti squash, 2 1/2 to 3 lb.
- 4 Tbs. (1/2 stick) unsalted butter
- Pinch of freshly grated nutmeg
- 1/3 cup grated Parmigiano-Reggiano cheese
- Salt and freshly ground pepper, to taste

Instructions:

- Place the whole squash in a large pot and add water to cover. Bring to a boil over high heat, reduce the heat to medium-low and simmer, uncovered, until the squash can be easily pierced with a knife, about 45 minutes.
- Meanwhile, in a saucepan over medium-high heat, melt the butter and cook it until it turns brown and just begins to smoke, 3 to 4 minutes. Remove immediately from the heat and stir in the nutmeg.
- When the squash is done, drain and set aside until cool enough to handle. Cut the squash in half lengthwise and, using a fork, scrape out the seeds and discard. Place the squash halves, cut sides up, on a serving platter. Using the fork, scrape the flesh free of the skin, carefully separating it into the spaghetti-like strands that it naturally forms. Leave the strands mounded in the squash halves. If the butter has cooled, place over medium heat until hot.
- To serve, drizzle the butter evenly over the squash. Sprinkle with the cheese and season with salt and pepper. Serve immediately.

2.17 Double Smoked Ham on Pellet Grill
Ingredients:

- 1 pre-cook cured smoked ham
- 2 liters of Pepsi, Coke, or Dr. Pepper

Instructions:

- Start by preheating your grill to 500 degrees.
- Place your ham long side down on the grill for 10 -20 minutes. You want to sear the ham, on all sides of the outside. So, rotate the ham around and build a nice sear all around.
- Once your ham is fully seared place in a pan and pour some pop over the ham. This is what you will use to baste throughout the cooking process.
- Drop the heat down to 225 degrees and baste your ham every 20-30 minutes for 4 hours.
- Once the 4 hours is up, pull the ham from the grill, and slice and serve.

2.18 Grilled Peach Salsa
Ingredients:

- 4 Ripe Peaches, Halved and Pitted
- 4 Heirloom Tomatoes
- 1 Bunch Cilantro
- 1 Jalapeno, Minced
- 2 Limes, Juiced
- 2 Cloves Garlic Minced
- 2 Tbsp Olive Oil
- Salt and Pepper to Taste

Instructions:

- When ready to cook, set temperature to High and preheat, lid closed for 15 minutes.
- Brush the cut side of the peaches with olive oil and season with salt. Place the peaches, cut side down, along the perimeter of the grill. Cook for 20 minutes or so until grill marks develop. Its best to pick peaches that are not too ripe and more on the firm side.
- Remove the peaches from the grill and dice when cool enough to handle. Place in a large bowl with diced tomatoes, minced cilantro, jalapeno, lime juice, garlic and olive oil and mix well. Taste and season with salt. Adjust with more lime juice if needed. Enjoy with your favorite chips!
- Serve with chips or on your favorite dishes. Enjoy!

2.19 Pizza Bites
Ingredients:

- 4 1/2 CUPS BREAD FLOUR, PLUS MORE FOR DUSTING
- 1 1/2 TBSP SUGAR
- 2 TSP INSTANT YEAST
- 3 TBSP EXTRA-VIRGIN OLIVE OIL
- 15 OZ LUKEWARM WATER
- PIZZA FILLING
- 1 CUP MOZARELLA CHEESE
- 8 OZ PEPPERONI, CUT INTO THIN STRIPS
- 1 CUP PIZZA SAUCE
- 1 EGG FOR EGG WASH

Instructions:

- For the Pizza Dough: Combine flour, sugar, salt, and yeast in food processor. Pulse 3 to 4 times until incorporated evenly. Add olive oil and water. Run food processor until mixture forms ball that rides around the bowl above the blade, about 15 seconds. Continue processing 15 seconds longer.
- Transfer dough ball to lightly floured surface and knead once or twice by hand until smooth ball is formed. Divide dough into three even parts and place each into a 1-gallon zip top bag. Place in refrigerator and allow to rise at least one day.
- At least two hours before baking, remove dough from refrigerator and shape into balls by gathering dough towards bottom and pinching shut. Flour well and place each one in a separate medium mixing bowl. Cover tightly with plastic wrap and allow to rise at warm room temperature until roughly doubled in volume.
- When ready to cook, set the temperature to 350°F and preheat, lid closed for 15 minutes.
- After the first rise remove the dough from the fridge and let come to room temperature. Roll dough on a flat surface. Cut dough into long strips 3" wide by 18" long.
- Slice pepperoni into strips.
- In a medium bowl combine the pizza sauce, mozzarella and pepperoni.
- Spoon 1 TBSP of the pizza filling onto the pizza dough every two inches, about halfway down the length of the dough. Dip a pastry brush into the egg wash and brush around pizza filling. Fold the half side of the dough (without the pizza filling) over the other the half that contains the pizza filling.
- Press down between each pizza bite slightly with your fingers. With a ravioli or pizza cutter, cut around each filling- creating a rectangle shape and sealing the crust in.
- Transfer each pizza bite onto a parchment lined cookie sheet. Cover with a kitchen towel and let them rise for 30 minutes.
- When ready to cook, preheat the grill to 350 F with the lid closed for 10-15 minutes.
- Brush the bites with remaining egg wash, sprinkle with salt and place directly on the sheet tray. Bake 10-15 minutes until the exterior is golden brown.
- Remove from grill and transfer to a serving dish. Serve with extra pizza sauce for dipping and enjoy!

2.20 Spicy Shrimp Skewers
Ingredients:

- 2 Lbs. Shrimp, Peeled, And Deveined
- 6 Oz Thai Chilies
- 6 Cloves Garlic
- 2 Tbsp Winemakers Blend Napa Valley Rub
- 1-1/2 Tsp Sugar
- 1-1/2 Tbsp White Vinegar
- 3 Tbsp Olive Oil
- Bamboo or Metal Skewers

Instructions:

- Place all **Ingredients:** besides shrimp in a blender and blend until a course textured paste is reached.
- Place shrimp in a bowl, add chili garlic mixture and place in fridge to marinate for at least 30 minutes.
- Remove from fridge and thread shrimp onto bamboo or metal skewers.

- When ready to cook, start the Traeger according to grill instructions. Set the temperature to 450 degrees F (set to 500 degrees F if using a WiFIRE enables grill) and preheat, lid closed, for 10 to 15 minutes.
- Place shrimp on grill and cook for 2 to 3 minutes per side or until shrimp are pink and firm to touch. Enjoy!

2.21 Traeger Jerk Shrimp
Ingredients:

- 1 Tbsp Brown Sugar
- 1 Tbsp Smoked Paprika
- 1 Tsp Garlic Powder
- 1/4 Tsp Ground Thyme
- 1/4 Tsp Ground Cayenne
- 1/8 Tsp Smoked Paprika
- 1 Tsp Sea Salt
- Zest Of 1 Lime
- 3 Tbsp Olive Oil
- 2 Lbs. Shrimp, Peel On

Instructions:

- Combine spices, salt, and lime zest in a small bowl and mix. Place shrimp into a large bowl, then drizzle in the olive oil, Add the spice mixture and toss to combine, making sure every shrimp is kissed with deliciousness.
- When ready to cook, set the temperature to 450°F and preheat, lid closed for 15 minutes
- Arrange the shrimp on the grill and cook for 2 – 3 minutes per side, until firm, opaque, and cooked through.
- Serve with lime wedges, fresh cilantro, mint, and Caribbean Hot Pepper Sauce. Enjoy!

2.22 Hellfire Chicken Wings
Ingredients:

- Hellfire Chicken Wings
- 3 Lbs. Chicken Wings
- 2 Tbsp. Vegetable Oil
- Rub
- 1 Tbsp. Paprika
- 2 Tsp. Brown Sugar
- 1 Tsp. Salt
- 1 Tsp. Black Pepper, Freshly Ground
- 1 Tsp. Cayenne Pepper
- 1 Tsp. Onion Powder
- 1 Tsp. Granulated Garlic
- 1 Tsp. Celery Seed
- Sauce
- 8 Tbsp. Butter, Unsalted
- 2 - 4 Jalapeno Peppers, Thinly Sliced Crosswise
- 1/2 Cup Cilantro Leaves
- 1/2 Cup Hot Sauce

Instructions:

- Cut the tips off wings and discard. Cut each wing into two pieces through the joint, giving you a meaty "drumette" and a "flat". Transfer to a large mixing bowl and pour the oil over the chicken
- Make the rub: In a small mixing bowl, combine the paprika, sugar, salt, black pepper, cayenne, onion powder, granulated garlic, and celery seed.
- Sprinkle over the chicken and toss gently with your hands to coat the wings.
- When ready to cook, set the temperature to 350°F and preheat, lid closed for 15 minutes
- Grill the wings for 35 to 40 minutes, or until the skin is crisp and golden brown and the chicken is cooked through, turning once halfway through the cooking time.
- Make the sauce: Melt the butter over medium-low heat in a small saucepan. Add the jalapeños and cook for 3-4 minutes. Stir in the cilantro & hot sauce.

- Pour the sauce over the wings and toss to coat. Enjoy!

2.23 Grilled Bison Sliders
Ingredients:

- 1 Lb. Ground Buffalo Meat
- 3 Cloves Garlic, Minced
- 2 Tbsp Worcestershire Sauce
- 1 Tsp Salt
- 1 Tsp Black Pepper

Instructions:

- Combine the buffalo meat, garlic, Worcestershire sauce, salt and pepper in a mixing bowl. Blend together with hands.
- Form meat into 8 small patties. Place on a plate and put in fridge.
- When ready to cook, set temperature to High and preheat, lid closed for 15 minutes.
- Remove patties from fridge and place on grill. Grill patties for 4 minutes on each side and remove from grill.
- If you want to add cheese, place sliced cheese on patties the last 2 minutes of cooking to melt.
- To toast buns, place buns on grill grate the last minute of cooking.
- Serve with sliced onions, pickles, tomatoes, lettuce and condiments of your choice. Enjoy!

2.24 Smoked Jalapeño Poppers
Ingredients:

12 Medium Jalapeños

6 Slices Bacon, Cut in Half

8 Oz Cream Cheese, Softened

1 Cup Cheese, Grated

2 Tbsp Traeger Pork & Poultry Rub

Instructions:

- When ready to cook, set temperature to 180°F and preheat, lid closed for 15 minutes.
- Slice the jalapeños in half lengthwise. Scrape out any seeds and ribs with a small spoon or paring knife.
- Mix softened cream cheese with Traeger Pork & Poultry rub and grated cheese.
- Spoon mixture onto each jalapeño half. Wrap with bacon and secure with a toothpick.
- Place the jalapeños on a rimmed baking sheet. Place on grill and smoke for 30 minutes.
- Increase the grill temperature to 375°F and cook an additional 30 minutes or until bacon is cooked to desired doneness. Serve warm, enjoy!

2.25 Easy Garlic Cheese Bombs
Ingredients:

- 4 1/2 Cups Bread Flour, Plus More for Dusting
- 1 1/2 Tbsp Sugar
- 2 Tsp Instant Yeast
- 3 Tbsp Extra-Virgin Olive Oil
- 15 Oz Lukewarm Water
- Cheese Filling
- 1 Lb. Block Mozzarella Cheese
- 4 Tbsp Butter
- 1 Tsp Garlic Salt
- 1 Tbsp Shredded Parmesan Cheese

Instructions:

- For the Pizza Dough: Combine flour, sugar, salt, and yeast in food processor. Pulse 3 to 4 times until incorporated evenly. Add olive oil and water. Run food processor until mixture forms ball that rides around the bowl above the blade, about 15 seconds. Continue processing 15 seconds longer.
- Transfer dough ball to lightly floured surface and knead once or twice by hand until smooth ball is formed. Divide dough into three even parts and place each into a 1-gallon zip top bag. Place in refrigerator and allow to rise at least for 24 hours.
- At least two hours before baking, remove dough from refrigerator and shape into balls by gathering dough towards bottom and pinching shut. Flour well and place each one in a separate medium mixing bowl. Cover tightly with plastic wrap and allow to rise at warm room temperature until roughly doubled in volume.
- Roll the pizza dough out into a rectangle ¼" thick. Cut into strips 2" thick. Then again to create 2x2 squares.
- Place one piece of cheese in the center of each dough square. Brush the edges with a little bit of water and fold the edges up securing tightly.
- Place the cheese balls seam side down on a parchment lined baking sheet.
- In a small bowl combine the melted butter, garlic salt and cheese.
- Brush each cheese ball with the butter mixture.
- When ready to cook, set the temperature to 350 °F and preheat, lid closed for 10-15 minutes.
- Place the sheet tray directly on the grill grate and bake for 20-30 minutes until light brown in color. Enjoy with marinara or your favorite dipping sauce.

2.26 Traeger Baked Corn Dog Bites

Ingredients:

- 1 Cup Milk at Room Temp
- 4 Tsp Active Dry Yeast
- 1/4 Cup Granulated Sugar
- 2 Cups All-Purpose Flour
- 1/2 Cup Yellow Corn Meal
- 1 Tsp Baking Soda
- 1/2 Tsp Mustard Powder
- 1/4 Cup Vegetable Oil
- 1/2 Tsp Cayenne Pepper
- 1 Egg, Lightly Beaten
- 15 Mini Hot Dogs
- 1 Tbsp Dried Mince Garlic
- 1 Tbsp Coarse Salt
- Ketchup & Mustard for Serving

Instructions:

- When ready to cook, set the temperature to 375°F and preheat, lid closed for 15 minutes.
- Combine milk, yeast and sugar in a bowl. Set aside for 5 minutes or until it starts to foam.
- Then add oil, salt, cayenne pepper, mustard powder, baking soda, corn meal, all-purpose flour. Mix with a spoon until combined then use your hands to knead into a dough.
- Transfer dough to a bowl and cover with plastic wrap and set aside for about 45 minutes- until dough rises and doubles in size.
- Remove dough from bowl and divide into 15 pieces. On a working surface dusted with flour, use a rolling pin to roll out each piece of dough into 3" x 3" pieces. Place each hot dog in the middle of the sheet of dough. Roll it in the dough and press edges to seal to make 15 mini corn dog bites.
- Transfer corn dog bites into a baking pan lined with parchment paper and brush each bite lightly with beaten egg. Sprinkle each bite with dried minced garlic and salt.
- Bake in Traeger until golden brown- about 30 min.
- Serve with ketchup and mustard or dipping sauce of your choice. Enjoy!

2.27 Baked Heirloom Tomato Tart

Ingredients:

- 1 Sheet Puff Pastry
- 2 Lbs. Heirloom Tomatoes, Various Shapes and Sizes
- 1/2 Cup Ricotta
- 5 Eggs
- 1/2 Tbsp Kosher Salt
- 1/2 Tsp Thyme Leaves
- 1/2 Tsp Red Pepper Flakes
- Pinch of Black Pepper
- 4 Sprigs Thyme
- Salt and Pepper, To Taste

Instructions:

- When ready to cook, set temperature to 350°F and preheat, lid closed for 15 minutes.
- Place the puff pastry on a parchment lined sheet tray, and make a cut ¾ of the way through the pastry, ½" from the edge.
- Slice the tomatoes and season with salt. Place on a sheet tray lined with paper towels.
- In a small bowl combine the ricotta, 4 of the eggs, salt, thyme leaves, red pepper flakes and black pepper. Whisk together until combined. Spread the ricotta mixture over the puff pastry, staying within ½" from the edge.
- Lay the tomatoes out on top of the ricotta, and sprinkle with salt, pepper and thyme sprigs.
- In a small bowl whisk the last egg. Brush the egg wash onto the exposed edges of the pastry.
- Place the sheet tray directly on the grill grate and bake for 45 minutes, rotating half-way through.
- When the edges are browned and the moisture from the tomatoes has evaporated, remove from the grill and let cool 5-7 minutes before serving. Enjoy!

2.28 Grilled Piña Colada

Ingredients:

- 7.5 Oz Light Rum
- 2 Oz Dark Rum
- 15 Oz Coconut Milk
- 1 Pineapple, Trimmed, Cored and Cut into Spears
- 5 Cups Ice

Instructions:

- When ready to cook, set temperature to High and preheat, lid closed for 15 minutes.
- Grill pineapple spears 10 minutes until lightly browned.
- Combine 3/4 of the grilled pineapple, coconut milk and both rums in the pitcher of a blender. Add ice and blend until smooth.
- Divide blender contents into four glasses and garnish with remaining grilled pineapple. Enjoy!

2.29 BBQ Chicken Nachos

Ingredients:

- 1-1/4 Lbs. Chicken Breasts, Boneless, Skinless
- Traeger Pork & Poultry Rub, As Needed
- 1/2 To 3/4 Cup Traeger Qu BBQ Sauce
- 24 Large Tortilla Chips
- 3 Cups Mexican Blend Shredded Cheese
- 1/2 Cup Black Olives, Sliced and Drained
- Pickled Jalapenos, Sliced
- 3 Scallions, Thinly Sliced
- 1 Cup Sour Cream

Instructions:

- Season the chicken breasts with the Traeger Pork and Poultry Rub.
- When ready to cook, set temperature to 350°F and preheat, lid closed for 15 minutes.
- Arrange the chicken breasts on the grill grate and cook, turning once halfway through the cooking time, for 25 to 30 minutes, or until the internal temperature when read on an instant-read meat thermometer is 170°F. Transfer to a cutting board and let rest for 3 minutes. Leave the grill on if you are making the nachos immediately.
- Dice the chicken into small cubes, 1/2-inch or less. Transfer to a mixing bowl and pour 1/2 cup of Traeger Regular Barbecue Sauce over the diced chicken. Stir gently to coat each piece.
- Set aside, or cover and refrigerate if not making the nachos immediately. Lay the tortilla chips in a single layer on a rimmed baking sheet or pizza pan. Sprinkle evenly with half the cheese and a few of the jalapenos (if using).
- Spoon barbecued chicken mixture on each chip. Top with black olives and more pickled jalapeno, if desired. Sprinkle the remaining half of the cheese evenly over the chips. Scatter the sliced onions over the chips.
- Put the baking sheet on the grill grate. Bake until the chips are crisp and the cheese is melted, 12 to 15 minutes. With a spatula, transfer the nachos to a plate or platter. Serve immediately with sour cream and pickled jalapenos. Enjoy!

2.30 Chinese BBQ Pork

Ingredients:

- Pork & Marinade
- 2 Pork Tenderloins, Silver Skin Removed
- 1/4 Cup Hoisin Sauce
- 1/4 Cup Honey
- 1 1/2 Tbsp Brown Sugar
- 3 Tbsp Soy Sauce
- 1 Tbsp Asian Sesame Oil
- 1 Tbsp Oyster Sauce, Optional
- 1 Tsp Chinese Five Spice
- 1 Garlic Clove, Minced
- 2 Tsp Red Food Coloring, Optional
- Five Spice Dipping Sauce
- 1/4 Cup Ketchup
- 3 Tbsp Brown Sugar
- 1 Tsp Yellow Mustard
- 1/4 Tsp Chinese Five Spice

Instructions:

- In medium bowl, whisk together marinade **Ingredients:** thoroughly, making sure brown sugar is dissolved. Add pork and marinade to glass pan or resealable plastic bag and marinate for at least 8 hours or overnight, turning occasionally to ensure all sides of pork are well coated.
- When ready to cook, set the temperature to 225°F and preheat, lid closed for 15 minutes.
- Remove pork from marinade and boil marinade in a saucepan over medium high heat on stove top for 3 minutes to use for basting pork. Cool slightly, then whisk in 2 additional Tablespoons of honey.
- Arrange the tenderloins on the grill grate and smoke pork until internal temperature reaches 145°F.
- Baste pork with reserved marinade half way through cooking. Remove pork from grill and, if desired, increase temperature to High and return pork to grill for a few minutes per side to slightly char and set the sauce. Alternatively, you can broil in the oven, just a couple minutes per side.
- For the 5 Spice Sauce: In a small saucepan over low heat, mix ketchup, brown sugar, mustard and five spice until sugar is dissolved and sauce is smooth. Let cool, and serve chilled or at room temperature.
- Serve pork immediately with Jasmine rice, or cool and refrigerate for later use as an appetizer, served with Five Spice dipping sauce and toasted sesame seeds. Enjoy!

2.31 Smoked Pickled Green Beans
Ingredients:

- 1 Lb. Green Beans, Blanched
- 1/2 Cup Salt
- 1/2 Cup Sugar
- 1 Tbsp Red Pepper Flake
- 2 Cups White Wine Vinegar
- 2 Cups Ice Water

Instructions:

- When ready to cook, set temperature to 180°F and preheat, lid closed for 15 minutes.
- Place the blanched green beans on a mesh grill mat and place mat directly on the grill grate. Smoke the green beans for 30-45 minutes until they've picked up the desired amount of smoke. Remove from grill and set aside until the brine is ready.
- In a medium sized saucepan, bring all remaining **Ingredients:** except ice water, to a boil over medium high heat on the stove. Simmer for 5-10 minutes then remove from heat and steep 20 minutes more. Pour brine over ice water to cool.
- Once brine has cooled, pour over the green beans and weigh them down with a few plates to ensure they are completely submerged. Let sit 24 hours before use.

2.32 Seared Lemon Garlic Scallops
- **Ingredients:**
- Scallops
- 1 Dozen U-20 Scallops
- Kosher Salt
- 1 Tbsp Butter
- 1 Tbsp Olive Oil
- Chopped Parsley, To Garnish
- Lemon Zest, To Garnish
- Garlic Butter
- 4 Tbsp Butter, Melted
- Juice Of 1 Lemon
- 1 Clove Garlic, Minced

Instructions:

- When ready to cook, set the temperature to 400°F and preheat, lid closed for 15 minutes.
- Remove the frill if it is still intact. Pat the scallops dry with a paper towel. Season liberally with salt and a bit of black pepper.
- When the grill is hot, place the butter and olive oil on the skillet. When the butter has melted, place the scallops on the skillet. Close the lid and cook for about 2 minutes until seared and browned on one side.
- While the scallops cook, combine the melted butter and garlic in a small bowl.
- Flip the scallops, spoon a couple tablespoons of garlic butter over the top and cook for 1 minute longer.
- Remove from the grill, add a little more garlic butter if desired and finish with parsley and lemon zest.

2.33 Baked Asparagus Pancetta Cheese Tart
Ingredients:

- 1 Sheet Puff Pastry
- 8 Oz Asparagus, Pencil Spears
- 8 Oz Pancetta, Cooked and Drained
- 1 Cup Cream
- 4 Eggs
- 1/4 Cup Goat Cheese
- 4 Tbsp Grated Parmesan
- 1 Tbsp Chopped Chives
- Black Pepper

Instructions:

- When ready to cook, set the temperature to 375°F and preheat, lid closed for 15 minutes.
- Place the puff pastry on a half sheet tray and score around the perimeter 1-inch in from the edges making sure not to cut all the way through. Prick the center of the puff pastry with a fork.
- Place the sheet tray directly on the grill grate and bake for 15-20 minutes until the pastry has puffed and browned a little bit.
- While the pastry bakes combine the cream, 3 eggs, both cheeses and chives in a small bowl. Whisk to mix well.
- Remove the sheet tray from the grill and pour the egg mixture into the puff pastry. Lay the asparagus spears on top of the egg mixture and sprinkle with cooked pancetta.
- Whisk remaining egg in a small bowl and brush the top of the pastry with the egg wash.
- Place back on the grill grate and cook for another 15-20 minutes until the egg mixture is just set.
- Finish tart with lemon zest, more chopped chives and shaved parmesan.

2.34 Smoked Deviled Eggs
Ingredients:

- 7 Hard Boiled Eggs, Cooked and Peeled
- 3 Tbsp Mayonnaise
- 3 Tsp Chives, Diced
- 1 Tsp Brown Mustard
- 1 Tsp Apple Cider Vinegar
- Dash of Hot Sauce
- Salt and Pepper, To Taste
- 2 Tbsp Bacon, Crumbled
- Paprika, For Dusting

Instructions:

- When ready to cook, set temperature to 180°F and preheat, lid closed for 15 minutes. For optimal flavor, use Super Smoke if available.
- Place cooked and peeled eggs directly on the grill grate and smoke eggs for 30 minutes. Remove from grill and allow eggs to cool.
- Slice the eggs lengthwise and scoop the egg yolks into a gallon zip top bag. Add mayonnaise, chives, mustard, vinegar, hot sauce, salt, and pepper to the bag.
- Zip the bag closed and, using your hands, knead all of the **Ingredients:** together until completely smooth.
- Squeeze the yolk mixture into one corner of the bag and cut a small part of the corner off. Pipe the yolk mixture into the hardboiled egg whites.
- Top the deviled eggs with crumbled bacon and paprika. Chill until ready to serve. Enjoy!

2.35 Baked Soft Pretzel with Beer Cheese Sauce
Ingredients:

- Soft Pretzel
- 1 1/2 Cups Warm Water (110-115°F)
- 1 Tbsp Sugar
- 1 Package Active Dry Yeast
- 4 1/2 Cups All Purpose Flour
- 2 Tbsp Kosher Salt
- 2 Oz Melted Unsalted Butter
- Cooking Oil Spray
- 10 Cups Water
- 2/3 Cup Baking Soda
- 1 Large Egg Yolk Beaten With 1 Tbsp Water
- Jacobsen Smoked Sea Salt, As Needed
- Beer Cheese Sauce
- 2 Cups Sharp Cheddar Cheese
- 1/2 Cup Cream Cheese, Room Temperature
- 1/2 Tbsp Worcestershire Sauce
- 2 Tsp Dijon Mustard
- 2 Cloves Garlic, Minced
- 1 Tsp Paprika
- 1/2 Cup Beer

Instructions:

- In the bowl of a stand mixer, combine the water and sugar and sprinkle the dry yeast on top. Let it sit for 5-6 minutes until it starts to foam on top.
- Add flour, salt, and butter to the bowl, and with the hook attachment mix on low until well combined. Then mix on medium for about 5 minutes until dough is smooth and pulls away from the sides.
- Remove dough from bowl and spray bowl well with cooking oil spray. Return dough to the bowl, cover with a cloth or plastic wrap and allow the dough to double in size.
- When ready to cook, set the Traeger to 350°F and preheat, lid closed for 15 minutes.
- While dough rises, bring to a boil 10 cups of water and the baking soda.
- When dough is ready, divide into 8 pieces. Roll each piece into a 24-inch rope.
- Form a U shape with each rope, holding each end of the rope and cross them over each other and press it down on the bottom of the U forming a pretzel.
- One by one, place each pretzel in the boiling water for 30 seconds. With a flat spatula take them out and place in a sheet pan.
- Brush pretzels with egg yolk and sprinkle with smoked sea salt. Bake in the Traeger for about 25-30 minutes.
- To make the Beer Cheese Sauce: In a food processor bowl, add cheddar cheese, cream cheese, Worcestershire sauce, Dijon mustard, garlic and paprika. Blend until finely chopped, add the beer slowly until is smooth.
- When pretzels are done serve with the beer cheese sauce. Enjoy!

2.36 Bacon Grilled Cheese Sandwich
Ingredients:

- 1 Lb. Applewood Smoked Bacon Slices, Cooked
- 8 Slices Texas Toast
- 16 Slices Cheddar Cheese
- Mayonnaise
- Butter

Instructions:

- When ready to cook, set the temperature to 350°F and preheat, lid closed for 15 minutes.
- Spread a little bit of mayonnaise on each piece of bread, place 1 piece of cheddar on a slice then top with a couple slices of bacon. Add another slice of cheese then top with the other piece of bread. Spread softened butter on the exterior of the top piece of bread.
- When the grill is hot, place the grilled cheese directly on a cleaned, oiled grill grate buttered side down. Then spread softened butter on the exterior of the top slice.
- Cook the grilled cheese on the first side 5-7 minutes until grill marks develop and the cheese has begun to melt. Flip the sandwich and repeat on the other side.
- Remove from the grill when the cheese is melted and the exterior is lightly toasted. Enjoy!

2.37 Stuffed Avocados

Ingredients:

- 4 Avocados, Halved, Pit Removed
- 8 Eggs
- 2 Cups Shredded Cheddar Cheese
- 4 Slices Bacon, Cooked and Chopped
- 1/4 Cup Cherry Tomatoes, Halved
- Green Onions, Sliced Thin
- Salt and Pepper, To Taste

Instructions:

- When ready to cook, set the temperature to High and preheat, lid closed for 15 minutes.
- After removing the pit from the avocado, scoop out a little of the flesh to make enough room to fit 1 egg per half.
- Fill the bottom of a cast iron pan with kosher salt and nestle the avocado halves into the salt, cut side up. The salt helps to keep them in place while cooking, like ice with oysters.
- Crack egg into each half, top with a hand full of shredded cheddar cheese, some cherry tomatoes and bacon. Season with salt and pepper to taste.
- Place the cast iron pan directly on the grill grate and bake the avocados for 12-15 minutes until the cheese is melted and the egg is just set.
- Remove from the grill and let rest 5-10 minutes. Enjoy!

2.38 Braised Backstrap Shredded Tacos

Ingredients:

- 4 Tbsp Grass Fed Butter
- 3 Cloves Fresh Garlic
- 4 Lbs. Large Cuts of Wild Game Neck, Shoulder or Arm Meat
- 3/4 Cup Bone Broth
- 2 Tbsp Traeger Prime Rib Rub
- 2 Tbsp Traeger Coffee Rub
- Sugar Lips Sriracha BBQ Glaze
- 4 Jalapeños
- 20 Tortillas
- 2 Bunches Cilantro, Chopped
- 3 Avocados, Sliced

Instructions:

- When ready to cook, set the temperature to 250°F and preheat, lid closed for 15 minutes
- Add the grass-fed butter and garlic to a large Dutch oven and place on the stovetop. Add the game meat to the Dutch oven and sear on all sides.
- Remove from heat and season with Traeger Prime Rib and Traeger Coffee rubs.
- Add the bone broth to the pot and cover. Wrap the seam of the lids tightly with foil.
- Place directly on the grill grate and cook for approximately 8 hours without peeking.
- Remove the lid and twist the meat with a fork. If the meat easily shreds, then drizzle Sriracha Sugar Lips on top and cover with the lid. If the meat doesn't fall apart yet, recover and continue to cook for another hour or until tender.
- Reduce grill temperature to 180°F. Place jalapeños directly on the grill grate and smoke the peppers for 20 minutes.
- With 10 minutes remaining, wrap a stack of tortillas in foil and set them in the Traeger to warm
- Remove Dutch oven from the grill and shred meat with two large forks. Mix in another drizzle of Sriracha Sugar Lips and cover pot.
- Remove tortillas and jalapeños from the grill and slice jalapeños.
- Build tacos with shredded backstrap, jalapeños and avocados. Garnish with cilantro. Enjoy!

CHAPTER 3: BEEF RECIPES

3.1 Blackened Saskatchewan Tomahawk Steak
Ingredients:

- 2 (40 Oz) Tomahawk Steaks
- 4 Tbsp Butter
- 4 Tbsp Blackened Saskatchewan Rub

Instructions:

- When ready to cook, set temperature to 225°F and preheat, lid closed for 15 minutes. For optimal flavor, use Super Smoke if available.
- Cover cold steaks in the Blackened Saskatchewan Rub. Let rest 10 minutes for the seasoning to adhere.
- Place steaks directly on grill grates and smoke for about 40 minutes, or until an internal temp reaches 119°F. Remove from grill and wrap tightly in foil to rest.
- Turn up temperature on the grill to 400°F- with a cast iron pan or griddle inside. When the pan is hot, add 2 Tbsp of butter and sear the first steak, about 2-4 minutes per side, or until the internal temperature reads 125°F - 130°F. Repeat with the other Tomahawk. Rest, slice, serve. Enjoy!

3.2 Traeger BBQ Brisket
Ingredients:

- 1 (12-14 Lb.) Whole Packer Brisket
- Traeger Beef Rub, As Needed

Instructions:

- Coat meat liberally with Traeger Beef Rub. When seasoned, wrap brisket in plastic wrap. Let the wrapped meat sit 12 to 24 hours in the refrigerator.
- When ready to cook, set the Traeger to 225°F and preheat, lid closed for 15 minutes.
- Place meat fat side down on the grill grate and cook for 6 hours or until internal temperature reaches 160°F. Remove brisket from the grill and wrap in foil.
- Place foiled brisket back on grill and cook until it reaches a finished internal temperature of 204°F this should take an additional 3-4 hours.
- Remove from grill and allow to rest in the foil for at least 30 minutes. Slice. Enjoy!

3.3 Garlic, Lemon, And Goat Cheese Mashed Potatoes
Ingredients:

- 1 Head of Garlic
- 1 Tsp Olive Oil
- 3 Lbs. Yukon Gold Potatoes, Peeled and Roughly Chopped
- 3/4 Cup Crumbled Goat Cheese
- 1/4 Cup Melted Butter, Plus More for Drizzling
- 3/4 Cup Heavy Whipping Cream
- Sea Salt & Freshly Cracked Black Pepper
- 2 Tbs Fresh Chives, Finely Diced

Instructions:

- When ready to cook, set the temperature to 350°F and preheat, lid closed, for 10 to 15 minutes.
- Using a sharp knife, slice about ⅛" off the top of the garlic head (leaving the root intact), exposing the individual garlic cloves. Drizzle the olive oil on top of the exposed garlic and season with a pinch of salt and pepper. Tightly wrap the bulb in

aluminum foil and roast on the Traeger for 30 - 35 minutes, until the cloves are soft. Remove the garlic cloves and mash into a paste with a fork.
- Meanwhile, bring a large stockpot of salted water to a boil over medium high heat. Add the potatoes and cook for 15 - 20 minutes, or until softened and hashable. Drain and return to the pot, stirring until dry. Remove from the heat and stir in the cream, goat cheese, lemon zest, garlic mash, and ¼ cup of butter. Mash until smooth, and if you like it, whip that business up with a whisk. Season with salt and pepper to taste. Garnish with extra chives and a generous drizzle of melted butter. Enjoy!

3.4 Traeger Prime Rib Roast
Ingredients:

- 1 (5-7 Bones) Prime Rib Roast
- Traeger Prime Rib Rub, As Needed

Instructions:

- Coat the roast evenly with the Traeger Prime Rib Rub and wrap in plastic wrap. Let sit in the refrigerator for 24 hours.
- When ready to cook, set the temperature to High and preheat, lid closed for 15 minutes.
- Place the prime rib fat side up, directly on the grill grate and cook for 30 minutes. Starting at a higher heat will help to develop a crispy, rendered crust.
- After 30 minutes, reduce the grill temperature to 325°F.
- Close lid and roast at 325°F for 3-4 hours or until cooked to desired internal temperature, 120°F for rare, 130°F for medium rare, 140°F for medium and 150°F for well done.
- Remove from grill and let rest 15 minutes before carving. Enjoy!

3.5 Italian Beef Sandwich
Ingredients:

- 1 Qty. (4 Lb.) Lean, Boneless Beef Roast (Sirloin or Top Round)
- Salt
- Pepper
- 4 Cloves Garlic, Thinly Sliced
- Traeger Prime Rib Rub
- 6 Cups Beef Broth
- 8 Hoagie-Style Buns (For Sandwiches)
- 6 Slices Swiss Cheese
- 1 Cup Bottled Giardiniera (Italian Pickled Vegetables; Optional), Chopped

Instructions:

- When ready to cook, set the temperature to 450°F and preheat, lid closed for 15 minutes.
- Season the roast liberally with salt, pepper and Traeger prime rib rub. Using a paring knife, make 10-15 slits in the roast every 1" or so. Insert a garlic clove into each slit.
- Place the roast directly on the grill grate and cook for about 1 hour flipping halfway through until browned well.
- Remove the roast from the grill and transfer to a deep Dutch oven. Pour the beef broth over the roast. Cover tightly with foil and place back on the grill. Reduce the grill temperature to 300°F and cook the roast for 3-4 hours or until it is fork tender.
- While the roast cooks, chop the giardiniera into small pieces.
- Remove the Dutch oven from the grill and shred removing any large bits of fat or connective tissue. Transfer the meat back to the Dutch over and stir to combine with the juices.
- Increase the grill temperature to high and preheat lid closed for 10 minutes.
- Place hoagie buns cut side up on a small sheet tray. Fill with the shredded roast and top with a slice of cheese. Transfer to the grill and cook for another 5-10 minutes or until the cheese is melted.
- Remove from the grill and top with chopped pickled veggies. Serve with remaining cooking liquid for dipping if desired. Enjoy!

3.6 Thai Beef Skewers
Ingredients:

- 1/4 Cup Vegetable Oil
- 1/4 Cup Soy Sauce
- 1 Juice of Lime
- 2 Cloves Garlic, Finely Minced
- 1 Tbsp. Fresh Ginger, Peeled and Minced
- 1 Tsp. Black Pepper, Freshly Ground
- 1/2 Beef Sirloin, Trimmed and Cut Into 1-1/4 Inch Dice
- 1/2 Red Bell Pepper, Stemmed, Seeded, And Cut Into 1/4 Inch Dice
- 1/2 Cup Dry-Roasted Peanuts (Salted or Unsalted), Coarsely Chopped
- 1 Traeger Skewers Set

Instructions:

- In a small bowl, whisk together the oil, soy sauce, lime juice, garlic, ginger, sugar, and black pepper. Transfer the meat to a large bowl or resealable plastic bag and pour the marinade over the meat, turning to coat each piece thoroughly. Refrigerate for 2 to 4 hours, or longer if desired.
- Drain the marinade off the sirloin cubes (discard the marinade) and pat them dry with paper towels. Thread the meat on the skewers, keeping the pieces close together to minimize exposure of the skewer to the heat. (You can also slip a folded length of aluminum foil under the exposed ends to protect them.)
- When ready to cook, set the temperature to 425°F and preheat, lid closed for 15 minutes.
- Arrange the skewers on the grill grate and grill for 2 to 4 minutes per side, or until the desired degree of doneness is reached. To serve, sprinkle with the diced red pepper and the chopped peanuts. Enjoy!

3.7 BBQ CHILI BURGER
Ingredients:

- Beef Chili
- 2.5 Lbs. Ground Beef
- 1 Large Onion, Diced
- 1 Tsp Kosher Salt
- 1 Can Chipotles in Adobo, Minced with Sauce
- 1/4 Cup Chili Powder
- 1-1/2 Tbsp Cumin Powder
- 3 Cloves Garlic, Peeled and Minced
- 1 Jalapeño Pepper, Minced
- 1 (14 Oz) Can Diced or Crushed Tomatoes
- 2 Cups Chicken Stock
- 1/8 Cup Flour
- 1/2 Tbsp Dark Chili Powder
- 1/2 Tbsp Ground Cinnamon
- Juice Of 1 Lime
- 1 Hershey's Chocolate Bar
- Salt and Pepper, To Taste
- Chili Burgers
- 2 Lbs. Ground Beef
- Traeger Beef Rub, As Needed
- 2 Cups Beef Chili or Preferred Chili
- 5 Hamburger Buns
- 5 Slices Cheddar Cheese
- 1 Red Onion, Sliced
- 1 Bag Frito Corn Chips

Instructions:

- For the Beef Chili: Heat a large Dutch oven on the stove top over medium-high heat. Cook the ground beef until browned and cooked through.

- Add all chili **Ingredients:** minus the chocolate and limes to the Dutch oven.
- When ready to cook, start the Traeger according to grill instructions. Set the temperature to 350 degrees F and preheat, lid closed for 10 to 15 minutes.
- Put the Dutch oven into the grill for 2 hours, stirring every hour. Remove Dutch oven from grill.
- Stir the lime juice and the chocolate into the chili. Set chili aside until ready to assemble the burgers.
- For the burgers: When ready to cook, set the temperature to 350°F and preheat, lid closed for 15 minutes.
- Form into 5 equal patties and season both sides with Traeger Beef Rub.
- Place patties directly on the grill grate and cook for 4-5 minutes per side, flipping once. Top each burger with cheese and cook for 1 minute more to melt.
- Remove from the grill and let rest 1-2 minutes.
- To build burger, place the patty on the bottom bun, add a scoop of chili, Fritos, red onion and finish with the top bun. Enjoy

3.8 Traeger Filet Mignon
Ingredients:

- 3 Filet Mignon Steaks
- 1 Tsp Salt
- 1 Tsp Pepper
- 2 Cloves Garlic, Minced
- 3 Tbsp Butter, Softened

Instructions:

- In a small bowl combine salt, pepper, garlic, and softened butter. Rub on both sides of filets. Let rest 10 minutes.
- When ready to cook, set the temperature to 450°F and preheat, lid closed for 15 minutes.
- Place steaks directly on the grill and cook for 5-8 minutes on each side, or until the filets reach an internal temperature of 135-140 degrees F for medium rare. Enjoy!

3.9 Whiskey Bourbon BBQ Cheeseburger
Ingredients:

- 3 Lbs. Ground Beef
- 1/2 Cup Brown Sugar
- Hot Sauce to Taste
- 1/2 Cup Whiskey Bourbon
- Traeger Rub as Needed
- 1 Lb. Bacon
- 4 Slices Cheddar Cheese
- 1 Red Onion, Sliced
- 4 Large Hamburger Buns

Instructions:

- In a medium bowl, combine ground beef and Traeger Rub and mix well using caution not to overwork or allow the beef to get too warm.
- Divide the ground beef in quarters and put each quarter in a 6" cake ring. Press down and form the beef into a patty.
- With a skewer, poke about 40 holes about ¾" of the way through each patty. Spread brown sugar all over the top of the patties then drizzle with hot sauce. Pour whisky over each burger, transfer to the fridge and let sit for about a half hour.
- When ready to cook, set temperature to 225°F and preheat, lid closed for 10-15 minutes.
- Remove burgers from the cake rings. When the grill is to temp, place bacon and burgers directly on the grill grate and cook until burgers internal temperature reaches 165 °F. In the last ten minutes of cooking, top with cheddar cheese to melt.
- Remove burgers and bacon from the grill and build your burger to your liking. Enjoy!

3.10 Steak Taco Salad

Ingredients:

- 1 Avocado
- 1 Jalapeno
- 1 Egg Yolk
- 1/2 Bunch Cilantro
- 1 Clove Garlic
- Juice Of 1 Lime
- 1 Cup Canola Oil

Salad

- 2- 8 Oz Snake River Farm Top Sirloin Steaks
- Traeger Coffee Rub as Needed
- 1 Ear of Corn Shucked
- 1/2 Tbsp Olive Oil
- Salt to Taste
- 2 Hearts Romaine
- 1 Can Black Beans, Drained and Rinsed
- 1/4 Cup Pico De Gallo
- 1 Jalapeno, Thinly Sliced
- 1 Tbsp Cilantro Leaves, Torn

Instructions:

- When ready to cook, set temperature to 180°F and preheat, lid closed for 15 minutes. For optimal flavor, use Super Smoke if available.
- Cut the avocado in half and place it cut side up, directly on the grill grate. Smoke for 15-20 minutes until desired smoke flavor is achieved. Remove from grill and set aside to cool.
- Scoop the flesh from the smoked avocado and place in the pitcher of a blender. Add remaining **Ingredients:** except for the oil and puree until smooth. With the motor running, gradually add the oil a little bit at a time until it has all been added and the mixture is emulsified. Season with salt and lime juice to taste.

FOR THE SALAD:

- Season the steaks with Traeger coffee rub as needed. Brush the corn cob with olive oil and season with kosher salt.
- When ready to cook set the temperature to 450 °F and preheat lid closed for 10-15 minutes.
- Place the steaks and corn next to each other on the grill. Cook the steaks for about 5-7 minutes per side or until the internal temperature registers 130 °F for medium rare. Remove from grill and set aside to rest. Allow the corn to cook for 15-20 minutes until the kernels are tender and the exterior is golden brown. This will take longer than the steaks to cook but should be done by the time the steaks have finished resting.
- Chop the lettuce into bite sized pieces and place in a serving bowl. Toss with as much dressing as desired. Cut the kernels from the cob and sprinkle over the top of the dressed salad. Add black beans, Pico, jalapeno, cilantro.
- Thinly slice the steak and place on top of the salad. This salad, as is, is gluten free and dairy free but top with cheese if desired. Enjoy!

3.11 Cowboy Cut Steak
Ingredients:

- 2 Ea. Snake River Farms Cowboy Cut Steak (2.5 Lbs. Each)
- Traeger Beef Rub to Taste
- Kosher Salt
- Gremolata
- 1 Bunch Parsley
- 2 Tbsp Chopped Mint
- 1 Tbsp Preserved Lemon, Minced
- 1 Clove Garlic Minced
- 1/4 Cup Olive Oil
- Juice Of 1 Lemon
- Salt and Pepper to Taste

Instructions:

- Season the steaks liberally with Traeger Beef rub and kosher salt.
- When ready to cook, set the temperature to 225 °F (with Super Smoke if using a WiFIRE enabled grill) and preheat lid closed for 10-15 minutes.
- Place steaks directly on the grill grate and cook for 45 minutes or until the internal temperature reaches 115°F.
- Remove steaks from the grill and let rest for 10 minutes.
- While the steaks are resting, increase the grill temperature to high (450-500 °F) and preheat, lid closed for 10-15 minutes.
- Place the steaks back on the grill and cook 5-7 minutes per side or until the internal reaches 130 °F for medium rare.
- For the gremolata:
- In a medium bowl combine all **Ingredients:** and stir well. Adjust seasoning to taste with salt and lemon juice.
- Remove from the grill and let rest 1 minutes before slicing. Spoon gremolata over sliced steak to serve. Enjoy!

3.12 Grilled Butter Basted Porterhouse Steak
Ingredients:

- 4 Tbsp Butter, Melted
- 2 Tbsp Worcestershire Sauce
- 2 Tsp Dijon Mustard
- 2 Porterhouse Steaks (16-20 Oz And At Least 1-1/2" Thick)
- Traeger Prime Rib Rub

Instructions:

- When ready to cook, set the temperature to 225°F and preheat, lid closed for 15 minutes.
- Combine the melted butter, Worcestershire sauce, and mustard and whisk until smooth. Brush on both sides of the steaks with a pastry brush. Season the steaks on both sides with Traeger Prime Rib Rub.
- When grill is to temperature, arrange the steaks on the grill grate and cook for 30 minutes.
- With tongs, transfer the steaks to a platter and increase the heat to 450°F
- When grill reaches 450°F, return the steaks to the grill grate and grill until your desired degree of doneness. 140 degrees F for medium-rare, about 2-3 minutes on each side.
- Baste with the butter Worcestershire sauce mixture once more if desired. Let rest for 3 minutes before serving. Enjoy!

3.13 Tin Foil Dinner
Ingredients:

- 8 Tbsp Butter, Cut into Cubes
- 4 Sprigs Thyme
- 1 Garlic Clove, Minced
- 2 Green Bell Pepper, Chopped
- 1 Sm. Red Onion, Chopped
- 2 Whole Russet Potatoes, Peeled and Chopped
- 1 Lb. Stew Meat
- 1 Tsp Fish Sauce

- 1 Tbsp Worcestershire Sauce
- 1 Tbsp Traeger Veggie Rub
- Salt and Pepper

Instructions:

- When ready to cook, set the temperature to 350°F and preheat, lid closed for 15 minutes.
- Peel and chop potatoes into cubes. Peel and chop onions, peppers, and garlic.
- Place the stew meat in a medium bowl. Add the fish sauce and Worcestershire Sauce and mix well. Season with salt, pepper and Traeger Veggie Rub. Mix again to distribute evenly.
- Tear 4 pieces of foil and lay on a flat surface. Divide the potatoes evenly between the four sheets of foil then follow with onion, bell pepper, garlic and the stew meat- top off with thyme. Top each packet with 2 TBSP of butter.
- Fold the foil up and wrap tightly.
- Place the packets on a sheet tray and transfer to the grill. Cook for 45 minutes to one hour or until potatoes are cooked through and stew meat is tender.
- Remove from the grill, open up the packet and top with fresh herbs if desired. Enjoy!

3.14 Roasted Hatch Chile Burger with Smoked Cheese Sauce
Ingredients:

- Smoked Cheese Sauce
- 16 Oz Velveeta Cheese
- 2 Cloves Garlic, Minced
- 1 Tbsp Butter
- 1 Tsp Franks Red Hot
- 1/4 Cup Milk
- Burgers
- 1 Tbsp Butter
- 1/2 Yellow Onion, Thinly Sliced
- 2 Cloves Garlic, Minced
- 1 Lb. Roasted Hatch Green Chiles, Peeled Deseeded, Cut into Strips
- 2 Lbs. Ground Beef
- 3 Tsp Traeger Beef Rub
- 4 Ea. Burger Buns

Instructions:

- When ready to cook, set temperature to 180°F and preheat, lid closed for 15 minutes.
- For the Smoked Cheese Sauce: Heat 1 Tbsp butter in a small oven safe pan over medium-high heat. Add minced garlic and sauté 30 seconds. Add Velveeta cheese and stir until melted then add hot sauce.
- Transfer the pan to the grill and smoke for 30 minutes. Remove from heat and set aside until ready to use.
- For the Chile-Onions: Heat 1 Tbsp butter in a sauté pan over medium heat. Add onion and cook until translucent and tender, about 5-7 minutes. Add garlic and roasted chiles and cook until chiles are warmed through. Remove from heat and set aside until the burgers are finished.
- Increase the grill temperature to High. For optimal results, set to 500 degrees F if available.
- For the burgers: Form ground beef into 4 equal patties and season with Traeger Beef Rub.
- Place directly on the grill grate and cook for 8-10 minutes, flipping once halfway through.
- Cut burger buns in half and place directly on the grill grate. Toast buns for 2-3 minutes. To build the burgers, place the patty on the bottom bun, pour smoked cheese sauce on top and finish with hatch chile onion mixture. Enjoy!

3.15 Grilled Tomahawk Steak
Ingredients:

- 2 Large Tomahawk Steaks
- 2 Tbsp Kosher Salt
- 2 Tbsp Ground Black Pepper
- 1 Tbsp Paprika
- 1/2 Tbsp Garlic Powder
- 1/2 Tbsp Onion Powder

- 1/2 Tbsp Brown Sugar
- 1 Tsp Ground Mustard
- 1/4 Tsp Cayenne Pepper

Instructions:

- In a small bowl, combine all **Ingredients:** for the rub. Season the steaks liberally with the rub and set steaks aside while the grill preheats.
- When ready to cook, set temperature to 225°F and preheat, lid closed for 15 minutes. For optimal flavor, use Super Smoke if available.
- Place the steaks directly on the grill grate and smoke for 45 minutes to 1 hour, until the internal temperature reaches 120°F.
- Remove from the grill and set aside to rest.
- Increase the grill temperature to 450°F.
- Place the steaks directly on the grill grate and cook 7-10 minutes per side, or until the internal temperature reaches 130°F.
- Remove from grill and let rest 5 minutes before serving. Enjoy!

3.16 Smoked Chili Rib Eye Steaks
Ingredients:

- 4 Rib Eye Steaks, 10-12 Oz Each
- 2 Large Garlic Cloves, Minced
- 1 Tsp Salt
- 2 Tbsp Chili Powder
- 2 Tbsp Worcestershire Sauce
- 2 Tbsp Olive Oil
- 1 Tsp Packed Brown Sugar
- 1 Tsp Ground Cumin

Instructions:

- Mash the garlic and salt into a paste in a small bowl; stir in the chili powder, Worcestershire sauce, olive oil, brown sugar and cumin. Rub all surfaces of the steaks with the mixture.

- Place the steaks and the remaining rub into a large resealable plastic bag and refrigerate for 4 hours or up to 2 days.
- When ready to cook, set the temperature to 225°F and preheat, lid closed for 15 minutes.
- Place the steaks on the grill grate and smoke for about 45 minutes (until the internal temperature reaches 120°F).
- Remove the steaks and set aside to rest. Increase the temperature to High and preheat, lid closed for 10-15 minutes.
- Return the steaks to the grill and cook until your desired doneness. We love a good medium-rare, which is about 135 to 140°F, or about 3 to 5 minutes on the first side and a minute or two on the second side.
- Let the steaks rest for 5 to 10 minutes before serving. Enjoy!

3.17 Smoked Bourbon Jerky
Ingredients:

- 1 (3 Lb.) Flank Steak
- 1 Cup Bourbon
- 1/2 Cup Brown Sugar
- 1/4 Cup Traeger Jerky Rub
- 1 Can Chipotle End Adobo
- 3 Tbsp Worcestershire Sauce
- 1/2 Cup Apple Cider Vinegar

Instructions:

- Roll flank steak up parallel to the grain. Slice, going with the grain, into 1/4" thick slices.
- Combine all **Ingredients:** for marinade in a medium bowl and mix well.
- Place sliced flank steak into a large Ziploc bag and pour marinade over steak. Place in refrigerator and marinate overnight.
- When ready to cook, set temperature to 180°F and preheat, lid closed for 15 minutes.
- Remove flank from the marinade and place on a jerky rack or directly on the grill grate.
- Smoke for about 6 hours or until steak has dried out but is still pliable. Remove from grill and let cool at room temperature, lightly covered for 60 minutes before eating.
- Store in an airtight container or Ziploc bag in the refrigerator. Enjoy!

3.18 Slow Roasted Shawarma
Ingredients:

- 5.5 Lbs. Top Sirloin
- 5.5 Lbs. Boneless Skinless Chicken Thighs
- 4.5 Lbs. Lamb Fat
- 4 Tbsp Traeger Rub
- 2 Large Yellow Onions
- Pita Bread
- Topping Options: Cucumber, Tomatoes, Tahini, Pickles, Fries, Israeli Salad
- A Double Skewer
- A Cast Iron Griddle

Instructions:

- *Plan ahead! Assemble the shawarma stack the night before you plan to cook it.
- Slice all the meat and fat into ½" slices and place into 3 bowls (pro tip: it's easier to slice if they are all partially frozen).
- Season each bowl with Traeger Rub and massage the rub into the meat.
- Place half an onion on the bottom of each half skewer to make a firm base. then add 2 layers from each bowl at a time. Try to make the stack symmetrical, more or less. Then put the other 2 half onions at the top. Wrap in plastic wrap and refrigerate overnight.
- When ready to cook, set temperature to 275°F and preheat, lid closed for 15 minutes.
- Lay the shawarma directly on the grill grate and cook for about 3-4 hours, rotating at least once.
- Remove from grill and increase the temperature to 445°F. While the grill preheats, place a cast iron griddle directly on the grill grate and brush with olive oil.
- When the griddle is hot place the whole shawarma on the cast iron and sear 5-10 minutes per side. Remove from grill, slice off the edges, then repeat with remaining shawarma.
- Serve in pita bread with your favorite toppings like cucumber, tomatoes, tahini, pickles, fries or Israeli salad.

- Enjoy!

3.19 Reverse Seared Rib Eye Caps
Ingredients:

- 1 1/2 Lb. Rib Eye Cap
- 2 Tbsp Traeger Coffee Rub
- 2 Tbsp Traeger Beef Rub

Instructions:

- Trim the Rib Eye Cap of excess silver skin and fat, if needed. Cut the cap into 4 equal portions and roll into steaks. Tie with butchers' twine to secure.
- In a small bowl, combine both rubs. Season the steaks liberally with the rub mixture and set aside while the grill heats up.
- When ready to cook, set temperature to 225°F and preheat, lid closed for 15 minutes. For optimal flavor, use Super Smoke if available.
- Place the steaks directly on the grill grate, and smoke for 30-45 minutes until the internal temperature reaches 120°F.
- Remove from the grill and set aside to rest.
- Increase the grill temperature to 450°F.
- Place the steaks directly on the grill grate and cook 3-4 minutes per side, or until the internal temperature reaches 130°F.
- Remove from grill and let rest 5 minutes before serving.
- Enjoy!

3.20 BBQ Beef Short Ribs
Ingredients:

- 4 Ea. (4 Bone) Beef Short Rib Racks
- 1/2 Cup Traeger Beef Rub
- 1 Cup Apple Juice

Instructions:

- If your butcher has not already done so, remove the thin papery membrane from the bone-side of the ribs by working the tip of a butter knife underneath the membrane over a middle bone. Use paper towels to get a firm grip, then tear the membrane off.
- Season both sides of ribs with Traeger Beef Rub.
- When ready to cook, set the Traeger to 225°F and preheat, lid closed for 15 minutes.
- Arrange the ribs on the grill grate, bone side down.
- Cook for 8-10 hours, spritzing or mopping with apple juice every 60 minutes until internal temperature reaches 205°F.
- Slice between ribs and serve immediately. Enjoy!

3.21 Grilled T-Bone Steaks with Bloody Mary Steak Sauce
Ingredients:

- 2 Large T-Bone Steaks
- 1 Tbsp Kosher Salt
- 1 Tbsp Black Pepper
- 1 Cup Smoked Bloody Mary Mix
- 1/2 White Onion, Small Dice
- 1 Clove Garlic, Minced
- Juice Of 1 Lemon
- 1 Tbsp Soy Sauce
- 2 Tbsp Brown Sugar
- 1 Tbsp Mustard
- 2 Tbsp Olive Oil

Instructions:

- When ready to cook, set temperature to 225°F and preheat, lid closed for 15 minutes. For optimal flavor, use Super Smoke if available.

- Season the steaks with salt and pepper and place directly on the grill grate and smoke for 60-90 minutes until the internal temperature reaches 125°F when an instant read thermometer is inserted into the thickest part of the steak.
- For the Steak Sauce: Place olive oil in a medium sauce pan over medium heat. Add onion and garlic and sauté 5 minutes until the onions are lightly browned and translucent. Add remaining **Ingredients:** and reduce the heat to a simmer. Simmer for 20-30 minutes until the mixture has reduced and thickened.
- Remove the steaks from the grill and increase the temperature to High.
- When the grill is hot, sear the stakes for 5 minutes on each side. Remove from the grill and let rest 10 minutes before serving.
- Serve steak with steak sauce on the side warm or room temperature. Enjoy

3.22 Grilled Thai Beef Salad
Ingredients:

- 1.5 Lb. Hanger or Skirt Steak
- Salt, To Taste
- Cracked White Pepper, To Taste
- 2-4 (Depending on Spice Preference) Fresh Hot Thai Chili Peppers (Or Jalapeños), Minced Very Thin
- 1 Garlic Clove, Chopped and Minced Fine
- 4 Tbsp Thai Fish Sauce
- 4 Tbsp Fresh Squeezed Lime Juice
- 1 Tbsp Toasted Sticky Rice Powder (Optional)
- 1 Tbsp Palm or Brown Sugar
- 1 Heart of Romaine Lettuce, Chopped
- 1 English Cucumber Without Seeds, Sliced Thin on A Bias Cut
- 1 Handful Fresh Mint Leaves, Roughly Chopped
- 6 Cherry Tomatoes, Halved
- 1 Small Red Onion, Sliced Very Thin
- 2 Green Onions Cut Into 1/4" Pieces
- 2 Sprigs Cilantro Without Stems, Roughly Chopped

Instructions:

- When ready to cook, set temperature to High and preheat, lid closed for 15 minutes.
- Season both sides of steak with salt and cracked white pepper. Brush the grill with canola oil to prevent steaks from sticking.
- Grill hanger steak until it reaches an internal temperature of 130°F for medium rare, about 5-10 minutes. Allow meat to rest then slice thin.
- For the Dressing: Mix together the garlic, chili peppers, fish sauce, lime juice and sugar in a small bowl. Add the toasted rice powder last. Note: If toasted rice powder is not accessible, use uncooked rice and dry roast in a pan over low heat until golden brown and grind into a powder with a mortar and pestle or food processor to add a nutty texture.
- Add the sliced hanger steak to the dressing and toss well.
- In another bowl, add all the herbs with the chopped romaine cucumbers and tomatoes and toss everything together with the dressing and the hanger steak.
- Add additional fish sauce, lime juice, sugar, toasted rice powder and chili peppers based on your taste preference.
- Garnish with cilantro and mint. Enjoy!

3.23 Grilled Ribeye with Green Butter
Ingredients:

- Ribeye Steak
- 3 Ribeye Steaks, 1 1/2-2" Thickness
- 1/4 Cup Kosher Salt
- 1/4 Cup Coarse Ground Black Pepper
- 3 Tbsp Onion Powder
- Green Butter
- 1 Stick Butter, Room Temperature
- 1 1/2 Tbsp Flat Leaf Parsley, Chopped
- 1/2 Tsp Garlic, Minced
- Pinch White Pepper
- Juice Of 1/2 Lemon

Instructions:

- When ready to cook, set the Traeger to 225°F and preheat, lid closed for 15 minutes.
- For the Green Butter: Combine all **Ingredients:** for the green butter and place in the fridge until ready to use.
- Combine the salt, pepper and onion powder. Rub the mixture on the steaks and place them on the grill.
- Cook until steaks reach an internal temperature of 120°F. This should take approximately 75-90 minutes.
- Remove steaks from the grill and tent with foil. Increase the grill temperature to High and let it come to temperature.
- When the grill is hot, place the steaks back on the grill for 4 minutes per side, adding a tablespoon of the green butter after the first flip.
- Top with green butter if desired. Enjoy!

3.24 Smoked Peppered Beef Tenderloin
Ingredients:

- 1(2-2 1/2 Lb.) Snake River Farms Beef Tenderloin Roast, Trimmed
- 1/2 Cup Dijon Mustard
- 2 Cloves Garlic, Minced to A Paste
- 2 Tbsp Bourbon or Strong Cold Coffee
- Jacobsen Salt, As Needed
- Coarsely Ground Black and Green Peppercorns, As Needed

Instructions:

- Lay the tenderloin on a large piece of plastic wrap.
- Combine the mustard, garlic, and bourbon in a small bowl. Slather the mixture evenly all over the tenderloin. Allow to sit at room temperature for 1 hour.
- Unwrap the plastic wrap and generously season the tenderloin on all sides with the salt and ground black and green peppercorns.
- When ready to cook, set temperature to 180°F and preheat, lid closed for 15 minutes.
- Arrange the tenderloin directly on the grill grate and smoke for 60 minutes.
- Increase the grill temperature to 400°F and roast the tenderloin until the internal temperature reaches 130°F, about 20 to 30 minutes depending on the thickness of the tenderloin. Do not overcook.
- Let rest for 10 minutes before slicing. Enjoy!

3.25 BBQ Sweet Pepper Meatloaf
Ingredients:

- 5 Lb. 80/20 Ground Beef
- 2 Eggs
- 1 Cup Plain Panko Bread Crumbs
- 1 Tbsp Kosher Salt
- 1 Tbsp Black Pepper
- 2 Tbsp Traeger Rub
- 1 Cup Finely Chopped Red Sweet Peppers
- 1 Cup Finely Chopped Green Onion
- 1 Cup Ketchup

Instructions:

- Thoroughly mix together the ground beef, eggs, plain panko bread crumbs, kosher salt, black pepper, Traeger rub, red sweet peppers and green onion.
- When ready to cook, set the temperature to 225°F and preheat, lid closed for 15 minutes.
- Mold the meat mixture into a loaf and season exterior with the Traeger rub.
- Place meatloaf directly on the grill grate and cook for 2 hours and 15 minutes.
- Increase the grill temperature to 375°F and cook until an internal temperature of 155°F.
- Glaze the meatloaf with ketchup and cook an additional 15 minutes.
- Allow to rest for 15 minutes before slicing. Enjoy!

3.26 Traeger Pot Roast Sandwich

Ingredients:

- Pot Roast
- 1 (3-4 Lb.) Chuck Roast
- Traeger Beef Rub, As Needed
- 2 Qtrs. Beef Stock
- 1 Carrot, Peeled and Chopped into Chunks
- 1 Stalk Celery, Chopped into Chunks
- 1 Small Yellow Onion, Peeled and Cut into Chunks
- 4 Cloves Garlic
- 2 Tbsp Cumin
- 2 Tbsp Chili Powder
- 2 Tbsp Garlic Powder
- 2 Tbsp Onion Powder
- 6 Slices Provolone
- 2 Loafs Crusty Bread, Such as Baguette or Sourdough
- Leek Marmalade
- 1/2 Cup 3 Leeks, Thinly Sliced, Washed and Dried
- 1/4 Cup Butter
- 1 Tbsp Yellow or Brown Mustard Seeds
- 1/4 Cup Sherry Vinegar
- 1/4 Cup Brown Sugar
- Salt, To Taste
- Horseradish Mayonnaise
- 1/2 Cup Mayonnaise
- Prepared Horseradish, To Taste

Instructions:

- When ready to cook, set the temperature to 400°F and preheat, lid closed for 15 minutes.
- Season the roast liberally with Traeger Beef rub and place on directly on the grill grate. Roast for 20-30 minutes until the outside is caramelized.
- Remove roast from the grill and place in a large pot. Reduce the grill temperature to 325°F.
- Add beef stock (the liquid should cover about 3/4 the height of the roast) and add carrot, celery, onion and spices. Stir to distribute evenly making sure there are no vegetables on top of the roast.
- Cover the pot and place back on the grill. Braise for 3-4 hours until the roast is fork tender.
- Remove the roast from the braising liquid and shred, discarding any large pieces of fat or sinew.
- For the Gravy: Strain the liquid and place back in the pot. Bring the liquid to a boil then reduce to a simmer. Thicken the liquid with cornstarch to desired consistency.
- Pour a bit of the gravy over the reserved shredded meat and reserve the rest to dip.
- Make sure leeks are washed well. The easiest way to do this is to slice the leeks, submerge them in a bucket of water and stir vigorously to remove the dirt. Lift the leeks out of the water into a strainer and shake off excess and dry.
- For the Leek Marmalade: Melt the butter in a medium sauce pan over medium high heat. Add leeks and reduce heat to medium. Cook the leeks stirring occasionally until completely softened and falling apart. Add the mustard seeds, vinegar and brown sugar and stir to combine. Simmer for 20-30 minutes until the liquid reduces and thickens. Season to taste with salt. Remove from heat and let cool.
- For the Horseradish Mayo: In a small bowl combine mayo and horseradish and set aside.
- Split loafs lengthwise and portion into 6-8 sandwiches.
- Spread a bit of the horseradish mayo and leek marmalade onto each half of the bread. Top each half with shredded beef and a slice of provolone.
- Place sandwich halves back on the grill (set at 325°F) long enough to melt the cheese, about 5 minutes.
- Remove from grill and serve open faced or with two halves together to make a sandwich. Serve with extra gravy to dip. Enjoy!

3.27 Grilled Steak Salad

Ingredients:

- 1 Ea. (1.5 Lb.) Black Flat Iron Steak
- Traeger Beef Rub
- 8 Oz Arugula
- 8 Oz Baby Spinach
- 1/4 Cup Cherry Tomatoes, Halved
- 1/2 Red Onion, Thinly Sliced
- 1/4 Cup Blue Cheese
- 2 Tbsp Balsamic Vinegar
- 4 Tbsp Extra Virgin Olive Oil
- Coarse Sea Salt and Fresh Black Pepper, To Taste

Instructions:

- When ready to cook, set temperature to High and preheat, lid closed for 15 minutes.
- Trim any sinew or silver skin from the flat iron steak. Season liberally with Traeger Beef rub and kosher salt.
- When the grill is hot, place steak directly on the grill grate. Cook for 10-15 minutes then flip and cook 10 minutes more. Remove from the grill when the internal temperature reaches 130°F when an instant read thermometer is inserted into the thickest part. Let steak rest 10 minutes before slicing.
- While the steak is resting, build the salad. In a large bowl combine the greens, tomatoes, onion and blue cheese. Drizzle with balsamic and olive oil and toss.
- Place salad on a large platter and top with sliced steak. Finish with a sprinkle of sea salt and fresh black pepper. Enjoy!

3.28 Smoked Corned Beef & Cabbage

Ingredients:

- 1 (3 To 5 Lb.) Corned Beef Brisket
- 1 Qtr. Chicken Stock
- 1 (12 Oz) Can Beer, Preferably A Pilsner or Lager
- 1/2 Cup (1 Stick) Butter, Cut into Slices
- 1/4 Tsp Garlic Salt
- 2 Tbsp Fresh Dill, Chopped
- 2 Cups Baby Carrots
- 1 Lb. Baby Potatoes or Fingerlings
- 1 Head Cabbage, Cut in Wedges

Instructions:

- When ready to cook, set the temperature to 180°F and preheat, lid closed for 15 minutes.
- Rinse brisket and pat dry. Place directly on the grill grate and smoke for 2 hours.
- Increase grill temperature to 325°F and preheat, lid closed.
- Remove brisket from grill and place in a roasting pan. Sprinkle seasoning packet on top. Pour chicken stock and dark beer over the roast and into the pan.
- Cover roasting pan with foil and place on the grill. Cook for 2 1/2 hours or until beef is fork tender.
- Remove foil and add carrots and potatoes to the roasting pan. Cover meat and vegetables with garlic salt and butter slices.
- Recover with foil and cook for an additional 20 minutes or until carrots and potatoes are just tender. Add cabbage, cover and return to grill for 20 minutes more.
- Remove vegetables from the pan to a bowl or serving platter. Slice beef and serve with potatoes, cabbage and carrots.
- Garnish with fresh dill and thyme if desired. Enjoy!

3.29 Traeger French Dip Sandwich
Ingredients:

- Roast Beef
- 1 (2-2.5 Lb.) Snake River Farms Manhattan Roast
- Traeger Beef Rub, As Needed
- Kosher Salt, As Needed
- Caramelized Onions
- 2 Yellow Onions, Thinly Sliced
- 1 Tbsp Butter
- Salt, To Taste
- Au Jus
- 1 Qtr. Good Quality Beef Stock
- 1 Sprig Thyme
- 1 Sprig Rosemary
- 4 Peppercorns
- 2 Cloves Garlic
- Sandwich
- 2 Baguettes Cut into Sandwich Sized Rolls, Or Hoagie Rolls
- Mayonnaise, As Needed
- 6 Slices Provolone Cheese

Instructions:

- When ready to cook, set the temperature to High and preheat, lid closed for 15 minutes.
- Season the roast liberally with Traeger Beef Rub and salt.
- Place roast directly on the grill grate and cook for 45 minutes until the exterior starts to caramelize and brown.
- Reduce the grill temperature to 325°F and continue to cook roast until the internal temperature reaches 125°F, about 75 minutes.
- Remove roast from grill and let rest for 15 minutes before slicing.
- After resting, thinly slice the meat on a meat slicer or with a very sharp knife. Set meat aside.
- For the Caramelized Onions: Place butter and onions in a sauté pan and cook over medium heat. Season liberally with salt and cook, stirring frequently until the onions are browned and caramelized. If the bottom of the pan starts to stick before the onions are completely cooked through, add 1 Tbsp of water, scrape up the browned bits with a wooden spoon and continue to cook. When completely softened and caramelized, remove from the heat and set aside until ready to build the sandwiches.
- For the Au Jus: Place the **Ingredients:** for the au jus in a pot and bring to a simmer. Cook for 30-45 minutes, season liberally with salt and strain the solids out.
- Toast the buns cut side down on the grill for 5-10 minutes until lightly browned.
- To build the sandwiches, place them toasted side up on a sheet tray. Spread the mayonnaise on the bun, top with the thinly sliced meat, then caramelized onions and cheese.
- Place the tray directly on the grill grate and cook just until the cheese is melted.
- Serve sandwiches hot with au jus. Enjoy!

3.30 3-2-1 BBQ Beef Cheek
Ingredients:

- 2 Ea. (About 2 Lb.) Beef Cheeks, Trimmed of Silver skin
- Traeger Beef Rub, As Needed
- 1/4 Cup Liquid of Your Choice (Beef Stock, Dark Beer Etc)
- 2 Tbsp Honey, Brown Sugar, Or Other Sweetener

Instructions:

- Make sure the beef cheeks are trimmed of all silver skin. Season liberally with Traeger Beef rub.
- When ready to cook, set temperature to 180°F and preheat, lid closed for 15 minutes.
- Place beef cheeks directly on the grill grate and cook until they reach an internal temperature of 165°F, about 3 hours. Remove from grill and place the cheeks in a small rimmed baking dish.
- Increase grill temperature to 225°F.

- In a small bowl, combine liquid and sweetener and stir until sweetener is dissolved. Pour mixture into the baking dish and return the cheeks to the grill to cook for an additional two hours.
- Remove cheeks from the grill and cover with foil. Return to the grill to cook for an additional hour or until the internal temperature reaches 205°F.
- Remove from the grill and allow the steam to escape. Wrap with foil again and let rest for 30 minutes before shredding or slicing. Enjoy!

3.31 Grilled Wagyu Burgers
Ingredients:

- 2 Lb. Snake River Farms Wagyu Ground Beef
- Salt and Pepper, To Taste
- Burger Buns
- Butter Lettuce
- Heirloom Tomatoes, Sliced
- Red Onion, Sliced
- American Cheese

Instructions:

- When ready to cook, set the temperature to High and preheat, lid closed for 15 minutes.
- Form six burger patties and season liberally with salt and pepper.
- When the grill is hot, place burger patties directly on the grill grate and cook for 4 minutes.
- Flip the burgers, top with cheese and cook for 4 minutes longer.
- Remove from grill and let rest 2 minutes.
- Build your burger and top with desired condiments. Enjoy!

3.32 Braised Italian Meatballs
Ingredients:

- 1 Lb. Ground Beef
- 1 Lb. Ground Pork
- 4 Oz Prosciutto, Finely Diced
- 1 Cup Fresh Bread Crumbs
- Kosher Salt
- 2 Tsp Fennel Seeds
- 1 Tsp Oregano
- 1 Cup Whole-Milk Ricotta Cheese
- 1/2 Cup Milk
- 3 Eggs, Whisked
- 1 (28 Oz) Can Crushed Tomatoes, In Their Juices
- Extra-Virgin Olive Oil
- 1/2 Cup Basil Leaves

Instructions:

- When ready to cook, set the temperature to 375°F and preheat, lid closed for 15 minutes.
- In a large mixing bowl, combine the ground beef, pork, prosciutto, bread crumbs, 2 tsp salt, fennel seed, and oregano.
- In a separate mixing bowl, combine the ricotta, milk, and eggs and whisk to combine.
- Using freshly washed hands, combine the meats with the bread crumbs, salt, and herbs until the mixture is evenly combined and the herbs are evenly incorporated.
- Slowly pour the liquid mixture over the meat and continue to use your hands to combine. The mixture will be tacky even when well mixed. Allow to sit for 10 minutes.
- Pro Tip: To check the seasoning of your mixture before cooking off the entire batch, form 1 2-inch patty and cook in a small sauté pan until cooked through, about 2 minutes per side. Taste and adjust the seasoning of the meat mixture as needed.
- Line a large baking sheet with parchment or Traeger butcher paper. Alternately, lightly grease the baking sheet.
- Using clean hands or an ice cream scoop, form meatballs into the size of golf balls.
- Arrange them on the baking sheet with a little space between each so they are not touching. The mixture should yield about 48 meatballs.
- Place the baking sheet directly on the grill and cook, turning the meatballs once, until cooked through when cut in half, about 20 minutes.
- Remove from the grill, add the second batch if necessary, and repeat.
- Reduce the grill temperature to 300°F.
- When the meatballs are cool enough to handle, place all of them in a large roasting pan. Pour the crushed tomatoes over the top. Sprinkle with an additional teaspoon of salt and drizzle 3 tbsp of olive oil over the top.
- Cover the pan tightly with aluminum foil. Place on the grill and cook, covered, for 60-90 minutes or until the tomatoes have absorbed some of the flavor from the meatballs and the meatballs are fork tender.
- Remove meatballs from the grill and sprinkle with basil. Alternately, the meatballs can be roasted, cooled, and refrigerated a day in advance, then brought to room temperature and braised in the tomato sauce before serving. Enjoy!

3.33 Grilled Piranha
Ingredients:

- 1 (2.5 Lb.) Snake River Farms Wagyu Piranha
- Kosher Salt

Instructions:

- Cut the piranha into steaks about 1-inch thick. Fold them in half to form a "C" shape with the fat cap on the outer edge.
- Thread the steaks onto a skewer one on top of the other. Season generously with coarse salt and leave at room temperature while the grill heats up.
- When ready to cook, set the temperature to High and preheat, lid closed for 15 minutes.
- Place the skewered steaks directly on the grill grate and cook for 5-7 minutes per side or until desired internal temperature is reached, 130°F for medium-rare.
- Let rest 5 minutes before slicing. Enjoy!

3.34 Reverse Seared Porterhouse Steak
Ingredients:

- 1-2 (About 2 Lb.) Dry Aged Porterhouse Steaks
- Kosher Salt
- 8 Cups Arugula
- Extra-Virgin Olive Oil
- Freshly Ground Pepper
- 3 Oz Parmigiano-Reggiano

Instructions:

- Two hours before cooking, remove the steaks from the refrigerator and allow to come to room temperature. Pat dry with a paper towel.
- When ready to cook, set temperature to 225°F and preheat, lid closed for 15 minutes. For optimal flavor, use Super Smoke if available.
- Season both sides of steak with a generous amount of salt. Place steaks on grill and cook for 30 to 45 minutes or until an instant read thermometer inserted in the thickest part of the meat reads 120°F.
- Remove steaks from grill and turn the grill temperature up to High. For optimal results, set to 500°F if available.
- Place the steaks back on grill and sear on both sides for 3 minutes or until desired internal temperature is reached, 125-130°F for medium rare. Remove from grill and let rest 10 minutes before slicing. Slice the meat against the grain into 1/2" thick slices.
- To serve, place the arugula on a large platter. Drizzle arugula with olive oil and sprinkle with salt. Place the sliced steak and its juices on top of the arugula.
- Add a fresh grinding of pepper over the steak and shave the Parmigiano-Reggiano over the top of the steak. Enjoy!

3.35 Reverse Seared Filet Mignon with Red Wine Reduction
Ingredients:

- Bacon Wrapped Filet Mignon
- 2 Ea. Filet Mignon
- 2 Slices Bacon
- Traeger Prime Rib Rub, As Needed
- Toothpicks
- Red Wine Reduction
- 1 Tbsp Butter
- 1 Shallot, Thinly Sliced
- 1/2 Cup Red Wine
- 1/2 Cup Beef Stock
- 1 Tsp Chopped Rosemary
- 1 Tbsp Cold Butter
- Salt, To Taste

Instructions:

- When ready to cook, set the temperature to 225°F and preheat, lid closed for 15 minutes.
- Wrap each filet with a slice of bacon and secure with a tooth pick. Season liberally with Traeger Prime Rib rub.
- Place steaks directly on the grill grate and cook until the internal temperature reaches 115°F, start checking after about 20 minutes.
- Remove steaks from grill and set aside. Increase grill temperature to High and let preheat 10 minutes.
- For the Red-Wine Reduction Sauce: In a sauté pan over medium heat, melt 1 Tbsp butter and shallots and sauté until translucent. Add red wine and beef stock and bring to a simmer. Reduce the heat and let simmer until reduced by half. Add rosemary, remove from heat and whisk in the 1 Tbsp cold butter. Season with salt to taste.
- When grill is hot, place steaks back on the grill and sear for 5-7 minutes on each side or until the internal temperature reaches 125°F for medium-rare.
- Remove from grill and let rest 5-7 minutes before serving.
- Serve steaks with your favorite sides and spoonful of red wine reduction sauce over the top. Enjoy!

3.36 Grilled Flank Steak with Peperomia
Ingredients:

- Flank Steak
- 1/4 Cup Olive Oil
- 2 Tbsp Red Wine Vinegar
- 2 Tbsp Brown Sugar
- 2 Tsp Salt
- 1 Tsp Fennel Seeds
- 1 Tsp Paprika
- 1/2 Tsp Freshly Ground Black Pepper
- 2 Cloves Garlic, Crushed
- 1 (2 Lb.) Flank Steak
- Peperomia
- 5 Red or Yellow Bell Peppers (Combination Preferred)
- 1/4 Cup Extra-Virgin Olive Oil, Plus More for Finishing
- Kosher Salt
- 1 Yellow Onion, Thinly Sliced
- 2 Small Fennel Bulbs, Core and Stems Removed, Thinly Sliced
- 2 Cloves Garlic, Peeled and Minced
- 1/4 Tsp Crushed Red Pepper Flakes
- 2 Tbsp Capers, Rinsed and Drained
- 2 Tbsp Sherry Vinegar
- 1/4 Cup Thinly Sliced Basil

Instructions:

- For the Marinade: Combine the olive oil, vinegar, sugar, spices, and the garlic in a baking dish that is large enough to hold the flank steak. Stir to combine.
- Add the flank steak to marinade and turn to coat. Cover with plastic wrap and refrigerate for 1-8 hours. Remove the meat from the refrigerator one hour before grilling.
- For the peperomia, when ready to cook, set temperature to High and preheat, lid closed for 15 minutes.
- Line a baking sheet with aluminum foil.
- Place the bell peppers in a large bowl. Drizzle with 1 Tbsp of the olive oil, sprinkle with a teaspoon of salt and toss until the peppers are well coated. Transfer to the prepared baking sheet.
- Roast for 15 minutes on the grill, turn the peppers, and continue roasting until the peppers are charred and soft, with their skins beginning to peel away, an additional 20 minutes.
- Return the peppers to the large bowl, cover tightly with plastic wrap, and let sit for 10 minutes. When the peppers are cool enough to handle, remove the stems, skin, and seeds. Cut the flesh into rough strips and set aside.
- In a large saute pan over medium heat, warm the remaining 4 Tbsp olive oil. Add the onion and fennel and cook, stirring occasionally, until softened, about 8 to 10 minutes.
- Add the garlic, crushed red pepper, and ½ tsp salt and cook, stirring constantly, until fragrant, about 1 minutes. Stir in the capers and vinegar and allow the vinegar to reduce for 1 minute. Remove from the heat and stir in the roasted peppers.
- Taste and adjust the salt and pepper as desired. If using immediately, finish with a generous drizzle of extra-virgin olive oil.
- To grill the steak, set the temperature to High on the grill and preheat, lid closed for 15 minutes.
- Remove the steak from the marinade and pat dry with paper towels. Place on the grill and cook, turning once, until the internal temperature reaches 135 degrees for medium-rare, about 10 minutes per side.
- Remove from the grill and allow to rest for 10 minutes before slicing.
- Serve flank steak with the peperomia. Enjoy!

3.37 Grilled Cheesesteak Sandwich
Ingredients:

- 1.5 Lbs. Snake River Farms New York Strip Slices
- Traeger Beef Rub, As Needed
- Salt and Pepper, To Taste
- 1 Tbsp Canola Oil
- 1 Green Bell Pepper, Sliced
- 1 Yellow Bell Pepper, Sliced
- 1 Red Bell Pepper, Sliced
- 1 Large Yellow Onion, Sliced into Rounds
- Provolone Cheese
- Hoagie Rolls

Instructions:

- When ready to cook, set the temperature to High and preheat, lid closed for 15 minutes.
- Place a cast iron griddle directly on the grill grate while the grill preheats.
- Season the peppers and onions liberally with salt and pepper. Season the strip slices with Traeger Beef rub.
- Lightly oil the cast iron griddle with 1 Tbsp canola oil. Add onions and season with salt.
- Sauté 5 minutes until translucent. Add peppers and sauté 10 minutes more until peppers are softened and cooked through.
- While the peppers and onions are cooking, place the seasoned steak strips directly on the grill grate next to the griddle and cook for 3 minutes per side until lightly browned and cooked through.
- Place buns cut side down on the top grill grate to toast.
- When the steak is done, transfer to the griddle to build the sandwiches. Place a pile of peppers and onions on top of each pile of steak and top with a slice of provolone.
- Close the lid and let the cheese melt. Using two spatulas, transfer each pile to the buns and serve hot. Enjoy!

3.38 Reverse Seared Ny Strip Steak
Ingredients:

- 4 (1-1/2" Inch Thick) New York Strip Steaks
- Traeger Beef Rub
- 4 Tbsp Butter

Instructions:

- When ready to cook, set the Traeger to 225°F and preheat, lid closed for 15 minutes. For optimal flavor, use Super Smoke if available.
- While the grill is coming up to temperature, season the steaks with Traeger Beef rub.
- Place the steaks in the grill and smoke for 60 minutes or until they reach an internal temperature of 105 to 110°F. Remove steaks from grill and set on the counter to rest.
- Increase the grill temperature to 450°F. For optimal results, set to 500°F if available and let it come up to temperature with the lid close, about 10 minutes.
- Return steaks to grill and sear for 4 minutes. Flip steaks and add 1 tbsp butter to each steak.
- Sear for another 4 minutes and check the internal temperature. The desired finish temperature is 130 to 135°F for medium-rare.Once desired temperature is reached, remove steaks from grill. Let rest 5 minutes. Enjoy!

3.39 Traeger Ny Strip Steak
Ingredients:

- 1 (14 Oz) New York Strip Steak
- Traeger Beef Rub
- 1 Cup Traeger Sweet & Heat BBQ Sauce

Instructions:

- Pour the Sweet & Heat BBQ Sauce into a shallow casserole dish, stirring to combine.
- Place the strip steak in the mixture, making sure the steak is coated evenly on both sides. Cover with plastic wrap and marinate in the refrigerator for a minimum of 3 hours to overnight.
- Remove the steak from the marinade and season with Traeger Beef rub. Let steaks come to room temperature before grilling, about 45 minutes.
- When ready to cook, set temperature to High and preheat, lid closed for 15 minutes.
- Place steak toward the front of the grill grate and cook for 4-5 minutes on each side until steaks reach desired internal temperature, 130°F for medium-rare.
- Remove from the grill and let rest for 5 minutes. Slice against the grain to serve. Enjoy!

3.40 Grilled Peppercorn Steaks with Mushroom Cream Sauce
Ingredients:

- Peppercorn Steaks
- 4 Beef Steaks, Preferably Beef Tenderloin Steaks
- 1/2 Cup Dijon Mustard
- 2 Cloves Garlic, Minced to A Paste
- 2 Tbsp Bourbon or Strong Cold Coffee
- Kosher Salt
- Black Pepper and Green Peppercorns, Coarsely Ground
- Mushroom Cream Sauce
- 1 Tbsp Olive Oil
- 16 Oz Cremini Mushrooms, Thinly Sliced
- 1 Clove Garlic, Minced
- 1/2 Cup White Wine
- 1/2 Cup Chicken Stock
- 1/2 Cup Heavy Cream
- Salt and Pepper, To Taste

Instructions:

- In a small bowl, add the mustard, garlic, bourbon, and Worcestershire sauce. Whisk to combine.
- Lay the steaks on a large piece of plastic wrap and slather the mixture evenly all over the tenderloin. Bring the sides of the plastic wrap over the tenderloin and wrap tightly. Allow to sit at room temperature for 60 minutes.
- Unwrap the plastic wrap and generously season the tenderloin on all sides with salt, ground black pepper and green peppercorns. Use your hands to pat the peppercorns into the steak.
- When ready to cook, set temperature to 180°F and preheat, lid closed for 15 minutes. For optimal flavor, use Super Smoke if available.
- Arrange the steaks directly on the grill grate and smoke for 60 minutes. Remove the steaks from the grill.
- Increase the grill temperature to High allow the grill to preheat with the lid closed.
- When grill is hot, return the steaks to the grill and cook until the internal temperature reaches 130°F on an instant-read meat thermometer, about 20 to 30 minutes, depending on the thickness of the steak. Do not overcook.
- For the Mushroom Cream Sauce: Heat olive oil in a large sauté pan over medium heat. Add sliced onions, being careful not to crowd the pan and sauté until softened and lightly browned. Add garlic and sauté 1 minute more. Add the white wine and chicken stock to the mushrooms and bring to a simmer. Simmer for 5-7 minutes then reduce the heat and stir in the cream. Season to taste with salt and pepper. Remove from heat and set aside.
- Transfer steaks to a platter and cover with foil. Let rest for 10 minutes before removing the foil and carving into thin slices.
- To serve, spoon the sauce directly onto the steaks. Enjoy!

3.41 BBQ Brisket Grilled Chees
Ingredients:

- 4 Oz Leftover Brisket
- 2 Slices Texas Toast
- 2 Slices American Cheese
- 1 Tbsp Butter, Room Temperature

Instructions:

- When ready to cook, set the temperature to High and preheat, lid closed for 15 minutes.
- Place a skillet or griddle directly on the grill grate with the flat side up to preheat.
- Butter one side of each piece of bread. Place the buttered side of one piece down on the skillet or griddle, top with one slice of American cheese, the brisket, second slice of cheese, then the other piece of toast buttered side up.
- Close the grill lid and let cook for 5-7 minutes. Flip the sandwich and cook for 5 minutes more.
- Remove from the grill and slice in half. Enjoy!

3.42 Smoked Pastrami Sandwich
Ingredients:

- Brine
- 1 (4-5 Lbs.) Beef Brisket Flat, Fat Trimmed To 1/4-Inch
- 1 Gallon Water
- 6 Cloves Garlic, Peeled and Smashed
- 5 Juniper Berries
- 3 Bay Leaves, Broken into Pieces
- 3/4 Cup Kosher Salt
- 1/2 Cup Brown Sugar
- 2 Tbsp Morton's Tender quick Curing Salt (Optional)
- Rub
- 1 Tbsp Whole Black Peppercorns
- 3 Tbsp Coarsely Ground Black Pepper
- 3 Tbsp Coriander Seeds
- 1 Tbsp Yellow Mustard Seeds
- 2 Bay Leaves
- 1/4 Cup Brown Sugar
- 2 Tbsp Sweet Paprika
- 1 Tbsp Kosher Salt
- 1 Tsp Ground Cinnamon
- 1/2 Tsp Ground Clove
- Sandwich
- 1/2 Cup Mayonnaise
- 2 Tsp Dijon
- 2 Tsp Horseradish
- 1 Clove Garlic, Minced
- Salt and Pepper
- Rye Bread
- Swiss Cheese

Instructions:

- Plan ahead! This recipe requires brining for 3 days and refrigeration overnight.
- For the Brine: Bring the water to a boil in a large pot. Stir in the garlic, juniper berries, bay leaves, salt, brown sugar, curing salt, if using, whole peppercorns and allspice berries. Let cool completely, then immerse the meat weighing it down with a plate if necessary. Refrigerate for 3 days.
- For the Rub: In a spice grinder or small food processor, combine the black pepper, coriander seeds, mustard seeds, and bay leaves and pulse until coarsely ground. Stir in the brown sugar, paprika, cinnamon, and clove.
- Remove the meat from the brine and rinse under cold running water and pat dry with paper towels. Sprinkle the rub on the brisket and cover tightly with plastic wrap. Refrigerate for 24 hours.
- When ready to cook, set temperature to 225°F and preheat, lid closed for 15 minutes.
- Remove the plastic wrap from the beef brisket and arrange on the grill grate. Smoke meat for 3 to 4 hours.
- Remove from grill and wrap in foil making sure to seal very well. Place back on grill and continue cooking for another 3 to 4 hours or until a thermometer inserted in the thickest part of the meat registers an internal temperature of 204°F.
- Remove from grill and rest in foil for at least 30 minutes before slicing. If you want cold pastrami, allow to cool completely, refrigerate until chilled and then slice. Enjoy!

3.43 Ultimate Loaded Nachos

Ingredients:

- 1 Bag Tortilla Chips
- 1/2 Cup Fresh Salsa
- 1 Lb. Kielbasa Sausage, Cooked and Sliced
- 1 Cup Cooked Chicken Breast, Shredded
- 1 Lb. Tri-Tip, Cooked and Cubed
- 1/4 Cup Black Olives, Sliced
- 1 Small Jar Jalapeños, Sliced
- 1/4 Cup Scallions, Sliced
- 1-1/2 Cup Cheddar Cheese
- 1/2 Cup Sour Cream
- 1/2 Cup Guacamole
- 1/4 Cup Cilantro

Introductions:

- When ready to cook, set the Traeger to 375°F and preheat, lid closed for 15 minutes.
- On a large tray, spread the tortilla chips evenly. First sprinkle the salsa on chips, then the Kielbasa sausage, chicken, and tri-tip.
- Top nachos with scallions, jalapeños, olives, and lastly the cheese.
- Place tray on the grill and bake for approximately 10 to 15 minutes, or until cheese melts and the nachos are heated through.
- Serve with sour cream, guacamole and cilantro. Enjoy!

3.44 Grilled London Broil with Blue Cheese Butter
Ingredients:

- London Broil
- 1/4 Cup Soy Sauce
- 1/4 Cup Water
- 1 Small Onion, Coarsely Chopped
- 1 Clove Garlic, Minced
- 2 Tbsp Red Wine Vinegar
- 2 Tbsp Vegetable Oil or Extra Virgin Olive Oil
- 1 Tbsp Ketchup
- 1 Tsp Worcestershire Sauce
- 1 Tsp Black Pepper, Freshly Ground
- 1 Tsp Sugar
- 1 (2 Lbs.) Top Round London Broil Steak
- Traeger Beef Rub
- Blue Cheese Butter
- 8 Tbsp Butter, Softened
- 1 Scallion, Finely Minced
- 1/4 Cup Crumbled Blue Cheese
- 1 Tsp Worcestershire Sauce
- Black Pepper, Freshly Ground

Instructions:

- For the Marinade: In a small mixing bowl, whisk together the soy sauce, water, onion, garlic, red wine vinegar, oil, ketchup, Worcestershire sauce, pepper and sugar.
- Place the meat in a large resealable plastic bag and pour the marinade over it. Refrigerate for 6 hours to overnight.
- Remove steak from the refrigerator and let it come to room temperature.
- For the Blue Cheese Butter: In a small mixing bowl, combine the butter, scallion, blue cheese, Worcestershire sauce, and pepper. Mix to combine with a wooden spoon. Cover and refrigerate if not using immediately.
- When steak is at room temperature, discarding the marinade and pat dry with paper towels.
- Season on all sides with Traeger Beef Rub.
- When ready to cook, set temperature to 180°F and preheat, lid closed for 15 minutes.
- Lay the steak directly on the grill grate and smoke for 60 minutes.
- Transfer steak to a platter. Increase grill temperature to High and preheat with the lid closed.
- When grill is hot, return steak to the grill and cook until desired internal temperature, 130°F for medium-rare, about 15 to 20 minutes.
- Let meat rest for 3 minutes, before thinly slicing on a diagonal. Serve with the Blue Cheese Butter. Enjoy!

3.45 Smoked Chili Con Queso
Ingredients:

- 1 (2 Lb.) Block Velveeta Cheese
- 1 Lb. Smoked Gouda Cheese
- 1 (10 Oz) Can Original Rote
- 1 (10 Oz) Can Diced Rote Fire Roasted Tomatoes and Green Chiles
- 1 (10 Oz) Can Cream of Mushroom Soup
- 1 Lb. Hot Pork Sausage
- 4 Tbsp Traeger Coffee Rub
- 1/2 Cup Chopped Cilantro

Instructions:

- Heat a medium cast-iron skillet over medium-heat and fully cook pork sausage breaking into small chunks as you go. Drain and discard fat reserving the sausage.
- When ready to cook, start the Traeger according to grill instructions. Set the temperature to 350 degrees F and preheat, lid closed, for 10 to 15 minutes.

- Use a 4 to 5-quart cast iron Dutch oven or another oven safe dish. Divide the block of Velveeta into 5-6 large pieces and cut the smoked gouda into small 1-inch cubes.
- Add the canned **Ingredients:** including the liquid. Add the meat and the Traeger Coffee Rub last.
- Smoke the queso for 45 minutes on the Traeger stirring three to four times. Add most of the cilantro the last 5 minutes of smoking.
- Sprinkle remaining cilantro on the top before serving. Enjoy!

3.46 Smoked Italian Meatballs
Ingredients:

- 1 Tsp Pepper
- 1 Tsp Parsley
- 1 Tbsp Oregano
- 1 Tsp Crushed Red Pepper
- 1 Tsp Kosher Salt
- 1 Tsp Onion Powder
- 1/2 Cup Parmesan Cheese, Grated
- 1 Lb. Ground Italian Sausage
- 1 Lb. Ground Beef
- 2 Eggs
- 1 Tbsp Worcestershire Sauce
- 1/2 Cup Bread Crumbs

Instructions:

- In a large bowl, mix together all the **Ingredients:** with hands until combined.
- Once all **Ingredients:** are mixed, shape the mixture into 1 1/2" meatballs. Place on a parchment lined baking sheet leaving space between each meatball.
- When ready to cook, set temperature to 180°F and preheat, lid closed for 15 minutes. For optimal flavor, use Super Smoke if available.
- Place the meatballs directly on the grill grate and smoke for 20 minutes.
- Increase the grill temperature to 350°F and cook for an additional 10 minutes, or until the internal temperature reaches 165°F.
- Serve meatballs over spaghetti noodles and top with your favorite marinara sauce. Enjoy!

3.47 Smoked Brisket Pot Pie
Ingredients:

- 2 Cups Leftover Brisket, Chopped
- 2 Tbsp Butter
- 2 Carrots, Peeled and Chopped
- 1 Yellow Onion, Chopped
- 1 Clove Garlic, Minced
- 1/2 Cup Frozen Peas
- 1 Cup Pearl Onions, Blanched and Peeled
- 2 Cups Beef Stock
- 1 Sheet of Frozen Pastry Dough
- 1 Egg

Instructions:

- In a medium stock pot melt the butter. When the butter is hot, add the carrots and saute 10-15 minutes until lightly browned.
- Add onion and cook 5-7 minutes until tender and translucent. Add the garlic and saute 30 seconds more until fragrant.
- Stir in the peas, onions and chopped brisket. Add beef stock and bring to a simmer.
- Cook until the liquid is reduced and thick enough to coat the back of a spoon. If the sauce doesn't thicken, add a slurry of cornstarch until thickened. Season with salt and pepper to taste.
- Pour brisket mixture into an oven proof baking dish. Place the pastry dough over the top making cuts in the top to vent.
- Mix the egg in a small bowl and brush the top of the pastry with the egg wash.

- When ready to cook, set the temperature to 350°F and preheat, lid closed for 15 minutes
- Place directly on the grill grate and bake for 45 minutes until the top is lightly browned and bubbling.
- Let stand 10 minutes before serving. Enjoy!

CHAPTER 4: LAMP RECIPES

4.1 Whole Rack of Lamb
Ingredients:

- 2 Lb. Rack of Grass-fed Lamb
- 1 Tbsp Kosher Salt
- 8 Cloves Fresh Garlic
- 1 Small Bunch Fresh Thyme
- 2 Tsp Olive Oil
- 1 Tsp Sherry Vinegar

Instructions:

- Process the fresh garlic and all the thyme leaves in your food processor with the salt, oil and vinegar. Rub this pasted all over the rack of lamb.
- When ready to cook, set the temperature to 450°F and preheat, lid closed for 15 minutes
- Lay the rack of lamb fat-side down on the grill and cook for 20 minutes. Turn over so the fat side is up and cook for an additional 10 minutes. Thermometer should be placed into the center of the lamb and should register 150-160°F.
- Let rest for 10 minutes. Slice the rack into chops and serve. Enjoy!

4.2 Slow Roasted Shawarma
Ingredients:

- 5.5 Lbs. Top Sirloin
- 5.5 Lbs. Boneless Skinless Chicken Thighs
- 4.5 Lbs. Lamb Fat
- 4 Tbsp Traeger Rub
- 2 Large Yellow Onions
- Pita Bread
- Topping Options: Cucumber, Tomatoes, Tahini, Pickles, Fries, Israeli Salad
- A Double Skewer
- A Cast Iron Griddle

Instructions:

- *Plan ahead! Assemble the shawarma stack the night before you plan to cook it.
- Slice all the meat and fat into ½" slices and place into 3 bowls (pro tip: it's easier to slice if they are all partially frozen).
- Season each bowl with Traeger Rub and massage the rub into the meat.
- Place half an onion on the bottom of each half skewer to make a firm base. then add 2 layers from each bowl at a time. Try to make the stack symmetrical, more or less. Then put the other 2 half onions at the top. Wrap in plastic wrap and refrigerate overnight.
- When ready to cook, set temperature to 275°F and preheat, lid closed for 15 minutes.
- Lay the shawarma directly on the grill grate and cook for about 3-4 hours, rotating at least once.

- Remove from grill and increase the temperature to 445°F. While the grill preheats, place a cast iron griddle directly on the grill grate and brush with olive oil.
- When the griddle is hot place the whole shawarma on the cast iron and sear 5-10 minutes per side. Remove from grill, slice off the edges, then repeat with remaining shawarma.
- Serve in pita bread with your favorite toppings like cucumber, tomatoes, tahini, pickles, fries or Israeli salad.
- Enjoy!

4.3 Roasted Leg of Lamb
Ingredients:

1 (7-8 Lb.) Leg of Lamb, Bone-In

1 Tbsp Garlic, Crushed

4 Cloves Garlic, Sliced Lengthwise

4 Sprigs Rosemary, Cut Into 1" Pieces

2 Tsp Olive Oil

2 Lemons

Salt and Pepper, To Taste

Instructions:

- Combine olive oil and the crushed garlic. Rub mixture on the leg of lamb.
- With a paring knife, make small 3/4-inch deep perforations in the lamb, about 2 dozen. Stuff the slivered garlic and cut rosemary sprigs into the perforations.
- Zest and juice the lemons, spreading the zest and juice evenly over the lamb. Season lamb with salt and pepper.
- When ready to cook, set temperature to High and preheat, lid closed for 15 minutes.
- Place the leg of lamb on the grill and cook for 30 minutes.
- Reduce grill temperature to 350°F and cook until the internal temperature reaches 130°F for medium-rare, about 60-90 minutes.
- Let the lamb rest for 15 minutes before carving. Enjoy!

4.4 Grilled Lamb Chops with Rosemary Sauce
Ingredients:

- 1/2 Cup Extra Virgin Olive Oil, Divided
- 1/4 Cup Onion or Shallot, Coarsely Chopped
- 2 Cloves Garlic, Coarsely Chopped
- 2 Tbsp Soy Sauce
- 2 Tbsp Balsamic or Sherry Vinegar
- 1 Tbsp Fresh Rosemary Needles
- 2 Tsp Dijon Mustard
- 1 Tsp Worcestershire Sauce
- Freshly Ground Black Pepper, As Needed

Instructions:

- In a small saucepan, sauté the onion and garlic in 1 tablespoon of olive oil over medium heat until softened and translucent. Do not let brown.
- Transfer to a blender jar. Add the soy sauce, vinegar, rosemary, mustard, and Worcestershire and blend. Season to taste with black pepper.
- Slowly drizzle in the remaining olive oil while the machine is running until the sauce is emulsified. Add a tablespoon of water if the sauce is too thick. Set aside.
- When ready to cook, set temperature to High and preheat, lid closed for 15 minutes.
- Brush the lamb chops on both sides with olive oil and season generously with salt and pepper.
- Grill until lamb chops reach an internal temperature of 135°F for medium-rare, about 4 to 6 minutes per side.
- Serve with the rosemary sauce for dipping. Enjoy!

4.5 Roasted Leg of Lamb with Red Wine Reduction
Ingredients:

- 1 (6-8 Lb.) Bone-In Leg of Lamb
- 10 Garlic Cloves, Peeled and Thinly Sliced
- 3 Tbsp Rosemary Leaves, Chopped
- 2 Tsp Thyme Leaves, Chopped
- 2 Tbsp Olive Oil
- 1 Tbsp Kosher Salt
- 1/2 Tsp Freshly Ground Pepper
- 1 Cup Red Wine
- 1 Tsp Kosher Salt
- 3 Tbsp Unsalted Butter

Instructions:

- Rinse lamb leg with water and pat dry. Using a sharp paring knife, create 20 1-inch slits all around the leg of lamb that are 1-inch deep. Place a sliver of garlic into each slit.
- Combine the chopped rosemary and thyme with the olive oil, salt, and pepper. Using your hands, coat the lamb evenly with the herb oil.
- Gently wrap lamb in saran wrap, place on a tray, and refrigerate for at least 4 hours to overnight. One hour before grilling, remove the lamb from the refrigerator.
- Remove the plastic wrap and place the lamb on a roasting rack above a large roasting pan. Pour the red wine and stock into the bottom of the pan, ensuring the liquid does not touch the meat. If it is close, only use half of the wine and stock.
- When ready to cook, set the temperature to High and preheat, lid closed for 15 minutes.
- Place the lamb in its roasting pan directly on the grill grate and roast for 20 minutes. Reduce the heat to 350°F and roast another hour or more, about 10 to 12 minutes per pound or until the temperature reaches 130°F when a meat thermometer is inserted into the thickest part of the leg away from the bone.
- Remove the meat from the grill and loosely tent with foil on a cutting board. Allow to rest for 15-20 minutes.
- Meanwhile strain the juices from the pan into a medium saucepan removing any excess fat that has dropped into the pan.
- Bring the juices to a boil, reduce to a simmer, and cook until it can coat the back of a spoon, about 10 minutes.
- Whisk in the butter and taste, adding more salt and pepper as needed.
- Carve the lamb and serve with the red wine jus. Enjoy!

4.6 Grilled Lamb Burgers with Pickled Onions

Ingredients:

- Pickled Onions
- 1/2 Red Onion, Thinly Sliced
- 6 Tbsp Lime Juice
- 1/2 Tsp Kosher Salt
- 1/2 Tsp Raw Cane Sugar
- Yogurt Sauce
- 1 Cup Greek Yogurt
- 2 Tbsp Lemon Juice
- 1 Garlic Clove, Minced
- 2 Tbsp Finely Chopped Herbs, Such as Mint, Dill and Parsley
- 1/2 Tsp Kosher Salt
- Lamb Burgers
- 1 Tbsp Olive Oil
- 1/2 Red Onion, Finely Diced
- 1 Lb. Ground Lamb
- 8 Oz Ground Pork
- 3 Tbsp Finely Chopped Mint
- 2 Tbsp Finely Chopped Dill
- 3 Tbsp Finely Chopped Parsley
- 4 Garlic Cloves, Minced
- 1 1/2 Tsp Ground Cumin
- 1 Tsp Ground Coriander
- 1 Tsp Kosher Salt
- 1/2 Tsp Freshly Ground Black Pepper
- 1 Sliced Tomato
- 6 Buns
- Sliced Cucumber
- Butter Lettuce

Instructions:

- To Pickle the Onions: Place the onion, lime juice, salt and sugar in a small bowl. Stir to combine, cover and let sit at room temperature for about 2 hours to soften. Refrigerate until ready to use.
- To make the Yogurt Sauce: In a small bowl, stir together the yogurt, lemon juice, garlic, herbs, and 1/2 tsp salt. Adjust the salt to taste. Cover and refrigerate until ready to serve, or for up to 2 days.
- To make the lamb burgers: In a small skillet over medium heat, warm the olive oil. Add the onion and cook, stirring frequently until softened, about 7 minutes. Transfer to a small plate to cool.
- In a large bowl, combine the lamb, pork, mint, dill, parsley, garlic, cumin, coriander, salt, pepper, and cooled onions. Gently mix with your hands. Do not overwork the meat.
- Divide the mixture into 6 equal balls. Press into patties and transfer to a parchment-lined baking sheet. If not cooking immediately, cover and refrigerate for up to 8 hours.
- When ready to cook, set the temperature to High and preheat, lid closed for 15 minutes.
- Place the burgers on the grill and cook until well-browned, about 2 to 3 minutes per side for medium-rare, or about 5 minutes per side for well done.
- Transfer burgers to a plate to rest for 5 minutes before serving.
- Place burgers on buns and top with a generous dollop of herbed yogurt sauce and some pickled onions.
- Add lettuce, sliced tomatoes or cucumbers if desired. Serve immediately. Enjoy!

4.7 Braised Lamb Shank
Ingredients:

- 4 Shanks Lamb
- Olive Oil, As Needed
- Traeger Prime Rib Rub
- 1 Cup Beef Broth
- 1 Cup Red Wine
- 4 Sprigs Fresh Rosemary and Thyme

Instructions:

- Season the lamb shanks liberally with Traeger Prime Rib Rub.
- When ready to cook, set the temperature to High and preheat, lid closed for 15 minutes.
- Place the shanks directly on the grill grate and cook for 20 minutes or until the exterior has browned.
- Transfer the shanks to a Dutch oven and pour in beef broth, wine, and add herbs. Cover with a tight-fitting lid and place back on the grill grate reducing the temperature to 325°F.
- Braise the shanks for 3-4 hours until the internal temperature is 180°F. Take care not to touch bone with the tip of the temperature probe or you will get a false reading.
- Carefully lift the lid and transfer the lamb and any accumulated juices to a platter or plates. Enjoy!

4.8 Greek Style Roast Leg of Lamb Recipe
Ingredients:

- One 6-7 Lbs. Leg of Lamb, Bone-In
- 8 Cloves Garlic
- 2 Sprigs Fresh Rosemary, Needles Stripped, Stems Discarded
- 1 Sprig (Or 1 Tsp. Dried) Fresh Oregano
- 2 Lemons, Juiced
- 6 Tbsp. Evo (Extra-Virgin Olive Oil)
- As Needed Coarse Salt (Kosher) And Black Pepper, Freshly Ground

Instructions:

- Using a paring knife, make a series of small slits in the leg.
- On a cutting board, finely mince the garlic, rosemary, and oregano with a chef's knife to make an herb and garlic paste. (Alternatively, put the garlic and herbs in a small food processor.)
- Stuff a small amount of the paste into each of the slits, driving it into the slit with a spoon handle or other utensil. Put the lamb on a rack inside a roasting pan. If desired, like the pan with foil for easier clean-up.
- Rub the outside of the lamb with the lemon juice, then the olive oil. Cover with plastic wrap and refrigerate for at least 8 hours, or overnight.
- Remove from the refrigerator and let the lamb come to room temperature.
- Remove the plastic wrap and season the lamb with salt and pepper. When ready to cook, start the Traeger grill on Smoke with the lid open until the fire is established (4 to 5 minutes). Set the temperature to 400F and preheat, lid closed, for 10 to 15 minutes.
- Roast the lamb for 30 minutes. Reduce the heat to 350F (300 if you have a manual controller) and continue to cook until the internal temperature in the thickest part of the meat - be sure the temperature probe is not touching bone - is about 140F for medium-rare, about 1 hour more, longer if you're cooking at 300F or prefer your lamb more well-done.
- Transfer the lamb to a cutting board and let rest for 15 minutes before slicing on a diagonal into thin slices.

4.9 Smoked Lamb Sausage
Ingredients:

- Smoked Lamb Sausage
- 2 Lb. Lamb Shoulder
- 1 Qty. (60 Inch) Hog Casing
- 1 Tbsp. Garlic
- 1 Tsp. Cumin
- 1 Tsp. Paprika
- 1/2 Tsp. Cayenne
- 2 Tbsp. Ground Fennel
- 1 Tbsp. Cilantro, Finely Chopped
- 1 Tbsp. Parsley, Finely Chopped
- 1 Tsp. Black Pepper
- 2 Tbsp. Salt
- Sauce
- 3 Cups Greek Yogurt
- 1 Lemon, Juiced
- 1 Clove Garlic
- 1 Cucumber, Peeled, Shredded, And Drained
- 1 Tbsp. Dill
- To Taste Salt & Pepper

Instructions:

- Cut the lamb shoulder into 2-inch pieces, and using a meat grinder, grind the meat.
- Lightly combine the lamb with all the spices in a bowl and refrigerate. It is important to refrigerate the ground lamb so the fat does not melt in order to give the sausage a good texture.
- Next, using a sausage horn, attach the hog casing and start to feed the sausage back through the grinder to fill the casing and twist into links. With a paring knife, prick holes all along the casing (this will allow steam to escape while cooking). Refrigerate. Combine all
- When ready to cook, start your Traeger on Smoke, with the lid open until the fire is established (4 to 5 minutes). Set the temperature to 225°F, place the prepared sausage on the grill grate and smoke it for 1 hour.
- Once the hour is up, remove the links from the grill and turn the grill up to High (450°F) and preheat (10-15 minutes). Once the grill has reached 450°F, place the links back on the grill and cook for 5 minutes on each side.
- Serve hot with yogurt sauce and roasted potatoes on the side. Enjoy!

4.10 Lamb Lollipops with Mango Chutney
Ingredients:

- Lamb Lollipops
- 6 Lamb Chops, Around 3/4-Inch-Thick, Frenched
- 2 Tbsp Olive Oil
- 1/2 Tsp Course Kosher Salt
- 1/2 Tsp Black Pepper, Freshly Cracked
- 2 Tbsp Fresh Mint, Chopped
- Mango Chutney
- 1 Mango, Peeled, Seeded and Chopped
- 3 Cloves Garlic, Chopped
- 1/2 Habanero Pepper, Seeded and Chopped, Or More to Taste
- 3 Sprigs Fresh Cilantro, Chopped
- 1 Tbsp Fresh Lime Juice
- 1 Teaspoon Salt
- 1/2 Tsp Pepper, Freshly Cracked

Instructions:

- If you can't purchase frenched lamb chops, using a sharp knife, cut and scrape the flesh and fat off the bone to make it look like a lollipop.
- Add all chutney Ingredients into a food processor and pulse about 15 times or until desired consistency; set aside. Chop mint and set aside.
- When ready to cook, start the Traeger grill on Smoke with the lid open until the fire is established (4 to 5 minutes). Set the temperature to High and preheat, lid closed, for 10 to 15 minutes.
- While grill preheats, on a baking sheet drizzle lamb lollipop with olive. Coat both sides. Season both sides with salt and pepper and allow to sit at room temperature for 5 to 10 minutes.
- Place the lamb pops directly on grill grate. Close lid and grill for 5 minutes. Flip over and grill for another 3 minutes or until a thermometer inserted into the thickest part of the meat registers an internal temperature of 130 degrees F.
- Remove from grill and allow to rest 10 minutes before serving.
- Spoon chutney over each lamb lollipop and sprinkle with fresh chopped mint. Enjoy!

4.11 Pistachio Crusted Lamb with Vegetables
Ingredients:

- Pistachio Crusted Lamb
- 2 Racks of Lamb
- 1 Tsp Herbs De Provence
- Salt and Ground Black Pepper, To Taste
- 1 Tbsp Vegetable Oil
- 2/3 Cups Pistachio Nuts, Chopped
- 2 Tbsp Dry Bread Crumbs
- 1 Tbsp Butter, Melted
- 1 Tsp Olive Oil
- 3 Tbsp Dijon Mustard
- Roasted Tri Color Carrots and Fingerling Potatoes
- 1 Lb. Fingerling Potato Medley
- 1 Bunch Tri Color Carrots, Peeled & Chopped
- 1 Tbsp Olive Oil
- 1/2 Tsp Kosher Salt
- 1/2 Tsp Ground Black Pepper
- 1 Clove Garlic, Minced
- 2 Tsp Fresh Time, Minced

Instructions:

- When ready to cook, start the Traeger grill on Smoke with the lid open until the fire is established (4 to 5 minutes). Set the temperature to High and preheat, lid closed, for 10 to 15 minutes.
- Pat the lamb dries with paper towels and generously season each rack of lamb with herbs de Provence, salt and black pepper.
- Peel carrots, cut into 1-inch pieces and add to a large mixing bowl. Add the potatoes, olive oil, salt, pepper, garlic, and thyme. Stir to combine.
- Place a large cast iron skillet on grill and add 1 tablespoon of vegetable oil. Close the lid and allow to preheat for 20 minutes.
- Place lamb in skillet and cook, browning on all sides, 6 to 8 minutes. Transfer lamb to a baking pan leaving skillet on grill and set aside.
- Stir pistachios, bread crumbs, butter, olive oil and a pinch of salt and black pepper in a bowl.
- Spread mustard on the fat-side of each rack of lamb. Pat pistachio mixture on top of mustard.
- Place racks of lamb directly on grill grate next to skillet. Add the seasoned potatoes to the skillet. Close lid and cook for 15 minutes.
- After 15 minutes, open the grill and stir the potatoes and carrots. Cover the racks of lamb loosely with foil.
- Continue cooking for another 5 to 10 minutes or until a thermometer inserted diagonally into the thickest part of the meat registers an internal temperature of 125 degrees F.
- Remove the lamb from grill with foil still intact and allow to rest for 10 minutes. Check potatoes with a fork to see if they are tender. If not, allow the potatoes and carrots to cook for another 5 minutes or until tender.
- Cut each rack of lamb into 4 double chops and serve with roasted carrots and potatoes. Enjoy!

4.12 Smoked Lamb Leg with Salsa Verde

Ingredients:

- Leg of Lamb
- 1 Leg of Lamb, Aitchbone Removed, Fat Trimmed To 1/4 Inch Thick, And Tied
- 1 Head of Garlic, Peeled
- 2 Tbsp Kosher Salt
- 2 Tbsp Fresh Rosemary, Chopped
- 1 Tsp Fresh Ground Black Pepper
- 1/4 Dry Red Wine, Or Beef Broth
- Green Garlic Salsa Verde
- 6 Green Garlic Cloves, Unpeeled
- 1 Tbsp Capers
- 1 Lb. Fresh Tomatillos, Husked, Rinsed
- 1 Small Onion, Quartered
- 5 Serrano Chiles
- 1/4 Cup Fresh Cilantro, Chopped
- 1 Tsp Sugar
- Kosher Salt to Taste
- 2 Tbsp Olive Oil
- 1 Cup Low Salt Chicken Broth
- 3 Tbsp Squeezed Lime Juice

Instructions:

- When ready to cook, start the Traeger grill on smoke with lid open until fire is established (4 to 5 minutes). Set the temperature to High and preheat, lid closed, for 10 to 15 minutes.
- Thread garlic onto skewer. Grill garlic, tomatillos, onion quarters, and chiles until dark brown spots form on all sides, about 9 minutes for onion, 6 minutes for tomatillos and chilies, and 4 minutes for garlic.
- Remove everything from grill and place the chiles directly into a Ziplock bag. Allow chiles to steam in bag for 15 minutes. Place a cast iron pan on grill, close lid and allow to preheat for 10 minutes.
- Peel garlic and remove skin from chiles. Coarsely chop the onion, chiles, and garlic. Transfer tomatillos, cappers and all vegetables into blender. Add cilantro and 1/2 teaspoon sugar. Puree until smooth. Season to taste with kosher salt.
- Add oil to preheated cast iron pan. Carefully add the tomatillo mixture and stir until slightly thickened, stirring often (about 2 minutes). Add broth and 2 tablespoons lime juice.
- Close lid and allow mixture to reduce until it measures about 2 1/2 cups (about 15-20 minutes). Season the Verde to taste with salt and more sugar and lime juice. Cool slightly, then cover and chill. Remove from grill and turn temperature dial to Smoke setting.
- Pat lamb dry and score fat by making shallow cuts all over with tip of a sharp small knife. Using a paring knife, make little incisions all over lamb and stuff with garlic cloves. Rub olive oil over lamb and liberally season with salt, pepper and rosemary. Let stand at room temperature for 30 minutes.
- Place leg of lamb in center of grill. Smoke lamb on the Smoke setting for 30 minutes.
- Increase temperature 350 degrees F and cook until a thermometer inserted into the thickest part of the meat registers 130 degrees F (about 1-1/2 hours).
- Transfer to a cutting board and let stand 15 to 25 minutes; the internal temperature will rise to 140 degrees F for medium-rare.
- Slice and serve with salsa Verde. Enjoy!

4.13 Armenian Style Lamb Shanks with Barley Risotto

Ingredients:

- 2 Tbsp Pomegranate Molasses
- 1/4 Cup Tomato Paste
- 1 Tbsp Garlic Powder
- 1 Tbsp Ground Cinnamon
- 1 Tsp Ground Fenugreek
- 1 Tsp Ground Cumin
- 1 Tsp Ground Cayenne
- 1 Tsp Ground Turmeric
- 3 Tbsp + 2 Tsp Kosher Salt
- 4 Lamb Hind Shanks
- 2 Qt Lamb or Beef Stock
- 1 Cup Pearled Barley
- 2 Tbsp Olive Oil
- 1 Medium Yellow Onion, Small Dice
- 1/2 Cup Grated Parmigiano Reggiano
- 2 Tbsp Butter

Instructions:

- In a small bowl, combine pomegranate molasses, tomato paste, garlic powder, cinnamon, fenugreek, cumin, cayenne, turmeric and 1 tbsp of the salt.
- Mix until the mixture turns into a uniform paste. Spice paste can be made up to a week in advance. Refrigerate if making ahead.
- Prepare lamb shanks by removing silver skin and large tendons. Evenly rub 1/4 of the spice paste on each shank and place shanks in refrigerator for at least 6 hours and up to 24 hours.
- To cook the lamb shanks: Place shanks in large cast iron skillet (or any oven proof vessel) and cover halfway with lamb stock.
- When ready to cook, start the Traeger grill on Smoke with the lid open until the fire is established (4 to 5 minutes). Set the temperature to 300 degrees F and preheat, lid closed, for 10 minutes.
- Cook for 7 to 8 hours turning shanks over every hour. Add more lamb stock to skillet as needed. Shanks are ready when the meat is tender and beginning to fall away from the bone.
- When the lamb is in its last hour of cooking, start the barley risotto. Heat 1 quart of the lamb or beef stock to a boil. Remove from heat and set aside.
- In a medium pot, heat olive oil and add onions to pot. Sauté onion until softened. Add barley and toast for about two minutes, stirring. Add 1 cup of stock, and the 2 tsp of salt.
- Cook, stirring occasionally, on low heat until the barley has fully absorbed the liquid. Repeat this step, adding 1/2 a cup of stock at a time until the barley is completely cooked through.
- Add parmigiano Reggiano and butter and stir to incorporate. Taste and add salt as needed.
- Serve lamb with barley risotto. Enjoy!

4.14 BBQ Lamb Wraps
Ingredients:

- Lamb
- 1 Leg of Lamb (6-7 Lb.)
- Juice of One Lemon
- Olive Oil
- Kosher Salt, To Taste
- Black Pepper, To Taste
- 1 Traeger Big Game Rub
- 12 Pitas
- 3 Roma Tomatoes, Sliced
- 1 Red Onion, Cut in Half and Sliced into Half Moons
- 8 Oz Feta Cheese, Crumbled
- Tzatziki Sauce
- 2 Cups Greek Yogurt
- 2 English Cucumbers Seeded and Finely Chopped
- 2 Cloves Garlic, Finely Minced
- Zest Of 2 Lemons
- Juice Of 2 Lemons
- 4 Tbsp Fresh Dill
- 2 Tbsp Fresh Mint
- Kosher Salt to Taste
- Black Pepper to Taste

Instructions:

- Remove from the refrigerator and let the lamb come to room temperature.
- Rub the outside of the lamb with the lemon juice, then the olive oil. Season with Traeger Big Game rub.
- When ready to cook, start the Traeger grill on Smoke with the lid open until the fire is established (4 to 5 minutes). Set the temperature to 400 degrees F and preheat, lid closed, for 10 to 15 minutes.
- Roast the lamb for 30 minutes. Reduce the heat to 350 degrees F and continue to cook until the internal temperature in the thickest part of the meat but not touching bone - is 140 degrees F for medium-rare.
- While lamb is roasting, combine all **Ingredients:** for tzatziki sauce in a mixing bowl and mix to combine. Place in fridge to chill.
- The last little bit of cooking, take the pittas and wrap in aluminum foil and place on grill to warm.
- Transfer the lamb to a cutting board and let rest for 15 minutes before slicing on a diagonal into thin slices.
- Build the wraps by filling a warm pitta with lamb, tzatziki sauce, diced tomato, red onion and feta crumble on top.
- Serve with fries and a side of the tzatziki. Enjoy!

4.15 Slow Roasted BBQ Lamb Shoulder
Ingredients:

- 1/4 Tsp Caraway Seeds
- 1/4 Tsp Coriander Seeds
- 1/4 Tsp Cumin Seeds
- 1 Tsp Dry Mint Leaves
- 2 Oz Ancho Chiles, Stemmed and Seeded
- 1 Tbsp Smoked Sweet Paprika
- 1 Tbsp Lemon Juice
- 3 Leg Garlic Cloves, 1 Clove Mashed to A Paste
- 1/4 Cup Extra Virgin Olive Oil
- Kosher Salt
- 3 Lb. Lamb Shoulder Roast on The Bone

Instructions:

- In a spice grinder, finely grind the caraway, coriander and cumin seeds.
- In a microwave-safe bowl, cover the ancho chilies with water and microwave on high for 2 minutes.
- Let cool slightly, then transfer soft chilies and 2 tablespoons of water to a blender. Add the grinded spices, paprika, lemon juice, the 2 garlic cloves, 2 tablespoons of the olive oil and 1 tablespoon of salt. Puree the harissa sauce until smooth.
- Set lamb in a medium roast pan and rub 1/2 cup of the harissa sauce all over the meat; let stand at room temperature for at least 2 hours.
- When ready to cook, start the Traeger grill on Smoke with the lid open until the fire is established (4 to 5 minutes). Set the temperature to 325 degrees F and preheat, lid closed, for 10 to 15 minutes.
- Add 1/2 cup of water to roasting pan and cover the pan loosely with foil. Cook the lamb for 2-1/2 hours, adding water to the pan a few times.
- Remove foil and cook for about 2-1/2 hours longer, until the lamb is brown and tender; occasionally spoon pan juices on top.
- Let stand for 20 minutes after removing from grill.
- Meanwhile, in a small bowl, combine the yogurt with cilantro, mashed garlic clove and 2 tablespoons of olive oil. Using a fork, pull the lamb off the bone in large chunks.
- Using your fingers, pull the lamb into smaller shreds and serve with the yogurt sauce and lettuce leaves, naan and the remaining harissa sauce. Enjoy!

4.16 Braised Lamb Shoulder Tacos

Ingredients:

- 3 Lb. Lamb Shoulder Roast
- 1/4 Tbsp Cumin Seeds
- 1/4 Tbsp Coriander Seeds
- 1/4 Tbsp Pumpkin Seeds
- 1 Tbsp Freshly Chopped Oregano
- 2 Oz Guajillo Peppers, Seeded
- 1 Tbsp Smoked, Sweet Paprika
- 1 Tbsp 1 T Lime Juice
- 3 Cloves Garlic, Roasted
- 1/4 Cup Evo
- Kosher Salt

Instructions:

- In a spice grinder, finely grind the seeds.
- In a microwave-safe bowl, cover the guajillo chilies with water and microwave on high for 2 minutes. Let cool slightly, then transfer soft chilies and 2 tablespoons of water to a blender.
- Add the ground spices, paprika, lime juice, oregano, the garlic cloves, 2 tablespoons of the olive oil and 1 tablespoon of salt. Puree the sauce until smooth.
- Set lamb in a medium roast pan and rub 1/2 cup of the sauce all over the meat; let stand at room temperature for at least 2 hours and up to 12 hours.
- When ready to cook, start the Traeger grill on Smoke with the lid open until the fire is established (4 to 5 minutes). Set the temperature to 325 degrees F and preheat, lid closed, for 10 to 15 minutes.
- Add 1/2 cup of water to roasting pan and cover the pan loosely with foil. Cook the lamb for 2-1/2 hours, adding water to the pan a few times.
- Remove foil and cook for about 2-1/2 hours longer, until the lamb is brown and tender; occasionally spooning the juices on top.
- Let stand for 20 minutes after removing from grill. Shred the meat when it's cool enough to handle and combine with remaining liquid in the bottom of the pan.
- Serve on corn tortillas, sprinkled with a squeeze of lime, sea salt, pickled radishes, and a sprig of cilantro. Enjoy!

4.17 Ultimate Grilled Lamb Burger
Ingredients:

- Roasted Red Pepper Mayo
- 1 Red Bell Pepper
- 1 Cup Mayo
- 2 Cloves Garlic
- 2 Tsp Fresh Lemon Juice
- 1 Tsp Kosher Salt
- 1/2 Tsp Black Pepper
- Ultimate Grilled Lamb Burger
- 2 Lb. Ground Lamb
- 1 Jalapeño, Seeded and Minced
- 6 Scallions, Minced
- 2 Tbsp Mint Leaves, Minced
- 2 Tbsp Dill, Minced
- 3 Cloves Garlic, Minced
- Kosher Salt and Black Pepper, To Taste
- 4 Slices Manchego Cheese
- 1 Cup Baby Arugula
- 1 Red Onion, Sliced
- 1 Large Ripe Tomato, Sliced
- 4 Brioche Buns

Instructions:

- When ready to cook, start the Traeger grill on Smoke with the lid open until the fire is established (4 to 5 minutes). Set the temperature to High and preheat, lid closed, for 10 to 15 minutes.
- Add the lamb, jalapeño, scallions, mint, dill, garlic, salt, and pepper to mixing bowl. Mix to combine.
- Form the lamb mixture into 4 to 8-ounce patties about ¾" inch thick. Set aside.
- Place the red bell pepper on preheated grill and cook for 20 minutes turning a quarter turn every 5 minutes or until it has charred a bit around the whole pepper.
- Remove the pepper from the grill and place in a large zip top bag and seal. After about 10 minutes, remove pepper from bag, cut in half, remove seeds and peel off skin.
- Add the roasted red pepper, mayo, lemon juice, garlic, salt and pepper to a food processor and process until smooth. Set aside.
- Place the lamb burgers on the grill still set to High, and cook for 5 minutes per side for medium or until desired doneness. The last minute of cooking, place your buns on the grill to toast and top burgers with a slice of cheese.
- Spread sides of toasted buns with mayo, add burgers to buns and top with arugula, onion and tomato. Serve with your favorite sides. Enjoy!

4.18 Grilled Lamb Kabobs
Ingredients:

- 3 Lbs. Boneless Leg of Lamb, Cut Into 2-Inch Cubes
- 1/2 Cup Olive Oil
- 1/2 Tbsp Kosher Salt
- 2 Tsp Freshly Ground Black Pepper
- 1/2 Cup Lemon Juice
- 1 Tbsp Lemon Zest
- 1 Tsp Cumin
- 2 Tbsp Fresh Mint, Chopped
- 1/2 Tbsp Fresh Cilantro, Chopped
- 2 Red Onions, Cut Into 8ths
- 15 Dried Apricots, Rehydrated
- 3 Traeger Flexible Skewers

Instructions:

- In a medium bowl, combine olive oil, salt, pepper, lemon juice, zest, cumin, mint and cilantro and mix well. Add lamb shoulder and toss to coat. Transfer to refrigerator and marinate over night.
- Remove lamb from marinade and thread lamb, apricots, and red onion alternating until the skewer is full.
- When ready to cook, start the Traeger grill on Smoke with the lid open until the fire is established (4 to 5 minutes). Set the temperature to 400 degrees F and preheat, lid closed 10-15 minutes.
- Lay skewers directly on the grill grate and cook for 8-10 minutes (for medium rare) or until the onions are lightly browned and lamb is cooked to desired temperature.
- Remove from grill and serve with your favorite side; quinoa, or rice are our favorites. Enjoy!

4.19 Roasted Rack of Lamb

Ingredients:

- 1 Rack (1-1/2 Lbs.) Lamb, Frenched
- 1/2 Cup Yellow Mustard
- 1 Tbsp Salt
- 1 Tsp Black Pepper, Ground
- 1 Cup Panko
- 1 Tbsp Italian Parsley, Minced
- 1 Tsp Sage, Minced
- 1 Tsp Rosemary, Minced

Instructions:

- Trim and clean the lamb if your butcher hasn't already done so. Rub the exterior with mustard and season generously with salt and pepper.
- In a shallow baking dish, combine breadcrumbs and herbs. Dredge the lamb in the breadcrumb mixture.
- When ready to cook, start the Traeger grill on Smoke with the lid open until the fire is established (4 to 5 minutes). Set the temperature to 450 degrees F (or 500 degrees F if using a WiFIRE enabled grill) and preheat lid closed for 10-15 minutes.
- Place the rack of lamb directly on the grill grate bone side down and cook for 20 minutes or until the internal temperature reaches 120 degrees F when an instant read thermometer is inserted into the thickest part of the lamb.
- Remove from the grill and let rest 5-10 minutes before slicing. Enjoy!

4.20 Grilled Butterflied Leg of Lamb

Ingredients:

- 1 Lemon, Juiced and Rinds Reserved
- 1/4 Cup Red Wine Vinegar
- 4 Cloves Garlic, Minced
- 2 Tbsp Fresh Or 2 Tsp Dried Rosemary, Minced
- 2 Tsp Fresh, or 1 Tsp Dried Fresh Thyme, Minced
- 1 Tsp Salt
- 1 Tsp Black Pepper, Freshly Ground
- 1 Cup Extra-Virgin Olive Oil
- 1 Onion, Sliced into Rings
- 1 (4-5 Lbs.) Leg of Lamb, Butterflied and Boneless

Instructions:

- For the Marinade: Cut the lemon into quarters and remove the seeds. Squeeze lemon juice into a mixing bowl and reserve the lemon rinds. Add the red wine vinegar, garlic, rosemary, thyme, salt and pepper and stir until the salt crystals dissolve. Whisk in the olive oil.
- Remove any netting from the lamb. Put the lamb into a large resealable plastic bag.
- Pour marinade into the bag, and add the onion and the reserved lemon rinds.
- Massage the bag to distribute the marinade and herbs. Refrigerate for several hours, or overnight.
- Remove the lamb from the marinade and pat dry with paper towels. Discard the marinade.
- When ready to cook, start the Traeger according to grill instructions. Set the temperature to High and preheat, lid closed, for 10 to 15 minutes.
- Arrange the lamb on the grill grate, fat-side down. Grill for 15 to 20 minutes per side or until the internal temperature reaches 135 degrees F for medium-rare.
- Let lamb leg rest for 5 minutes before slicing. To serve, slice thinly across the grain. Enjoy!

4.21 Braised Irish Lamb Stew
Ingredients:

- 4 Lbs. Lamb Shoulder, Boneless, Cut Into 1-Inch Pieces
- Salt and Pepper, To Taste
- 1/4 Cup Flour
- 1/4 Cup Butter, Room Temp
- 8 Oz Bacon, Chopped
- 2 Cloves Garlic, Minced
- 1/2 Cup White Wine
- 4 Cups Beef Stock
- 2 Bay Leaf
- 2 Sprigs Thyme
- 1 Sprig Rosemary
- 1 Onion, Small Dice
- 2 Carrots, Peeled, Cut Into 1/2-Inch Pieces
- 2 Large Potatoes, Peeled, 1/2-Inch Dice

Instructions:

- When ready to cook, start the Traeger on Smoke with the lid open until the fire is established (4 to 5 minutes). Set the temperature to 350 degrees F and preheat, lid closed, for 10-15 minutes.
- Season lamb with salt and pepper. Heat 2 Tbsp olive oil in a Dutch oven over medium heat. Brown lamb in batches and set aside.
- Add bacon and cook 15-20 minutes stirring occasionally until lightly browned. Remove bacon and discard all but 2 Tbsp of the bacon fat.
- Add fat back to the Dutch oven and onions and saute until translucent. Add garlic and cook 30 seconds more. Transfer lamb and bacon back to the pan and deglaze with white wine using a wooden spoon to scrape up all the browned bits on the bottom of the pan.
- Add stock, herbs, potatoes and carrots and bring to a simmer. Cover and transfer to the grill. Let stew cook for 1-1/2 to 2 hours or until the lamb is tender and falling apart.
- Remove stew from grill and place back on the stove top over medium heat. Mix butter and flour together in a small bowl and whisk into the stew. Let cook 5-10 minutes or until the stew is thick enough to coat the back of a spoon.
- Season with salt and pepper to taste. Remove bay leaves and springs from thyme and rosemary and serve. Enjoy!

CHAPTER 5: CHICKEN RECIPES

5.1 Hellfire Chicken Wings
Ingredients:

- Hellfire Chicken Wings
- 3 Lbs. Chicken Wings
- 2 Tbsp. Vegetable Oil
- Rub
- 1 Tbsp. Paprika
- 2 Tsp. Brown Sugar
- 1 Tsp. Salt
- 1 Tsp. Black Pepper, Freshly Ground
- 1 Tsp. Cayenne Pepper
- 1 Tsp. Onion Powder
- 1 Tsp. Granulated Garlic
- 1 Tsp. Celery Seed
- Sauce
- 8 Tbsp. Butter, Unsalted
- 2 - 4 Jalapeno Peppers, Thinly Sliced Crosswise
- 1/2 Cup Cilantro Leaves
- 1/2 Cup Hot Sauce

Instructions:

- Cut the tips off wings and discard. Cut each wing into two pieces through the joint, giving you a meaty "drumette" and a "flat". Transfer to a large mixing bowl and pour the oil over the chicken
- Make the rub: In a small mixing bowl, combine the paprika, sugar, salt, black pepper, cayenne, onion powder, granulated garlic, and celery seed.
- Sprinkle over the chicken and toss gently with your hands to coat the wings.
- When ready to cook, set the temperature to 350°F and preheat, lid closed for 15 minutes
- Grill the wings for 35 to 40 minutes, or until the skin is crisp and golden brown and the chicken is cooked through, turning once halfway through the cooking time.
- Make the sauce: Melt the butter over medium-low heat in a small saucepan. Add the jalapeños and cook for 3-4 minutes. Stir in the cilantro & hot sauce.
- Pour the sauce over the wings and toss to coat. Enjoy!

5.2 Buffalo Chicken Thighs
Ingredients:

- 4-6 Boneless, Skinless Chicken Thighs
- 1 Cup Buffalo Wing Sauce
- 4 Tbsp. Butter
- Traeger Pork & Poultry Rub, As Needed
- Bleu Cheese Crumbles, For Serving
- Ranch Dressing, For Serving

Instructions:

- When ready to cook, set the temperature to 450°F and preheat, lid closed for 15 minutes.
- Generously season the chicken thighs with your desired Traeger seasoning and place directly on the grill grate. Cook for 8-10 minutes, flipping once.
- In a small saucepan, cook the wing sauce and the butter over medium heat stirring occasionally.
- Dip the cooked chicken thighs into the wing sauce and butter mixture, turning to coat both sides evenly.

- Return the sauced chicken thighs to the grill and cook for an additional 4-5 minutes or until the internal temperature reads 175 degrees on a meat thermometer.
- Sprinkle with the Bleu cheese and drizzle with the ranch dressing (optional). We like to serve ours as sliders on toasted buns with all the fixings. Enjoy!

5.3 Beer Braised Chicken Tacos with Jalapeño Relish

Ingredients:

- Jalapeño Relish
- 3 Jalapeños, Seeded and Diced
- 1/4 Cup Red Onion, Finely Diced
- 1 Clove Garlic, Minced
- 2/3 Cup White Wine Vinegar
- 1/3 Cup Water
- 1 Tbsp Sugar
- 1 Tbsp Salt
- Pickled Cabbage
- 2 Cups Shredded Red Cabbage
- 1/2 Cup White Wine Vinegar
- 1 Tbsp Salt
- 1 Tbsp Sugar
- Braised Chicken
- 2 Lbs. Boneless Skinless Chicken Thighs
- 1 Tbsp Olive Oil
- 1 Tsp Salt
- 1 Tsp Black Pepper
- 1/2 Yellow Onion, Small Dice
- 1 Jalapeño, Deseeded and Chopped
- 1 Clove Garlic, Minced
- 1 Tsp Chili Powder
- 1 Tsp Garlic Powder
- 4 Tbsp Adobo Sauce
- 1 Ea. Chipotle Chile In Adobo
- Juice Of 2 Limes
- 1 (12 Oz) Can Model Beer
- Tacos
- 8-12 Small Flour Tortillas
- Cotija Cheese
- Cilantro
- Your Favorite Hot Sauce

Instructions:

- For the jalapeño relish, combine all **Ingredients:** in a non-reactive dish and set aside.
- To make the pickled cabbage, combine all **Ingredients:** in a non-reactive dish and set aside.
- Transfer both the relish and pickled cabbage to the refrigerator and let sit a couple hours to overnight.
- Season chicken thighs generously with salt and pepper. Heat 1 Tbsp olive oil in a Dutch oven over medium-high heat. Place chicken thighs skin side down and brown in batches. Remove from heat and set aside.
- Add 1 Tbsp butter to the Dutch oven and set over medium-high heat. When butter is melted, add onion and jalapeño and sauté 3-5 minutes until translucent. Add minced garlic and sauté 30 seconds or until fragrant.
- Add chili powder, adobo sauce, chipotle chile and lime juice. Add chicken thighs back to the Dutch oven and pour in beer.
- When ready to cook, set the Traeger to 350°F and preheat, lid closed for 15 minutes.
- Place Dutch oven in the grill and braise for 30 minutes or until chicken is tender and falls apart. Remove chicken from braising liquid and shred.
- To build the tacos, place shredded chicken on tortilla, top with jalapeño relish, cabbage, cotija, cilantro, and finish with hot sauce. Enjoy!

5.4 Slow Roasted Shawarma
Ingredients:

- 5.5 Lbs. Top Sirloin
- 5.5 Lbs. Boneless Skinless Chicken Thighs
- 4.5 Lbs. Lamb Fat
- 4 Tbsp Traeger Rub
- 2 Large Yellow Onions
- Pita Bread
- Topping Options: Cucumber, Tomatoes, Tahini, Pickles, Fries, Israeli Salad
- A Double Skewer
- A Cast Iron Griddle

Instructions:

- *Plan ahead! Assemble the shawarma stack the night before you plan to cook it.
- Slice all the meat and fat into ½" slices and place into 3 bowls (pro tip: it's easier to slice if they are all partially frozen).
- Season each bowl with Traeger Rub and massage the rub into the meat.
- Place half an onion on the bottom of each half skewer to make a firm base. then add 2 layers from each bowl at a time. Try to make the stack symmetrical, more or less. Then put the other 2 half onions at the top. Wrap in plastic wrap and refrigerate overnight.
- When ready to cook, set temperature to 275°F and preheat, lid closed for 15 minutes.
- Lay the shawarma directly on the grill grate and cook for about 3-4 hours, rotating at least once.
- Remove from grill and increase the temperature to 445°F. While the grill preheats, place a cast iron griddle directly on the grill grate and brush with olive oil.
- When the griddle is hot place the whole shawarma on the cast iron and sear 5-10 minutes per side. Remove from grill, slice off the edges, then repeat with remaining shawarma.
- Serve in pita bread with your favorite toppings like cucumber, tomatoes, tahini, pickles, fries or Israeli salad.
- Enjoy!

5.5 BBQ Chicken Nachos
Ingredients:

- 1-1/4 Lbs. Chicken Breasts, Boneless, Skinless
- Traeger Pork & Poultry Rub, As Needed
- 1/2 To 3/4 Cup Traeger Qu BBQ Sauce
- 24 Large Tortilla Chips
- 3 Cups Mexican Blend Shredded Cheese
- 1/2 Cup Black Olives, Sliced and Drained
- Pickled Jalapenos, Sliced
- 3 Scallions, Thinly Sliced
- 1 Cup Sour Cream

Instructions:

- Season the chicken breasts with the Traeger Pork and Poultry Rub.
- When ready to cook, set temperature to 350°F and preheat, lid closed for 15 minutes.
- Arrange the chicken breasts on the grill grate and cook, turning once halfway through the cooking time, for 25 to 30 minutes, or until the internal temperature when read on an instant-read meat thermometer is 170°F. Transfer to a cutting board and let rest for 3 minutes. Leave the grill on if you are making the nachos immediately.
- Dice the chicken into small cubes, 1/2-inch or less. Transfer to a mixing bowl and pour 1/2 cup of Traeger Regular Barbecue Sauce over the diced chicken. Stir gently to coat each piece.
- Set aside, or cover and refrigerate if not making the nachos immediately. Lay the tortilla chips in a single layer on a rimmed baking sheet or pizza pan. Sprinkle evenly with half the cheese and a few of the jalapenos (if using).
- Spoon barbecued chicken mixture on each chip. Top with black olives and more pickled jalapeno, if desired. Sprinkle the remaining half of the cheese evenly over the chips. Scatter the sliced onions over the chips.
- Put the baking sheet on the grill grate. Bake until the chips are crisp and the cheese is melted, 12 to 15 minutes. With a spatula, transfer the nachos to a plate or platter. Serve immediately with sour cream and pickled jalapenos. Enjoy!

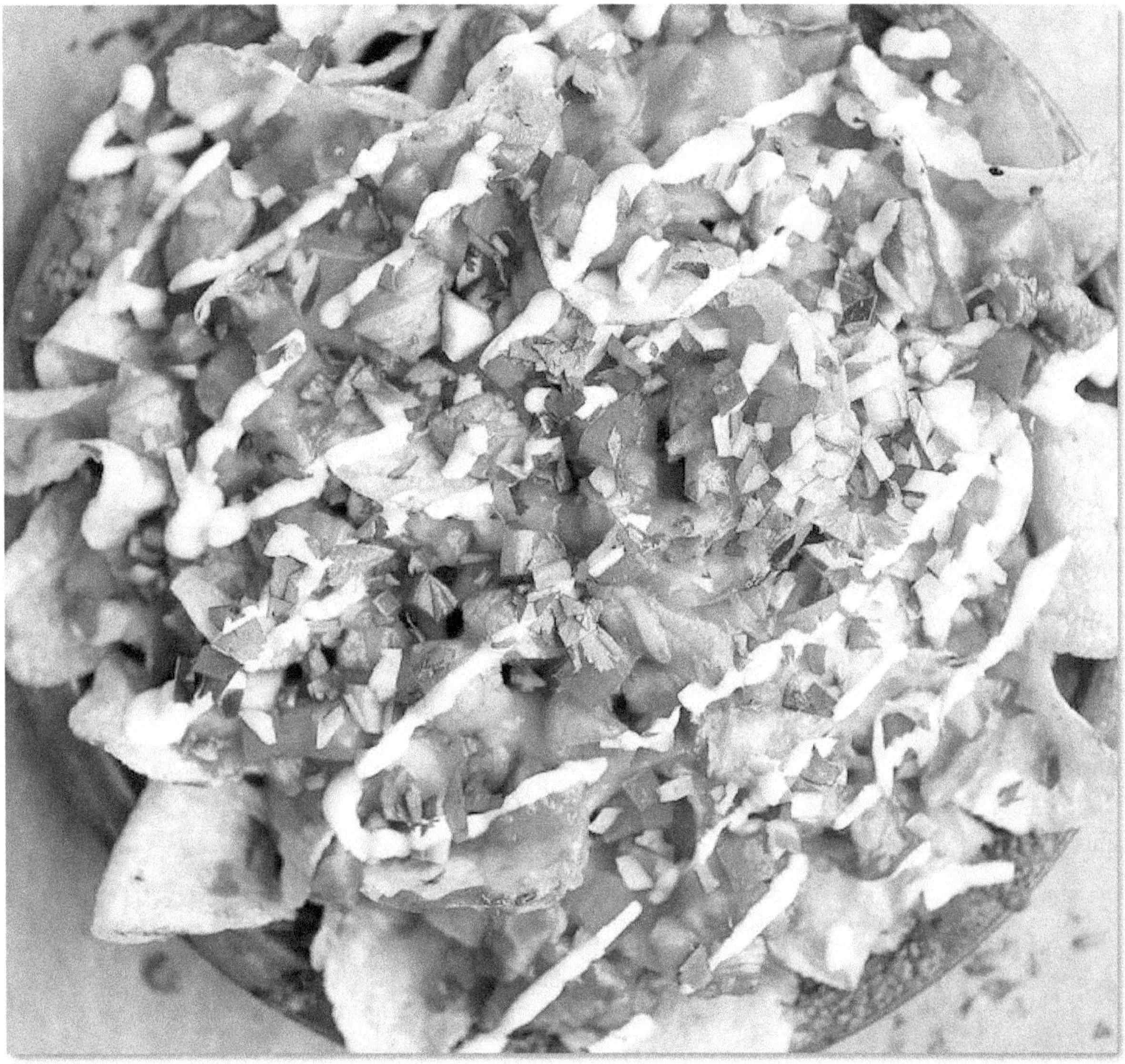

5.6 Spicy BBQ Chicken
Ingredients:

- 1 Whole Chicken
- 6 Thai Chiles
- 2 Tbsp Sweet Paprika
- 1 Scotch Bonnet
- 2 Tbsp Sugar
- 3 Tbsp Salt
- 1 White Onion
- 5 Garlic Cloves
- 4 Cups Grape Seed Oil

Instructions:

- Puree the Thai chilies, paprika, scotch bonnet, sugar, salt, onion, garlic, and grape seed oil together until smooth.
- Smother the chicken with mixture and let rest in fridge overnight.
- When ready to cook, set the Traeger to 300°F and preheat, lid closed for 15 minutes.
- Place chicken on grill breast side up and smoke for 3 hours or until it reaches an internal temperature of 165°F in the breast.
- Remove from grill and allow to rest for 10 to 15 minutes before slicing. Serve with sides of choice. Enjoy!

5.7 Traeger BBQ Half Chickens
Ingredients:

- 1 Ea. (3-3 1/2 Lb.) Young Fresh Chicken
- Traeger Apricot BBQ Sauce
- Traeger Summer Shandi Rub

Instructions:

- Place the chicken, breast side down, on a cutting board with the neck pointing away from you. Cut along one side of the backbone, staying as close to the bone as possible, from the neck to the tail.
- Repeat on the other side of the backbone then remove it. Open the chicken and slice through the white cartilage at the tip of the breastbone to pop it open. Cut down either side of the breast bone then use your fingers to pull it out.
- Flip the chicken over so it is skin side up and cut down the center splitting the chicken in half. Tuck the wings back of each chicken half.
- Season on both sides with Traeger Summer Shandi rub.
- When ready to cook, set the temperature to 375°F and preheat, lid closed for 15 minutes.
- Place chicken directly on the grill grate skin side up and cook until the internal temperature reaches 160 degrees F, about 60-90 minutes.
- Brush the BBQ sauce all over the chicken skin and cook for an additional 10 minutes.
- Remove from grill and let rest 5 minutes before serving. Enjoy!

5.8 Smoked Deviled Eggs
Ingredients:

- 7 Hard Boiled Eggs, Cooked and Peeled
- 3 Tbsp Mayonnaise
- 3 Tsp Chives, Diced
- 1 Tsp Brown Mustard
- 1 Tsp Apple Cider Vinegar
- Dash of Hot Sauce
- Salt and Pepper, To Taste
- 2 Tbsp Bacon, Crumbled
- Paprika, For Dusting

Instructions:

- When ready to cook, set temperature to 180°F and preheat, lid closed for 15 minutes. For optimal flavor, use Super Smoke if available.
- Place cooked and peeled eggs directly on the grill grate and smoke eggs for 30 minutes. Remove from grill and allow eggs to cool.
- Slice the eggs lengthwise and scoop the egg yolks into a gallon zip top bag. Add mayonnaise, chives, mustard, vinegar, hot sauce, salt, and pepper to the bag.
- Zip the bag closed and, using your hands, knead all of the **Ingredients:** together until completely smooth.
- Squeeze the yolk mixture into one corner of the bag and cut a small part of the corner off. Pipe the yolk mixture into the hardboiled egg whites.
- Top the deviled eggs with crumbled bacon and paprika. Chill until ready to serve. Enjoy!

5.9 Pickled Brined Hot Chicken Sandwich

Ingredients:

- Pickle Brined Chicken
- 2 Cups Leftover Pickle Juice
- 8 Ea. Boneless Skinless Chicken Thighs
- Salt and Pepper, As Needed
- 1 Cup Flour
- 1/2 Cup Tapioca Flour
- 1 Cup Buttermilk
- 2 Tsp Franks Red Hot Sauce
- 1 Egg
- Butter Hot Sauce
- 1/2 Cup Butter, Melted
- 1/2 Cup Franks Red Hot Sauce
- 2 Tsp Cayenne
- 1/2 Tsp Dark Brown Sugar
- 1 Tsp Black Pepper
- 1 Tsp Garlic
- 1 Tsp Paprika
- Sandwich
- Shredded Cabbage Slaw
- Traeger Smoked Pickles
- 4 Sesame Seed Buns

Instructions:

- In a medium bowl, combine pickle juice and chicken thighs. Weigh them down if necessary, to make sure they are completely submerged. Place in the refrigerator to brine overnight.
- When ready to cook, set the temperature to High and preheat, lid closed for 15 minutes.
- Place a cast iron pan with 1/2-inch canola oil on the grill grate while the grill preheats.
- Remove the chicken thighs from the pickle brine and pat dry.
- In a medium bowl combine both flours and a pinch of salt. Mix well to combine.
- In another bowl combine the buttermilk, hot sauce, egg and a pinch of salt. Mix well to combine.
- Season the chicken thighs with salt. Dip the thighs in the flour mixture, then buttermilk, then back into the flour mixture. Transfer to a wire rack and repeat with the remaining thighs.
- Place wire rack directly on the grill grate next to the cast iron of oil and bake chicken for 15 minutes or until the internal temperature reaches 150°F.
- As chicken pieces come to temperature, transfer them 2 or 3 at a time to the preheated oil to crisp the coating and finish cooking.
- For the Butter Hot Sauce: While the chicken is cooking, melt the butter and combine with the hot sauce, brown sugar, cayenne, garlic powder, paprika and black pepper in a medium bowl. Set aside.
- Remove chicken from the oil when the internal temperature reaches 165°F and dunk in the butter hot sauce mixture.
- Build the sandwiches with buns, mayonnaise, pickles, cabbage slaw and hot chicken. Enjoy!

5.10 Baked Chicken Cordon Bleu
Ingredients:

- 4 Ea. (4-5 Oz) Boneless, Skinless Chicken Breasts
- 8 Slices Prosciutto or Ham
- 8 Slices Swiss Cheese
- 1/3 Cup All-Purpose Flour
- Salt, As Needed
- Freshly Ground Black Pepper, As Needed
- 1 Cup Dry Breadcrumbs, Preferably Panko
- 1/4 Cup Grated Parmesan Cheese
- 2 Tbsp Melted Butter
- 2 Tsp Fresh Thyme Leaves
- 2 Eggs

Instructions:

- Spray a baking sheet with nonstick cooking spray. Set aside.
- Butterfly each chicken breast and place between two pieces of plastic wrap. Evenly pound with the flat side of a meat mallet, being careful not to tear the chicken, until chicken is 1/4-inch thick.
- Lay each chicken breast on a fresh piece of plastic wrap. Season chicken with salt and lay 1 to 2 slices of cheese on each breast followed by prosciutto or ham, then 1-2 more slices of cheese.
- Roll the chicken breast up like you would roll a burrito. Using the bottom piece of plastic wrap as an aid, fold the bottom of the breast up about an inch, then fold in the sides. Roll tightly.
- Wrap in the plastic wrap and tightly twist the ends to shape and compress the chicken. Repeat with the remaining chicken breasts. Chill in the refrigerator for 60 minutes.
- While chicken chills, season the flour with salt and pepper and put in a shallow dish.
- Combine the breadcrumbs, parmesan cheese, butter, and thyme. Season with salt and pepper and put in a second shallow dish.
- Whisk the eggs in a separate third dish.
- Arrange your workspace in this order: flour, eggs, breadcrumbs. Put the prepared baking sheet next to the breadcrumbs.
- Remove the plastic wrap from the chicken breasts. Coat each lightly with flour then dip in the egg.
- Finally, roll in breadcrumbs, patting them to make them adhere. Arrange on the baking sheet.
- When ready to cook, set the temperature to 375°F and preheat, lid closed for 15 minutes.
- Place the baking sheet with the chicken on the grill. Bake for 30-40 minutes, or until the coating is golden brown and the chicken is cooked through.
- Serve whole or slice crosswise into pinwheels with a sharp serrated knife. Enjoy!

5.11 Roasted Teriyaki Wings
Ingredients:

- 2 1/2 Lbs. Large Chicken Wings
- 1/2 Cup Soy Sauce
- 1/4 Cup Water
- 1/4 Cup Brown Sugar
- 2 Tbsp Rice Wine Vinegar
- 2 Scallions
- 1 Clove Garlic, Minced
- 2 Tsp Sesame Oil
- 2 Tbsp Fresh Ginger, Smashed
- 1 Tbsp Sesame Seeds, Lightly Toasted

Instructions:

- Cut the wings into three pieces through the joints. Discard the wing tips, or save for chicken stock.
- Transfer the remaining chicken drumettes and flats to a large resealable plastic bag or a bowl.
- For the Marinade: In a small saucepan, combine the soy sauce, water, brown sugar, vinegar, scallions, garlic, sesame oil, and ginger. Bring to a boil, then reduce the heat and simmer for 10 minutes.
- Cool completely, then pour over the chicken wings. Seal the bag and refrigerate for several hours, or overnight. Drain the wings, discarding the marinade.
- When ready to cook, set the temperature to 350°F and preheat, lid closed for 15 minutes.
- Cook for 45 to 50 minutes, or until the skin is brown and crisp and the meat is no longer pink at the bone.
- Turn once during the cooking time to prevent the wings from sticking to the grill grate. Remove from grill.
- Sprinkle with sesame seeds to serve. Enjoy!

5.12 Smoked Korean Wings
Ingredients:

- Brine
- 1 Gallon Water
- 1 Cup Sea Salt
- 1/2 Cup Sugar
- 1 Lemon, Halved
- 1 Head Garlic, Halved
- 4 Sprigs Thyme
- 10 Peppercorns
- Wings
- 3 Lb. Chicken Wings
- 2 Tbsp Olive Oil
- Sauce
- 1/2 Cup Gochujang Hot Pepper Paste#1
- 1/4 Cup Soy Sauce
- 1/3 Cup Honey
- 2 Tbsp Rice Wine Vinegar
- 2 Tbsp Fresh Squeezed Lime Juice
- 2 Tbsp Toasted Sesame Oil
- 1/4 Cup Butter, Melted
- 4 Cloves Garlic, Minced
- 1 Tbsp Ginger, Peeled and Grated

Instructions:

- For the Brine: To a stockpot, add 1 gallon of water, salt, and sugar, and stir well. Bring to a boil then remove from the heat and stir in the lemon, garlic, thyme, and peppercorns. Cool to room temperature, then submerge the wings. Cover and refrigerate for 2 to 4 hours.
- When ready to cook, set the temperature to 375°F and preheat, with the lid closed for 15 minutes.
- Remove the wings from the brine and dry them completely with paper towel. Discard brine.
- Toss the wings with the olive oil coating them completely.
- Place the wings directly onto the grill grate and cook to an internal temperature of 165°F, about 45 to 60 minutes.
- For the Sauce: In a bowl, combine all the sauce **Ingredients:** and whisk until smooth. Heat over medium-heat until the sauce just comes to a simmer, then remove from heat and set aside.
- Toss the cooked wings with 2/3 of the sauce, the green onions, peanuts, and sesame seeds.
- Serve wings with fresh cilantro, lime wedges, and extra sauce for dipping. Enjoy!

5.13 Roasted Buffalo Wings

Ingredients:

- Chicken Wings
- 4 Lbs. Chicken Wings
- 1 Tbsp Corn Starch
- Traeger Chicken Rub, As Needed
- Kosher Salt, To Taste
- Buffalo Sauce
- 1/4 Cup Spicy Mustard
- 1/2 Cup Franks Red Hot Sauce
- 6 Tbsp Unsalted Butter

Instructions:

- When ready to cook, set the temperature to 375°F and preheat, lid closed for 15 minutes.
- While grill is preheating, dry off chicken wings with a paper towel. Place wings in a large bowl and sprinkle with cornstarch, Traeger Chicken Rub and salt to taste. Mix to coat both sides of the chicken wings.
- When the grill has heated, place the wings on the grill and cook for 35 minutes total, turning halfway through cook time.
- Check the internal temperature of the wings at 35 minutes. The internal temperature should be at least 165°F. However, an internal temperature of 175-180°F will yield a better texture.
- For the Buffalo Sauce: In another pot add the Franks Red Hot, mustard and butter. Whisk to combine and heat through on the stove top.
- Keep sauce warm while the wings are cooking. When wings are done, pour the buffalo sauce over the wings, turning with tongs to coat.
- Cook for an additional 10-15 minutes on the grill for the sauce to set.
- Serve wings with ranch or blue cheese dressing. Enjoy!

5.15 Roasted Tequila-Lime Wings

Ingredients:

- Wings
- 3 Lbs. Chicken Wings
- 2 Tsp Ancho Chile Powder
- 2 Tsp Brown Sugar
- 1 Tsp Granulated Garlic
- 1 Tsp Cumin
- 1 Tsp Kosher Salt
- 1 Tsp Chili Powder
- 2 Tbsp Vegetable Oil
- Glaze
- 1/4 Cup Honey
- 1/4 Cup Pineapple Juice
- 3 Tbsp Tequila
- 1-1/2 Tbsp Hot Sauce
- 1-1/2 Tbsp Butter
- 1-1/2 Tbsp Fresh Lime Juice

Instructions:

- When ready to cook, set temperature to High and preheat, lid closed for 15 minutes.
- If you bought whole chicken wings, remove the tip and separate the drumettes and wings from each other. Pat them dry. Discard the wing tips or save them for chicken stock.
- Combine all of the dry rub **Ingredients** in a medium bowl. Add the oil and whisk to combine. Add the chicken wings and toss well to coat.
- For the Glaze: Combine glaze **Ingredients** in a small saucepan. Bring to a boil over medium heat. Cook until mixture is reduced by about 1/3 and begins to thicken, about 3 minutes. Keep the syrup warm while waiting to glaze.
- Place the wings directly on the grill grate and cook, turning once, until the internal temperature of the wings reaches 155-160°F, about 20 minutes.
- Brush the wings with the glaze and continue to cook until the internal temperature reaches 165-175°F, about 5-10 minutes longer.
- Serve warm. Enjoy!

5.16 Smoked Chicken Tikka Masala
Ingredients:

- Marinade
- 6 Garlic Cloves, Minced
- 1 Thumb-Sized Knob of Ginger, Finely Diced
- 4 Tsp Ground Turmeric
- 2 Tsp Garam Masala
- 2 Tsp Ground Coriander
- 2 Tsp Ground Cumin
- 2 Tsp Ground Chili
- 1 1/2 Cups Whole Milk Yoghurt
- 1 Tbsp Kosher Salt
- 2 Lb. Chicken Breasts, Cut Into 1-Inch Strips
- Tikka Masala Sauce
- 3 Tbsp Ghee or Clarified Butter
- 1 Medium Onion, Finely Diced
- Finely Diced Cilantro Stems 1/4 Cup
- Tomato Paste 1/4 Cup
- 6 Cardamom Pods, Crushed
- 1 (28 Oz) Can Crushed Tomatoes
- 2 Cups Heavy Whipping Cream
- 1-2 Sliced Fresh Chilies, For Garnish
- 1/2 Cup Fresh Cilantro, For Garnish
- 1 Cup Creamy Yogurt
- Cooked Basmati Rice, To Serve

Instructions:

- Prepare the spice mixture by combining the garlic, ginger and all the spices in a small bowl. Mix well and set aside.
- For the Marinade: In a large bowl, combine the sliced chicken breast, yogurt, 1/2 the spice mixture, and kosher salt. Mix well.
- Cover with plastic wrap and chill in the fridge overnight for marinated chicken perfection.
- When ready to cook, set the temperature to High and preheat with the lid closed for 15 minutes.
- For the Sauce: Heat a high-sided, oven-safe pan over medium-heat and melt the ghee. Add the onion, cilantro stems, cardamom, and a pinch of salt, and cook until the onion softens, about 5 minutes. Add the tomato paste and remaining spice mixture, and cook for 2 minutes. Pour in the tomatoes and season with another pinch of salt. Bring the sauce to a simmer and cook for about 8 minutes, until thickened.
- While the sauce is cooking, add the marinated chicken pieces to the grill and cook for 2 minutes per side, until just starting to turn to beautifully golden brown. Remove and set aside.
- Reduce grill heat to 350°F. Stir the cream into the sauce mixture, then fold in the chicken. Transfer the curry to the grill and cook, lid closed, for 35 to 40 minutes, until the chicken is cooked through and the curry is thick and glorious.

- Divide the cooked basmati rice onto plates, then top with curry. Garnish with yogurt, fresh chilies and cilantro. Enjoy!

5.17 Roasted Rosemary Orange Chicken
Ingredients:

- 1 (3-4 Lbs.) Chicken, Backbone Removed
- 1/4 Cup Olive Oil
- 2 Oranges, Divided
- Zest Of 1 Orange
- 2 Tsp Dijon Mustard
- 3 Tbsp Chopped Rosemary Leaves
- 2 Tsp Kosher Salt

Instructions:

- Rinse the chicken and pat dry with paper towels.
- For the Marinade: In a medium bowl, combine the olive oil, juice from the oranges (about 1/4 cup of freshly squeezed juice), the orange zest, Dijon mustard, rosemary leaves and salt. Whisk to combine.
- Place the chicken in a shallow baking dish large enough to be fully opened in one piece.
- Pour the marinade over the chicken ensuring it is covered with the marinade. Cover with plastic wrap and refrigerate for a minimum of 2 hours or up to overnight, turning once during the process.
- When ready to cook, set temperature to 350°F and preheat, lid closed for 15 minutes.
- Remove the chicken from the marinade and place on the grill, skin side down. Cook for 25-30 minutes until the skin is well-browned, then flip.
- Continue to grill chicken until the internal temperature of the breast reaches 165°F and the thigh reaches 175°F, about 5-15 minutes longer.
- Let rest 10 minutes before carving. Enjoy!

5.18 Loaded Grilled Chicken Tacos
Ingredients:

- Grilled Chicken
- 2 Lbs. Boneless-Skinless Chicken Breasts
- 2 Tbsp Olive Oil
- 2 Tsp Chili Powder
- 1 Tsp Smoked Paprika
- 1/2 Tsp Ground Cumin
- 1/4 Tsp Ground Cayenne
- 1 1/2 Tsp Kosher Salt Kosher Salt
- 1 Tsp Fresh Cracked Black Pepper
- Pico De Gallo
- 1 1/2 Lbs. Ripe Plum Tomatoes, Diced
- 1 Medium Red Onion, Diced
- 1/2 Cup Fresh Cilantro Leaves, Chopped
- Juice Of 1 Lime
- Kosher Salt, To Taste
- Guacamole
- 2 Ripe Avocados
- 1 Tbsp Fresh Squeezed Lime Juice
- 1/4 Cup Finely Diced Red Onion
- 2 Tbsp Finely Chopped Cilantro Leaves
- 1/2 Cup Sour Cream
- 1 Tsp Chili Powder
- 1 Tbsp Fresh Squeezed Lime Juice
- Pinch of Kosher Salt
- Toppings
- 10-12 Flour Tortillas
- 1 Lime, Cut into Wedges

- 1-2 Jalapenos, Sliced
- Handful of Fresh Cilantro
- Hot Sauce

Instructions:

- For the Marinade: Combine the chicken breasts, olive oil, spices, zest, salt, and pepper in freezer bag and give everything a good mix. Chill in the fridge for at least 4 hours (overnight is best).
- When ready to cook, set temperature to High and preheat, lid closed for 15 minutes.
- Place the chicken breasts on the hot grill and cook, lid closed, for 25 to 30 minutes, until crispy, golden, and the chicken reaches an internal temperature of 165°F.
- Rest the grilled chicken for 5 minutes before slicing into thin strips.
- While the chicken is on the grill, prepare the Pico, guacamole, and spiked sour cream.
- For the Pico: Combine all the Pico **Ingredients** in a small bowl and mix well. Set aside.
- For the Guacamole: Peel and carefully remove the pit from the avocados. Smash the avocado in a bowl until smooth, leaving a few chunks for texture, then add the remaining guacamole **Ingredients** and give everything a good mix.
- For the Spiked Sour Cream: Combine all the spiked sour cream **Ingredients** in a small bowl and mix well.
- Divide the sliced grilled chicken on warm tortillas, then hit each with fresh Pico, guacamole, and a dollop of spiked-sour cream.
- Top each taco with sliced jalapeño and fresh cilantro, and serve with lime wedges and hot sauce. Enjoy!

5.19 Grilled Thai Chicken Burgers with Papaya Slaw
Ingredients:

- Papaya Slaw
- 6 Oz Shredded Green Papaya (From 1 Medium Papaya)
- 1/2 Red Onion, Thinly Sliced
- 2 Tsp Grated Lime Zest
- 3 Tbsp Plus 2 Tsp Fresh Lime Juice
- 1 Tbsp Fish Sauce
- 1 Tbsp Brown Sugar
- Chicken Burger
- 1 Lb. Ground Chicken Thigh Meat
- 1/2 Cup Panko or Gluten Free Bread Crumbs
- 1/4 Cup Coconut Cream (Thick Milk Solids From 1 Can Chilled Coconut Milk)
- 1/2 Cup Chopped Fresh Cilantro
- 2 Garlic Cloves, Minced
- 2 Tsp Kosher Salt
- 1 Tsp Ground Cumin
- 1 Tsp Freshly Ground Black Pepper
- 1/2 Tsp Ground Ginger
- 1/2 Cup Mayonnaise
- 1 1/2 Tsp Curry Powder
- 1 Tbsp Vegetable Oil
- 8 Large Leaves Butter Lettuce Or 4 Hamburger Buns

Instructions:

- For the Papaya Slaw: In a medium bowl, combine the papaya, onion, 3 Tbsp of the lime juice, fish sauce and the brown sugar. Cover and refrigerate until ready to use, up to 3 hours.
- In a large bowl, stir together the ground chicken, breadcrumbs, coconut cream, cilantro, garlic, ginger, salt, pepper, cumin, lime zest, and remaining 2 tsp lime juice until thoroughly combined. Refrigerate for 20 minutes. If the mixture seems too wet or dry adjust with breadcrumbs or coconut milk until it stays together.
- Meanwhile, in a small bowl, stir together the mayonnaise and curry powder. Set aside.
- When ready to cook, set temperature to High and preheat, lid closed for 15 minutes.
- Using your hands, form the chicken mixture into four equal patties.
- Brush each burger with the vegetable oil on both sides. Cook for 4-5 minutes per side, or until the burgers reach 165°F internally. Remove from the grill and allow to rest for a few minutes before serving.
- Place each burger on a leaf of lettuce then top with curry mayonnaise and pickled papaya slaw. Top with a second lettuce leaf and serve.
- Alternatively, use regular hamburger buns and pile high with the burgers, curry mayonnaise and papaya slaw. Enjoy!

5.20 Baked Buffalo Chicken Dip
Ingredients:

- 1 (8 Oz) Package Cream Cheese, Softened
- 1/2 Cup Sour Cream
- 1/2 Cup Mayonnaise
- 2 Tbsp Dry Ranch Seasoning
- 1 Tsp Kosher Salt
- 1/2 Cup Franks Red Hot Sauce
- 2 Cups Chicken, Cooked and Shredded
- 1 Cup Cheddar Cheese, Shredded
- 1 Cup Mozzarella Cheese, Shredded
- Blue Cheese, To Taste
- Crumbled Bacon, To Taste

Instructions:

- When ready to cook start the Traeger grill on Smoke with the lid open until fire is established (4-5 minutes). Set the temperature to 350 degrees F and preheat, lid closed for 10-15 minutes.
- In the bowl of a stand mixer, combine cream cheese, sour cream, mayonnaise, ranch, salt, and hot sauce and mix with the paddle attachment until combined.
- Fold together the cheddar and mozzarella cheese and shredded chicken. Transfer to an oven proof dish and top with blue cheese and crumbled bacon.
- Place directly on the grill grate and cook for 20-30 minutes until the top is golden brown and dip is bubbling.
- Serve with chips, crackers, crostini, or sliced vegetables. Enjoy!

5.21 Tomatillo Braised Chicken
Ingredients:

- Tomatillo Salsa
- 1 Lb. Tomatillos, Husks Removed and Rinsed
- 1 White Onion, Quartered Through the Root End and Skin Removed
- 3 Jalapeños, Halved Lengthwise, Seeded If Preferred
- 2 Tbsp Olive Oil
- Kosher Salt
- 3 Tbsp Lime Juice
- 2 Tbsp Chopped Cilantro
- Braised Chicken
- 8 Bone-In, Skin-On Chicken Thighs
- 6 Bone-In, Skin-On Chicken Breasts
- Kosher Salt
- Freshly Ground Pepper
- 1/2 Cup Chicken Stock
- 2 Cups Tomatillo Salsa

Instructions:

- When ready to cook, set the temperature to 350°F and preheat, lid closed for 15 minutes.
- Place the tomatillos, onion, and jalapeños in a large bowl and add the olive oil and 1/2 tsp salt. Toss to coat evenly, then place in a grilling basket or a baking sheet.
- Grill, turning the vegetables occasionally, until they begin to char and soften, about 5 to 10 minutes. Remove the vegetables from the grill as they are ready.
- Transfer to the same bowl to catch their juices and allow them to cool to room temperature.
- Place the cooled vegetables along with their juices in a blender and add the lime juice, cilantro, and another pinch of salt. Pulse until the mixture reaches the texture of a salsa. Taste, adding more salt or lime juice as desired.
- Rinse the chicken and pat dry with paper towels. Sprinkle with salt and pepper on both sides.
- Place the chicken skin side down on the grill grate and cook until the skin is golden brown and very crispy, 10-15 minutes. Turn, cooking the other side for 5 minutes, then transfer the chicken to a plate.
- Place the grilled chicken legs in a Dutch oven or cast iron and add chicken stock and salsa Verde. Cover the pan and place directly on the grill grate.
- Cook for 1 1/2 to 2 hours until the chicken is fork tender. Enjoy!

5.22 Grilled Sticky Ginger Chicken Thighs
Ingredients:

- Marinade
- 1/2 Cup Grated Onion
- 1/2 Cup Peanut Oil
- 1/3 Cup Rice Vinegar
- 2 Tbsp Water
- 2 Tbsp Grated Fresh Ginger
- 2 Tbsp Ketchup
- 4 Tsp Soy Sauce
- 2 Tsp Sugar
- 2 Tsp Lemon Juice
- 1/2 Tsp Minced Garlic
- Chicken Thighs
- 4-6 Chicken Thighs
- 3 Green Onion Stalks
- 2 Limes
- Sesame Seeds, To Garnish

Instructions:

- Combine all sauce **Ingredients:** in a large bowl and set aside.
- Place chicken thighs into a zip lock bag and add approximately 3/4 of the dressing to cover. Place in the refrigerator to marinate for at least 1 hour.
- When ready to cook, set temperature to High and preheat, lid closed for 15 minutes.
- Place marinated chicken thighs on the grill grate, skin side down. Cook for 10 minutes, flip and cook another 10 minutes.
- Cut limes and green onions and place on chicken. Cook for an additional 5 minutes. Enjoy!

5.23 BBQ Game Day Chicken Wings and Thighs
Ingredients:

- 8-10 Chicken Thighs
- 20-30 Chicken Wings
- 1/2 Cup Olive Oil
- 1/2 Cup Traeger Chicken Rub

Instructions:

- When ready to cook, set the Traeger to 375°F and preheat, lid closed for 15 minutes.
- Place thighs and wings in a large bowl. Add the olive oil and Traeger Chicken rub and mix well. Cover bowl and refrigerate for 3 to 8 hours.
- Place chicken directly on the grill grate and cook for 45 minutes. Check the internal temperature of the chicken, it is considered done at 165°F however, a finished temperature of 175 to 180°F results in a better texture in dark meat.
- Once the finished temperature is reached, remove chicken from the grill and let rest for 5 to 10 minutes before serving. Enjoy!

5.24 Baked Garlic Parmesan Wings
Ingredients:

- Chicken Wings
- 5 Lbs. Chicken Wings
- 1/2 Cup Traeger Chicken Rub
- Sauce
- 1 Cup Butter
- 10 Cloves Garlic, Finely Diced
- 2 Tbsp Traeger Chicken Rub
- Garnish
- 1 Cup Parmesan Cheese, Shredded

- 3 Tbsp Parsley, Chopped

Instructions:

- When ready to cook, set temperature to High and preheat, lid closed for 15 minutes.
- In a large bowl, toss the wings with the Traeger Chicken rub.
- Place wings directly on the grill grate and cook for 10 minutes. Flip wings and cook for an additional 10 minutes. Check the internal temperature of the wings, finished desired temperature is 165-180 degrees F.
- To make the Garlic Sauce: While the chicken is cooking, combine butter, garlic and remaining rub in a medium sized saucepan and cook over medium heat on a stove top. Cook sauce for 8-10 minutes, stirring occasionally.
- When wings are finished cooking, remove from grill and place in a large bowl. Toss wings with the garlic sauce, parmesan cheese and parsley. Enjoy!

5.25 Roasted Habanero Wings
Ingredients:

- 4 Lbs. Chicken Wings
- 1 White Onion, Peeled and Chopped
- 2/3 Cup Sliced Green Onions, White and Light Green Parts Only, Plus 2 Tbsp for Garnish
- 2 Cloves Garlic, Peeled and Minced
- 1/4 Cup Vegetable Oil
- 2 Tbsp Low-Sodium Soy Sauce or Tamari
- 2 Tbsp Habanero or Other Hot Pepper Sauce
- 1-1/2 Tsp Salt
- 1-1/2 Tsp Ground Allspice
- 1 Tsp Ground Black Pepper
- 1/2 Tsp Dried Thyme
- 1/2 Tsp Ground Cinnamon
- 1 Habanero Pepper, Seeds Removed

Instructions:

- Cut off the tips of the wings and discard or save for making stock. Cut the wings into drumette and flat sections.
- To make the Marinade: Combine the onion, green onions and scallions in a food processor and puree until it is the texture of a thick paste. Add the oil, soy sauce, hot pepper sauce, the salt and all of the spices, and half or all of the habanero pepper, depending on how much heat you prefer. Process until all **Ingredients** are combined. Reserve some of the marinade for basting and set aside.
- Arrange the wings in a shallow baking dish and pour the marinade over the wings, tossing with tongs to ensure wings are evenly coated in sauce. Cover and refrigerate wings. Allow them to marinate for at least 6 hours or up to overnight, turning the wings at least twice.
- When ready to cook, set the Traeger to 350°F and preheat, lid closed for 15 minutes.
- Remove the wings from the marinade and discard what is left of the marinade.
- Place the wings directly on the grill grate and cook for 30 minutes, baste the wings with the reserved marinade and flip.Close the lid and continue cooking for another 20 minutes, or until the wings are browned and crispy and have reached an internal temperature of at least 165°F.Garnish wings with the remaining green onions and serve immediately.

5.26 Smoked Chicken Tikka Drumsticks
Ingredients:

- Chicken Tikka Drumsticks
- 1 Tbsp Smoked Paprika
- 1 Tbsp Garam Masala
- 1 Tbsp Ground Cumin
- 1 Tbsp Ground Coriander
- 1 Tsp Turmeric
- 1 Tsp Ground Cayenne
- 1/2 Medium Spanish Onion, Diced
- 1 Thumb-Sized Piece of Ginger, Peeled and Roughly Chopped
- 6 Cloves Garlic, Chopped
- 1/2 Cup Greek Yogurt
- Juice Of 1/2 A Lemon
- 1/4 Cup Olive Oil
- 12 Chicken Drumsticks
- Curry Lime Yogurt
- 1-1/2 Cups Greek Yogurt
- 1 Tbsp Curry Powder
- 1 Tbsp Fresh Squeezed Lime Juice
- Pinch of Sea Salt
- Garnishes
- Fresh Cilantro
- 1/2 Small Red Onion, Thinly Sliced
- 1 Lime, Cut into Wedges
- 1-2 Sliced Green or Red Chilies

Instructions:

- For the Marinade: In the base of a food processor, combine the spices, ginger, garlic, onion, yogurt, lemon juice, oil, and salt, and pulse until smooth.
- Place the chicken in a large bowl, pour over the marinade, then massage chicken until every nook and cranny of the chicken is coated. Cover with plastic wrap and chill in the fridge overnight (at least 12 hours).
- When ready to cook, set the temperature to High and preheat, lid closed for 15 minutes.
- Place the chicken directly on the grill grates and cook for 45-50 minutes, until crispy and wood-fire grilled to perfection (or until it reaches an internal temperature of 165°F).
- For the Curry Lime Yogurt: While the chicken is grilling, combine all of the yogurt **Ingredients** in a small bowl and mix well. Chill in the fridge until ready to serve.
- Garnish with fresh cilantro and sliced red onion and serve with curry lime yoghurt, fresh lime wedges, and if you like it extra spicy, sliced chilies. Enjoy!

5.27 Lemon Rosemary Beer Can Chicken
Ingredients:

- 1 (3-3.5 Lbs.) Whole Chicken
- 1 Lemon
- 1 Tsp Kosher Salt
- 1 Tsp Ground Pepper
- 1 Tsp Fresh Rosemary, Chopped Fine
- 1 (12 Oz) Can Beer

Instructions:

- When ready to cook, set temperature to High and preheat, lid closed for 15 minutes.
- Coat the chicken inside and out with the juice from one lemon. In a small bowl, combine the salt, pepper and rosemary and sprinkle on the inside and out of chicken.
- Empty half of the beer from the can and place the can on a solid surface. Place the chicken atop the beer can tucking the legs in the front.

- Carefully place the chicken directly on the grill grate using the legs to support if needed. Alternatively, place the chicken atop the beer can on a sheet tray for a more stable surface, then place the sheet tray directly on the grill grate.
- Cook the chicken until an instant read thermometer reads 165°F when inserted in the thickest part of the breast, about 60 minutes.
- Let the chicken rest 10 minutes before carving.
- Serve with Chardonnay or any of your favorite medium body red or white wines. Enjoy!

5.28 Ultimate Traeger Thanksgiving Sandwich
Ingredients:

- 1 French Bread Loaf
- Mayonnaise
- Dijon Mustard
- Leftover Turkey Gravy
- Leftover Smoked Turkey
- Shredded White Cheddar Cheese
- Leftover Stuffing
- Cranberry Sauce

Instructions:

- Slice French bread loaf in half and toast on the grill if desired. Spread mayonnaise and Dijon mustard on both halves of the bread.
- Mix to combine leftover smoked turkey and gravy. Layer on top of one bread half.
- Layer remaining **Ingredients** in this order: shredded white cheddar cheese, stuffing and cranberry sauce.
- Top sandwich with other bread half. Slice in half to serve. Enjoy!

5.29 Baked Thanksgiving Shepherd's Pie
Ingredients:

- 1lb Ground Beef
- 2 Cups Leftover Mashed Potatoes
- 1 Cup Leftover Green Beans
- 1 Cup Leftover Stuffing
- 1 Cup Leftover Gravy
- 1 1/2 Lb. Leftover Turkey
- 2 Tbsp Canola Oil
- 1 Cup Chopped Onions
- 2 Cloves Garlic, Minced
- 1 Tsp Kosher Salt
- 1/2 Tsp Freshly Ground Black Pepper
- 2 Tbsp All-Purpose Flour
- 2 Tsp Tomato Paste
- 1 Cup Chicken Broth
- 1 Tsp Worcestershire Sauce
- 2 Tsp Freshly Chopped Rosemary Leaves
- 1 Tsp Freshly Chopped Thyme

Instructions:

- When ready to cook, set temperature to High and preheat, lid closed for 15 minutes.
- Place canola oil in a medium sauté pan over medium-high heat. Once the oil shimmers, add the onion and sauté just until softened and lightly brown, about 3-4 minutes. Add the garlic and stir to combine.
- Add the beef, salt and pepper and cook until browned and cooked through, approximately 3 minutes.
- Sprinkle the onions with the flour and toss to coat, continuing to cook for another minute. Add the tomato paste, leftover gravy, chicken broth, Worcestershire, rosemary and thyme. Stir to combine.
- Bring to a boil, then reduce the heat to low. Cover and simmer 10-12 minutes or until the sauce is thickened slightly.
- Add the leftover turkey, green beans and stuffing to the mixture and spread evenly into an 11 x 7-inch glass baking dish.
- Top with the mashed potatoes, starting around the edges to create a seal to prevent the mixture from bubbling up and smooth with a rubber spatula.
- Place directly on the grill grate and bake for 25 minutes or just until the potatoes begin to brown. Remove to a cooling rack for at least 15 minutes before serving. Enjoy!

5.30 Roasted Cornish Game Stuffed Hens
Ingredients:

- 2 Tbsp Butter
- 1 Pint Wild Mushrooms, Cleaned
- 1/2 Yellow Onion, Diced
- 1 Stalk Celery, Diced
- 1 Clove Garlic, Minced
- 1 Cup Wild Rice
- 1 1/2 Cups Chicken Stock
- 2 Sprigs Thyme, Leaves Removed
- Salt & Pepper as Needed
- 1/2 Tbsp Fresh Sage, Minced
- 4 Cornish Game Hens
- 1/4 Cup Traeger Fin & Feather Rub

Instructions:

- Melt butter in a medium sauce pan and add wild mushrooms. Cook for 10 minutes until softened and lightly browned.
- Add onion and celery and cook 5 minutes until translucent. Add garlic and cook 30 seconds more until fragrant.
- Add rice and stock and bring to a simmer. Cook for about 20 minutes or until rice is tender. Add herbs and season with salt and pepper.
- Stuff 1/4 to 1/2 cup of rice mixture into each bird truss the legs together. Season the exterior of the Cornish game hens liberally with rub.
- When ready to cook, set temperature to 375°F and preheat, lid closed for 15 minutes.
- Place the birds directly on the grill grate and cook for 30 minutes or until the internal temperature registers 165°F with an instant read thermometer.
- Remove from grill and let rest for a few minutes before serving. Enjoy!

5.31 Baked Chicken Pot Pie
Ingredients:

- 2 Tbsp Butter
- 1 Small Yellow Onion, Diced
- 1 Stalk Celery, Diced
- 2 Tbsp Flour
- 2 Cups Homemade Chicken or Turkey Gravy
- 1/2 Cup Cream or Milk
- 1-1/2 Cups Frozen Peas and Carrots, Thawed
- 2 Tsp Dry Sherry (Optional)
- 1/2 Tsp Traeger Pork & Poultry Rub
- 1/4 Tsp Dried Thyme Leaves
- 3-4 Cups Cooked Skinless Chicken or Turkey Meat, Diced
- Salt and Pepper, To Taste
- Flour, For Dusting as Needed
- 1 Sheet Frozen Puff Pastry
- 1 Egg, Beaten With 1 Tbsp Water

Instructions:

- Melt the butter in a large saucepan over medium heat. Add the onion and celery and cook 3 to 5 minutes, or until the onion is translucent. Sprinkle with flour and stir to coat.
- Slowly stream in the chicken stock whisking out any lumps. Add milk or cream and bring to a simmer. Let simmer for a few minutes until slightly thickened, the mixture should coat the back of the spoon. Add the peas and carrots, sherry, Pork and Poultry Rub, thyme leaves, and chicken and simmer for 5 to 10 minutes.
- Coat cast iron skillet with cooking spray and fill with the pot pie filling.
- Unroll the puff pastry sheet on a lightly floured countertop. Let thaw slightly.
- Cover the top of the cast iron with the puff pastry crimping any overhang. Make several small slits in the center to let the steam escape. Brush lightly with the egg wash.
- Transfer the pot pie to the grill.
- Set the temperature to 400°F and preheat, lid closed for 15 minutes.
- Bake the pot pie for 30 minutes, or until the puff pastry is nicely browned and the filling is bubbling. Serve immediately. Enjoy!

5.32 Grilled Chicken Fajitas
Ingredients:

- Cast Iron Fajita Plate
- 2 Ea. Boneless Skinless Chicken Breasts
- 1/2 Tbsp Cumin
- 1/2 Tbsp Chili Powder
- Juice Of 1 Lime
- Salt and Pepper, To Taste
- 1 Small Yellow Onion, Sliced
- 1 Green Bell Pepper, Sliced
- 1 Red Bell Pepper, Sliced
- 1 Tbsp Olive Oil
- Tortillas, To Serve

Instructions:

- Place chicken breasts in a Ziploc bag and add cumin, chili powder, lime juice and salt and pepper. Transfer to the refrigerator and marinate for 1 hour.
- When ready to cook, set temperature to High and preheat, lid closed for 15 minutes.
- Place fajita skillet directly on the grill grate and preheat for 30 minutes. Place olive oil in the pan and add the onions and peppers, season with salt and pepper and close the lid.
- Cook 10 minutes or until lightly browned and cooked through.

- Lay the chicken breast directly on the grill grate next to the skillet and cook 10-15 minutes flipping halfway through until the internal temperature reaches 165°F.
- Remove chicken breast from grill and let rest before slicing.
- Serve sliced chicken with peppers and onions on the fajita plate with tortillas and choice of toppings. Enjoy!

5.33 Smoked Chicken with Chimichurri
Ingredients:

- Chicken Legs
- 6 Whole Bone-In Chicken Legs
- 2 Tbsp Olive Oil
- 1 Tbsp Paprika
- 1 Tbsp Coriander Seeds, Crushed in A Mortar and Pestle
- Zest Of 1 Lime
- 1 1/2 Tsp Sea Salt
- 1 Tsp Freshly Cracked Black Pepper
- 1-2 Limes, Halved, For Serving
- Chimichurri
- 1 Cup Fresh Flat-Leaf Parsley Leaves
- 1 Cup Fresh Cilantro Leaves
- 1 Jalapeño, Halved and Seeds Removed
- 1/2 Medium Spanish Onion, Finely Diced
- 3 Cloves Garlic, Peeled
- 3 Tbsp Fresh Squeezed Lime Juice
- 2 Tbsp Red Wine Vinegar
- 1/3 Cup Extra Virgin Olive Oil
- 1/2 Tsp Sea Salt
- 1/2 Tsp Freshly Cracked Black Pepper

Instructions:

- In a large bowl, massage the chicken legs with the olive oil, paprika, coriander, lime zest, salt, and pepper. For maximum delicious, cover and marinade in the fridge overnight.
- When ready to cook, set the temperature to 425°F and preheat lid closed, for 15 minutes.
- Put the chicken directly on the grill grate, skin side up. Cook for 40-45 minutes or until chicken reads 165°F on an instant-read thermometer.
- *Note: This chimichurri recipe makes extra leftover goodness. Perfect for grilled steak, fish, sandwiches, you name it.
- To make the Chimichurri: Combine all **Ingredients** in the base of a food processor and pulse until smooth & creamy.
- Serve grilled chicken legs with the chimichurri, an extra squeeze of fresh lime juice and your favorite side dish. Enjoy!

5.34 Grilled Sriracha Wings
Ingredients:

- Sweet & Spicy Sriracha Wings
- 2 Tbsp Traeger Chicken Rub
- 2 Tsp Garlic Powder
- 1 Tbsp Sesame Oil
- 2 Lbs. Thawed of Fresh Chicken Wings
- Sauce
- 5 Tbsp Butter, Melted
- 1/3 Cup Dark Brown Sugar
- 1/4 Cup Sriracha
- 2 Tbsp Soy Sauce
- 2 Tbsp Lime Zest
- 1 Tbsp Garlic, Crushed
- 1 Tbsp Ginger, Crushed
- 1 Tbsp Cilantro, Chopped
- 1 Tbsp Toasted Sesame Seeds
- 1 Tbsp Juice from Limes

Instructions:

- When ready to cook, set the Traeger to 325°F and preheat, lid closed for 15 minutes.
- Combine Traeger Chicken rub, garlic powder, sesame oil, and wings. Toss to coat.
- Place the wings directly on the grill grate and cook for 25 to 30 minutes, or until the chicken reaches an internal temperature of 160°F.
- While wings are cooking, combine all the sauce **Ingredients** except for the cilantro and sesame seeds.
- Once wings reach an internal temperature of 160°F, remove from grill and increase the grill temperature to High.
- While grill heats, toss the cooked wings in half of the sauce mixture (just enough to coat them) and place back on the grill for 10 to 15 minutes, or until sauce sets.
- Top wings with chopped cilantro and sesame seeds and serve with the remaining sauce on the side. Enjoy!

5.35 Whole Smoked Chicken
Ingredients:

- Brine
- 1/2 Cup Kosher Salt
- 1 Cup Brown Sugar
- 1 Gallon Water
- Whole Chicken
- Traeger Big Game Rub
- 1 Tsp Garlic, Minced
- 1 (3 To 3 1/2 Lb.) Whole Chicken
- 1 Lemon, Halved
- 1 Medium Yellow Onion, Quartered
- 3 Whole Garlic Cloves
- 4-5 Sprigs Thyme

Instructions:

- For the Brine: Dissolve the kosher salt and brown sugar in 1 gallon of water. Once dissolved, place the chicken in the brine and refrigerate overnight. Make sure chicken is fully submerged weighing it down if necessary.
- When ready to cook, set the Traeger to 225°F and preheat, lid closed for 15 minutes.
- While the grill preheats, remove the chicken from the brine and pat dry. Rub with the minced garlic and Big Game rub.
- Next, stuff the cavity with the lemon, onion, garlic and thyme. Tie the legs together.
- Place chicken directly on the grill grate and smoke for 2-1/2 to 3 hours or until an instant read thermometer reads 160°F when inserted into the thickest part of the breast.
- The finished internal temperature will rise to 165°F in the breast as the chicken rests. Enjoy!

5.36 Grilled Honey Garlic Wings
Ingredients:

- 2-1/2 Lbs. Chicken Wings
- Traeger Pork & Poultry Rub, As Needed
- 4 Tbsp Butter
- 1/2 Cup Hot Sauce
- 1/4 Cup Honey
- 2-3 Cloves Minced Garlic
- 1 1/2 Cups Blue Cheese or Ranch Dressing

Instructions:

- Start by segmenting the wings into three pieces, cutting through the joints. Discard the wing tips or save them to make a stock.
- Lay out the remaining pieces on a rimmed baking sheet lined with nonstick foil or parchment paper. Season well with Traeger Pork and Poultry rub.
- When ready to cook, set temperature to 350°F and preheat, lid closed for 15 minutes.
- Place the baking sheet with wings directly on the grill grate and cook for 45-50 minutes or until they are no longer pink at the bone.
- To make the sauce: Melt butter in a small saucepan. Add the garlic and sauté for 2-3 minutes. Add in the honey and hot sauce and cook for a few minutes until completely combined.

- Keep sauce warm while the wings are cooking. When wings are done, pour the spicy honey-garlic sauce over the wings, turning with tongs to coat.
- Place wings back on the grill and cook for an additional 10-15 minutes to set the sauce5.37 Roasted Beer Can Chicken

5.37 Traeger Chicken Rub

Ingredients:

- 1 (3-5 Lb.) Whole Chicken
- Traeger Chicken Rub, As Needed
- 1 Can Beer

Instructions:

- Tuck the wing tips back and truss the chicken legs together.
- Season chicken generously with Traeger Chicken Rub, including the cavity.
- Open the can of beer and set the chicken on top of the beer. Make sure all but the bottom 1-1/2" of the beer can is in the cavity of the chicken.
- When ready to cook, set the Traeger to 350°F and preheat, lid closed for 15 minutes.
- Place chicken on a sheet tray and place directly on the grill grate. Cook for 60-75 minutes or until the internal temperature registers 165°F in the thickest part of the breast.
- Remove from the grill and let rest 5-10 minutes before carving. Enjoy!

5.38 Competition BBQ Chicken Thighs

Ingredients:

- 20 Bone in Chicken Thighs (Approximately 1/2 Lb. Each)
- 3 Sticks Melted Butter
- 6 Oz Traeger Big Game Rub
- 20 Oz Low Sodium Chicken Broth
- 24 Oz Traeger Apricot BBQ Sauce

Instructions:

- Peel skin off the thighs. With kitchen shears remove the fat on each side of the chicken thighs.
- Trim 1/4" off the bottom and top bone knuckle of the chicken thighs. Trim so that the thighs are uniform in size.
- Trim skin to fit now trimmed thighs. Place the skin back on the thighs.
- Once done with all thighs, inject 1/2 oz of low sodium chicken broth into each side of the thigh and let rest for 60 minutes.
- While resting, season the top of the chicken thighs with Traeger Big Game Rub. Place in a refrigerator or cold cooler until ready to cook.
- Place thighs in a large disposable pan and add the melted butter to the pan as a braising liquid.
- When ready to cook, set temperature to 250°F and preheat, lid closed for 15 minutes.
- Slide the whole disposable pan of chicken on the grate and cook for one hour. After one hour, wrap the top of the disposable pan in aluminum foil and cook for another hour or until the internal temperature reaches 165°F.
- Once thighs reach internal temperature of 165°F, use tongs to remove each chicken thigh and dunk it into heated Traeger Apricot BBQ sauce.
- Place back in a clean disposable pan and cook for an additional 20 minutes. Remove from grill and let rest for 10 minutes before serving. Enjoy!

5.39 Roasted Sweet Thai Chili Wings

Ingredients:

- Wings
- 3 To 4 Lbs. Chicken Wings, Drumettes And Flappers Preferred, Separated Over the Entire Wing
- Meat Church Holy Gospel Seasoning, As Needed
- Toasted Sesame Seeds, To Garnish
- Sliced Green Onions, To Garnish
- Sweet Thai Chili Sauce
- 1/2 Cup Sugar
- 1/2 Cup Rice Vinegar

- 1/4 Cup Water
- 3 Tbsp Fish Sauce
- 2 Tbsp Cooking Sherry
- 4 Cloves Garlic, Minced Fine
- 1/2 Tbsp To 1 Tbsp Dried Crushed Chili Pepper, Depending on Desired Heat Level
- 1 1/2 Tbsp Cornstarch, Dissolved In 4 Tbsp Water

Instructions:

- For the Thai Chili Sauce: Place all **Ingredients** except the cornstarch in a sauce pan and whisk to combine. Bring the mixture to a slight boil and simmer for 10 minutes. Reduce heat and add the cornstarch and water mixture. Stir until thickened, about 2-3 minutes. Remove sauce from heat while wings cook.
- When ready to cook, set temperature to High and preheat, lid closed for 15 minutes.
- This temperature will help get the wings crisper than a lower temperature cooks which can lead to rubbery skin.
- If you bought the whole wing, remove the tip and separate the drumette and wing from each other. Pat them dry. Season the wings moderately on all sides with Meat Church Holy Gospel Rub. This is a blend of our Holy Cow and our Gospel All-Purpose rubs. It is amazing as the base for chicken.
- Place wings directly on the grill grate and cook for a total time of 20 minutes. Flip the wings halfway through the cook. I like to get as many tasty bites of char on my wings and flipping them will help achieve this on an additional side.
- Using an instant thermometer to test the internal temperature of chicken wings. The finished temperature should be between 165 -180°F after about 20 minutes. While chicken is safe to eat at 165°F, it is ok to take wings even further as it is difficult to dry them out.
- To finish the wings, toss wings in the sweet Thai chili sauce. Place them back on Traeger for 5 minutes to allow sauce to set. This will prevent the sauce from running all over you when trying to eat.
- Remove and allow to cool slightly. Enjoy!

5.40 BBQ Chicken Thighs
Ingredients:

- 6 Bone-In Chicken Thighs, Skin On
- Traeger Big Game Rub
- Salt and Ground Black Pepper, To Taste

Instructions:

- When ready to cook, set the Traeger to 350°F and preheat, lid closed for 15 minutes.
- While grill is heating, trim excess fat and skin from chicken thighs. Season with a light layer of salt and pepper and a layer of Traeger Big Game rub.
- Place chicken thighs on the grill grate and cook for 35 minutes. Check internal temperature, chicken is done at 165°F, but there is enough fat that they will stay moist at an internal temperature of 180°F and the texture is better.
- Remove from the grill and let rest for 5 minutes before serving. Enjoy!

5.41 Smoked Chicken Leg & Thigh Quarters
Ingredients:

- 8 Connected Chicken Leg and Thigh Pieces
- 3 Tbsp Olive Oil
- Traeger Pork & Poultry Rub, To Taste

Instructions:

- Rinse the chicken pieces under cold running water and pat dry with paper towels.
- Place the chicken pieces in a large mixing bowl. Pour oil over the chicken to coat each piece, then season to taste with the rub. Massage the chicken pieces to encourage the oil and seasonings get under the skin.
- Cover and refrigerate for at least 1 to 2 hours.
- When ready to cook, set temperature to 180°F and preheat, lid closed for 15 minutes.
- Remove the chicken from the refrigerator, letting any excess oil drip back into the bowl. Arrange the chicken on the grill grate and smoke for 1 hour.
- Increase grill temperature to 350°F and continue to roast the chicken until the internal temperature in the thickest part of a thigh is 165°F, or the chicken is golden brown and the juices run clear, about 50 to 60 minutes.

- Allow the chicken to rest for 8-10 minutes and serve. Enjoy!

5.42 Smoked Wings
Ingredients:

- 24 Wings (Sectioned)
- 12 Oz Italian Dressing
- 3 Oz Traeger Chicken Rub
- 8 Oz Traeger Chili Barbecue Sauce

Instructions:

- Wash all wings and place into resealable bag.
- Add Italian Dressing to the resealable bag containing the wings. Place in refrigerator and allow to marinate for 6-12 hours.
- When ready to cook, set the Traeger to 225°F and preheat, lid closed for 15 minutes.
- Remove wings from marinade and shake off excess marinade. Season all sides of the wings with Traeger Chicken Rub and let sit for 15 minutes before putting wings on the Traeger.
- Cook wings to an internal temperature of 160°F.
- Remove the wings and toss in Chili Barbecue Sauce.
- Increase the temperature to 375°F and preheat. Once at temperature, place the wings on the Traeger and sear both sides getting the internal temperature of the chicken wings to at least 165°F.
- Remove the wings from the smoker and let rest for 5 minutes.
- Serve with your favorite side wing dressing or sauce. Enjoy!

5.43 Chicken Parmesan Sliders with Pesto Mayonnaise
Ingredients:

- 2 Lbs. Ground Chicken
- 1 Cup Parmesan Cheese, Shredded
- 1 Tbsp. Worcestershire Sauce
- A Few Grinds Black Pepper, Freshly Ground
- 1 Cup Mayonnaise
- 2 Tbsp. Prepared Pesto Sauce
- 12 Slider Buns, Split
- 3 Roma Tomatoes, Thinly Sliced
- 1 Small Red Onion, Thinly Sliced
- For Serving Fresh Spinach or Arugula Leaves, Washed, And Dried

Instructions:

- Line a baking sheet with plastic wrap. In a large mixing bowl, combine the ground chicken, the Parmesan, the Worcestershire, and a few grinds of black pepper. Wet your hands with cold water, and use them to mix the **Ingredients.**
- Divide the meat mixture in half, then form six 2-inch patties out of each half. Place the patties on the baking sheet, cover with another sheet of plastic wrap, and refrigerate for at least 1 hour.
- Combine the mayonnaise and pesto in a small bowl and whisk together. Cover and refrigerate until serving time.
- When ready to cook, start the Traeger grill on Smoke with the lid open until the fire is established (4 to 5 minutes). Set the temperature to 300F and preheat, lid closed, for 10 to 15 minutes.
- Arrange the chicken patties on the grill grate and grill, turning once, until the patties are cooked through (165F), about 30 minutes.
- To serve, put a chicken patty on the bottom of a slider bun and top with a dollop of the pesto mayonnaise. Add tomato, onion, and spinach as desired. Replace the top of the bun and skewer with a frilled toothpick, if desired.

5.44 Chicken Picadillo Empanadas

Ingredients:

- 1 Lb. Chicken, Shredded
- 2 Carrots
- 2 Stalks Celery
- 1 Tbsp Vegetable Oil
- Salt and Pepper
- 1/4 Cup Water
- 1 Tsp Chicken Bouillon
- 1 Small Can Tomato Juice
- 1 Egg, Scrambled
- 2 Rolls Pie Crust
- 1 Large Oven Safe Pan

Instructions:

- Start the Traeger on Smoke with the lid open until a fire is established (4-5 minutes). Then turn temperature to 450 degrees F and preheat, lid closed, for 10 to 15 minutes.
- Chop carrots and celery. Set a large oven safe skillet into your Traeger, heat oil in skillet and cook carrots and celery. Add salt and pepper. Cook until carrots and celery soften, about 5 to 10 minutes, stirring occasionally.
- Once vegetables soften, add chicken, tomato juice, water and chicken bouillon. Cook an additional 5-10 minutes or until sauce starts to thicken.
- Turn the heat down to 350 degrees F.
- Roll out pie crusts and cut circles about 4" in diameter.
- Place some filling in the middle of the dough and rub a little egg wash on one half of the circle's edge. This will ensure a good seal when you fold it over and press.
- Fold dough over and press to make half-moon pastries.
- Brush the top of the pastries with a little egg wash and a dash of salt. Transfer them to the grill.
- Grill for 10-15 minutes at 350 degrees F. When golden brown, serve with cilantro lime sour cream! Enjoy!

5.45 Chicken Salad

Ingredients:

- 1 Qt. Cold Water
- 1/4 Cup Kosher Salt
- 4 Large Chicken Breasts, Boneless
- 4 Chicken Thighs, Bone-In
- 1/2 Red Bell Pepper, Finely Diced
- 1/2 Green Bell, Finely Diced
- 2 Scallions, Thinly Sliced
- 1 To 2 Tbsp. Pickled Jalapeno Peppers, Minced
- 1 Cup Mayonnaise
- 1 Tbsp. Fresh Lime Juice
- 1 Tsp. Ground Cumin
- 1 Tsp. Black Pepper, Freshly Ground
- 1/2 Tsp. Garlic Salt
- 2 Tbsp. Fresh Cilantro Leaves, Minced

Instructions:

- For the brine, in a large saucepan or mixing bowl, combine the water and salt and stir until the salt crystals dissolve. Add the chicken breasts and thighs. Cover and refrigerate for 2 to 4 hours.
- Drain, but do not dry the chicken: Smoke clings better to wet surfaces.
- When ready to cook, start the Traeger grill on Smoke with the lid open until the fire is established (4 to 5 minutes).
- Arrange the chicken on the grill grate and smoke for 30 minutes. Increase the temperature to 350F and continue to cook the chicken until the juices run clear and the internal temperature when read on an instant-read meat thermometer is 165F, 25 to 30 minutes.
- Transfer to a cutting board and let cool. Dice the chicken, discarding any skin, bones, or gobbets of fat.

- Transfer to a mixing bowl. Add the red and green bell peppers, the scallions, and pickled jalapenos. Stir gently to distribute the **Ingredients** set aside.
- In a mixing bowl, whisk together the mayonnaise, lime juice, cumin, black pepper, and garlic salt. Stir in the cilantro.
- Add the dressing to the chicken mixture and stir gently until well-combined.
- Transfer to a serving bowl. Dust with paprika. Serve immediately, or cover and chill for up to 3 days. Enjoy!

CHAPTER 6: TURKEY RECIPES

6.1 Herb Roasted Turkey
Ingredients:

- 8 Tbsp. Butter, Room Temperature
- 2 Tbsp. Mixed Herbs Such as Parsley, Sage, Rosemary, And Marjoram, Chopped
- 1/4 Tsp. Black Pepper, Freshly Ground
- 1 (12-14 Lbs.) Turkey, Thawed If Previously Frozen
- 3 Tbsp. Butter
- As Needed Traeger Pork and Poultry Rub
- 2 Cups Chicken or Turkey Broth

Instructions:

- In a small mixing bowl, combine the 8 tablespoons of softened butter, mixed herbs, and black pepper and beat until fluffy with a wooden spoon. (You can make the herbed butter several days ahead: Cover and refrigerate, but bring to room temperature before using).
- Remove any giblets from the turkey cavity and save them for gravy making, if desired. Wash the turkey, inside and out, under cold running water. Dry with paper towels. Place the turkey on a roasting rack in a roasting pan. Tuck the wings behind the back, and tie the legs together with butcher's string.
- Using your fingers or the handle of a wooden spoon, gently push some of the herbed butter underneath the turkey skin onto the breast halves, being careful not to tear the skin. Massage the skin to evenly distribute the herbed butter.
- Rub the outside of the turkey with the melted butter and sprinkle with the Traeger Pork and Poultry Rub. Pour the chicken broth in the bottom of the roasting pan.
- When ready to cook, set temperature to 325°F and preheat, lid closed for 15 minutes.
- Put the roasting pan with the turkey directly on the grill grate. Roast the turkey for 3 hours. Insert the probe from the meat thermometer in the thickest part of the thigh, but not touching bone. Cook until internal temperature reaches 165°F. The turkey should also be beautifully browned with crisp skin. If the temperature is less than that, or if your turkey is not browned to your liking, let it roast for another 30 minutes, then check the temperature again. Repeat until the turkey is fully cooked.
- When the turkey is done, carefully transfer it to a cutting board and let it rest for 20 to 30 minutes. Do not tent it with aluminum foil or the skin will lose its crispness. Use the drippings that have accumulated in the bottom of the roasting pan to make gravy, if desired. Carve the turkey and serve.

6.2 Smoked Bourbon & Orange Brined Turkey
Ingredients:

- Traeger Orange Brine (From Kit)
- Traeger Turkey Rub (From Kit)
- 1.25-2.5 Gallons Cold Water
- 1 Cup Bourbon
- 1 Tbsp. Butter, Melted
- 1 Tbsp. Grand Marnier Or Other Orange-Flavored Liquor

Instructions:

- Mix Traeger Orange Brine seasoning (from Orange Brine & Turkey Rub Kit) with one quart of water. Boil for 5 minutes. Remove from heat, add 1 gallon of cold water and bourbon. Refrigerate until completely cooled.
- Place turkey breast side down in a large container. Pour cooled brine mix over bird. Add cold water until bird is submerged. Refrigerate for 24 hours.
- Remove turkey and disregard brine. Blot turkey dry with paper towels. Combine butter and Grand Marnier and coat outside of turkey.
- Season outside of turkey with Traeger Turkey Rub (from Orange Brine & Turkey Rub Kit).
- When ready to cook, set temperature to 225°F and preheat, lid closed for 15 minutes.
- Smoke turkey, breast up, for 2 hours. Increase temperature to 350°F and roast turkey until the internal temperature of the thickest part of the high reaches 165F, 2 to 3 hours, depending on size of turkey.
- Let rest 20 to 30 minutes before serving. Enjoy!

6.3 Traeger Leftover Turkey Soup
Ingredients:

- 1 Turkey Carcass
- 16 Cups Cold Water
- 2 Large Celery Ribs, Sliced
- 2 Large Carrots, Scraped and Sliced
- 2 Red Onions, Quartered
- 10 Sprigs Fresh Flat Parsley Leaf
- 1 Tbsp. Peppercorn
- 2 Tsp. Fresh Thyme

Instructions:

- Strip a turkey carcass of all meat; set aside in a container.
- Break up the bones of the turkey carcass and place them in a large pot. Add any turkey skin or other assorted "bits" that are not edible meat. For the best taste, make the stock the day after the turkey has been cooked. Pour in the cold water and turn heat to high; bring to a boil.
- Once the stock has come to a boil, add all remaining **Ingredients** and turn heat down until the bubbles barely break the surface. Let simmer for 3 to 4 hours, stirring occasionally. The broth tastes best when reduced to 7 or 8 cups of stock.
- When the stock is ready, strain it through a fine-meshed sieve into a large bowl; if your sieve is not fine, line it first with cheesecloth. Discard the bones and veggies you used to make the stock (all their flavor is now in the stock).
- Refrigerate stock, covered, for several hours or preferably overnight. You can either make soup the next day, or freeze the stock; make sure you skim off the solidified fat before you either make soup or freeze the stock.
- When ready to make the actual soup, heat up the homemade stock on the stovetop. Dish stock into individual bowls. Add shredded turkey, desired vegetables (such as chopped celery and red onions), fresh herbs (such as rosemary and thyme) and freshly ground pepper.

6.4 Smoked Turkey
Ingredients:

- Smoked Turkey by Rob cooks
- 1 (12-14 Lb.) Turkey, Fresh or Thawed
- 3/4 Lb. (3 Sticks) Unsalted Butter
- 1 (5 Gal) Bucket or Stock Pot
- Foil Pan, Large Enough for Turkey
- Heavy Duty Foil
- Brine
- 2 Cups Kosher Salt
- 2 Cups Sugar
- 2-Gals (1/2 Gal Is Ice) Water
- Rub
- 1/2 Cup Kosher Salt
- 1/2 Cup Coarse Ground Black Pepper

Instructions:

- This method requires an overnight brining so collect everything the day before your meal.
- The afternoon before, prepare your brine by adding the kosher salt and sugar to a medium saucepan. Cover with water and bring to a boil. Stir to dissolve the salt and sugar. Pour salt and sugar concentrate into a bucket, add ice and water up to 2 gallons.
- Prepare your turkey by removing the neck, gizzards and truss, if pre-trussed. Trim off excess skin and fat near the cavity and neck. Place the turkey in bucket with the brine. If it floats, place a plate or two on top to keep the turkey submerged. Cover bucket and place in fridge until ready to cook the next afternoon.
- When ready to cook, set temperature to 180°F and preheat, lid closed for 15 minutes.
- Remove your turkey from the brine. Remember there's a cavity full of water so make sure to do this over the sink, otherwise you'll have brine all over the place. Set your turkey down on a cookie sheet to prepare it for the smoker.
- Mix up the kosher salt and pepper in a shaker, sprinkle the rub on all parts of the turkey, don't sprinkle inside the cavity! There is no need to tie up the legs and wings with this method. The fan in the Traeger pushes air all around the turkey during the cook.

- Put the turkey on the grill at 180°F for 2 hours, 225°F for the next hour, and finally 325°F to finish it off. Place it so the legs and thighs are towards the hotter area of your smoker and the breast to the cooler side. Check the turkey after a couple hours for color. When it reaches your desired color place it in the foil pan.
- Cut the butter up into squares and pile them on the turkey.
- Wrap in heavy-duty foil and put it back on the smoker. Cook until temperature in the breast reaches 165°F and the thigh reaches 180°F.
- Remove from smoker and allow it to rest for 30 minutes before carving.

6.5 Smoked Turkey Legs
Ingredients:

- 1 Gal Warm Water
- 1/2-Gal Cold Water
- 4 Cups Ice
- 1 Cup Traeger BBQ Rub
- 1/2 Cup Curing Salt
- 1/2 Cup Brown Sugar
- 1 Tbsp Allspice Berries, Crushed (Optional)
- 1 Tbsp Whole Black Peppercorns
- 2 Bay Leaves
- 2 Tsp Liquid Smoke
- 4 Turkey Legs

Instructions:

- In a large stockpot, combine one gallon of warm water, the rub, curing salt, brown sugar, allspice (if using), peppercorns, bay leaves and liquid smoke.
- Bring to a boil over high heat to dissolve the salt granules. Cool to room temperature.
- Add cold water and ice; chill in the refrigerator. Add the turkey legs, making sure they're completely submerged in the brine.
- After 24 hours, drain the turkey legs and discard the brine. Rinse the brine off the legs with cold water, then dry thoroughly with paper towels. Brush off any clinging solid spices.
- When ready to cook, set temperature to 250°F and preheat, lid closed for 15 minutes.
- Lay the turkey legs directly on the grill grate. Smoke for 4-5 hours, or until the internal temperature reaches 165°F on an instant-read meat thermometer. Make sure the probe doesn't touch bone or you'll get a false reading.
- The turkey legs should be deeply browned. Don't be alarmed if the meat under the skin is pinkish: That's a chemical reaction to the cure and the smoke.
- Serve immediately. Enjoy!

6.6 Traditional Thanksgiving Turkey
Ingredients:

- 1 (18-20lb) Turkey
- 1/2 Lb. Butter, Softened
- 8 Sprigs Thyme
- 6 Cloves Garlic, Minced
- 1 Sprig Rosemary, Rough Chop
- 1 Tbsp Cracked Black Pepper
- 1/2 Tbsp Kosher Salt

Instructions:

- In a small bowl, combine butter with the minced garlic, thyme leaves, chopped rosemary, black pepper and kosher salt.
- Prepare the turkey by separating the skin from the breast creating a pocket to stuff the butter-herb mixture in.
- Cover the entire breast with 1/4" thickness of butter mixture.
- Season the whole turkey with kosher salt and black pepper. As an option, you can also stuff the turkey cavity with Traditional Stuffing.
- When ready to cook, set the temperature to 300°F and preheat, lid closed for 15 minutes.
- Place turkey on the grill and roast for 3-4 hours. Check the internal temperature, the desired temperature is 175°F in the thigh next to the bone, and 160°F in the breast.

- Turkey will continue to cook once taken off grill to reach a final temperature of 165°F in the breast.
- Let rest for 10-15 minutes before carving. Enjoy!

6.7 Turkey Jalapeno Meatballs
Ingredients:

- Turkey Jalapeño Meatballs
- 1 1/4 Lbs. Ground Turkey
- 1 Jalapeño Pepper, Deseeded and Finely Diced
- 1/2 Tsp Garlic Salt
- 1 Tsp Onion Powder
- 1 Tsp Salt
- 1/2 Tsp Ground Black Pepper
- 1/4 Tsp Worcestershire Sauce
- Cayenne Pepper, Pinch
- 1 Large Egg, Beaten
- 1/4 Cup Milk
- 1/2 Cup Plain Bread Crumbs Or Panko
- Glaze
- 1 Cup Canned Jellied Cranberry Sauce
- 1/2 Cup Orange Marmalade
- 1/2 Cup Chicken Broth
- 1 Tbsp Jalapeño Pepper, Minced
- Salt, To Taste
- Ground Black Pepper, To Taste

Instructions:

- In a separate small bowl, combine the milk and bread crumbs.
- In a large bowl, mix together turkey, garlic salt, onion powder, salt, pepper, Worcestershire sauce, cayenne pepper, egg and jalapeños.
- Add the bread crumb milk mixture to the bowl and combine. Cover with plastic and refrigerate for up to 1 hour.
- When ready to cook, set the temperature to 350°F and preheat, lid closed for 15 minutes
- Roll the turkey mixture into balls, about one tablespoon each and place the meatballs in a single layer on a parchment lined baking sheet.
- Cook meatballs until they start to brown, flipping occasionally until they reach an internal temperature of 175 degrees F and all sides are browned (about 20 minutes).
- Glaze: Combine cranberry sauce, marmalade, chicken broth, and jalapeños and cook over medium heat in a small saucepan on the stovetop. Cook until **Ingredients:** are incorporated.
- Half way through meatball cook time, brush the meatballs with the cranberry glaze.
- Transfer meatballs to a serving dish with cranberry glaze on the side. Serve immediately. Enjoy!

6.8 Wild Turkey Southwest Egg Rolls
Ingredients:

- 2 Cups Leftover Wild Turkey Meat
- 1/2 Cup Corn
- 1/2 Cup Black Beans
- 3 Tbsp Taco Seasoning
- 1/2 Cup White Onion, Chopped
- 4 Cloves Garlic, Minced
- 1 Poblano Pepper (Or 2 Jalapeño Peppers), Chopped
- 1 Can Rote Tomatoes & Chiles
- 1/2 Cup Water
- 12 Egg Roll Wrappers

Instructions:

- Add olive oil to a large skillet and heat on the stove over medium heat. Add onions and peppers and sauté 2-3 minutes until soft. Add garlic, cook 30 seconds, then Rote and black beans. Reduce heat and simmer.
- Pour taco seasoning over meat and add 1/3 cup of water and mix to coat well. Add to veggie mixture and stir to mix well. If it seems dry, add 2 tbsp water. Cook until heated all the way through.
- Remove from the heat and transfer the mixture to the fridge. The mixture should be completely cooled prior to stuffing the egg rolls or the wrappers will break.
- Place spoonful of the mixture in each wrapper and wrap tightly. Repeat with remaining wrappers. When ready to cook, set temperature to High and preheat, lid closed for 15 minutes.
- Brush each egg roll with oil or butter and place directly on the Traeger grill grate. Cook until the exterior is crispy, about 20 min per side.
- Remove from Traeger and cool. Serve. Enjoy!

6.9 Smoked Wild Turkey Breast
Ingredients:

- Brine
- 2 Lbs. Turkey Breast and Deboned Thigh, Tied with Skin On
- 1 Cup Brown Sugar
- 1/4 Cup Salt
- 2 Tbsp Cracked Pepper
- 4 Cups Cold Water
- BBQ Rub
- 2 Tbsp Garlic Powder
- 2 Tbsp Onions, Dried
- 2 Tbsp Black Pepper
- 2 Tbsp Brown Sugar
- 1 Tbsp Cayenne Pepper
- 2 Tbsp Chili Powder
- 1/4 Cup Paprika
- 1 Tbsp Salt
- 2 Tbsp Sugar
- 2 Tbsp Cumin, Ground

Instructions:

- For the Brine: In a large glass bowl combine brown sugar, salt, pepper and water. Add turkey and weigh down to completely submerge if necessary. Transfer to the refrigerator and brine for 12-24 hours.
- Remove turkey from the brine and discard the brine.
- When ready to cook, set the temperature 180°F and preheat lid closed for 15 minutes.
- Combine **Ingredients** for the BBQ Rub. Season turkey with rub and place directly on the grill grate skin side up.
- Smoke for 5-8 hours or until the internal temperature reaches 160°F degrees when an instant read thermometer is inserted into the center.
- Remove from the smoker and let rest for 10 minutes. Turkey will continue to cook once taken off grill to reach a final temperature of 165°F in the breast.
- Slice and serve with your favorite sides. Enjoy!

6.10 Grilled Wild Turkey Orange Cashew Salad
Ingredients:

- Turkey Breast
- 2 Wild Turkey Breast Halves, Without Skin
- 1/4 Cup Teriyaki Sauce
- 1 Tsp Fresh Ginger
- 1 (12 Oz) Can Blood Orange Kill Cliff or Similar Citrus Soda
- 2 Tbsp Traeger Chicken Rub
- Cashew Salad
- 4 Cups Romaine Lettuce, Chopped
- 1/2 Head Red or White Cabbage, Chopped
- 1/2 Cup Shredded Carrots

- 1/2 Cup Edamame, Shelled
- 1 Smoked Yellow Bell Pepper, Sliced into Circles
- 1 Smoked Red Bell Pepper, Sliced into Circles
- 3 Chive Tips, Chopped
- 1/2 Cup Smoked Cashews
- Blood Orange Vinaigrette
- 1 Tsp Orange Zest
- Juice From 1/2 Large Orange
- 1 Tsp Finely Grated Fresh Ginger
- 2 Tbsp Seasoned Rice Vinegar
- 1 Tsp Honey
- 1/4 Cup Light Vegetable Oil

Instructions:

- For the Marinade: Combine teriyaki sauce, Kill Cliff soda and fresh ginger. Pour marinade over turkey breasts in a Ziplock bag or dish and seal. Marinate in the refrigerator for 6 to 24 hours, turning occasionally.
- When ready to cook, set temperature to 375°F and preheat, lid closed for 15 minutes.
- Remove turkey from the refrigerator, drain the marinade and pat turkey dry with paper towels.
- Place turkey into a shallow oven proof dish and season with Traeger Chicken Rub.
- Place dish in the Traeger and cook for 30-45 minutes or until the breast reaches an internal temperature of 160°F.
- Remove the breast from the grill and wrap in Traeger Butcher Paper. Let turkey rest for 10 minutes. While turkey is resting, prepare salad.
- Assemble salad **Ingredients** in a bowl and toss to mix. Combine all **Ingredients** in list for vinaigrette.
- After resting for 10 minutes, slice turkey and serve with cashew salad and blood orange vinaigrette. Enjoy!

6.11 Baked Cornbread Turkey Tamale Pie
Ingredients:

- Filling
- 2 Cups Shredded Turkey
- 2 Cobs of Corn
- 1 (15 Oz) Can Black Beans, Rinsed and Drained
- 1 Yellow Bell Pepper
- 1 Orange Bell Pepper
- 2 Jalapeños
- 2 Tbsp Cilantro
- 1 Bunch Green Onions
- 1/2 Tsp Cumin
- 1/2 Tsp Paprika
- 1 (7 Oz) Can Chipotle Sauce
- 1 (15 Oz) Can Enchilada Sauce
- 1/2 Cup Shredded Cheddar Cheese
- Cornbread Topping
- 1 Cup All-Purpose Flour
- 1 Cup Yellow or White Cornmeal
- 1 Tbsp Sugar
- 2 Tsp Baking Powder
- 1/2 Tsp Salt
- 3 Tbsp Butter
- 1 Cup Buttermilk
- 1 Large Egg, Lightly Beaten

Instructions:

- For the filling: Mix to combine filling **Ingredients** Place in the bottom of a butter greased 10-inch pan.

- For the cornbread topping: In a mixing bowl, combine the flour, cornmeal, sugar, baking powder, and salt. Melt the butter in a small saucepan. Remove butter from the heat and stir in the milk and egg. Make sure the mixture isn't too hot or the egg will curdle.
- Add the milk-egg mixture to the dry **Ingredients** and stir to combine. Do not over mix.
- To assemble Tamale Pie: Fill the bottom of a butter greased 10-inch pan with the shredded turkey filling. Top with the cornbread topping and smooth to the edges of pan.
- When ready to cook, set the temperature to 375°F and preheat, lid closed for 15 minutes.
- Place directly on the grill grate and cook for 45-50 minutes or until the cornbread is lightly browned and cooked through. Enjoy!

6.12 BBQ Pulled Turkey Sandwiches
Ingredients:

- 6 Turkey Thighs, Skin-On
- 1 1/2 Cups Chicken or Turkey Broth
- Traeger Pork & Poultry Rub
- 1 Cup Traeger BBQ Sauce, Or More as Needed
- 6 Buns or Kaiser Rolls, Split and Buttered

Instructions:

- Season turkey thighs on both sides with the Traeger Pork & Poultry rub.
- When ready to cook, set temperature to 180°F and preheat, lid closed for 15 minutes.
- Arrange the turkey thighs directly on the grill grate and smoke for 30 minutes.
- Transfer the thighs to a sturdy disposable aluminum foil or roasting pan. Pour the broth around the thighs. Cover the pan with foil or a lid.
- Increase temperature to 325°F and preheat, lid closed. Roast the thighs until they reach an internal temperature of 180°F.
- Remove pan from the grill, but leave grill on. Let the turkey thighs cool slightly until they can be comfortably handled.
- Pour off the drippings and reserve. Remove the skin and discard.
- Pull the turkey meat into shreds with your fingers and return the meat to the roasting pan.
- Add 1 cup or more of your favorite Traeger BBQ Sauce along with some of the drippings.
- Recover the pan with foil and reheat the BBQ turkey on the Traeger for 20 to 30 minutes.
- Serve with toasted buns if desired. Enjoy!

6.13 Roasted Spatchcock Turkey
Ingredients:

- 1 (18-20 Lb.) Whole Turkey
- 4 Tbsp Traeger Turkey Rub
- 1 Tbsp Jacobsen Sea Salt
- 4 Cloves Garlic, Minced
- 3 Tbsp Parsley, Chopped
- 1 Tbsp Rosemary, Chopped
- 2 Tbsp Thyme Leaves, Chopped
- 2 Scallions, Chopped
- 3 Tbsp Olive Oil

Instructions:

- When ready to cook, set temperature to High and preheat, lid closed for 15 minutes.
- On a cutting board, combine garlic, parsley, thyme, rosemary, and scallions. Chop together until the mixture forms a paste. Set aside.
- To spatchcock the turkey: With a large knife or shears, cut the bird open along the backbone on both sides, through the ribs and remove the backbone.
- Once the bird is open, split the breastbone to spread the bird flat; this will allow it to roast evenly.
- With the bird breast side up, season the exterior with half the Traeger Turkey Rub then follow with 2/3 the herb mixture rubbing it into the bird. Drizzle with olive oil.
- Flip the bird and season generously with the remaining Traeger Turkey Rub.
- Place the turkey directly on the grill grate and cook for 30 minutes.

- Reduce the temperature on the grill to 300°F and continue to cook for 3-4 hours or until the internal temperature reaches 160°F in the breast.
- The finished internal temperature should reach 165°F, but the temperature will continue to rise after the bird is removed from the grill.
- Let the bird rest 20-25 minutes before carving. Enjoy!

6.14 Spatchcocked Maple Brined Turkey
Ingredients:

- 1 (12-14 Lbs.) Turkey, Thawed If Frozen
- 5 Qtrs. Hot Water
- 1 1/2 Cups Kosher Salt
- 3/4 Cup Bourbon
- 1 Cup Pure Maple Syrup
- 1/2 Cup Brown Sugar
- 1 Onion, Peeled and Quartered Through the Root End
- 3 To 4 Strips Orange Peel
- 3 Bay Leaves, Broken into Pieces
- 2 Tbsp Black Peppercorns
- 1 Tbsp Whole Cloves
- 3 Qtrs. Ice
- 1 Cup Butter, Melted
- Traeger Pork & Poultry Rub, As Needed
- Sprigs of Fresh Sage and Thyme, To Garnish
- Orange Wedges, Lady Apples, Or Kumquats, To Serve

Instructions:

- Note: Do not use a kosher turkey or a self-basting turkey for this recipe as they have already been enhanced with a salt-solution.
- For the Brine: In a large stockpot or container, combine the hot water, kosher salt, bourbon, 3/4 cup of the maple syrup, brown sugar, onion, bay leaves, orange peel, peppercorns, and cloves and stir until well mixed. Add the ice.
- Rinse the turkey, inside and out, under cold running water. Remove giblets and discard or save for another use. Some turkeys come with a gravy packet as well; remove it before roasting the bird.
- Add the turkey to the brine and refrigerate 8 to 12 hours, or overnight. Weight with a bag of ice to keep the bird submerged.
- Drain and pat dry with paper towels; discard the brine.
- To spatchcock the turkey: With a large knife or shears, cut the bird open along the backbone on both sides, through the ribs and remove the backbone.
- Once the bird is open, split the breastbone to spread the bird flat; this will allow it to roast evenly.
- Combine the melted butter and the remaining 1/4 cup of maple syrup and divide in half. Brush half of the mixture on the bird and sprinkle with Traeger Pork & Poultry Rub or salt and black pepper.
- Set aside the other half of the mixture until ready to use.
- When ready to cook, set the temperature to 350°F and preheat, lid closed for 15 minutes.
- Roast the turkey until the internal temperature in the thickest part of the breast reaches 165°F, about 2-3 hours.
- Brush with the remaining butter-maple syrup glaze the last 30 minutes of cooking.
- Let the turkey rest for 15 to 20 minutes before carving. Garnish, if desired, with fresh herbs and or kumquats. Enjoy!

6.15 Homemade Turkey Gravy

- **Ingredients:**
- 4 Cups Homemade Chicken Stock
- 2 Large Onions Cut Into 8th
- 4 Carrots, Rough Chop
- 4 Celery Stalks
- 8 Sprigs Thyme
- 8 Cloves Garlic, Peeled and Smashed
- 1 Turkey Neck
- 1 Cup Flour
- 1 Stick Butter, Cut into About 8 Pieces
- 1 Tsp Kosher Salt
- 1 Tsp Cracked Black Pepper

Instructions:

- When ready to cook, set the temperature to 350°F and preheat with the lid closed, for 15 minutes.
- In a large roasting pan, place turkey neck, onion, celery, carrot, garlic and thyme. Add 4 cups of chicken stock and sprinkle with salt and pepper.
- Place the prepped turkey on the rack into the roasting pan and place in the Traeger.
- Cook for 3-4 hours or until the breast reaches 160°F. Once taken off the grill, the turkey will continue to cook and will reach a finished internal temperature of 165°F.
- Strain the drippings into a saucepan and simmer on low.
- In a larger saucepan combine butter and flour with a whisk stirring until golden tan. This takes about 8 minutes, stirring constantly.
- Next whisk the drippings into the roux and cook until it comes to a boil. Season with salt and pepper and serve hot. Enjoy!

6.16 Roasted Honey Bourbon Glazed Turkey

Ingredients:

- Turkey
- 1 (16-18 Lbs.) Turkey
- 1/4 Cup Traeger Fin and Feather Rub
- Whiskey Glaze
- 1/2 Cup Bourbon
- 1/2 Cup Honey
- 1/4 Cup Brown Sugar
- 3 Tbsp Apple Cider Vinegar
- 1 Tbsp Dijon Mustard
- Salt and Pepper, To Taste

Instructions:

- When ready to cook, set the temperature to 375°F and preheat, lid closed for 15 minutes.
- Truss the turkey legs together. Season the exterior of the bird and the cavity with Traeger Fin and Feather Rub.
- Place the turkey directly on the grill grate and cook for 20-30 minutes at 375°F or until the skin begins to brown.
- After 30 minutes, reduce the temperature to 325°F and continue to cook until internal temperature registers 165°F when an instant read thermometer is inserted into the thickest part of the breast, about 3-4 hours.
- For the Whiskey Glaze: Combine all **Ingredients** in a small saucepan and bring to a boil. Reduce the temperature and let simmer 15-20 minutes or until thick enough to coat the back of a spoon. Remove from heat and set aside.
- During the last ten minutes of cooking, brush the glaze on the turkey while on the grill and cook until the glaze is set, about 10 minutes.
- Remove from grill and let rest 10-15 minutes before carving. Enjoy!

6.17 Roasted Autumn Brined Turkey Breast
Ingredients:

- 6 Cups Apple Cider
- 2 Cloves Garlic, Smashed
- 1/3 Cup Brown Sugar
- 1 Tbsp Allspice
- 1/3 Cup Kosher Salt
- 3 Bay Leaves
- 4 Cups Ice Water
- 1 Turkey Breast
- 1/2 Cup Plus Two Tbsp Unsalted Butter, Softened
- Traeger Pork and Poultry Rub

Instructions:

- For the Brine: In a large pot, combine 4 cups of the apple cider, the garlic cloves, brown sugar, allspice, salt, and bay leaves. Simmer on stove top for 5 minutes, stirring often.
- Take off stove top and add in the ice water.
- Place turkey in the brine and add water as needed until the turkey is fully submerged. Cover and refrigerate overnight.
- For the Cider Glaze: Boil the remaining 2 cups of apple cider in a saucepan until reduced to 1/4 cup, about 30-45 minutes. Whisk in butter and cool completely.
- After turkey has brined overnight, drain turkey and rinse.
- Using your fingers, take two tablespoons of the softened butter and smear it under the skin of the breast. Lightly season the turkey breast with Traeger Pork & Poultry Rub.
- When ready to cook, set the temperature to 325°F and preheat, lid closed for 15 minutes.
- Cook turkey until it reaches an internal temperature of 160°F, about 3-4 hrs. After the first 20 minutes of cooking, brush turkey with the cider glaze.
- If the breast starts to get too dark, cover it with foil. Let stand 30 minutes before carving. Enjoy!

6.18 Ultimate Smoked Turkey
Ingredients:

- 1 (18-20 Lb.) Turkey
- 1 Traeger Turkey Brine Kit
- 1/2 Cup Traeger Pork & Poultry Rub
- 1/2 Lb. Softened Butter

Instructions:

- The day before, brine the turkey according to the Traeger Turkey Brine Kit package directions.
- Remove from brine, rinse and pat dry. Season the inside cavity with Traeger Pork & Poultry Rub.
- Prepare the turkey by separating the skin from the breast creating a pocket to stuff the softened butter in. Cover the entire breast with 1/4-inch thickness of butter.
- Transfer to the fridge and let chill for at least 1 hour.
- Remove from the fridge and truss the legs and tuck the wing tips back around the bird.
- When ready to cook, set the Traeger to 225°F and preheat, lid closed for 15 minutes.
- Place the turkey in a roasting pan and place directly on the grill grate. Cook until the internal temperature reaches 100-110°F.
- Increase the temperature on the grill to 350°F and continue to cook until an instant read thermometer registers 160°F when inserted in the thickest part of the breast, about 3 to 4 hours total cook time. Turkey will continue to cook once taken off grill to reach a final temperature of 165°F in the breast.
- Remove the bird from the grill and let rest for at least 15 minutes before carving. Enjoy!

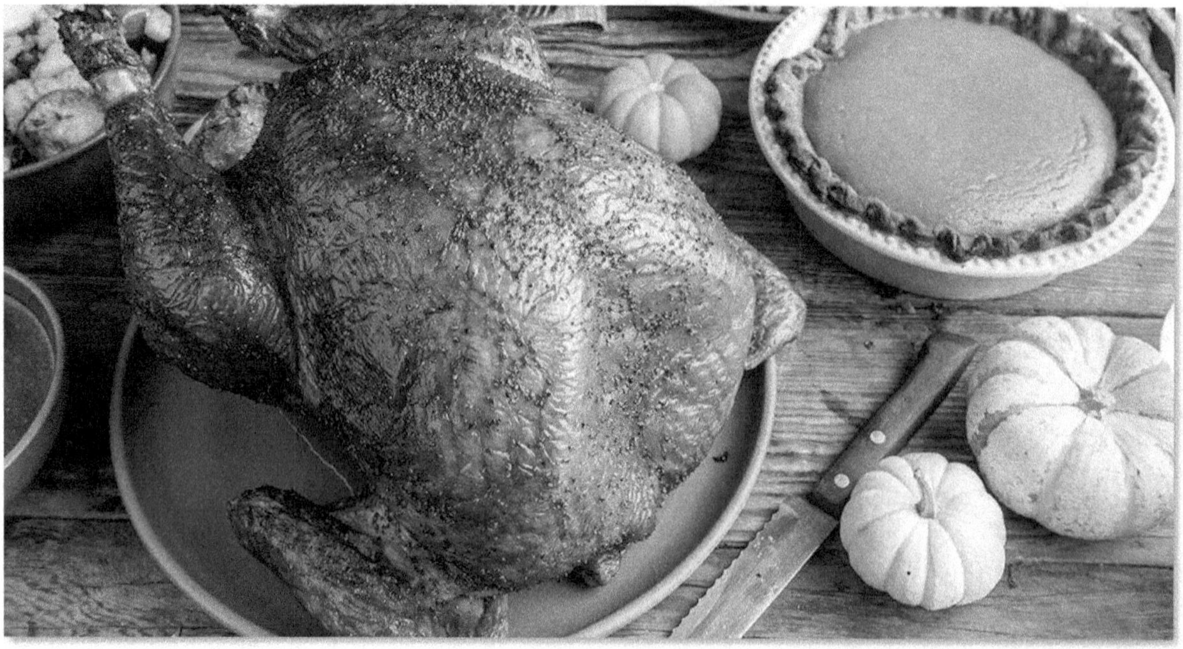

6.19 Smoked Wild Turkey Jerky
Ingredients:

- 3 Lb. Turkey Breast, Thinly Sliced
- 2 Cups Soy Sauce
- 1 Cup Brown Sugar
- 5 Garlic Cloves, Chopped
- 2 Tbsp Fresh Ginger, Chopped
- 1 Tbsp Ground Black Pepper
- 3 Tbsp Honey

Instructions:

- Combine all **Ingredients** in a large zip lock bag. Mix well. Place zip lock bag in a bowl and place in the refrigerator for 12 to 24 hours.
- When ready to cook, set temperature to 180°F and preheat, lid closed for 15 minutes.
- Drain the marinade and place the turkey strips on the grill.
- Let smoke for 4 hours or until the jerky is dry. Enjoy!

6.20 BBQ Chicken Breasts
Ingredients:

- 4-6 Boneless Skinless Chicken Breast
- 1 1/2 Cups Traeger Sweet & Heat BBQ Sauce
- Salt and Pepper, To Taste
- 1 Tbsp Chopped Parsley, To Garnish

Instructions:

- Place chicken breasts and 1 cup of Traeger Sweet & Heat BBQ sauce in a Ziploc bag and marinate overnight.
- Set temperature to High and preheat, lid closed for 15 minutes.
- Remove chicken from marinade and season with salt and pepper.
- Place directly on the grill grate and cook for 10 minutes on each side flipping once or until internal temperature reaches 150°F.
- Brush remaining sauce on chicken while on the grill and continue to cook 5-10 minutes longer or until a finished internal temperature of 165°F.
- Remove from grill and let rest 5 minutes before serving. Sprinkle with chopped parsley. Enjoy!

6.21 Beer-Brined Turkey
Ingredients:

- 1 (12-14 Lb.) Turkey
- 3 (12-Oz.) Cans or Bottles Dark Beer or Apple Cider
- 4 Qt. Cold Water
- 1-1/2 Cup Kosher Or 3/4 Cup Table Kosher Salt or Table Salt
- 1 Cup Dark Brown Sugar
- 3 Cloves Garlic, Smashed
- 1 Tbsp. Whole Black Peppercorns
- 1 Onion, Peeled and Cut into Quarters
- 4 Sprigs Each Fresh Rosemary, Thyme, Parsley, And Sage
- 3 Bay Leaves
- 2 Stalks Celery, Sliced Into 2" Pieces
- 1 Apple, Cut into Wedges
- Vegetable Oil, As Needed

Instructions:

- Thaw the turkey, if frozen, 3 days before you plan to eat the bird. Remove the giblets, if any.
- For the brine, in a large 5-gallon bucket or clean cooler, combine the beer, water, salt, and brown sugar and stir with a long-handled wooden spoon until the salt and sugar crystals are dissolved. Add the garlic and peppercorns.
- Add the turkey. Keep it submerged with a heavy pot lid or resealable bags of ice. Refrigerate for at least 8 hours.
- Remove the bird from the brine. Dry the turkey thoroughly, inside and out, with paper towels. Discard the brine.
- Put the onion, herbs, bay leaves, celery, and apple in the main cavity and tie the legs together with butcher's twine. Fold the wings behind the bird's back. Oil the outside of the bird.
- Put the turkey on a rack in a sturdy roasting pan. If you don't care to save the drippings, you can put the turkey directly on the grill grate.
- When ready to cook, set temperature to 350°F and preheat, lid closed for 15 minutes
- Put the roasting pan with the turkey on the grill grate and roast for 2-1/2 to 3 hours, or until a temperature probe inserted in the thickest part of the thigh reads 165°F.
- Let the turkey rest for 20 minutes before carving.
- *Cook times will vary depending on set and ambient

6.22 Cooking A Full Turkey on A Wood Pellet Grill & Smoker
Ingredients:

- 1 Eighteen Pound Turkey
- Dry Brine
- 6 tbsp Kosher Salt
- 2 tbsp Baking Soda
- Turkey Rub
- 1 cup Kosher Salt
- 1 cup Granulated Garlic
- 1 tbsp McCormick Poultry Seasoning

Instructions:

- Combine 6 tablespoons Morton's kosher salt with two tablespoons of baking powder in a bowl. Carefully pat your turkey dry with paper towels.
- Generously sprinkle it on all surfaces with the salt mixture by picking up the mixture between your thumb and fingers, holding it six to ten inches above the bird and letting the mixture shower down over the surface of the turkey for even coverage. The turkey should be well-coated with salt, though not completely encrusted. Leave in refrigerator for 24 hours.
- Prepare the smoker loading it up with either Apple or Cherry wood pellets but use whatever you think will work for you.
- Prepare an 8 to 18 lb. thawed or fresh turkey by removing the giblets and neck, draining the juices, and drying with paper towels. The turkey should be completely thawed for even, safe cooking. Do not stuff your turkey. Brush the skin with olive oil and insert an oven-safe meat thermometer deep into the lower thigh.
- Preheat the smoker to 275F degrees. Place the turkey breast side up on the grill. Place an oven thermometer alongside the turkey to monitor its temperature. I use a remote thermometer so you can monitor the temperature and also set an alarm when it hits 165 degrees (done).
- Try to plan for about 15-18 minutes per pound when you smoke at around 275F-300F degrees. If you like the skin to be crispy raise temperature to 300F.
- Check the temperature of your turkey after 3½ hours. Your turkey must pass through a critical range of 40F to 140F in 4 hours or less. If the internal temperature is low after 3½ hours, take your turkey off the smoker and finish it in the oven.
- When done, remove the turkey from the smoker, protecting your hands with BBQ Gloves, and let stand for 15 minutes before carving.

CHAPTER 7: PORK RECIPES

7.1 Smoked Traeger Pulled Pork
Ingredients:

- 1 (6 To 9 Lb.) Whole Bone-In Pork Shoulder
- Traeger Big Game Rub
- 2 Cups Apple Cider

Instructions:

- When ready to cook, set the temperature to 250°F and preheat, lid closed for 15 minutes.
- While the Traeger comes to temperature, trim excess fat off pork butt. Generously season with Traeger Big Game Rub on all sides.
- Put pork butt fat side up directly on the grill grate and cook until the internal temperature reaches 160°F, about 3-5 hours. Remove the pork butt from the grill.
- On a large baking sheet, stack 4 large pieces of aluminum foil on top of each other, ensuring they are wide enough to wrap the pork butt entirely on all sides. If not, overlap the foil pieces to create a wider base.
- Place the pork butt in the center on the foil, then bring up the sides of the foil a little bit before pouring the apple cider on top of the pork butt. Wrap the foil tightly around the pork, ensuring the cider does not escape.
- Place the foil-wrapped pork butt back on the grill fat side up and cook until the internal temperature reaches 204°F, in the thickest part of the meat, about 3-4 hours longer depending on the size of the pork butt.
- Remove from the grill. Allow the pork to rest for 45 minutes in the foil packet. Remove the foil and pour off any excess liquid into a fat separator.
- Place the pork in a dish large enough to pull the meat, removing and discarding the bone and any excess fat. Add separated liquid back to pork and season to taste with additional Big Game Rub.
- Serve alone, in your favorite recipes, or on sandwiches. Refrigerate leftover pork in a covered container for up to 4 days. Enjoy!

7.2 Smoked Pig Shots Recipe
Ingredients:

- 1 Block Cream Cheese
- 2 Large Green Chile Peppers, diced (Substitute 1 Can Diced Green Chiles)
- 8 Oz Cheese, Shredded
- 1 Tbsp Chili Powder
- 2 Tbsp Meat Church Honey Hog
- 1 Package Thick Cut Bacon
- 1 Package of Your Favorite Smoked Sausage
- Toothpicks

Instructions:

- When ready to cook, start the Traeger grill on Smoke with the lid open until the fire is established (4 to 5 minutes). Set the temperature to 350 degrees F and preheat, lid closed, for 10 to 15 minutes.
- Allow the cream cheese to soften. Mix cream cheese, chiles, shredded cheese, chili powder and Honey Hog thoroughly in a mixing bowl. Set aside. Slice sausage into 1/2-inch slices.
- Cut bacon strips in half. Wrap bacon around the sausage, creating a bowl and secure with a toothpick.
- Fill the bowl with the cream cheese mixture. Top with more Honey Hog BBQ rub.
- Place the pig shots on the Traeger until the bacon is crispy and golden brown, about 45 to 60 minutes.
- Remove the pig shots from the grill and cool for 10 minutes, cream cheese will be hot. Enjoy!

7.3 Grilled German Sausage with A Smoky Traeger Twist
Ingredients:

- 4 Lbs. Ground Pork (80% Lean 20% Fat)
- 1 Lb. Ground Veal or Ground Beef
- 2 Tbsp Jacobsen Salt
- 1 Tsp Instacart Or Morton's Tender quick Curing Salt
- 1 Tbsp Ground Nutmeg
- 2 Tsp Ground Mace
- 1 Tsp Ground Ginger
- 1 Cup Cold Milk
- 2 Eggs
- 1 Cup Non-Fat Dry Milk Powder

Instructions:

- Combine salt, tender quick, nutmeg, mace and ginger in a large pitcher or small bowl.
- Add the milk and eggs and beat until well combined. Pour the egg mixture over the ground meat and mix gently.
- Using your hands, mix in the milk powder until evenly distributed.
- Form the meat into sausage links.
- When ready to cook, set the temperature to 450°F and preheat, lid closed for 15 minutes.
- Smoke for approximately 2 hours or until the internal temperature reaches 175 degrees F.
- Serve immediately or refrigerate until ready to serve. Enjoy!

7.4 Texas Style Smoked Pulled Pork
Ingredients:

- 1/2 cup kosher salt USE KOSHER, NOT TABLE SALT
- 1/2 cup ground black pepper
- 1/3 cup paprika
- 1/2 cup brown sugar
- 2 tbsp granulated garlic
- 2 tbsp granulated onion
- 2 tbsp cayenne pepper
- 1 tbsp celery salt
- PULLED PORK
- 8-10 lb. pork shoulder butt
- 2 tbsp yellow mustard
- 1 cup apple cider vinegar/apple juice in a spritzer bottle

Instructions:

- Prepare your pork butt. trimming any excess fat leaving about 1/4 inch of fat on the fat cap side. Trim off any unwanted glands or cartridge as well. Pat dry with a paper towel, then spread a light coat of mustard.
- With your rub ingredients combined, liberally coat your pork butt. You shouldn't see anything but your rub on the pork.
- Preheat your smoker to 235. Place your pork butt, fat side up on the grates. Close the smoker and don't peek for about 2 hours. Spritz every hour after the 2-hour mark.
- At around the 4-5-hour mark start probing for temperature. When you get to about 160, it's time to wrap. Taking a couple 18×30 sheets of aluminum foil. Remove your pork butt from the grates with a towel and place on the foil fat side down; spritz one more time. Wrap as tightly as possible so that you don't lose any of that bark. Double wrap so that the foil doesn't tear on the grates.
- At this point your pork butt has taken all the smoke it's going to get. You can either leave the temperature at 235, or increase to around 275 to speed up the process. Place the pork butt fat side down onto the grate and close. Probe for tenderness and temperature at the 7- or 8-hour mark until the internal temperature is around 200-205. If you can easily pull the blade from the meat, you're ready to take off the grill.
- Keep wrapped and let rest of the grill for about 30-45 minutes. Pull away and enjoy!

7.5 Spice Rubbed Pork Tenderloin
Ingredients:

- 2 pork tenderloins
- 2 tsp dried oregano
- 1 tsp cumin
- 1 tsp chili powder
- 1 tsp paprika
- 4 garlic cloves, minced or pushed through a press
- ½ C lime juice
- ¾ C fresh orange juice
- 2 tsp orange rind, finely grated
- ¼ C olive oil
- ¼ C fresh mint leaves, minced
- ¼ C fresh cilantro leaves, minced
- ½ tsp salt
- Grinding of fresh pepper

Instructions:

- In a small bowl, mix oregano, cumin, chili powder and paprika together. Divide into two equal portions. Set one portion aside for later use.
- Pat tenderloins dry with paper towel and coat the meat with half of the rub. Gently massage it into the surface of the meat then place the tenderloins into a food safe, re-sealable plastic bag.
- In a small bowl combine the orange juice, orange rind, lime juice, olive oil, mint, cilantro and garlic. Pour this marinade mixture over the tenderloins and seal the bag. Refrigerate for at least 4 hours or overnight, turning the bag occasionally.
- Preheat the Memphis Wood Pellet Grill to 375 degrees F.
- Remove tenderloins from the bag and pat dry. Add salt and pepper to the reserved portion of spice mixture. Sprinkle over the tenderloin and rub gently into the surface of the meat.
- Place seasoned pork tenderloin on the lower rack of the pre-heated Memphis Pellet Grill. Close the lid and cook until the internal temperature of the meat reaches 145 degrees F (about 35 minutes).
- Remove from grill and rest for 5-10 minutes before serving.

7.6 Apple Cider Braised Smoked BBQ Pulled Pork
Ingredients:

- 7–9 lb. bone-in pork butt/shoulder roast
- RUB
- 4 tablespoons brown sugar
- 1 tablespoon garlic powder
- 1 tablespoon onion powder
- 1 tablespoon kosher salt
- 1/2 tablespoon pepper
- 1.5 tablespoons smoked paprika
- 2 teaspoons dry mustard
- 1 tablespoon coriander
- 1 tablespoon chili powder
- SPRAY
- 1/2 cup apple cider
- 1/2 cup apple cider vinegar
- BRAISING
- 2 cups apple cider
- 3–4 sweet, crisp red apples, peeled and sliced
- 2 onions, sliced
- SAUCE
- 1 cup ketchup
- 1/2 cup apple jelly
- 1/4 cup apple cider

- 1 tablespoon apple cider vinegar
- 1 teaspoon liquid smoke
- 1/2 tablespoon Worcestershire sauce
- 1 teaspoon chili powder
- 1/2 teaspoon onion powder
- 1 cup pan juices from roast (fat separated)

Instructions:

- Pat roast dry. Combine all rub ingredients and pat on all sides of roast, rubbing in well. Cover roast and let sit overnight in the fridge.
- When ready to cook, preheat smoker to 225 degrees and smoke roast directly on grill for 5 hours. While cooking, combine spray ingredients in a clean spray bottle and spritz roast all over once every hour.
- While roast is smoking, combine all sauce ingredients and whisk together in a pan. Set aside until pan juices are ready.
- After smoking, transfer your roast to either your slow cooker (if it will fit, remember you have more stuff going in there!) or a roasting pan, or disposable roasting pan (if you'll continue cooking on the smoker.)
- Place apples, onions, and 2 cups apple cider around the roast in the roasting pan. Cover with lid, or tightly with foil. Cook in slow cooker on high for 6-7 hours (or low for more like 8-10 if you want/need to drag it out, overnight for example.) If you are cooking in the oven, set temperature to 275 degrees. In the smoker, you can increase temperature to 275 as well. Cook until internal temperature reaches 200-210 degrees, usually about 6-7 hours.
- Let pork rest, covered for at least 15 minutes (longer is just fine) before discarding bones, separating fat, etc.
- Pour pan juices into a fat separator. Pour 1 cup of juices into your BBQ sauce and bring to a simmer. Simmer for about 15 minutes until slightly thickened.
- Pour a little of the remaining juices over shredded pork. Use a slotted spoon to grab the onions and apples and mix them in with the pork. Serve alone or on rolls or over rice. Freezes great! Excellent on nachos, pizzas, and more.

7.7 Bourbon Brown Sugar Smoked Pork Loin

Ingredients:

For the pork:

- 1 center-cut piece of pork loin (2½ to 3 pounds)
- 3 tablespoons Tennessee whiskey
- 2 tablespoons of your favorite barbecue rub
- 3 tablespoons Dijon mustard
- ½ cup firmly packed brown sugar
- 4 slices bacon

For the glaze:

- 3 tablespoons salted butter
- 3 tablespoons brown sugar
- 3 tablespoons Dijon mustard
- 3 tablespoons Tennessee whiskey
- Barbecue sauce (optional), for serving

Instructions:

- Butterfly the pork loin: Using a very sharp knife, cut the roast almost in half lengthwise through one side (stop about 1 inch from the opposite side). Open the roast up as you would a book. Sprinkle the inside of the roast with 1 tablespoon of the whiskey and let it marinate for 5 minutes. Sprinkle a third of the rub over the inside of the roast. Spread the mustard on top with a spatula, then sprinkle the brown sugar on top of the mustard. Sprinkle the remaining 2 tablespoons of whiskey on top of the brown sugar. Fold the roast back together (like closing a book) and sprinkle the remaining rub over the outside.
- Cut four 12-inch pieces of butcher's string. Position the pieces of string on the work surface so that they are parallel and roughly 2 inches apart. Place a slice of bacon across the strings so that it is perpendicular to and in the center of them. Set the roast on top of the bacon, positioning its long side parallel to the bacon. Place a slice of bacon on top of the roast. Press the remaining 2 slices against the long sides of the roast. Tie each piece of string together around the roast so that they hold the slices of bacon against it. Set the pork roast aside.
- Make the glaze: Combine the butter, brown sugar, mustard, and whiskey in a saucepan and boil until syrupy, 4 to 6 minutes. Set the glaze aside.

- Set up the grill for indirect grilling and preheat to medium. If using a gas grill, place all of the wood chips or chunks in the smoker box or in a smoker pouch and run the grill on high until you see smoke, then reduce the heat to medium. If using a charcoal grill, place a large drip pan in the center, preheat the grill to medium, then toss all of the wood chips or chunks on the coals.
- When ready to cook, place the pork roast on the hot grate, over the drip pan and away from the heat and cover the grill. Cook the roast until cooked through, 1 to 1½ hours. To test for doneness, insert an instant-read meat thermometer into the side of the roast: The internal temperature should be about 160°F. Start basting the roast with some of the glaze after 30 minutes and continue basting every 15 minutes. If you are using a charcoal grill and the pork is not done after 1 hour, you'll need to add 12 fresh coals to each side.
- Transfer the cooked roast to a cutting board and let it rest for 5 minutes, then remove and discard the strings. Slice the roast crosswise and drizzle any remaining glaze over it. If you like, serve barbecue sauce alongside.

CHAPTER 8: SEAFOOD RECIPES

8.1 Spicy Shrimp Skewers
Ingredients:

- 2 Lbs. Shrimp, Peeled, And Deveined
- 6 Oz Thai Chilies
- 6 Cloves Garlic
- 2 Tbsp Winemakers Blend Napa Valley Rub
- 1-1/2 Tsp Sugar
- 1-1/2 Tbsp White Vinegar
- 3 Tbsp Olive Oil
- Bamboo or Metal Skewers

Instructions:

- Place all ingredients besides shrimp in a blender and blend until a course textured paste is reached.
- Place shrimp in a bowl, add chili garlic mixture and place in fridge to marinate for at least 30 minutes.
- Remove from fridge and thread shrimp onto bamboo or metal skewers.
- When ready to cook, start the Traeger according to grill instructions. Set the temperature to 450 degrees F (set to 500 degrees F if using a WiFIRE enables grill) and preheat, lid closed, for 10 to 15 minutes.
- Place shrimp on grill and cook for 2 to 3 minutes per side or until shrimp are pink and firm to touch. Enjoy!

8.2 Baja-Style Fish Tacos
Ingredients:

- 1 Lb. White Fish Such as Cod, Monkfish, Or Halibut (Skinless)
- 2 Limes
- 2 Tsp. Dijon-Style Mustard
- 1/2 Tsp. Salt
- 1/2 Tsp. Black Pepper, Freshly Ground
- 1/2 Cup Vegetable Oil, Or Olive Oil
- 2 Cloves Garlic, Minced
- As Needed Traeger Cajun Rub
- 8 Corn Tortillas
- For Serving Shredded Cabbage, Diced Red Onions, Cilantro Leaves, Pickled Jalapeno Slices, Diced Avocado, Pico De Gallo Or Salsa, Sour Cream

Instructions:

- Juice one lime. Cut the other lime in wedges; set aside until serving time.
- Make the marinade: In a small mixing bowl, combine the lime juice, mustard, and salt and pepper. Slowly whisk in the oil, then stir in the garlic.
- Place the fish in a resealable plastic bag, pour the marinade over it, and refrigerate for no more than 1 hour.
- When ready to cook, start the Traeger grill on Smoke with the lid open until the fire is established (4 to 5 minutes). Set the temperature to 400F (High on a 3-position controller) and preheat, lid closed, for 10 to 15 minutes.
- Remove the fish from the marinade and pat off any excess marinade with paper towels. Season generously on both sides with Traeger Cajun Rub.
- Arrange the fish on the grill grate and grill until the fish is opaque and flakes easily when pressed with a fork. (There is no need to turn it.) Remove to a cutting board and cut into bite-size chunks. Meanwhile, warm the tortillas on the Traeger until pliant and hot.
- Arrange the fish, tortillas, and suggested accompaniments on a large platter. Garnish with the reserved lime wedges. Serve immediately.

8.3 Traeger Jerk Shrimp
Ingredients:

- 1 Tbsp Brown Sugar
- 1 Tbsp Smoked Paprika
- 1 Tsp Garlic Powder
- 1/4 Tsp Ground Thyme
- 1/4 Tsp Ground Cayenne
- 1/8 Tsp Smoked Paprika
- 1 Tsp Sea Salt
- Zest Of 1 Lime
- 3 Tbsp Olive Oil
- 2 Lbs. Shrimp, Peel On

Instructions:

- Combine spices, salt, and lime zest in a small bowl and mix. Place shrimp into a large bowl, then drizzle in the olive oil, Add the spice mixture and toss to combine, making sure every shrimp is kissed with deliciousness.
- When ready to cook, set the temperature to 450°F and preheat, lid closed for 15 minutes
- Arrange the shrimp on the grill and cook for 2 – 3 minutes per side, until firm, opaque, and cooked through.
- Serve with lime wedges, fresh cilantro, mint, and Caribbean Hot Pepper Sauce. Enjoy!

8.4 Traeger Smoked Mussels
Ingredients:

- Mussels
- 1/4 Cup Butter
- 1 Tbsp Smoked Paprika
- 4 Garlic Cloves, Minced
- 1 Cup Apple Cider
- 3 Lbs. Mussels, Cleaned & Scrubbed
- Fresh Lemons & Crusty Bread to Serve
- Salsa Verde
- 1 Small Bunch Fresh Chives
- 1 Small Bunch Tarragon
- 1 Small Bunch Basil
- 1 Small Bunch Flat-Leaf Parsley
- 1 Garlic Clove, Peeled and Roughly Chopped
- Juice Of 1/2 Lemon
- 200 MLX Extra-Virgin Olive Oil
- Sea Salt & Fresh Crackled Black Pepper

Instructions:

- When ready to cook, set the temperature to 350°F and preheat, lid closed for 15 minutes
- Heat a cast-iron (or oven-safe) pan over medium heat, and melt the butter. When melted, add the garlic and cook for 30 seconds (keep watch that it doesn't burn), then pour in the apple cider and bring to a simmer. Add the mussels, cover with a tight-fitting lid, and transfer to the Traeger. Cook for 8 – 10 minutes, or until the mussels have opened (discard any mussels that do not open).
- While the mussels are cooking, crack on with the salsa Verde. Combine the fresh herbs and garlic in a food processor (or high-powered blender) and finely chop. Add the lemon juice and season with salt and pepper. With the blender running on low, drizzle in the olive oil in a slow & steady stream until thick and glorious.
- Serve up those beautiful wood-fire kissed mussels with the salsa Verde, lemon wedges, and crusty bread. Enjoy!

8.5 Grilled Lobster Tails

Ingredients:

- 2 Lobster Tails, 8-10 Oz Each
- 8 Tbsp Butter
- 2 Tbsp Lemon Juice
- 1 Tsp Paprika
- 1/4 Tsp Garlic Salt
- 1/4 Tsp Old Bay Seasoning
- 1/4 Tsp Freshly Ground Black Pepper
- 2 Tbsp Fresh Parsley, Chopped

Instructions:

- Prepare the lobster by cutting down the middle of the tough shell toward the tail with kitchen shears. Using your fingers, gently pry the meat from the shell, keeping it attached at the base of the tail. Lift the meat so it is resting on top of the split shell (again, keeping it attached at the base of the tail).
- Make a slit down the middle of the meat to butterfly it open on top. Place the lobster tails on a rimmed baking sheet.
- Melt the butter in a small saucepan over medium-low heat. Whisk in the lemon juice, paprika, garlic salt, Old Bay Seasoning, pepper, and parsley.
- Pour about 1 tablespoon of the butter mixture over each lobster tail. Keep the remaining butter mixture warm.
- When ready to cook, set temperature to High and preheat, lid closed for 15 minutes.
- Remove the lobster tails from the baking sheet and arrange them directly on the grill grate. Cook for 25 to 30 minutes, or until the meat is white and opaque.
- Transfer lobster tails to a platter and serve with the reserved butter mixture. Enjoy!

8.6 Garlic Salmon

Ingredients:

- 1 2-3 Lb. Salmon Filet, Skin On
- 1/4 Cup Olive Oil
- 2 Tbsp Garlic, Minced
- 1/2 Tbsp Parsley, Minced
- Traeger Fin & Feather Rub
- Lemon Wedges, For Serving

Instructions:

- Line a baking sheet with butcher paper or parchment. Place the salmon skin side down on the baking sheet and season the filet with the Traeger Fin & Feather Rub. In a small bowl combine olive oil, garlic, and parsley. Set aside.
- When ready to cook, set temperature to High and preheat, lid closed for 15 minutes.
- Brush the salmon with the garlic mixture and transfer the baking sheet to the grill. Cook until the internal temperature reaches 140°F (about 20-25 minutes), or until the fish flakes easily.
- Remove from the grill and brush with any extra garlic mixture you may have and serve with lemon wedges. Enjoy!

8.7 Grilled Penang Curry Salmon

Ingredients:

- Penang Curry Salmon
- 1 (12 Oz) Jar Thai fusions Penang Curry
- 1 (4-7 Lb.) Salmon Fillet
- 2 Sprigs Thai Basil, Roughly Chopped
- 1/2 Red Bell Pepper Sliced Thinly, Lengthwise
- 1 Lime, Sliced into Thin Crosscut Pieces
- Mussels with Prawns (Optional)
- 1/2 Lb. Prawns, Shelled and Deveined
- 1/2 Lb. Mussels Debearded And Washed
- Handful Thai Basil, Chopped

Instructions:

- Season both sides of the salmon with salt and pepper.
- Brush a little canola oil on the salmon fillet and marinate with a 1/2 cup of Thai fusions Penang Curry in a shallow pan. Cover and marinate at room temperature for about 30 minutes.
- When ready to cook, set temperature to High and preheat, lid closed for 15 minutes.
- Brush some canola oil onto the grill so the salmon won't stick. Place salmon fillet directly on the grill grate and brush on about another 1/4 cup of Thai fusions Penang Curry and top with sliced red bell pepper and lime slices.
- Grill salmon until an internal temperature of 145°F, about 10-15 minutes.
- For the Mussels and Prawns: Pour last 1/4 cup of Penang Curry into a sauce pan, add prawns, mussels, Thai basil and cover sauce pan and finish on the Traeger. When the mussels have opened, take off the grill and set aside.
- Take salmon off the grill as gently as possible and top salmon with mussels and prawns if desired. Garnish with Thai basil. Enjoy!

8.8 Seared Lemon Garlic Scallops
Ingredients:

- Scallops
- 1 Dozen U-20 Scallops
- Kosher Salt
- 1 Tbsp Butter
- 1 Tbsp Olive Oil
- Chopped Parsley, To Garnish
- Lemon Zest, To Garnish
- Garlic Butter
- 4 Tbsp Butter, Melted
- Juice Of 1 Lemon
- 1 Clove Garlic, Minced

Instructions:

- When ready to cook, set the temperature to 400°F and preheat, lid closed for 15 minutes.
- Remove the frill if it is still intact. Pat the scallops dry with a paper towel. Season liberally with salt and a bit of black pepper.
- When the grill is hot, place the butter and olive oil on the skillet. When the butter has melted, place the scallops on the skillet. Close the lid and cook for about 2 minutes until seared and browned on one side.
- While the scallops cook, combine the melted butter and garlic in a small bowl.
- Flip the scallops, spoon a couple tablespoons of garlic butter over the top and cook for 1 minute longer.
- Remove from the grill, add a little more garlic butter if desired and finish with parsley and lemon zest. Enjoy!

8.9 Whole Grilled Red Snapper
Ingredients:

- Red Snapper
- 1 Whole Red Snapper, Rinse and Pat Dry
- 2 Tbsp Olive Oil
- 1/2 Tbsp Kosher Salt
- 1 Tsp Black Pepper
- 1/4 Cup Butter, Melted
- 1/4 Cup Harissa
- Salad
- 1 Bunch Watercress, Trimmed and Washed
- 2 Cherry Peppers, Thinly Sliced
- 3 Scallions, Thinly Sliced
- 2 Tbsp Chopped Cilantro
- 2 Tbsp Mint Leaves Torn
- 2 Limes, Juiced
- 1 Tsp Brown Sugar
- 1/4 Tsp Fish Sauce
- 1/4 Cup Olive Oil
- Salt and Pepper, To Taste

Instructions:

- In a medium bowl combine melted butter and harissa.
- When ready to cook, set the temperature to High and preheat, lid closed for 15 minutes.
- Coat the exterior of the fish with olive oil and season with salt and pepper on both sides. Place fish directly on the grill grate, brush with the harissa-butter mixture and cook for 15-20 minutes.
- While the fish cooks, prepare the salad. In a small bowl combine the lime juice, brown sugar, fish sauce, salt and pepper. While whisking, slowly stream in olive oil. In a medium bowl combine the watercress, peppers, scallions, cilantro and mint. Wait to dress the salad until ready to serve.
- Flip the fish and brush the other side with harissa-butter mixture. Close the lid and continue to cook 10-15 minutes more until the internal temperature registers 145°F.

- Carefully remove the fish from the grill and place on a serving platter. Drizzle the dressing over the greens, season to taste with salt and pepper and mix to coat.
- Pile the salad over the top of the fish and drizzle the fish with remaining dressing if desired. Enjoy!

8.10 Roasted Halibut in Parchment

Ingredients:

- 4 Ea. (4 Oz) Fish Fillets, Such as Salmon, Halibut or Snapper, Pin Bones Removed
- Extra-Virgin Olive Oil
- Kosher Salt and Freshly Ground Pepper
- 2 Lemons, Preferably Meyer, Ends Trimmed, Cut Into 12 Slices
- Kernels From 2 Ears of Corn
- 16 Asparagus Spears, Bottoms Trimmed, Sliced Into 1/2-Inch Pieces
- 2 Tbsp Finely Chopped Assorted Herbs, Such as Basil, Chives, Or Parsley
- Equipment: 4 Pieces Parchment Paper

Instructions:

- When ready to cook, set the temperature to High and preheat, lid closed for 15 minutes.
- Cut four pieces of parchment paper or Traeger butcher paper each 18" long.
- Place a fish fillet on the center of a piece of parchment. Season with a pinch each of salt and pepper, then drizzle with olive oil. Place three lemon slices on the fillet, overlapping them slightly to cover the fish.
- Sprinkle one-fourth each of the corn, asparagus, and tomatoes (if using) evenly around the fish, then drizzle with a little olive oil and season again with a small pinch each of salt and pepper.
- Bring the long sides of the paper together, and fold the top edges down together to create a 1-inch seal, then continue to fold down tightly over the fish and vegetables.
- Twist the open ends of the parchment in opposite directions to prevent steam from escaping.
- Repeat the process with the remaining ingredients and parchment and place the packets on a baking sheet. If not cooking immediately, refrigerate for up to 4 hours.
- Place the baking sheet on the Traeger and bake until the packets are lightly browned and have puffed up, about 15 minutes.
- Transfer each packet to a plate and let stand for 5 minutes. Using sharp scissors, cut an X into the center of each packet and carefully pull back the parchment and sprinkle with the herbs.
- Serve immediately. Enjoy!

8.11 Grilled Lobster with Lemon Garlic Butter Recipe

Ingredients:

- Grilled Lobster
- (4) 1 1/2 Lb. Live Lobsters
- 2 Tbsp 2 T Olive Oil
- 2 Lemons, Sliced
- Flat Leaf Parsley, To Serve
- Lemon Garlic Butter
- 3/4 Cup Butter, Softened
- 2 Tbsp Flat Leaf Parsley, Finely Diced
- 1 Tbsp Minced Shallot
- 2 Cloves Garlic, Minced
- 1 Tbsp Lemon Juice
- 1 Tbsp Lemon Zest
- 1/2 Tsp Sea Salt
- 1/2 Tsp Fresh Cracked Black Pepper

Instructions:

- Bring a large stockpot of water to a rapid boil. Working in batches as necessary, submerge the lobster in the water head first, then cover with a lid. Cook for 5 minutes, then transfer to an ice-bath to cool and stop the cooking process.
- In a small saucepan, melt the butter over medium low heat. When melted, add the remaining ingredients and whisk together until smooth. Set aside.
- Using a very sharp knife, split the lobster into 2 halves. Clean out the tomalley from the body and discard. Brush the lobster halves all over with olive oil.
- When ready to cook, set temperature to High and preheat, lid closed for 15 minutes.
- When hot, place the lobsters on the grill, flesh side down, and cook for 4 minutes. Turn, and spoon about 2 tsp of compound butter onto each lobster half. As the butter begins to melt, baste with a brush all over the flesh. Cook for 4-5 minutes until cooked through and coated in melted butter.
- Serve immediately with sliced lemons and parsley. Enjoy!

8.12 BBQ Oysters
Ingredients:

- BBQ Oysters
- 12 Oysters, Shucked
- 1 Bunch Green Onions, Chopped
- 8 Oz Shredded Pepper Jack Cheese
- 1/4 Cup Seasoned Bread Crumbs
- Traeger Sweet & Heat BBQ Sauce
- Compound Butter
- 1 Lb. Butter, Unsalted
- 1 Tbsp Meat Church the Gospel or Honey Hog BBQ Rub
- 1/2 Bunch Green Onions, Minced
- 2 Cloves Garlic, Minced

Instructions:

- When ready to cook, start the Traeger according to grill instructions. Set the temperature to 375 degrees F and preheat, lid closed, for 10 to 15 minutes.
- For the compound butter: Allow the butter to soften. Combine butter, garlic, onion and BBQ Rub thoroughly.
- Lay the butter on parchment paper or plastic wrap. Roll it up to form a log and tie each end with butcher's twine. Place in the freezer for an hour to solidify. You can use this butter on any grilled meats to enhance the flavor. You can also use a high-quality butter to replace the compound butter.
- Shuck the oysters keeping all of the juice in the shell.
- Sprinkle the oysters with bread crumbs and place directly on the Traeger. Cook them for 5 minutes. You will be looking for the edge of the oyster to start to curl slightly.
- After 5 minutes place a spoonful of butter in the oysters. After the butter melts, add a pinch of pepper jack cheese.
- Remove the oysters after 6 minutes on the grill total. Top oysters with a squirt of BBQ sauce and a few chopped onions. Allow to cool for 5 minutes, then enjoy!

8.13 Maple Glazed Salmon
Ingredients:

- 1/2 C + 3 Tbsp soy sauce
- 1 C maple syrup (the real stuff)
- Really fresh thick salmon, skin on (I prefer Sockeye, however, that is the strongest of the selection. If you're working with some people you hope to convert, the farm-raised stuff is a little lighter.)

Instructions:

- Mix a 1/2 C of soy with a 1/2 C of maple syrup in a dish big enough that the salmon fits flat but not so deep that the skin is covered.
- Put in the fridge. This isn't a "longer is better" type of meat to marinate, so 15 minutes per inch should suffice with at least 30 minutes total, regardless of size. (For 2 inches, 45-60 minutes is a safe window.)

- Set grill to 400 degrees F and lightly oil just enough of the grate to accommodate the fish flesh side down.
- Heat 1/2 C of maple syrup and 3 Tbsp of soy sauce in a skillet pan (not cast iron and not non-stick) until the glaze thickens a bit. Note: You can also have some fun here. Brown sugar, honey, mustard and cherry juice can all be mixed around for good flavors. Even adding some spice to the party can change this dish around.
- Brush the salmon with the glaze and put it flesh side down on the hot grill and shut the lid.
- Flip fish after a few minutes. If it is ready to be turned over (and you've oiled your grill grates), it shouldn't stick.
- Cook the salmon until the internal temperature reaches 140 degrees F. Less is fine, more is okay, but understand that a little rare for fresh salmon will never hurt you, but a little too much will destroy the meal.

8.14 Lemon Garlic Smoked Salmon Recipe
Ingredients:

- 6 5 oz Prime Waters Seafood Salmon Filets
- 4 tbsp softened butter
- 2 tsp lemon juice
- 1 tsp lemon zest
- 1 tsp salt
- 1 tsp pepper
- 1 clove garlic minced

Instructions:

- Preheat wood pellet smoker to 350 degrees F
- Combine all of the ingredients (except the salmon) in a bowl and mix well.
- Add a generous amount of the butter mixture on top of each filet of salmon, and top with lemon slices if desired
- Add each filet to the wood pellet grill and cook until an internal temperature of 125 degrees is reached.
- Remove the filets from the grill and tent with aluminum foil. Let rest for 10 minutes before serving.
- Garnish with lemon slices and additional spices for presentation

8.15 Easy and Flavorful Smoked Tilapia
Ingredients:

- 6 tilapia fillets
- 3 tbsp./45 ml vegetable oil
- 2 tbsp./30 ml fresh lemon juice
- 1/2 tsp./2.5 ml garlic powder
- 1 tsp./5 ml kosher salt
- 1/2 tsp./2.5 ml lemon pepper

Instructions:

- Prepare smoker for a 2-hour smoke.
- Wash fish and remove all bones. Combine oil, lemon juice, garlic powder, salt, and lemon pepper in a small bowl. Brush liquid mixture onto both sides of the tilapia fillets.
- Place in the smoker for 1 1/2 to 2 hours.
- When finished, remove from heat and serve.

CHAPTER 9: DESSERTS RECIPES

9.1 Strawberry Shortbread

Ingredients:

- 1 Qt. Strawberries, Washed, Stemmed, And Sliced
- To Taste, About 1 To 2 Tbsp. Sugar, For Strawberries
- 1 To 2 Tsp. Grand Marnier Or Triple Sec (Optional)
- 2 Cups, Plus More for Flouring Board All-Purpose Flour
- 2 To 3 Tbsp. Sugar
- 1 Tbsp. Baking Powder
- 1/4 Tsp. Salt
- 1/4 Tsp. Cinnamon
- 2 Tbsp. Butter, Cold, Cubed
- 2 Tbsp. Shortening, Cold
- 2/3 Cup Milk or Half and Half
- As Needed Butter, Melted
- For Serving Sweetened Whipped Cream

Instructions:

- In a mixing bowl, combine the strawberries and sugar to taste (1 to 2 tablespoons are usually enough to sweeten the berries). Add the Grand Marnier, if using, and stir, crushing some of the berries slightly to release their juices. Cover and refrigerate until serving time.
- Sift the 2 cups of flour, sugar, baking powder, salt, and cinnamon into a mixing bowl. (Or just put the ingredients into the bowl and whisk to combine.) Cut the butter and shortening into the dry ingredients with a pastry blender, fork, or knife until the mixture is reduced to pea-size clumps. Make a well in the center, and pour in the milk. Stir until just combined. Do not overmix.
- Lightly flour a cutting board or countertop and dump the shortcake mixture onto it. Knead lightly to bring the dough together. Pat into a 1/2-inch thick circle and cut rounds out with a biscuit cutter or an upended glass. Transfer to an ungreased baking sheet. Brush the tops of the shortcakes with the melted butter.
- When ready to cook, start the Traeger grill on Smoke with the lid open until the fire is established (4 to 5 minutes). Set the temperature to 425F or High and preheat, lid closed, for 10 to 15 minutes.
- Put the pan with the shortcakes on the grill grate and close the lid. Bake for 10 minutes, or until the shortcakes have risen and are nicely browned. Let cool slightly, then slit in half with a knife. Divide the strawberries between the bottom halves of the shortcakes, then replace the tops. Top with sweetened whipped cream.

9.2 Leave No Trace Chocolate-Chunk Oatmeal Cookies

Ingredients:

- 1 Cup Old-Fashioned Rolled Oats (Not Instant or Quick-Cooking)
- 1 Cup All-Purpose Flour
- 1/2 Tsp. Baking Powder
- 1/2 Tsp. Baking Soda
- 1/4 Tsp. Salt
- 1/2 Cup (1 Stick) Butter, Softened
- 1/2 Cup Peanut Butter (Smooth or Chunky)
- 1/2 Cup Sugar
- 1/2 Cup Brown Sugar, Firmly Packed
- 1 Large Egg
- 1 1/2 Tsp. Vanilla
- 1 Generous Cup Semi-Sweet Chocolate Chunks or Chips, Coarsely Chopped

Instructions:

- When ready to cook, set temperature to 225°F and preheat, lid closed for 15 minutes.
- Line a sturdy rimmed baking sheet with parchment paper.

- Spread the oats in an even layer on the baking sheet. Place the baking sheet on the grill grate and smoke the oats, stirring once. Remove from the grill. Increase the temperature of the Traeger to 375°F
- In the meantime, make the cookie dough: Let the smoked oats cool completely. Lift the sides of the parchment paper up and tip the oats into a mixing bowl. (Return the parchment paper to the baking sheet; you'll reuse it for the cookies.) Add the flour, baking powder, baking soda, and salt and stir to combine. Set aside.
- In another bowl - such as the bowl of a stand mixer - combine the butter, peanut butter, and sugar.
- Mix on medium-high speed (you can use a hand-held mixer or a wooden spoon and elbow grease) until the mixture is light and fluffy.
- Beat in the egg and vanilla. Gradually add the oatmeal-flour mixture using low speed. Stir in the chocolate chunks by hand.
- Drop the dough by heaping tablespoons onto the prepared baking sheet and flatten slightly with the back of a tablespoon.
- Bake for about 12 minutes, or until the cookies have spread and are lightly browned. Remove the baking sheet from the grill. Let the cookies firm up for a minute or two, then transfer to a wire cooling rack to cool.
- Repeat with the remainder of the dough. Store in an airtight container. Enjoy!

9.3 Double Chocolate Chip Brownie Pie

Ingredients:

- 1 Cup Butter
- 1 Cup Brown Sugar
- 1 Cup Sugar
- 2 Tsp. Vanilla
- 4 Eggs
- 2 Cups All-Purpose Flour
- 2/3 Cup Cocoa Powder
- 1 Tsp. Baking Soda
- 1 Tsp. Salt
- 1 1/2 Cup Semi-Sweet Chocolate Chips, Divided
- 3/4 Cup White Chocolate Chips
- 3/4 Cup Nuts (Optional)
- 1, 8-Oz. Hot Fudge Sauce
- 1-2 Tbsp. Guinness

Instructions:

- Coat the inside of a 10-inch pie plate with non-stick cooking spray.
- When ready to cook, set the temperature to 350°F and preheat, lid closed for 15 minutes.
- Melt 1/2 cup of the semi-sweet chocolate chips in the microwave. Cream together butter, brown sugar and granulated sugar. Beat in the eggs, adding one at a time and mixing after each egg, and the vanilla. Add in the melted chocolate chips.
- On a large piece of wax paper, sift together the cocoa powder, flour, baking soda and salt. Lift up the corners of the paper and pour slowly into the butter mixture.
- Beat until the dry ingredients are just incorporated. Stir in the remaining semi-sweet chocolate chips, white chocolate chips, and the nuts. Press the dough into the prepared pie pan.
- Place the brownie pie on the grill and bake for 45-50 minutes or until the pie is set in the middle. Rotate the pan halfway through cooking. If the top or edges begin to brown, cover the top with a piece of aluminum foil.
- In a microwave-safe measuring cup, heat the fudge sauce in the microwave. Stir in the Guinness.
- Once the brownie pie is done, allow to sit for 20 minutes. Slice into wedges and top with the fudge sauce. Enjoy

CHAPTER 10: SPECIALTIES

10.1 Baked Wood-Fired Pizza
Ingredients:

- Dough
- 2/3 Cup Warm Water (Between 100-110°F)
- 2 1/2 Tsp Active Dry Yeast
- 1/2 Tsp Granulated Sugar
- 1 Tsp Kosher Salt
- 1 Tbsp Oil
- 1 3/4 To 2 Cups All Purpose Flour
- 1/4 Cup Fine Cornmeal
- Toppings
- 1 Large Grilled Portobello Mushroom, Sliced
- 1 Jar Pickled Artichoke Hearts, Chopped
- 1 Cup Fontina Cheese, Shredded
- 1/2 Cup Shaved Parmigiano, Divided
- Chopped Roasted Garlic, To Taste
- 1/4 Cup Olive Oil
- Banana Peppers, To Taste
- Traeger Pizza Kit

Instructions:

- In a glass bowl, stir together the warm water, yeast, and sugar. Let stand until the mixture starts to foam, about 10 minutes.
- In a mixer, combine 1 3/4 cup flour, sugar, and salt. Stir oil into the yeast mixture. Slowly add the liquid to the dry ingredients while slowly increasing the mixers speed until fully combined. The dough should be smooth and not sticky.
- Knead the dough on a floured surface, gradually adding the remaining flour as needed to prevent the dough from sticking, until smooth, about 5-10 minutes. Form the dough into a ball.
- Apply a thin layer of olive oil to a large bowl. Place the dough into the bowl, and coat the dough ball with a small amount of olive oil. Cover and let rise in a warm place for about 1 hour, or until doubled in size.
- When ready to cook, set temperature to High and preheat, lid closed for 15 minutes.
- Place a pizza stone in the grill while it preheats.
- Punch the dough down and roll it out into a 12-inch circle on a floured surface.
- Spread the cornmeal evenly on the pizza peel. Place the dough on the pizza peel and assemble the toppings evenly in the following order: olive oil, roasted garlic, fontina, portobello, artichoke hearts, parmigiano and banana peppers.
- Carefully slide the assembled pizza from the pizza peel to the preheated pizza stone and bake until the crust is golden brown, about 10-12 minutes. Enjoy!

10.2 Braised Rabbit Stew
Ingredients:

- 1 (3 Lb.) Rabbit
- 2 Tbsp Butter
- 1 Medium Yellow Onion, Chopped
- 2 Cloves Garlic, Minced
- 1 Carrot, Peeled, Chopped
- 1 Stalk Celery, Chopped
- 2 Tbsp Flour
- 1 Sprig Thyme
- 2 Bay Leaves
- 1 Cup Red Wine
- 4 Cups Rabbit or Chicken Stock
- Salt and Pepper, To Taste

Instructions:

- Heat 1 tablespoon olive oil in Dutch oven over medium-high heat. When the oil is hot, brown the rabbit pieces in batches until golden brown and set aside.
- Add 2 tablespoons butter to the pan and when the butter is melted add the onion, carrot and celery. Saute 10 minutes until carrots are tender and onions are translucent. Add garlic and saute 1 minute more.
- Sprinkle flour over onion mixture, stir well, and cook for 1 minute more. While stirring, pour in red wine and chicken stock and place rabbit pieces back in making sure they're covered at least 3/4 of the way. Add bay leaves and thyme and bring liquid to a simmer.
- When ready to cook start the Traeger grill on smoke with the lid open until fire is established (4-5 minutes). Set the temperature to 300 degrees F and preheat, lid closed 10-15 minutes.
- Cover and transfer to the grill. Cook for 2 hours or until the rabbit is completely tender and pulls away from the bone. Top with some chopped parsley and serve with crusty bread. Enjoy!

10.3 Grilled Duck Breasts
Ingredients:

- 4 (6 Oz) Boneless Duck Breasts
- 1/4 Cup Traeger Big Game Rub

Instructions:

- Using a sharp knife, score the skin of the duck so it has a 1/4-inch diamond pattern.
- Season both sides of the duck with Traeger Big Game Rub.
- When ready to cook, set temperature to High and preheat, lid closed for 15 minutes.
- Place the duck breasts, skin side down, on the grate. Close the lid and cook for 15-20 minutes, or the internal temperature reaches 130-135°F (for medium rare) when an instant read thermometer is inserted into the thickest part of the breast.
- Remove from grill and allow to rest for 5 minutes. Slice against the grain and serve in thick slices. Enjoy!

10.4 Smoked Dry Rubbed Baby Back Ribs
Ingredients:

- 1/4 Cup Dark Brown Sugar
- 1/4 Cup Sea Salt
- 1/4 Cup Pimento (Spanish Smoked Paprika)
- 2 Tbsp Black Pepper
- 2 Tsp Granulated Onion
- 2 Tsp Granulated Garlic
- 1 Tsp Ground Cumin
- 1/2 Tsp Cinnamon
- 1/4 Tsp Ground Nutmeg
- Baby Back Ribs:
- 4 Racks (8 To 10 Lbs. Total) Baby Back Ribs
- 2 Cups Traeger Qu BBQ Sauce

Instructions:

- For the rub, combine all the rub ingredients in a small bowl and whisk to mix.
- If your butcher has not already done so, remove the thin silver skin from the bone-side of the ribs by working the tip of a butter knife or screwdriver underneath the membrane over a middle bone. Use paper towels to get a firm grip, then pull the membrane off.
- Sprinkle the rub over both sides of the ribs. Gently pat the seasonings onto the meat, but do not rub vigorously. You will need about 1-1/2 tablespoons of rub for each side.
- When ready to cook, start the Traeger grill on Smoke with the lid open until the fire is established (4 to 5 minutes). Set the temperature to 250 degrees F and preheat, lid closed, for 15 minutes.
- Place the ribs bone-side down on the grill grate. Smoke the ribs until browned, very tender, and the meat has shrunk back from the ends of the rib bones by 1/4-1/2 inch, about 3-1/2 to 4-1/2 hours.

- Remove the ribs from the grill grate and let rest. Increase the temperature of the Traeger to 375 degrees F and allow to preheat.
- Brush the ribs with Traeger Qu BBQ Sauce. Grill for 6 to 8 minutes per side, or until the sauce has set.
- Cut each rack into halves or individual ribs for serving. Enjoy

CHAPTER 11: TRICKS, TIPS, TOOLS & COOKING TIME

11.1 Tools
Here are some accessories that I own and use to make my cooking experiences easier and more enjoyable.

- DIGITAL MEAT THERMOMETER—I cannot stress the importance of a good digital thermometer.
- SET OF KNIVES AND SCISSORS—Make sure you have a great set of sharp knives to use on raw and cooked meats.
- FLAME ZONE, OPEN FLAME TECHNOLOGY, DIRECT FLAME —Many wood pellet smoker-grill manufacturers now provide the technology for direct-flame grilling
- SEARING GRATES—There are different types of searing grates available depending on your unit.
- CHICKEN LEG/WING HANGER—Simply the best way to smoke/cook chicken legs and/or wings to perfection is with these hangers
- RIB RACK—A rib rack allows you to cook four to eight slabs of St. Louis– style, baby back, or spare ribs at one time
- TEFLON-COATED FIBERGLASS MATS—These indirect cooking mats keep food from sticking to grill grates and allow for easy cleanup
- BARBECUE INSULATED GLOVES—I use light, flexible insulated rubber gloves to protect my hands while handling and removing food directly from the grill, and pulling hot pork butts.
- MEAT SLICER—For precise meat slicing I use a 7-inch-blade meat slicer to eliminate the time-consuming process of slicing food by hand. For example, it works great to thinly slice tri-tip roasts for exquisite tri-tip sandwiches
- NONSTICK GRILLING TRAY—Great for grilling, roasting, or baking items like vegetables, fish, and small or delicate foods. Cleans easily with soap and water.
- PIZZA PADDLE—Your wood pellet smoker-grill cooks crispy, hot, delicious take-and-bake pizzas or made-from-scratch pies
- PIG TAIL FOOD FLIPPER—This tapered shaft has a sharp, spiral snare at the tip designed to lightly pierce the edge of any food to flip or move without trouble. Use it for steaks, chops, ribs, chicken, etc.

11.2 Cooking Tips & Tricks
Following are the cooking tips and tricks in wood pallet smoker grill.

11.2.1 Quality Meat and Seasonings
Don't overlook your friendly neighborhood butcher shop for great and custom cuts of meats, poultry, and sausages, as well as wonderful rubs, seasonings, and barbecue sauces.

11.2.2 FTC
A number of my recipes call for FTC resting the meat. This important acronym stands for "Foil–Towel–Cooler" and is a common method used for holding and/or resting cooked meats, such as pork butts, brisket, and turkey, in order to redistribute the juices into the meat. It produces a moist and tender finished product. Pitmasters, professionals, caterers, and restaurants use industrial units like a Cambro, for example, to achieve these results. FTC is lovingly referred to as the poor man's Cambro.

11.2.3 USDA Minimum Internal Temperatures
Cook all food to these minimum internal temperatures as measured with a digital food thermometer before removing from the heat source. You may choose to cook to higher temperatures for reasons of personal preference.

11.2.4 Indirect and Direct Grill Setup
All wood pellet smoker-grills are designed primarily for indirect cooking. Indirect cooking uses deflected heat to cook more slowly and evenly. As mentioned before, the heat deflector is a stainless-steel plate that sits above the firepot.

11.2.5 Recommended Wood Pellet Flavors
The wood pellets I recommend are just that, a recommendation. When you see multiple pellet recommendations my preferred pellet flavor for that recipe is always listed first. If you have another flavor profile you would like to accomplish, feel free to substitute it.

11.2.6 Prepping for The Grill
The prep section is all the work you do before bringing the food to the grill. The number one priority in the prep cycle is planning ahead. Give yourself plenty of time, read the recipe, and research any step or procedure you might have questions about.

11.2.7 Cooking Times
Cooking times in this book are given for planning purposes and can vary depending on what type of grill you have or what temperature your meat started at. Always determine the cooking time by the internal temperature reading of your food and not the cook time I have provided.

11.2.8 Preheating
Times for preheating your wood pellet smoker-grill may vary due to manufacturer-dependent startup procedures. The key is to run a few tests and know your grill.

11.2.9 Thawing Food
In order to be safe and prevent illness, always thaw food in the refrigerator; submerge it in cold water, changing the water every 30 minutes making sure the food stays submerged; or use the defrost setting in a microwave. Do not thaw your frozen food on the countertop.

11.2.10 Internal Temperature
Always cook to internal temperatures preferably using a digital instant-read thermometer like a Thermapen or equivalent unit. Probe thermometers should be inserted before placing the protein on the grill and should be placed in the thickest part of the meat, not touching the bone.

The Ultimate Traeger Grill Smoker Cookbook

The Complete How-To Cookbook for Your Wood Pellet Grill and Smoker, with 200 Flavorful Recipes Plus Tips and Techniques for Beginners and Advanced Pitmasters

PETER DEVON

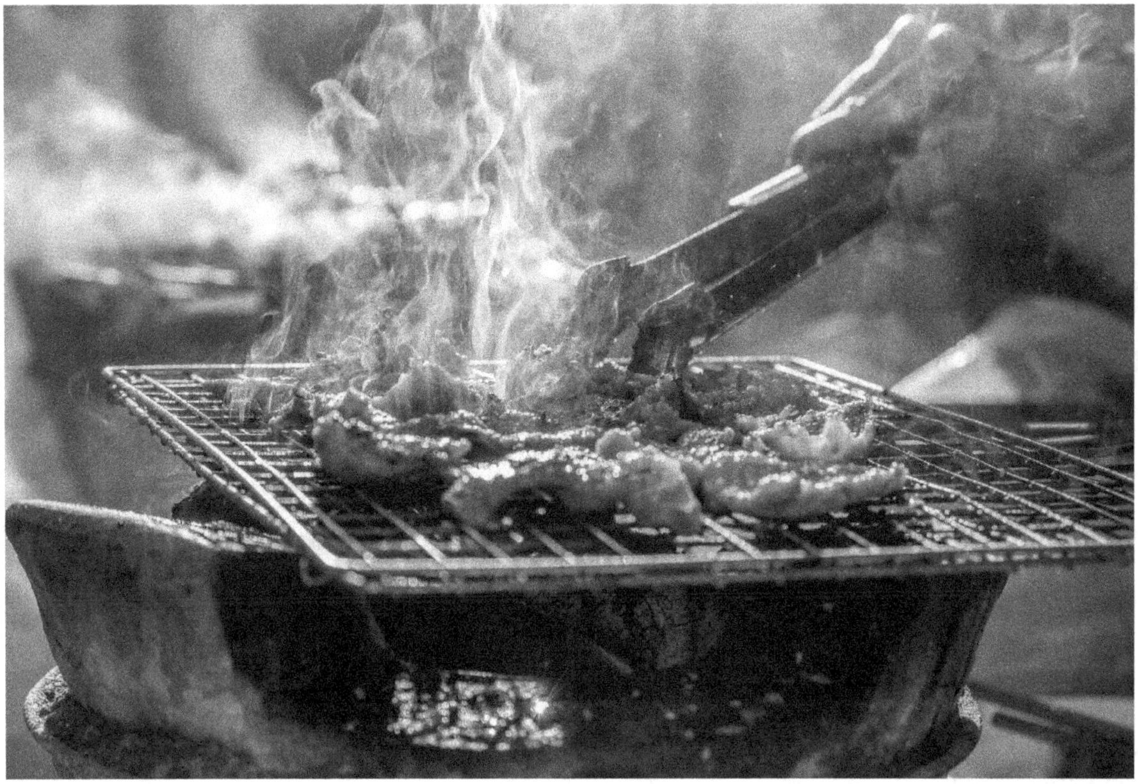

Chapter 1: Introduction

If you like to eat barbecue on a summer night and linger on the mouthwatering tang of the best-smoked burgers, spare ribs, or timber fried noodles afterward, Traeger Grill s is the correct location for you. There's the north run of the mill roughly Traeger Grill s. It's always been recognized among the very best on earth with its sumptuous al fresco Traeger Grill systems. They don't use charcoal or gas to supply better and healthy choices by applying indirect heat in preparing meals. As opposed to utilizing propane or charcoal, Traeger Grill s utilizes a quarter-inch wood pellet that looks a good deal like giant horse pills and may quickly and burn approximately 8500 BTUs per pound produce their beef, vegetables, and fish hot and packed with flavor. A particular high temperature is required to cook the hamburgers and hotdogs perfectly. On the flip side, cooking varied meals like fish, poultry, brisket, and poultry entails a suitable method in supervising the warmth to prevent undercook food.

What's more, Traeger Grill s showcase direct and safe means of the cook. Throughout indirect cook, the food is split out of the fire us a barrier. Accord to experts, cook meals not directly produce flexibility as it offers a person the capability to correct or place in timber to accommodate an individual's flavor of meals. By comparison, cook meals directly utilize no obstacles so that it may lead to overcooked food. Direct Traeger Grill can cause burn and charr of meals, which makes it unhealthy to consume and may result in undesirable health issues. The conversion from amino acids into carcinogens cancer-because chemicals may happen. This is precisely what makes Traeger Grill s distinctive and different. The Traeger pellet Traeger Grill s is an ideal option if you would like to invest quality time with your nearest and dearest and revel in flavorsome food. These Traeger Grill s is made to offer a healthful and secure alternative in cook since it utilizes natural wood pellets rather than charcoal or gas.

Additionally, it uses indirect heat when cooked to prevent charred food, leading to cancer or injury to our body and reducing the number of fats from the meals while creating the superb smoky tang. With it, you do not need to be bothered about the health hazard and mess. Moreover, its automated system makes these users friendly and convenient. You do not need to devote a good deal of time view over the Traeger Grill; instead, you have to begin the Traeger Grill and place the necessary temperature to cook your meals.

Purchasing Guide for a Traeger Grill

While purchase a Traeger Grill, a considerable portion of your choice will depend upon your budget and what you are able. Just remember that based on how many times you utilize your Traeger, you will also have to devote a couple of hundred dollars per year, or even more, for wood pellets to run your Traeger Grill. How many folks do you expect to cook? The number of people may decide how large of a barbecue you purchase. For a household of two adults and two children, or much less, I believe that you can handle any of the more significant sized Traeger Grill s. For larger families or households with older kids that consume more, the larger Traeger Grill dimensions are likely a much better match since you're able to manage more meals simultaneously. Also, think about where you anticipate placing your Traeger Grill. You may be fortunate enough to have a condominium that permits Traeger Grill son balconies. However, your patio may only have sufficient room to accommodate a giant-sized Traeger Grill. Traeger has made this choice an easy one for you to browse since they have included the Traeger Grill capability right in the title of every Traeger Grill. The number after the Traeger Grill version consistently indicates the size of this Traeger Grill capability in square inches.

To put it differently, the Ironwood 880 includes 880 square inches of the Traeger Grill area. The Guru 780 contains 780 square inches of the Traeger Grill area. The Timberline 1300 includes 1300 square inches of the Traeger Grill area. Remember, the larger the Traeger Grill, the longer pellets it will have to heat it. Consequently, if you believe you're merely likely to be cook for two or three people regularly, you may be west cash on pellets seek to warm up a giant Traeger Grill.

On the contrary, it may be a better choice to obtain the Traeger Grill and apply the sav s towards more pellets. In my view, this is among the most significant factors as it is mostly going to ascertain what size and features you want. If you seek to throw a block party or cookout with different racks of ribs, pork butts, or large briskets, then a larger Traeger Grill more inner property is best to accommodate the more oversized format of those cuts of beef. Each of the series includes two Traeger Grill dimensions: a bigger one and a bigger one. The Traeger Grill s in each line are always cheaper than the larger ones, as anticipated. More about the detailed comparisons under. It is essential to understand that every Traeger essentially works the same. They use the power to burn 100% organic timber pellets that are engineered. There's not any gas, natural gas, or charcoal included. All you will need is access to an electric socket and Traeger-brand wood pellets. Unlike many traditional Traeger Grill s, Traeger utilizes indirect heat for cook meals (no direct heat or flame-to-food cook). The fire pit has a heated pole and little fan. Since the pellets get warm from the bar, the enthusiast introduces oxygen along with the pellets glow. Above it's the greased pan, which grabs any drip s that drop while the food cooks, and transmits it to some skillet or bucket.

The simplest way to understand that a Traeger would be to consider it as an outside convection oven with Traeger Grill, smoke, Traeger Grill, and back abilities. It's by far the most versatile and user-friendly barbecue I've ever cooked with. The Pro Series Traeger Grill s will be the most economical. The Timberline is the costliest, and also, the Ironwood is someplace in between. You are purchasing a Traeger Grill is sort of like buying a vehicle. You may buy the baseline version, which includes regular features, the midline version with a sunroof and leather chairs, or even the fully-loaded variant that accompanies each of the above and a 21-speaker sound system, 20" chrome rims, along with a larger engine. Each update includes a cost. If you only have the budget for the entry Professional Str or top-of-the-line Timberline, I honestly think You're making a Superb decision purchase a Traeger.

Tips for Maintaining Your Traeger Grill

When triggered, creosote makes a scorching flame. Airborne dust particles will undergo the cook room, and a few of these airborne contaminants will collect on the flue liner, very similar to creosote, which might be conducive to some flame. The smokestack exhaust should be inspected at least two times per year to ascertain when a creosote or grease buildup has happened. Additionally, grease drip s in the meals will fall on the dirt drain pan and be emptied to the dirt drain and then from the Traeger Grill throughout the dust drain tube to accumulate in the skillet. Grease will collect in everyone these locations. The dirt drain, the dirt drain tube, and the dust bucket ought to be inspected at least two times per year for grease buildup signs. Once creosote or grease has been collected, it should be eliminated to decrease fire probability. Remove (unscrew) the chimney cap assembly on the surface of the flue pipe. When the chimney cap assembly was eliminated, it may be washed us warm, soapy water with a biodegradable degreaser. Scrape the creosote and dirt accumulation from the interior of the horizontal and vertical segments of the flue pipe with a rigid, nonmetallic instrument. A wooden paint stir rod, by way of instance, would function for this particular undertaking. When the creosote and dirt residue have been loosened in the flue pipe liner, a lot of it could be eliminated with paper towels or disposable rags. Don't spray water or liquid cleansers on the interior of your Traeger Grill. When the flue pipe was cleaned, then replace the chimney cap assembly.

Accumulated grease is simpler to wash off when the Traeger Grill is still warm--not hot. Take care not to burn off. Gently wash out the dirt from this V-shaped dirt drain and grease drain tube. If an excessive amount of grease is permitted to accumulate from the V-shaped grease drain or plug in the dirt drain tub, a grease fire can result. We recommend clean these places regularly. Eliminate the porcelain-coated Traeger Grill grates along with the dirt drain pan. This will give access to this V-shaped grease drain and grease drain tube opens within the Traeger Grill. Scrape the dirt accumulation from within the conical dirt drain and grease drain tube with a rigid, nonmetallic instrument. Many of this loosened dirt can be pushed through the dirt drain tube and slip into the dirt bucket. Wipe up remaining dirt residue with paper towels or disposable rags. Paper towels or disposable rags may also be used to wash some of the dirt from the Grill's inside surfaces inside surfaces. Line your earth bucket us aluminum foil for simple cleanup. Empty is sometimes based on the quantity of usage. Change the aluminum foil onto the dirt drain pan regularly (sometimes after every use, determined by which has been cooked).

Clean Your Traeger Grill

A Traeger Grill was designed to continue provided that you keep and run it securely continuously. What's more, you always have to wash it regularly to get rid of the build-up of carbon and dirt accumulation. Nobody would like to taste rancid dirt or rancid carbon in their majestically cooked legumes or fish kebabs. Whenever dirt burns, it generates acrid smoke, which can mess up your food. Before you cook, you have to do some cleanup to maintain your Traeger Grill or Traeger Grill is act in a great state, prevent off-flavors, and prolong your stove's life span. Then, the system requires maintenance and comprehensive cleanup. Should you always use that, then you want to do a thorough clean three or four times annually before story it to get winter? These hints below will direct you on how to wash a Traeger Grill efficiently. Spray the dirt catch bucket utilize vegetable spray once you're prepared to drain it. Afterward, the drip s will slip out easily. Take a few paper towels so that you can swab the inside of your bucket.

Drain the dirt once the weather is warm on a more regular basis. Therefore, it doesn't turn rancid. Or place into a cottage cheese container and then toss it out as necessary. The simplest way of clean your ceramic coated grids would be for one to have a bit of aluminum foil and rub it over the grids. Be careful not to burn yourself! Take advantage of a long sleeve forehead mitt so you can guard your hand and forearm. Vacuum outside your pellet ash from around and in the firepot and underside of your cook room. It is possible to use a vegetable brush to remove built a scale onto the interior of your Traeger Grill. The simplest way of massive cleans the cook grids will be to set them within the self-clean oven and then turn the knob to begin the cleanup. Both the range and cook grids will be sterile without have a great deal of elbow grease. This is very helpful when the cook grids are encrusted with the residue of meals. Another way of clean the cook grids is by merely putting them in an extreme yard debris bag. You include one-half cup of ammonia and then seal the bag shut. Lay the cook grids level immediately. Eliminate the grids the following day, thoroughly rinse with warm water, and they'll be fine and very tidy. The ammonia helps to dissolve the dirt on the cook grids. If you're experiencing a stainless steel Traeger Grill, then never forget to dust off the Traeger Grill before you begin to cook. It is possible to use a moist cloth to conduct this job. Otherwise, the dirt will cook in the metal and only discolor it. Be sure the foil is closely wrapped around the borders to help maintain even airflow.

Chapter 2: Beef & Lamb Recipes

Flank Steak with Tomato Sauce Marinated
Ingredients

- 1 Tablespoon Fresh Chopped Rosemary
- 1 Teaspoon Salt
- ½ Teaspoon Freshly Ground Pepper
- 1 Medium Tomato
- 1 Shallot
- 60 ml Red Wine Vinegar
- 2 Tablespoons Fresh Chopped Marjoram
- 680 Grams of Flank Steak

Instructions

- In a blender put the tomato, shallot (which have both been chopped), the marjoram, rosemary, salt and pepper. Blend until they form a smooth paste and set aside covered in the refrigerator. If there is any of the puree remain in the blender scrape it out into a sealable plastic bag into which you then put the steak.
- Make sure that you spend time move the steak around in the bag so that it is all coated in the puree. Once all the steak has been coated you now place it in the bag into the refrigerator and leave it to marinate for between 4 and 24 hours. The longer you leave the meat marinate in the puree the more flavor it will take on. Once the allotted time has passed you should now get the barbecue heated up and set the Traeger Grill above the heat at a height that it cooks the meat on a medium heat.
- Also make sure that you oil the rack first. Once the barbecue is heated up enough you should Traeger Grill the steaks for between 4 to 5 minutes per side if you want yours medium rare or 6 to 7 minutes if you want yours to be medium. You should only turn the steaks one makes sure that you brash the side that is already cooked with some of the sauce you reserved earlier. As soon as the second side of the steak has been cooked you should turn it over again and brush it with more of the puree and then remove from the heat and place on a clean plate.
- Now allow it to rest for 5 minutes before then thinly cut the steak crosswise. Before serve you should spoon on the rest of the puree.

Grilled Steak with Marinated Wine
Ingredients

- 1 Large Shallot (Finely Chopped)
- 1 Teaspoon Worcestershire Sauce
- 450 Gram Skirt Steak (Which has been trimmed and cut into 4 pieces)
- ½ Teaspoon Freshly Ground Pepper
- 120ml Reduced Sodium Beef or Chicken Broth
- 3 Tablespoons Whiskey
- 1 Teaspoon Freshly Chopped Thyme
- 3 Tablespoons Dijon Mustard
- 2 Tablespoons Light Brown Sugar
- ¼ Teaspoon Salt

Instructions

- Preheat your barbecue to a medium high heat. Whilst the barbecue is heat up you can prepare the sauce. To do this you need to combine in a saucepan the whiskey, mustard, brown sugar, shallot, thyme and Worcestershire sauce.
- Mix all these Ingredients to the boil then reduce the heat so that a lively simmer is maintained. It is important that you stir this sauce frequently to prevent it stick to the sides of the saucepan and burn Keep it simmer for around 6 to 10 minutes until it has been reduced down by about half.
- Then remove from the heat. Now you need to cook the steaks on the barbecue. But before you do sprinkle both sides with the salt and pepper. If you want yours to be medium you should cook each steak for between 1.5 and 3 minutes on each side. However, you should cook them for less time if you want yours to be medium rare. Once they have been cooked for the recommended about of time remove them from the Traeger Grill and let them rest for 5 minutes before serve with the sauce.

Beef Shoulder Tenders Marinated Chimichurri Sauce
Ingredients

- 1 teaspoon dried red pepper flakes, or more to taste
- 1/4 cup red wine vinegar
- Salt and freshly ground black pepper to taste
- Traeger Beef Rub, or coarse salt and freshly ground black pepper
- 1/4 cup fresh parsley leaves, coarsely chopped
- 1/2 cup extra-virgin olive oil
- 2 beef shoulder tenders, 10 to 12 ounces each
- 3 cloves garlic, coarsely chopped
- 2 teaspoons dried oregano

Instructions

- Season the shoulder tenders with Traeger Beef Rub and set aside. Make the chimichurri: In a blender jar or small food processor, combine the parsley, garlic, oregano, dried red pepper flakes, and red wine vinegar. Pulse until blended.
- Add salt and pepper to taste. Let the mixture sit for 20 minutes for the flavors to develop. Then slowly blend in the olive oil. When ready to cook, start the Traeger Grill on Smoke with the lid open until the fire is established (4 to 5 minutes). Set the temperature to 450 degrees F (High) and preheat, lid closed, for 10 to 15 minutes.
- Arrange the shoulder tenders on the Traeger Grill grate. Turn after 10 minutes to put Traeger Grill marks on the other side. Traeger Grill to the desired degree of doneness, 5 to 10 minutes more for medium-rare (135 degrees F on an instant read meat thermometer). Transfer the meat to a cut board and let it rest for 3 minutes. Carve it on a diagonal into slices 3/4-inch thick. If desired, pour some of the chimichurri over the meat and serve the rest of the sauce on the side. Or serve the sauce separately.

Traeger Grill Beef Balsamic Steak
Ingredients

- 1 Small Onion (minced)
- 2 Tablespoons Worcestershire Sauce
- 1 Tablespoon Dijon Mustard
- 2 Gloves Garlic (minced)
- 900gram Sirloin Steak (Should be about an inch thick)
- 240ml Water
- 120ml Soy Sauce

- 2 Tablespoons Balsamic Vinegar
- ¼ Teaspoon Hot Sauce

Instructions

- Please the steak either into a glass dish or a bag that is sealable. Now combine the rest of the Ingredients above in a bowl or a jug and whisk thoroughly. Once you have combined all the Ingredients above together you then pour of the steak and leave to marinate for between 1 and 12 hours.
- When you are ready to cook the steak, you should get your barbecue heated up and cook it over a medium to high heat.
- When the barbecue is at the right temperature you should remove the steak from the marinade and place it on the Traeger Grill cook it on each side for between 5 and 7 minutes if you like it medium. Any leftover marinade should be discarded and once the steak is cooked to the way you or your guests like it you can now remove it from the heat and serve.

Beef Strip Steak with Ground Pepper

Ingredients

- 4 Strip Steaks,
- Kosher or Sea Salt
- Freshly Ground Pepper
- 1 Inch Thick (About 12 Ounces Each)
- Extra-Virgin Olive Oil

Instructions

- Prepare a hot fire in a charcoal Traeger Grill or preheat a gas Traeger Grill on high. Remove the steaks from the refrigerator 20 to 30 minutes before Traeger Grill and place them on a large, rimmed back sheet. Rub the steaks on both sides with olive oil. Liberally season the steaks on both sides with salt and pepper.
- Oil the Traeger Grill grate. Place the steaks directly over the hot fire. Traeger Grill the steaks on one side, 4 minutes for rare or 6 minutes for medium-rare.
- Turn and cook for 4 minutes more, or until an instant-read thermometer registers 120°F for rare or 130° to 135°F for medium-rare. Remove the steaks from the Traeger Grill and let rest for 5 minutes before serve.

Indian Pot Chuck Roast

Ingredients

- 1 large onion, peeled and coarsely chopped
- 2 cloves garlic, minced
- 1 cup beef broth
- 3- to 4-pound boneless chuck roast
- 1 teaspoon dried oregano, preferably Mexican
- 1 teaspoon cumin
- Traeger Fajita Rub, or salt
- 2 tablespoons oil
- 1 10-ounce can dice tomatoes with green chiles
- 2 teaspoons chile powder, or more to taste
- freshly ground black pepper

Instructions

- Generously season the roast on all sides with the Traeger Fajita Rub. Heat a large skillet over medium-high heat. Add the oil. When the oil shimmers, sear the roast on all sides. Transfer the roast to a lidded casserole or back   dish large enough to hold it. Reduce the heat to medium and add the onions, stir occasionally.
- Cook for 5 minutes, or until the onions begin to soften. Add the garlic and cook for 2 minutes more. Add the beef broth, stir   to scrape up the brown bits from the bottom of the pan. Then add the tomatoes, chile powder, oregano, and cumin and bra   to a simmer. Add salt and pepper to taste.
- Tip the onion-tomato mixture over the meat. Put the lid on the casserole. If us   a back   pan, cover it tightly with aluminum foil. When ready to cook, start the Traeger Grill on Smoke with the lid open until the fire is established (4 to 5 minutes). Set the temperature to 250 degrees F and preheat, lid closed, for 10 to 15 minutes.
- Put the casserole or pan on the Traeger Grill grate. Roast until the meat is very tender, 3 to 4 hours. (Be careful when lift   the casserole lid or foil as steam will escape.) Slice and serve with the tomato-onion gravy.

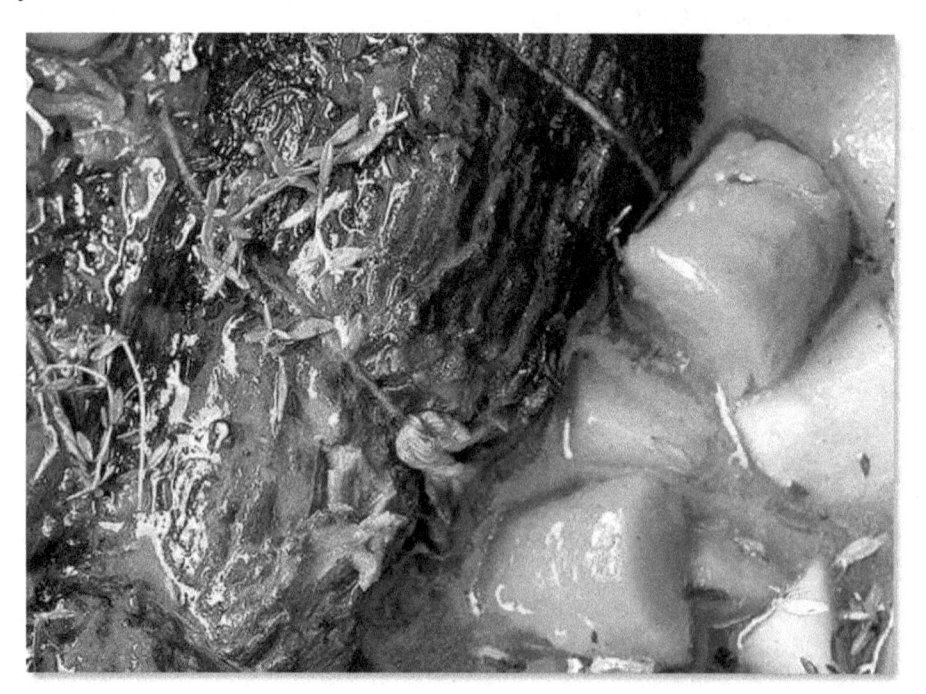

Traeger Grill Meatball Kebabs
Ingredients

- 115gram Dried Bread Crumbs
- 60ml Milk
- 75gram Parmesan Cheese (grated)
- 2 Gloves Garlic (Minced)
- 2 Tablespoons Dried Parsley
- 450gram Ground Beef
- 1 Large Onion (cut into 1-inch pieces)
- ½ Teaspoon Salt
- ½ Teaspoon Black Pepper
- 1 Large Red or Yellow Bell Pepper (cut into 1-inch pieces)
- 1 Tablespoon Dried Basil

- 2 Eggs

Instructions

- In a small bowl mix the bread crumbs and mil and let stand for 5 minutes. After five minutes squeeze the bread crumbs to help remove any excess milk and then combine this with the beef, cheese, herbs, garlic, salt, pepper and eggs and blend them together well.
- After combine all these Ingredients together, you shape the meat into around 16 to 18 meatballs. They should measure around ½ inch. Once you have created the meatballs you place them onto skewers one at the time and in between each one place a piece of onion and pepper.
- Now you need to place the kebabs on to your Traeger Grill that is lightly oiled to prevent them from stick and cook them on a medium heat for around 10 minutes. Remember to rotate them every 2 to 3 minutes to ensure that they are cooked evenly. Once they have been cooked properly you can remove them from the heat and serve.

Easy Traeger Grill Veal Chops
Ingredients

- 2 Teaspoons Freshly Chopped Thyme
- ½ Teaspoon Salt
- ½ Teaspoon Black Pepper
- 6 Veal Chops (Should be about 1 ½ inches thick)
- 3 Tablespoons Extra Virgin Olive Oil

Instructions

- Preheat heat the barbecue and cook the veal chops on a medium to high heat. Whilst the barbecue is heat up you can now prepare the chops.
- The first then you need to do is coat the veal chops in the olive oil before then sprinkle over them (both sides) the thyme, salt and pepper.
- Once you have done this you now place them on the barbecue Traeger Grill and cook on each side for between 7 and 8 minutes. Once they have been cooked for the allotted time remove from heat and serve.

Traeger Grill Beef Quesadillas
Ingredients

- 689gram Monterey Jack Cheese
- 8-10 Flour Tortillas
- 57gram Freshly Chopped Cilantro
- 229gram Sliced Roast Beef
- 1 Can Black Beans (drained and rinsed)
- 3 Tablespoons Lime Juice
- 172gram Salsa

Instructions

- Turn on the barbecue so it is heated up to the right temperature for you to then cook these quesadillas properly. Whilst the barbecue is heat up in a bowl combine the salsa, cilantro and lime juice and then set to one side.
- However, before you do set it aside mix a third of this mixture with the beans in a separate bowl. Now you are ready to start make the quesadillas.

- Onto one of the tortillas places some of the sliced roast beef and cheese before then top off with a spoonful of the beans and salsa mix. Fold the tortilla over and place on the barbecue Traeger Grill and cook for between 4 and 5 minutes turn them over once. Remove them from the heat as they turn golden brown and serve with the other salsa mix you made earlier.

Lime Salty Marinated Garlic Steaks
Ingredients

- 1 Teaspoon Garlic Powder
- 1 Teaspoon Cumin Powder
- 1 Teaspoon Freshly Ground Pepper
- 1 Teaspoon Ground Coriander
- 2 x 226gram Round Eye Steaks (measure 1 inch thick)
- Juice from 1 Lime
- 1 Teaspoon Salt

Instructions

- In a bowl combine together the lime juice, garlic powder, cumin, coriander, salt and pepper. Next trim of any fat that is visible from the steaks and place them in a plastic bag that can be resealed.
- But before close the bag up pours in the mix you made earlier ensure that the steaks have been coated well and leave in the refrigerator for 30 minutes. Whilst the steaks are marina you can start heat up the Traeger Grill ready for cook.
- Once the 30 minutes has passed you can remove the steaks from the bag and place them on the Traeger Grill. Cook each side of the steak for 4 to 5 minutes before serve them.

Traeger Grill Beef with Pepper Coat, Herb and Garlic
Ingredients

- 1 Tablespoon Salt
- 8 Large Garlic Cloves Minced
- 2 Tablespoons Freshly Minced Rosemary
- 1 Tablespoon Dried Thyme Leaves
- 2.26Kg Whole Beef Tenderloin
- 6 Tablespoons Olive Oil
- 2 Tablespoons Coarsely Ground Black Pepper

Instructions

- You need to prepare the beef first. This means trim off any excess fat with a sharp knife before fold over the thinnest part of the meat so that it is about the same thickness as the rest. Of course, if you want you could ask your butcher to do this for you. They will then tie it with butchers' twine as well. It is also important that you snip the silver skin on the meat, as this will prevent it from bow when it is cook.
- Once the meat is prepared now you need to mix the other Ingredients together and then rub these all over the meat. Place the meat in the refrigerator whilst you prepare the barbecue to cook it on.
- If you are us a charcoal Traeger Grill then build the fire on just one half of it. However, if you are us a gas barbecue turn the burners up high for 10 minutes. Before you place the meat on to the Traeger Grill make sure that you coat it well with oil us a cloth that is soaked in oil between a pair of tongs.
- Once the Traeger Grill has been coated with oil place the beef onto it and close the lid. After 5 minutes you now need to turn the meat over and repeat the same process. After the meat has been seared

(sealed) on both sides you now need to place it on to the side of the charcoal Traeger Grill which is cooler or if us a gas barbecue turn off the heat directly underneath the meat. Cook for around 45 to 60 minutes or when a thermometer is inserted the internal temperature of the beef has reached 130 degrees Fahrenheit.
- Once it has cooked for the time stated now remove it from the heat and let it stand for 15 minutes (cover it over) before car.

Beef with Chili Garlic Sauce
Ingredients

- 1 Tablespoon Honey
- 1 Glove Garlic Minced
- 1 Teaspoon Sesame Oil (Optional)
- 1 Teaspoon Chili Garlic Sauce
- 900gram Flank Steak
- 240ml Hoisin Sauce
- 2 Tablespoons Fresh Lime Juice
- ½ Teaspoon Crushed Red Pepper Flakes
- ¼ Teaspoon Freshly Ground Black Pepper
- 1 Tablespoon Toasted Sesame Seeds
- 1 Teaspoon Salt
- 1 Teaspoon Freshly Peeled and Grated Root
- 2 Chopped Green Onions

Instructions

- At an angle thinly slice the steak across the grain so you are creating slices that measure around 1.25 inches thick. Next in a bowl whisk together the hoisin sauce, lime juice, honey, garlic, salt, sesame oil, chili garlic sauce, red pepper flakes and pepper.
- Then pour into a plastic resealable bag and into this also put the steak and move it around so it is well coated by the marinade.
- Then place in the refrigerator for between 2 to 12 hours to allow the meat to become infused with the marinade. When you want to cook the steak, you should preheat your barbecue to a medium to high heat and thread the slices of meat on to skewers. If you are us wooden skewers soak them in water for around 30 minutes, as this will prevent them from burn when you place them on the Traeger Grill.
- Any leftover marinade should then be discarded. Cook the meat on the barbecue for between 2 and 3 minutes on each side depend on how you like your beef to be cooked. 2 minutes for rare to medium and 3 minutes for well done. Once the steak has been cooked sprinkle them with the toasted sesame seeds and chopped green onions before serve.

Beef Crackers Burgers
Ingredients

- 1 Egg (Lightly Beaten)
- 172gram Saltine Crackers (Crushed)
- 1 Chopped Onion
- 900gram Lean Ground Beef
- 1 Pack of Ranch Dress Mix

Instructions

- In to a bowl place the ground beef, the dress mix, the egg, crushed crackers and onion. Combine well together before then form them into hamburger patties.
- You should be making the burgers as you allow the barbecue to heat up to a high temperature. Once the burgers are ready and the barbecue has reached the desired you now place them on it. It is a good idea to coat the Traeger Grill with some oil first to prevent the burgers stick to it.
- You should cook each side of the burger for 5 minutes and when done you serve them in a sesame topped bun.

Traeger Grill Thai Beef Kebabs with Soya Sauce
Ingredients

- 1 Tablespoon Rice Wine Vinegar
- 1 Tablespoon Roasted Sesame Seeds
- 1 Small Onion (cut into 1-inch pieces)
- 120ml Vegetable or Olive Oil
- 2-3 Teaspoons Curry Powder
- 450-gram Beef Sirloin (cut into 1-inch pieces)
- 1 Bell Pepper (cut into 1-inch pieces)
- 2 Teaspoons Soy Sauce
- 2 Teaspoons Sesame Oil
- 1 Teaspoon Hot Sauce
- 1 Teaspoon Cumin Powder
- 1 Teaspoon Sugar
- 2 Gloves Minced Garlic
- 2 Teaspoons Dry Mustard
- ½ Teaspoon Salt
- ½ Teaspoon Paprika
- ¼ Teaspoon Black Pepper

Instructions

- Place the meat into a large sealable plastic bag and put to one side whilst you make the marinade. Best to place it in the refrigerator.
- To make the marinade you combine all the Ingredients above together in a bowl or jug. Once combined remove the meat from the refrigerator and pour the marinade directly into the bag and move the meat around to ensure that it is coated well.
- Replace the bag back in the refrigerator and leave it therefore for between 3 and 6 hours to allow the meat to become infused with the marinade.
- When the allotted time has passed now remove the meat from the bag discard it and the marinade. On to skewers you now place meat, onions and bell pepper alternately.
- If you are us wooden skewers then soak them in water for around 30 minutes, as this will prevent them from burn when placed on the barbecue. To cook the kebabs place them on a Traeger Grill over a medium to high heat and cook for 10 to 12 minutes, remember to turn them occasionally. Once they are cooked remove from heat and serve.

Pineapple Lamb Kebabs
Ingredients

- 680gram Boneless Lamb Cut Into 1 Inch Cubes
- 3 Bell Peppers (1 Red, 1 Yellow and 1 Green) Deseeded and Cut Into 1
- 60ml Red Wine
- 1 Teaspoon Freshly Ground Black Pepper
- ½ Teaspoon Ground Ginger (Fresh If Possible)
- 2 Tablespoons Olive Oil
- 2 Tablespoons Teriyaki Sauce
- 4 Cloves of Garlic Minced
- 2 Medium Red Onions Cut Into 1 Inch Pieces
- 8 Cap Mushrooms
- 1 Pineapple Cut Into 1 Inch Pieces
- Grated Rind Of 1 Lemon

Instructions

- In a bowl mix together all the marinade Ingredients then place to one side. Now on to skewers thread pieces of the lamb, peppers, onions, mushrooms and pineapple. Alternate between each item and if you are us wooden skewers then make sure that they have been soaked in some water for at least 30 minutes before you start make the kebabs.
- As you make each kebab place them in a shallow dish and when all have been made you can now pour over the marinade. Pour over the marinade a little at the time and turn the kebabs over to ensure that every part of them is coated in the marinade. Now cover and place in the refrigerator for at least 8 hours.
- Whilst they are in the refrigerator make sure that you turn them over occasionally to ensure that all sides of the kebabs remain coated in the marinade. After remove the lamb kebabs from the refrigerator you should start your barbecue up this will then allow time for the kebabs to reach room temperature and will help to make cook them much easier.
- You should cook them over a medium heat so place the Traeger Grill about 6 inches above the heat source. Prior to place the kebabs on the Traeger Grill apply a little olive to prevent the kebabs from stick to it. Then brush with some of the left-over marinade and cook for between 12 and 15 minutes. Whilst they are cook make sure that you turn them over at least 3 times to ensure that they cooked evenly through. Once they are cooked serve immediately to your guests.

Beef Loin Steak

Ingredients

- 2 Beef Top Loin Steaks (1 ½ Inch Thick)
- 60ml Olive Oil
- 57gram Freshly Cut Basil
- 1 Tablespoon Freshly Cut Oregano
- 1 to 2 Teaspoons of Freshly Cracked Black Pepper
- 2 Medium Red or Yellowing sweet Peppers
- 1 Tablespoon Olive Oil
- Salt and Pepper to Season
- 114gram Freshly Cut Parsley
- ½ Teaspoon Salt

Instructions

- In a bowl mix the olive oil, basil, parsley, oregano, cracked black pepper and salt to create the marinade. Before rub the mixture made up over the steak (both sides) you need to trim off any fat. Once coated in the marinade you need to place them on a clean plate (covered) and put in the refrigerator for one hour.
- Whilst the steak is in the refrigerator slice up the pepper before then coat with olive oil, salt and pepper. Put these to one side ready for when you start cook. As soon as you remove the steak from the refrigerator start up the barbecue. This will allow time for the meat to come up to room temperature make it much easier to cook.
- If you want your steaks to be medium rare cook for between 15 and 19 minutes (turn once during this time). However, if you want your steaks to be medium then cook for between 18 and 23 minutes.
- Put the peppers on to Traeger Grill around 10 minutes before you take the meat off. You should turn them once during this time to sure that they are cooked well. After the time for cook the steaks has passed remove from heat place on a clean plate sprinkle with rest of herb mixture before cover and leave to stand for 10 minutes. To serve you simple slice the steak across the grain and then top off with some of the peppers.

Thyme Rib Steak

Ingredients

- 2 Teaspoons Crushed Dried Thyme
- 2 Teaspoons Crushed Dried Oregano
- 1 ½ Teaspoons Lemon Pepper Season
- 1 Teaspoon Salt
- 4 x 285-340gram Rib Eye Steaks (Cut 1 Inch Thick)
- 1 Tablespoon Olive Oil
- 1 Tablespoon Paprika
- 1 Tablespoon Garlic Powder
- ½ to 1 Teaspoon Freshly Ground Black Pepper
- ½ to 1 Teaspoon Cayenne Pepper

Instructions

- Trim any excess fat from the steak then brush with the olive oil. Also snip the edges of the steak before coat to prevent them curl up when Traeger Grill on the barbecue. In a bowl combine the other

Ingredients together before then sprinkle over the meat evenly before then rub it into the meat with your fingers.
- Place on a clean plate and cover the steaks once both sides have been coated in the dry mixture before then place in a refrigerator for 1 hour.
- To cook the steaks, remove from refrigerator whilst the barbecue is heat up and when ready cook them directly over a medium heat and cook until they are done to the way you and your guests like to eat them.
- For steaks that are medium rare cook for between 11 and 15 minutes, turn them once. Whilst if you want yours cooked to medium then keep then on the Traeger Grill for between 14 and 18 minutes. Again, turn them over once during this time.

Red Wine Beef Kebabs
Ingredients

- 2 Tablespoons Red Wine Vinegar
- 1 Tablespoon Cook Oil (Vegetable Is Best)
- 1 Tablespoon Jamaican Jerk Season
- 2 Ripe Plantains (Peeled Then Cut Into 1 Inch Chunks)
- 340gram Boneless Sirloin Steak (Cut To 1 Inch Thick)
- 1 Medium Sized Red Onion (Cut into Wedges)

Instructions

- Trim any excess fat from the meat before then cut into 1-inch thick pieces then place to one side whilst you make the marinade for it.
- Into a bowl place the vinegar, oil and jerk season. Use a whisk to make sure that all the Ingredients have been combined well together.
- Now divide the mixture into two separate amounts and use one half of the mixture to coat the steak. Then leave the steak to marinate in this mixture whilst you prepare the plantain and onion to make the skewers. To make the kebabs you thread on to them meat, plantain and onion.
- Make sure you leave a gap of about ¼ inch between each item placed on the skewer. Then brush the onions and plantain with the other half of the marinade mixture. In order to cook the kebabs, you place them directly over the coals or turn the burners down to a medium heat and Traeger Grill for between 12 and 15 minutes. It is important that you turn the kebabs occasionally to ensure that they are cooked evenly.

Pearl Continental Barbecued Steak
Ingredients

- 60ml Chili Sauce
- 60ml Fish Sauce
- 1 ½ Tablespoons Dark Sesame Oil
- 1 Tablespoon Freshly Grated Ginger Root
- 907gram Flank Steak
- 2 Gloves Garlic (Peeled and Crushed)

Instructions

- In to a bowl pour the chili sauce, fish sauce, sesame oil, grated Ginger root and garlic and mix well together.

- Nonwinged aside a few tablespoons of this mixture, as you will use it to baste the meat whilst it is on the barbecue.
- Next you must score the meat and then place it in a shallow dish before then pour over the remainder of the marinade you made earlier. Turn the meat over to ensure that it coated in the sauce completely.
- Then cover the meat and place in the refrigerator for no less than 3 hours. To cook the steak, you need to heat the barbecue up to a high temperature. Then just before place the meat on to the barbecue brush the Traeger Grill lightly with oil to prevent the meat from stick to it. Now Traeger Grill the meat for around 5 minutes on each side to have meat that is medium rare. Of course, if you want your meat to be cooked to medium or well-done levels then cook on each side for a little cooker.
- Whilst cook brush over some more of the marinade you put to one side. When cooked let stand for a few minutes before then serve.

Indian Rib Eye Steak
Ingredients

- 280gram Marbled Rib Eye Steak
- 2 Teaspoons Garlic Powder
- 1 Teaspoon Salt
- 1 Teaspoon Freshly Ground Black Pepper
- 700ml Cola Flavored Drink
- 950ml Barbecue Sauce
- 8 Slices Bacon

Instructions

- Score the steaks on both sides us a sharp knife so that a diamond pattern is formed. Also make cuts into the fatty areas of the steak with the tip of the knife. Nonwinged the steak with a small amount of the garlic powder, salt and pepper before then rub it into the scores you made previously.
- Do this to both sides of the steak. Now place the steak into a shallow dish and pour over them the cola flavored drink, cover and leave in the refrigerator to marinate for 4 hours. You should turn the steaks over every hour.
- Also, during the last hour of marina you should now cover the steak in a thin layer of the barbecue sauce. After the steaks have marinated for 4 hours, they are now ready to cook they should be cooked on the barbecue over a high heat. However, before you place them on the Traeger Grill make sure that it has been lightly oiled. Now cook on each side for about 4 minutes or until burnt.
- Once this has been done either reduce the heat by turn the burners down or by mov the steak to a cooler part of the barbecue. Once you have moved the heat has been reduced place on top the bacon strips close the lid and then cook each side for 10 minutes. During the last few minutes of cook again spread over a thin layer of barbecue sauce. Cook until the sauce has become dried out and created a glazed effect to the meat.

Garlic-Traeger Grill Flank Steak
Ingredients

- 1 Teaspoon Red Pepper Flakes
- ¼ Cup Hoisin Sauce
- 2 Tablespoons Plum Sauce
- 1 Flank Steak, 1¼ to 1½ Pounds, Trimmed of Fat
- 2 Teaspoons Minced Garlic

Instructions

- Prepare a hot fire in a charcoal Traeger Grill or preheat a gas Traeger Grill on high. Remove the flank steak from the refrigerator 20 to 30 minutes before Traeger Grill and place it on a large, rimmed back sheet. In a small bowl, stir together the hoisin and plum sauces, garlic, and red pepper flakes.
- Liberally rub the steak on both sides with the mixture. To create a cool zone, bank the coals to one side of the Traeger Grill or turn off one of the burners. Oil the Traeger Grill grate. Place the flank steak directly over the hot fire. Cover the Traeger Grill and sear the steak on one side for 3 to 4 minutes. Turn, re-cover, and cook for 3 minutes more. Move the flank steak to the cooler part of the Traeger Grill, cover, and Traeger Grill for about 4 minutes longer, or until an instant-read thermometer registers 120°F for rare or 130° to 135°F for medium-rare.
- Transfer the steak to a car board and let rest for 5 minutes. Cut the meat across the grain into ¼-inch-thick slices. Divide the slices evenly among warmed dinner plates and spoon any accumulated juices over the top. Serve immediately.

Garlic and Oregano Traeger Grill Strip Steak
Ingredients

- 1 Tablespoon Dried Crushed Oregano
- ¼ Teaspoon Salt
- ¼ Teaspoon Freshly Ground Pepper
- 4 Strip Steaks (1 Inch Thick)
- 3 Gloves of Garlic Minced
- 1 ½ Tablespoons Olive Oil

Instructions

- In a small bowl combine together the oil, garlic, oregano, salt and pepper then slather over the steak on both sides.
- Then place them in a dish that you cover and put in the refrigerator for 2 to 3 hours to allow the steak to become infused with the marinate.
- It is important that when cook these steaks you do so on the highest heat possible on the barbecue. Place them on the barbecue Traeger Grill and cook each site for between 6 to 8 minutes. Once both sides have been cooked remove from heat and serve.

Beef Steak with Capers, Olives, and Red Bell Peppers
Ingredients

- ¼ Teaspoon Freshly Ground Pepper; Plus, More for Season
- 3 Red Bell Peppers, Quartered, Seeded, And Defibbed
- 1 Cup Cergol Or Sicilian Green Olives, Pitted and Halved
- ¼ Cup Capers, Rinsed and Drained
- 2 Porterhouse Steaks, 1½ Inches Thick (About 1½ Pounds Each) 1 Tablespoon
- Extra-Virgin Olive Oil; Plus, More for The Rub
- Kosher or Sea Salt
- 1 Tablespoon Minced Fresh Flat-Leaf Parsley

Instructions

- Prepare a hot fire in a charcoal Traeger Grill or preheat a gas Traeger Grill on high. Remove the steaks from the refrigerator 20 to 30 minutes before Traeger Grill and place them on a large, rimmed back sheet.

- Rub the steaks on both sides with olive oil. Liberally season the steaks on both sides with salt and pepper. Place the bell peppers in a bowl and toss with just enough olive oil to coat them lightly. In another bowl, combine the olives, capers, parsley, and ¼ teaspoon freshly ground pepper. Set aside. Oil the Traeger Grill grate.
- Place the peppers directly over the hot fire. Cover the Traeger Grill and cook, turn once, until dark brown Traeger Grill marks appear and the peppers are crisp-tender, 4 to 5 minutes. Transfer the peppers to a cut board. Oil the Traeger Grill grate again and place the steaks directly over the hot fire. Traeger Grill the steaks on one side, 5 minutes for rare or 6 minutes for medium-rare. Turn and cook for 5 minutes more, or until an instant-read thermometer registers 120°F for rare or 130° to 135°F for medium-rare.
- Transfer the steaks to a car board and let rest for 5 minutes. While the steaks are rest, cut the Traeger Grill ed peppers lengthwise into ½-inch-wide strips and add to the bowl with the olives. Add 1 tablespoon olive oil and toss gently to combine.
- Arrange overlap slices of steak on warmed dinner plates or a platter, and spoon the bell pepper mixture over the top. Serve immediately.

Traeger Grill Chipotle Steak
Ingredients

- 2 Tablespoons Finely Ground Dark-Roast Coffee
- Ground Chipotle Chile For Dust
- 4 Rib-Eye Steaks, 1½ Inches Thick (About 10 Ounces Each)
- Extra-Virgin Olive Oil
- Finish Salt

Instructions

- Prepare a hot fire in a charcoal Traeger Grill or preheat a gas Traeger Grill on high. Remove the steaks from the refrigerator 20 to 30 minutes before Traeger Grill and place them on a large, rimmed back sheet. Rub the steaks on both sides with olive oil. Liberally season the steaks on both sides with the coffee and chile, lightly press the season s into the meat. Oil the Traeger Grill grate.
- Place the steaks directly over the hot fire. Traeger Grill the steaks on one side, 4 minutes for rare or 6 minutes for medium-rare. Turn and cook for 4 minutes more, or until an instant-read thermometer registers 120°F for rare or 130° to 135°F for medium-rare. Remove the steaks from the Traeger Grill and let rest for 5 minutes. Sprinkle the steaks generously with fleur de sell just before serve.

Skirt Steak with Garlic
Ingredients

- Freshly Ground Pepper
- 2 Large Cloves Garlic
- ¼ Cup Fresh Lemon Juice
- ½ Cup Extra-Virgin Olive Oil
- 1 Teaspoon Red Pepper Flakes
- ½ Teaspoon Ground Cumin
- ½ Teaspoon Kosher or Sea Salt
- 2 To 2½ Pounds Skirt Steak, Trimmed of Excess Fat
- 2 Tablespoons Extra-Virgin Olive Oil
- 2 Large Cloves Garlic, Minced
- Kosher or Sea Salt

- ½ Teaspoon Sugar
- 1 Cup Packed Fresh Flat-Leaf Parsley Leaves

Instructions

- Prepare a hot fire in a charcoal Traeger Grill or preheat a gas Traeger Grill on high. Remove the steaks from the refrigerator 20 to 30 minutes before Traeger Grill and place them on a large, rimmed back sheet. In a small bowl, combine the 2 tablespoons olive oil and the garlic. Rub the steaks on both sides with the mixture.
- Lightly season the steaks on both sides with salt and pepper. While the Traeger Grill is heat, make the chimichurri: In a food processor fitted with the metal blade, combine the garlic, red pepper flakes, cumin, ½ teaspoon salt, and sugar and process until the garlic is minced. Add the parsley and lemon juice and pulse until the parsley is finely chopped. With the machine run, pour the ½ cup olive oil through the feed tube and process until the sauce is well blended. Set aside. Oil the Traeger Grill grate.
- Place the steaks directly over the hot fire. Traeger Grill the steaks on one side until nicely seared, about 2 minutes for rare and 3 minutes for medium-rare. Turn and cook until seared, 2 to 3 minutes more. Skirt steaks are too thin to yield an accurate read with an instant-read thermometer. Instead, cut into the steak at its thickest part to check for doneness. Transfer the steaks to a car board and let rest for 5 minutes.
- Cut the meat across the grain into ¼-inch-thick slices. Arrange overlap slices of steak on warmed dinner plates or a platter, and spoon any accumulated juices over the top. Spoon about half of the chimichurri over the meat, and place the rest in a bowl for pass. Serve immediately.

Traeger Grill Potatoes with Blue Cheese Sauce
Ingredients

- Sea Salt
- Freshly Ground Pepper
- Traeger Grill Potatoes
- Crumbled Blue Cheese Sauce
- 2 To 2½ Pounds Skirt Steak, Trimmed of Excess Fat
- 2 Tablespoons Extra-Virgin Olive Oil
- 2 Large Cloves Garlic, Minced

Instructions

- Prepare a hot fire in a charcoal Traeger Grill or preheat a gas Traeger Grill on high. Ten minutes after the coals are lit, bank the coals to one side or turn one of the burners too low to create a cool zone. Remove the steaks from the refrigerator 20 to 30 minutes before Traeger Grill and place them on a large, rimmed back sheet.
- In a small bowl, combine the olive oil and garlic. Rub the steaks on both sides with the mixture. Lightly season the steaks on both sides with salt and pepper.
- While the Traeger Grill is heat, put the potatoes on to cook (see headnote) and make the blue cheese sauce. Oil the Traeger Grill grate. Place the steaks directly over the hot fire. Traeger Grill the steaks on one side until nicely seared, about 2 minutes for rare and 3 minutes for medium-rare. Turn and cook until seared, 2 to 3 minutes more. Skirt steaks are too thin to yield an accurate read with an instant-read thermometer. Instead, cut into the steak at its thickest part to check for doneness. Transfer the steaks to a car board and let rest for 5 minutes.
- Cut the meat across the grain into ¼-inch-thick slices. Arrange overlap slices of steak on warmed dinner plates or a platter, and spoon any accumulated juices over the top. Serve the roasted potatoes

on the side, spoon   about half of the blue cheese sauce over the potatoes. Place the rest of the sauce in a bowl for pass. Serve immediately.

Traeger Grilled Onions Steaks
Ingredients

- 1½ Tablespoons Balsamic Vinegar
- 1½ Tablespoons Worcestershire Sauce
- 1 Tablespoon Extra-Virgin Olive Oil
- 1¼ to 1½ Pounds Hanger Steak, Trimmed of Fat
- 1½ Tablespoons Soy Sauce
- 1 Teaspoon Coarsely Ground Pepper
- Walla Walla Sweet Onions

Instructions

- Prepare a hot fire in a charcoal Traeger Grill or preheat a gas Traeger Grill on high. Remove the steaks from the refrigerator 20 to 30 minutes before Traeger Grill and place them in a back   dish just large enough to hold them. In a small bowl, stir together the soy sauce, vinegar, Worcestershire sauce, olive oil, and pepper. Pour the marinade over the steaks and turn to coat both sides.
- While the Traeger Grill is heat, prepare the onions. Oil the Traeger Grill grate. Place the steaks directly over the hot fire.
- Traeger Grill the steaks on one side until nicely seared, 3 minutes for rare or 4 minutes for medium-rare. Turn and cook until seared, 3 to 4 minutes more, or until an instant-read thermometer registers 120°F for rare or 130° to 135°F for medium-rare.
- Transfer the steaks to a car board and let rest for 5 minutes. While the steaks are rest, Traeger Grill the onions. Cut the meat across the grain into ½-inch-thick slices. Arrange overlap   slices of steak on warmed dinner plates, and spoon any accumulated juices over the top. Serve the onions on the side.

Grilled Chuck Roast
Ingredients

- 2 Teaspoons Salt
- 350ml Beer (Canned or Bottled)
- 3 Teaspoons Minced Garlic

- 3 Teaspoons Freshly Thinly Sliced Ginger Root
- 1 Onion (Finely Chopped)
- 3 Teaspoons Coarsely Ground Black Pepper

Instructions

- Into a large bowl mix together the barbecue sauce with the teriyaki sauce, beer, garlic, Ginger, onion, coarsely ground black pepper and salt. Then place the roast into the marinade just made, cover and put into the refrigerator for 6 hours. It is important that turn the meat often whilst in the refrigerator to ensure that all of it is well coated.
- You need to preheat your barbecue to allow you to cook the meat us the indirect heat method. Once the barbecue has had sufficient time to heat up now remove the meat from the marinade before then place on the barbecue Traeger Grill on thread onto a spit. You should cook the meat for around 2 hours or until the temperature inside has reached 145 degrees Fahrenheit. Whilst the meat is cook take the rest of the sauce, which you marinated the meat in originally and pour into a saucepan. Now heat it up until it starts to boil, and then cook for 5 minutes so it becomes reduced.
- You will then use this sauce for bast the meat whilst it is cook. It is important that you baste the meat regularly during the last hour of cook. Once the time for cook has elapsed remove from heat and allow to stand for 15 minutes before you then slice and serve. Remember to keep the meat covered whilst it is rest.

Buffalo Burgers with Cheese

Ingredients

- Mayonnaise
- Ketchup
- Relish
- Pickles
- 4 Sesame-Seed Hamburger Buns, Split
- 4 Lettuce Leaves
- 1 Large Tomato, Sliced
- 1 Walla Walla Or Other Sweet Onion, Cut into Paper-Thin Slices
- 1½ Pounds Ground Buffalo
- 3 Tablespoons Plus 1 Teaspoon Traeger Grill Every Day Spice Rub
- 2 Tablespoons Canola Oil
- 4 Slices Pepper Jack Cheese

Instructions

- Prepare a hot fire in a charcoal Traeger Grill or preheat a gas Traeger Grill on high. In a large bowl, combine the ground buffalo with 2 tablespoons of the spice rub, mix well. Divide into 4 equal portions, and shape each portion into a patty 1 inch thick. Pat each patty on both sides with a teaspoon of the spice rub.
- Refrigerate the patties while the Traeger Grill heats. Oil the Traeger Grill grate. Brush the burgers on both sides with the canola oil. Place the burgers directly over the hot fire and sear on one side, about 4 minutes. Turn and sear on the other side until juicy and medium-rare, about 4 minutes more.
- About a minute before the burgers are done, place a slice of cheese on top of each burger, cover the Traeger Grill, and let the cheese melt. Place the buns, cut side down, on the Traeger Grill to toast during the last minute the burgers are cook. Serve the burgers on the toasted buns with the lettuce, tomato, onion, and mayonnaise. Pass the ketchup, relish, and pickles.

Grilled Big Beef Burger with Cheese

Ingredients

- 1 Large Tomato, Sliced
- Mayonnaise
- Pickles
- 1½ Teaspoons Freshly Ground Pepper
- 4 Tablespoons Crumbled Blue Cheese
- 2 Tablespoons Canola Oil
- 4 Sesame-Seed Hamburger Buns, Split
- 4 Lettuce Leaves
- 1½ Pounds Freshly Ground Chuck
- 3 Tablespoons Grated Yellow Onion
- 1 Tablespoon Minced Fresh Thyme

Instructions

- Prepare a hot fire in a charcoal Traeger Grill or preheat a gas Traeger Grill on high. In a large bowl, combine the beef, onion, thyme, and pepper and mix thoroughly. Divide into 4 equal portions and shape each portion into a ball.
- Press your thumb into the top of a ball, make a depression about 1 inch deep. Spoon 1 tablespoon of the cheese into the depression, press the beef over the cheese to enclose it, and shape the ball into a patty 1 inch thick.
- Repeat to form 3 more patties. Refrigerate the patties while the Traeger Grill heats. Oil the Traeger Grill grate. Brush the burgers on both sides with the canola oil. Place the burgers directly over the hot fire and sear on one side, 4 to 5 minutes.
- Turn and sear on the other side until juicy and medium-rare, about 4 minutes more. Place the buns, cut side down, on the Traeger Grill to toast during the last minute the burgers are cook. Serve the burgers on the toasted buns with the lettuce, tomato, and mayonnaise. Pass the pickles.

Barbecued Steaks with Parsley

Ingredients

- 4 flat iron steaks, each 1/2- to 3/4-inch thick
- 2 tablespoons minced parsley
- Traeger Beef Rub, or your favorite barbecue rub

Instructions

- Season the steaks well on both sides with Traeger Beef Rub. Rub the season in with your f errs. When ready to cook, start the Traeger Grill on Smoke with the lid open until the fire is established (4 to 5 minutes).
- Set the temperature to 450 degrees F (High) and preheat, lid closed, for 10 to 15 minutes. Arrange the steaks on the Traeger Grill grate and Traeger Grill, turn once, for 8 to 10 minutes for medium-rare, or 11 to 13 minutes for medium, turn once halfway through Traeger Grill. Transfer to a platter or plates and sprinkle with parsley. Let the steaks rest 2 minutes before serve to give the juices a chance to redistribute themselves.

Traeger Grilled Beef Tenderloin

Ingredients

- Traeger Beef Rub or Prime Rib Rub, or coarse salt and freshly ground black pepper
- 1/3 cup Dijon-style mustard
- 1 teaspoon Worcestershire sauce
- 1 teaspoon dried thyme leaves or 1 tablespoon fresh thyme leaves
- 2 tablespoons extra virgin olive oil (divided use)
- 1 2- to 3-pound filet of beef, trimmed, preferably center cut

Instructions

- Heat a large skillet, preferably cast iron, on the stovetop over medium-high heat. Add one tablespoon of the olive oil to the pan. Season the meat with the Traeger Beef Rub. When the oil is shimmer, put the meat into the pan, sear it well on all sides. (Don't forget the ends: Carefully hold the meat upright with tongs.)
- Transfer the meat to a rimmed back sheet. In a small bowl, combine the mustard, thyme, Worcestershire sauce, and the remain tablespoon of olive oil and mix well. Brush or slather the mustard mixture over the outside of the filet. When ready to cook, start the Traeger Grill on Smoke with the lid open until the fire is established (4 to 5 minutes). Set the temperature to 400 degrees F and preheat, lid closed, for 10 to 15 minutes.
- Put the filet directly on the Traeger Grill grate and roast for 25 to 30 minutes, or until an instant read meat thermometer registers an internal temperature of 135 degrees F (for medium rare). Cook less time if you prefer your meat rarer than that, or more time if you like it well-done. Transfer to a cut board and let the meat rest, tented with aluminum foil, for 5 minutes before slice and serve.

Traeger Grilled Smoked Beef T-Bones

Ingredients

- Your favorite Traeger Rub, or coarse salt and freshly ground black pepper
- 4 T-bone steaks (14- to 16-ounces each), at least 1-inch thick
- 4 tablespoons butter, at room temperature

Instructions:

- Season the steaks on both sides with the Traeger Rub. When ready to cook, start the Traeger Grill on Smoke with the lid open until the fire is established (4 to 5 minutes). Arrange the steaks on the Traeger Grill grate and smoke for 30 minutes.
- Set the temperature to 450 degrees F (High), and preheat, lid closed, for 10 to 15 minutes. Cook the steaks to your desired degree of doneness, turn once, about 15 to 20 minutes for medium-rare (135 degrees F), longer if you prefer your steaks more done. Top each with a pat of butter. Let the steaks rest for 3 minutes and serve.

Traeger Grilled Prime Rib with Cream

Ingredients

- Horseradish Cream (recipe follows)
- Large roast pan with a meat rack
- One 3-to-4-pound prime rib
- Traeger Prime Rib or Beef Rub, or equal parts of kosher salt and coarsely ground black pepper
- Granulated garlic (optional)
- Butcher's str

Instructions

- Allow the roast to come to room temperature before Traeger Grill. Tie it at intervals with butcher's str. (This keeps it from separate along the inner fat line as it cooks.) Season the roast well with the Traeger Prime Rib or Beef Rub, or the salt/ pepper mixture. Sprinkle with the granulated garlic, if desired. Use your f errs to pat the season s into the meat. Place the meat rack in the roast pan; put the roast, bone-side down and uncovered, on the rack.
- When ready to cook, start the Traeger Grill on Smoke with the lid open until the fire is established (4 to 5 minutes).
- Set the temperature to 450 degrees F (High) and preheat, lid closed, for 10 to 15 minutes. Roast for 30 minutes. Reduce the temperature to 300 degrees F, and continue to cook until the internal temperature in the thickest part of the meat reads 130 degrees F (for medium-rare) as read on an instant-read meat thermometer. (Figure on roughly 18 to 20 minutes per pound total cook time.)

Traeger Grilled Brisket
Ingredients

- 1/4 cup apple cider vinegar
- 2 tablespoons Worcestershire sauce
- 1 6-pound brisket flat, trimmed
- Traeger Beef Rub, or your favorite barbecue rub
- 2 cups beef broth, beer, or cola
- Traeger Texas Spicy Barbecue Sauce, or your favorite barbecue sauce

Instructions

- Season the brisket on both sides with the Traeger Beef Rub. Make the mop sauce: In a clean spray bottle, combine the beef broth, beer, or cola with the vinegar and Worcestershire sauce. When ready to cook, start the Traeger Grill on Smoke with the lid open until the fire is established (4 to 5 minutes). Arrange the brisket fat-side up on the Traeger Grill grate and smoke for 3 to 4 hours, spray with the mop sauce every hour.
- Set the temperature to 225 degrees F and continue to cook the brisket, spray occasionally with mop sauce, until an instant-read thermometer inserted in the thickest part of the meat reads 190 to 195 degrees F. (This will likely take 4 to 6 hours more, or even longer. Be patient and don't rush the process.) Foil the meat and let it rest for 30 minutes, preferably in an insulated container lined with thick bath towels or newspapers so the meat stays hot. Slice with a sharp knife across the grain into pencil-width slices. Serve the barbecue sauce separately on the side.

Grilled Lamb Burgers
Ingredients

- 1 Garlic Clove Minced
- Cucumber Slices
- Tomato Slices
- Onion Slices
- ½ Teaspoon Crushed Dried Rosemary
- ½ Teaspoon Salt (To Taste)
- ¼ Teaspoon Freshly Ground Pepper
- 450gram Ground Lamb
- 1 Tablespoon Dijon Mustard
- 1 Tablespoon Fresh Lemon Juice
- 1 Tablespoon Minced Onion

- 4 Hamburger Rolls or Pitta Breads

Instructions

- In a bowl mix together the ground lamb, mustard, lemon juice, onion, garlic, rosemary, salt and pepper. You can of course combine these Ingredients by hand otherwise you may want to consider us a food processor. Once all the above Ingredients have been combined together you now need to divide into four equal portions and then form patties out of each one. It is important that whilst you are making these Greek burgers that you turn the barbecue on or light the coals so it is at the right temperature for you to then cook the burgers. Before you place the burgers on the Traeger Grill lightly oil its surface with some olive oil and Traeger Grill until you notice the burgers are no longer pink in color.
- On average you should expect it to take around 10 minutes for these burgers to be cooked properly. Remember to turn them over at least once. Just before you take the burgers off the Traeger Grill place the pitta breads or burger buns on it to become warmed through. Then when they are ready place the burgers on them and top with slices of cucumber, tomato and onion. You may also want to consider add a light yogurt and mint dress to them as well.

Flank Steak with Crouton Salad
Ingredients

- Kosher or Sea Salt Freshly Ground Pepper
- ½ Cup Extra-Virgin Olive Oil
- 1½ Tablespoons Fresh Lemon Juice
- 1½ Tablespoons Coarse-Grain Mustard
- 1 Flank Steak, 1¼ to 1½ Pounds, Trimmed of Fat
- 2 Tablespoons Extra-Virgin Olive Oil
- 1 Teaspoon Minced Garlic
- 1½ Tablespoons Prepared Horseradish
- 2 Tablespoons Capers, Rinsed and Drained
- 3 Cups ¾-Inch-Cubed Day-Old Baguette or Artisanal Bread, Lightly Toasted
- 2 Cups Loosely Packed Fresh Flat-Leaf Parsley Leaves
- 1 Teaspoon Freshly Ground Pepper
- ½ Teaspoon Kosher or Sea Salt
- ½ Teaspoon Sugar
- 1 Cup Baby Arugula Leaves

Instructions

- Prepare a hot fire in a charcoal Traeger Grill or preheat a gas Traeger Grill on high. Remove the flank steak from the refrigerator 20 to 30 minutes before Traeger Grill and place it on a large, rimmed back sheet. In a small bowl, combine the 2 tablespoons olive oil and the garlic. Rub the steak on both sides with the mixture and season with salt and pepper. While the Traeger Grill is heat, make the salad: In a large bowl, whisk together the ½ cup olive oil, lemon juice, mustard, horseradish, pepper, salt, and sugar. Stir in the capers and set aside. Oil the Traeger Grill grate. Place the flank steak directly over the hot fire.
- Cover the Traeger Grill and sear the steak on one side, 4 minutes for rare or 6 minutes for medium-rare. Turn, re-cover, and cook for 4 minutes more, or until an instant-read thermometer registers 120°F for rare or 130° to 135°F for medium-rare. Transfer the steak to a car board and let rest for 5

minutes. While the steak is rest, toss the salad. Give the dress a last-minute stir, then add the bread cubes, parsley, and arugula to the bowl and toss gently to mix. Cut the meat across the grain into ¼-inch-thick slices. Divide the slices evenly among warmed dinner plates and spoon any accumulated juices over the top. Arrange a mound of salad to the side of the steak or on top of the slices. Serve immediately.

Traeger Grilled Barbecued Brisket
Instructions

- 9x13-inch aluminum foil disposable pan
- Aluminum foil
- A clean spray bottles
- 1 teaspoon garlic salt
- 1/4 cup Traeger Prime Rib Rub
- 1 tablespoon ground coffee
- 1 cup cold brewed coffee
- 1 cup Texas beer
- 2 tablespoons brown sugar
- 1 tablespoon chile powder
- 1 4- to 5-pound center cut brisket flat, trimmed
- Traeger Texas Spicy Barbecue Sauce

Instructions

- Make the mop sauce: Combine the coffee, beer, brown sugar, chile powder and garlic salt in a bowl and whisk to dissolve any salt or sugar crystals. Transfer to a clean spray bottle and set aside. In a small bowl, mix the Traeger Prime Rib Rub and the ground coffee. Rub this mixture on the brisket, cover all surfaces. When ready to cook, start the Traeger Grill on Smoke with the lid open until the fire is established (4 to 5 minutes). Put the brisket directly on the Traeger Grill grate and smoke for 2 hours.
- Spray the brisket with the mop sauce and transfer to a disposable aluminum foil pan. Increase the temperature to 275 degrees F and continue to cook for 4 to 5 hours, spray every hour with the mop sauce. If at any point the brisket appears to be dry out, cover it tightly with aluminum foil. (Discontinue mop if you do this.) When done, the internal temperature of the brisket will be 185 to 190 degrees F (anything less, and your brisket will be tough). Let rest for 20 to 30 minutes before car against the grain (see Note below) into pencil-thick slices. Serve, if desired, with barbecue sauce on the side. Good accompaniments include baked beans and biscuits or cornbread.

Smoked Beef Brisket with Apricot Barbecue Sauce
Ingredients

- 1 bottle Traeger Apricot Barbecue Sauce, or your favorite fruit-based barbecue sauce
- 1/4 cup Dijon-style mustard
- 1 corned beef brisket flat, 3 to 4 pounds, with a fat cap at least ¼ inch thick

Instructions

- Remove the corned beef brisket from its package and discard the spice packet, if any. When ready to cook, start the Traeger Grill on Smoke with the lid open until the fire is established (4 to 5 minutes). Set the temperature to 275 degrees F and preheat, lid closed, for 10 to 15 minutes. Put the corned beef brisket directly on the Traeger Grill grate, fat side up, and cook for 2 hours.

- Meanwhile, combine the barbecue sauce and the mustard in a medium bowl, whisk to mix. Pour half of the barbecue sauce-mustard mixture in the bottom of a disposable aluminum foil pan. With tongs, transfer the brisket to the pan, fat-side up. Pour the remainder of the barbecue sauce-mustard mixture over the top of the brisket, us a spatula to spread the sauce evenly. Cover the pan tightly with aluminum foil. Return the brisket to the Traeger Grill and continue to cook for 2 to 3 hours, or until the brisket is tender.
- The internal temperature should be 185 degrees F on an instant-read meat thermometer. Allow the meat to rest for 15 to 20 minutes. Slice across the grain into 1/4-inch slices with a sharp knife and serve immediately. If desired, spoon some of the sauce over each serve.

Grilled Beef Jerky with Cup Soy Sauce
Ingredients

- 2 teaspoons garlic powder
- 1 teaspoon onion powder
- 1 teaspoon freshly ground black pepper
- 1/2 cup soy sauce
- 1/2 cup beer, cola, or water
- 1/4 cup Worcestershire sauce
- 2 pounds trimmed beef top or bottom round, sirloin tip, or flank steak

Instructions

- In a mix bowl, combine the soy sauce, water, Worcestershire sauce, garlic powder, onion powder, and pepper and whisk to mix. With a sharp knife, slice the beef into 1/4- inch thick slices against the grain. (This is easier if the meat is partially frozen.) Trim any fat or connective tissue. Put the beef slices in a large resealable plastic bag. Pour the soy sauce mixture over the beef, and massage the bag so that all the slices get coated with the marinade. Seal the bag and refrigerate for several hours, or overnight. When ready to cook, start the Traeger Grill on Smoke with the lid open until the fire is established (4 to 5 minutes). Remove the beef from the marinade and discard the marinade.
- Dry the beef slices between paper towels. Arrange the meat in a s le layer directly on the Traeger Grill grate. Smoke for 4 to 5 hours, or until the jerky is dry but still chewy and somewhat pliant when you bend a piece. Transfer to a resealable plastic bag while the jerky's still warm. Let the jerky rest for an hour at room temperature. Squeeze any air from the bag, and refrigerate the jerky. It will keep for several weeks.

Traeger Prime Mignons
Ingredients

- Traeger Prime Rib Rub, or coarse salt and freshly ground black pepper
- 2 filets mignons, each about 1-1/4 inch thick

Instructions

- Season the steaks with the Traeger Prime Rib Rub, pat it on with your f retypes. When ready to cook, start the Traeger Grill on Smoke with the lid open until the fire is established (4 to 5 minutes).
- Set the temperature to 450 degrees F (High) and preheat, lid closed, for 10 to 15 minutes. Arrange the steaks on the Traeger Grill grate. Cook for 7 minutes. Turn with tongs, and cook for 5 to 7 minutes more, or until the internal temperature reaches 135 degrees F on an instant-read meat thermometer inserted through the side toward the center of the steak. (Adjust the time if you prefer your meat more well-done.) Transfer to a platter or plates and let rest for 2 minutes before serve.

Style Mustard Steak
Ingredients

- 1 tablespoon Dijon-style mustard
- 1/2 onion, sliced
- 1 clove garlic, minced
- 1 flank steak, 1-1/2 to 2 pounds
- 1/2 cup vegetable oil or extra-virgin olive oil
- 1/4 cup red wine vinegar
- Traeger Beef Rub or Prime Rib Rub, or salt and freshly ground black pepper

Instructions

- In a small bowl, whisk together the oil, vinegar, and mustard. Lay the flank steak in a back dish large enough to hold it. Season the flank steak on both sides with the Traeger Beef Rub, pat the season down with your f retypes. Pour the oil mixture over it, turn to coat, then top with the onions and garlic.

- Marinate, covered with plastic wrap and refrigerated, for 4 to 8 hours, turn once. When ready to cook, start the Traeger Grill on Smoke with the lid open until the fire is established (4 to 5 minutes). Set the temperature to 450 degrees F (High) and preheat, lid closed, for 10 to 15 minutes. Lift the flank steak from the marinade (discard the marinade and solids) and pat dry with paper towels. Arrange the steak at a diagonal directly on the Traeger Grill grate. Traeger Grill for 6 minutes, then turn. Continue Traeger Grill for 6 to 8 minutes more. (The exact time will depend on the thickness of your steak.) Transfer the steak to a cut board and let rest for 5 minutes. Preseason with Traeger Beef Rub, if desired. Slice thinly on the diagonal across the grain. Serve immediately.

London Asada Marinade Broil
Ingredients

- Traeger Carne Asada Marinade, or your favorite beef marinade
- 1 2-1/2 to 3-pound beef top round shoulder

Instructions

- Put the beef and the Traeger Carne Asada Marinade in a large resealable plastic bag. Turn to coat. Refrigerate for several hours, or overnight. When ready to cook, start the Traeger Grill on Smoke with the lid open until the fire is established (4 to 5 minutes). Set the temperature to 450 degrees F (High) and preheat, lid closed, for 10 to 15 minutes.
- Remove the meat from the marinade. If desired, pour the marinade in a small saucepan and bra to a boil over high heat. Boil for two minutes, then remove from the heat. Strain, and let cool. Now you can use the marinade as a sauce. Keep warm.
- Pat the meat dry with paper towels. Put the meat on the Traeger Grill grate and Traeger Grill 8 to 10 minutes per side, turn once with tongs, or until an instant-read meat thermometer inserted into the thickest part reads 135 degrees F for rare. (Traeger Grill a few minutes longer if you prefer your London Broil medium-rare.) Let the meat rest for 3 minutes before slice thinly on a diagonal against the grain. Serve the warmed marinade as a sauce, if desired.

Barbecue Bourbon Whiskey Steak
Ingredients

- 200g Dark Brown Sugar
- 4 x 200g Rump, Fillet or Sirloin Steaks
- 240ml Bourbon Whiskey

Instructions

- You need to lightly score the surface of each steak with the tip of a sharp knife on one side (diagonally). Then place into a shallow dish with the side you have scored fac upwards. Now you must pour the bourbon over the steaks and then over the top sprinkle on the dark brown sugar before then rub it in.
- Once you have done the above you must now cover the steak up and place in the refrigerator and leave for 1 to 3 hours for the marinate to infuse into the meat. Around 15 minutes before you take the steaks out of the refrigerator you should get your barbecue go. Once the barbecue is hot enough and you have placed the Traeger Grill about 6 inches above the heat you can place the steaks on to the Traeger Grill sugar side down.
- Allow them to cook for around 4 to 5 minutes or until the sugar has caramelized. Whilst the steak is going you should baste the side of the steak that is towards you with the remain marinade before then turn it over. Just as with the previous side you should cook it again for around 4 to 5 minutes

or cook until it is done to how you or your guests like it. Once the steak is ready serve immediately with a fresh green salad.

Traeger Grilled Beef Roast in Olive Oil
Ingredients

- Traeger Beef Shake or Rub or Prime Rib Rub, or salt and coarse black pepper
- 1 beef chuck, rump, or sirloin tip roast, 3 to 3-1/2 pounds
- 2 tablespoons vegetable oil or extra-virgin olive oil
- 2 cups beef broth

Instructions

- Rub the roast on all sides with the oil and place on a rack in a roast pan, fat-side up. Season well with the Traeger Beef Shake. Pour the beef broth in the bottom of the pan. When ready to cook, start the Traeger Grill on Smoke with the lid open until the fire is established (4 to 5 minutes). Set the temperature to 450 degrees F (High) and preheat, lid closed, for 10 to 15 minutes. Cook the roast for 25 to 30 minutes, or until the outside is seared.
- Reduce the temperature to 225 degrees F and continue cook, 2 to 3 hours, or until medium-rare (135 degrees F on an instant-read meat thermometer). Let it reach 155 degrees F if you prefer your meat well-done. Tent the roast with aluminum foil and let the meat rest for 10 minutes before slice across the grain into thin slices. Serve with the pan drip s, if desired.

Beef Ribs in Barbecue Sauce
Ingredients

- Traeger Texas Spicy Barbecue Sauce, or your favorite barbecue sauce
- 2 7-bone racks beef long ribs (back ribs), 5 to 6 pounds total
- Traeger Prime Rib Rub, or your favorite barbecue rub

Instructions

- If your butcher has not already done so, remove the thin papery membrane from the bone-side of the ribs by work the tip of a butter knife or a screwdriver underneath the membrane over a middle bone. Use paper towels to get a firm grip, then tear the membrane off. Season the ribs with Traeger Prime Rib Rub.
- When ready to cook, start the Traeger Grill on Smoke with the lid open until the fire is established (4 to 5 minutes). Smoke the ribs, meat-side up, for 2 hours. Set the temperature to 225 degrees F. Continue to cook the ribs for 3 to 4 hours more, or until the meat is tender. If desired, wrap the ribs tightly in foil partway through the cook time. The last 30 minutes, carefully remove the ribs from the foil and brush them liberally with Traeger Texas Spicy Barbecue Sauce, and return to Traeger Grill. Transfer the ribs to a cut board and let them rest for a few minutes before car them into individual ribs.

Santa Maria-Style Tri-Tip with Garlic
Ingredients

- Traeger Beef Rub or 1-1/2 teaspoons each salt, freshly ground black pepper, and
- garlic powder
- 1 tri-tip roast, 1-1/2 to 2 pounds

Instructions

- Season the meat well on all sides with the Traeger Beef Rub. When ready to cook, start the Traeger Grill on Smoke with the lid open until the fire is established (4 to 5 minutes). Set the temperature to 425 degrees F and preheat, lid closed, for 10 to 15 minutes.
- Lay the tri-tip directly on the Traeger Grill grate and cook for 45 to 50 minutes. (Do not overcook or the tri-tip with be tough and dry.) Transfer to a cut board and tent with aluminum foil. Let the tri-tip rest for 15 minutes before car across the grain into broad, thin slices.

Chili-Glazed Garlic Meat
Ingredients

- 2 eggs
- 1/2 cup milk
- 2 teaspoons Worcestershire sauce
- 1/4 cup finely minced onion
- 1 tablespoon Traeger Cajun Rub, or your favorite barbecue rub
- 1 teaspoon garlic powder
- 1-1/2 pounds ground beef
- 1/2-pound ground pork
- 1 cup dried bread crumbs
- 2 whole carrots, peeled, trimmed, cut into lengths the width of your loaf pan
- 1/2 cup Traeger Chili Sauce, or your favorite chili sauce

Instructions

- In a large mix bowl, combine the ground beef, ground pork, bread crumbs, onion, Traeger Cajun Rub, and the garlic powder. In another bowl, beat the eggs lightly. Add milk and Worcestershire sauce. Add the liquid Ingredients to the meat mixture, and mix with your hands. Lay a few of the carrot pieces down in the loaf pan; the carrots will become a natural rack for the meat.
- Form the meat into a loaf shape and lay it on top of the carrots. When ready to cook, start the Traeger Grill on Smoke with the lid open until the fire is established (4 to 5 minutes). Set the temperature to 350 degrees F and preheat, lid closed, for 10 to 15 minutes. Put the loaf pan on the Traeger Grill rack. Bake the meatloaf for 50 to 60 minutes, or until the internal temperature reads 160 degrees F when read on an instant-read meat thermometer. Spread the Traeger Chili Sauce on top of the meatloaf the last 10 minutes of cook. Transfer the meatloaf to a cool rack and let cool for 10 minutes. Carefully remove it from the loaf pan. (Discard the carrots.) Slice into 1/2-inch slices for serve.

Traeger Chili Beef Short Ribs
Ingredients

- 1 large sweet onion, thinly sliced into r s
- 3 to 4 pounds boneen short ribs, or 2-1/2 pounds of boneless short ribs
- Salt
- 1 bottle Traeger Chili Barbecue Sauce, or your favorite chili sauce
- 1 cup good-quality root beer soda, such as Dr. Brown's or Hanne's, plus more as needed
- 1 tablespoon fresh thyme leaves, chopped
- Freshly ground black pepper
- • A 9x13-inch aluminum foil disposable back pan or other back pan
- Aluminum foil

Instructions

- In a medium bowl, combine the Traeger Chili Barbecue Sauce, the root beer, and the thyme leaves. Arrange the onions evenly in the bottom of the pan. Season the short ribs on all sides with salt and pepper. Lay in a s le layer on top of the onions. Pour the chili-root beer sauce evenly over the ribs.
- Cover the pan tightly with aluminum foil. When ready to cook, start the Traeger Grill on Smoke with the lid open until the fire is established (4 to 5 minutes). Set the temperature to 300 degrees F and preheat, lid closed, for 10 to 15 minutes. Put the pan of ribs on the Traeger Grill grate and cook for 2-1/2 to 3 hours, or until the ribs are tender but not fall off the bone. Add a bit more root beer to the pan if the dish doesn't seem saucy enough. Serve immediately with polenta or mashed potatoes. Short ribs render a fair amount of fat, so if it concerns you, refrigerate the ribs in the sauce overnight. The fat will have solidified on top, and can be removed and discarded before reheat the ribs.

White Vinegar Barbecued Ribs
Ingredients

- 2 tablespoons brown sugar
- 1 tablespoon granulated sugar or honey
- 2 cloves garlic, minced
- 1/2 cup soy sauce
- 1/2 cup water
- 2 tablespoons white vinegar or rice vinegar
- 1 scallion (green onion), trimmed and coarsely chopped
- 2 teaspoons sesame oil
- 1 ripe pear, peeled, cored, and coarsely chopped
- 1 1-inch piece fresh Ginger, peeled and sliced into coins
- 1 teaspoon Traeger Beef Shake, or salt
- 1-1/2 pounds crosscut beef short ribs (flanked), or see substitutions above

Instructions

- Make the marinade: Combine the soy sauce, water, vinegar, brown sugar, granulated sugar, garlic, pear, Ginger, scallion, and sesame oil in a blender and pulse several times. Lay the beef in a s le layer in a back dish and season on both sides with Traeger Beef Shake. Pour the marinade over the beef, turn the beef over to coat both sides. Cover and refrigerate for several hours, or overnight.
- When ready to cook, start the Traeger Grill on Smoke with the lid open until the fire is established (4 to 5 minutes). Set the temperature to 450 degrees F (High) and preheat, lid closed, for 10 to 15 minutes. Remove the beef from the marinade; discard marinade. Arrange the beef on the Traeger Grill grate and Traeger Grill, 2 to 3 minutes per side, or until the meat is cooked to your like. (In Korea, they prefer their short ribs well-done.) Transfer to a platter or plates and serve immediately.

Lamb Chops with Raisin Sauce
Ingredients

- 57gram Butter
- 128gram Apple Sauce
- 85gram Dark Raisins
- 1 Tablespoon Olive Oil
- 384gram Chopped Onion
- 1 Crushed Garlic Clove
- 6 Lamb Chops (Each weigh around 115gram)
- 1 Teaspoon Salt to season meat

- Sauce
- 2 Tablespoons Curry Powder
- 1 Teaspoon Dried Thyme
- ½ Lemon Seeded and Finely Chopped (Peel as Well)
- 384gram Apples Peeled, Cored and Chopped
- 85gram Golden Raisins
- 1 Tablespoon Ground Coriander
- 1 Tablespoon Ground Cumin
- 2 Teaspoons Salt to Season
- 2 Teaspoons White Pepper to Season
- 1 Tablespoon Water (If Needed)

Instructions

- In a saucepan place the butter, olive oil, onions and garlic and cook them over a medium heat until the onions have turned translucent. This should take around 8 minutes to happen. Once the onions are ready you stir in the rest of the Ingredients to make the sauce and bra the mixture to the boil. As soon as the mixture has started to boil you now need to turn the heat down and cover the saucepan and let the mixture simmer for a while. You should check the sauce regularly and stir it also to make sure that it doesn't stick to the saucepan. You will know when it is ready because it will have the consistency of apple sauce and the raisins will start to break apart.
- Expect this part of the process to take an hour to happen. However, if you notice the mixture is become thick then stir in the tablespoon of water. Once the sauce is ready you can now go ahead and cook the lamb chops. However, before you place on the Traeger Grill make sure that it has been lightly oiled and that the chops have been seasoned with some salt. Leave them on the Traeger Grill until the outside has started to turn a golden brown, which should be around 3 to 5 minutes for each side. Of course, how long you cook them for will depend on whether you want the meat to be medium rare or medium inside. To further help test if they are ready insert a meat thermometer into the chop make sure it isn't touching the bone and the internal temperature should have reached 145 degrees Fahrenheit. When the lamb chops are cooked place on clean plates and in a small bowl beside them place the sauce made earlier.

Traeger Grill Lamb with Ground Cinnamon
Ingredients

- 1 Teaspoon Ground Cinnamon
- 1 Teaspoon Ground Black Pepper
- 4 Lamb Chops
- 32gram Brown Sugar
- 2 Teaspoons Dried Tarragon
- 1 Teaspoon Garlic Powder
- ½ Teaspoon Salt

Instructions

- In a bowl place the sugar, Ginger, cinnamon, tarragon, pepper, garlic powder and salt and mix well together. Now take this season mixture and rub well into the lamb chops on both sides then place on a place and cover. Then place in the refrigerator for an hour. To cook the lamb chops you must remove them from the refrigerator whilst the barbecue is heat up to bra them back up to room temperature and they need to be cooked on a high heat.

- As usual brush the Traeger Grill of the barbecue with some oil first before lay the chops on it. Then cook the chops on each side for around 5 minutes or until they are cooked the way you like them. Once they are cooked allow them to rest for a few minutes before serve with a salad and some new potatoes.

Better Burgers with Barbecue Sauce
Ingredients

- 1/4 cup Traeger Regular Barbecue Sauce, or your favorite barbecue sauce
- 3 tablespoons butter, melted
- Sweet onion slices
- Tomato slices
- Dill pickle chips
- 4 Kaiser rolls, split
- Lettuce leaves
- 2 pounds ground chuck, 80/20 or 85/15 (lean to fat ratio)
- 2 teaspoons Traeger Beef Rub, or substitute your favorite barbecue rub
- 1 cup mayonnaise

Instructions

- Make sure the meat is well-chilled before handle. Combine the ground beef and Traeger Beef Rub in a medium bowl. Wet your hands with cold water, and mix gently. Divide the meat into four equal portions. Rewet your hands with cold water, and form each portion into a patty about 4 inches in diameter and 3/4-inch thick. (Try not to overwork the meat.) Us your thumbs, make a shallow wide depression on the top of each burger. (This prevents the burger from develop a bulge in the middle.)
- Combine the mayonnaise and the barbecue sauce in a shallow bowl and refrigerate until serve time. Brush the cut sides of the Kaiser rolls with the melted butter. When ready to cook, start the Traeger Grill on Smoke with the lid open until the fire is established (4 to 5 minutes). Set the temperature to 425 degrees F and preheat, lid closed, for 10 to 15 minutes. Arrange the burgers directly on the Traeger Grill grate, depression-side down. Cook for 10 minutes, then flip. Cook for 10 to 15 minutes more, or until an instant-read meat thermometer (put the probe through the side of the burger) registers 160 degrees F. Meanwhile, lightly toast the buns, cut sides down. Watch carefully as buttered bread can easily burn. Spread the cut sides of the buns with the mayonnaise sauce. Put a burger on each bun bottom, and top with lettuce, onion, tomato, and pickle. Finish with the top of the bun. Serve immediately.

Traeger Grill Lamb Chops with Minced Garlic
Ingredients

- ½ Teaspoon Ground Black Pepper
- 1 Tablespoon Minced Garlic
- 1 Thinly Sliced Onion
- 900gram Lamb Chops
- 60ml Distilled White Vinegar
- 2 Teaspoons Salt
- 2 Tablespoons Olive Oil

Instructions

- In a large resealable bag place the vinegar, salt, pepper, garlic, onion and olive oil and shake well to ensure that all the Ingredients have been combined together properly.

- Then into the bag you place the chops again shake the bag vigorously as this will help to ensure that the chops have been thoroughly coated with the marinate. Once this has been done you place the bag into the refrigerator and leave there for 2 hours. When it comes to cook the lamb chops you should remove them from the refrigerator whilst the barbecue is heat up. This will ensure that they come up to room temperature ensure that they then cook properly. When you remove the lamb chops from the marinade to place on the lightly oiled Traeger Grill if you notice any pieces of onion stuck to them leave them in place.
- Then Traeger Grill them until they are cooked to the level of doneness you require. Around 3 minutes for each side should be enough for them to be medium. Once cooked allow to rest for a short while before then serve to your guests.

Lamb Kofta Kebabs with chopped Parsley
Ingredients

- 3 Tablespoons Grated Onion
- 3 Tablespoons Freshly Chopped Parsley
- 1 Tablespoon Ground Coriander
- ¼ Teaspoon Cayenne Pepper
- ¼ Teaspoon Freshly Ground Black Pepper
- 1 Teaspoon Ground Cumin
- 450gram Ground Lamb Meat
- 4 Garlic Cloves Minced
- 1 Teaspoon Salt
- ½ Teaspoon Ground Cinnamon
- ½ Teaspoon Ground All Spice

Instructions

- With a mortar and pestle ground the garlic into a paste with the salt then the place these Ingredients into a bowl with the onion, parsley, coriander, cumin, cinnamon, all spice, cayenne pepper, Ginger and black pepper then to this bowl add the ground lamb meat. Once all the above Ingredients have been combined together divide it in to 28 small pieces and form them into balls.
- To make the Kofta kebabs take one of the balls of meat and thread it on to the top of a wooden skewer that has been soak in water for ½ hour. Then very slowly start to flatten the meat down the skewer until a 2-inch oval is created. Do this with all 28 balls of meat and then place them on a clean plate, cover and put in to the refrigerator for between 30 minutes and 12 hours.
- To cook the Lamb Kofta Kebabs you need to ensure that the temperature of the barbecue is of a medium heat and the Traeger Grill has been lightly oiled. Once the barbecue has reached the right temperature place the kebabs on the Traeger Grill and cook for around 6 minutes, make sure that you turn them over regularly.

Butterflied Leg Mushroom Soy Sauce
Ingredients

- 50ml Mushroom Soy Sauce
- ½ Teaspoon Freshly Ground White Pepper
- ½ Teaspoon Freshly Ground Black Pepper
- 4 Tablespoons Minced Garlic
- 2 Tablespoons Honey
- ½ Teaspoon Sesame Oil

- 2.26Kg Boneless Butterflied Leg of Lamb
- 75ml Hoisin Sauce
- 6 Tablespoons Rice Vinegar
- 64gram Minced Green Onions
- 1 Tablespoon Toasted Sesame Seeds

Instructions

- Place the hoisin sauce, rice vinegar, green onions, mushroom soy sauce, honey, garlic, sesame oil, sesame seeds, white and black pepper into a resealable plastic bag and shake vigorously as this will help to ensure that all the Ingredients are mixed together properly. Once you have made the marinade now place the leg of lamb into the bag also and seal it and move the bag around to ensure that all the meat is coated in the marinade. After do this you should place the bag in the refrigerator for at least 8 hours.
- But it is best to leave it in the bag in the refrigerator overnight. Whilst the barbecue is heat up you should now remove the meat from the refrigerator and leave it in the bag until the barbecue is hot enough to cook the meat on it. Before place the meat on the Traeger Grill brush some oil over its surface and then place the lamb on top. Any marinade left over should be discarded. You should be look to cook each side for of the meat for around 15 minutes or until you feel it done to the way you enjoy eat lamb.
- If you are unsure if the lamb is ready and you have a meat thermometer then insert this to check the internal temperature. The meat should be ready when the internal temperature has reached 145 degrees Fahrenheit. As soon as the lamb is cooked remove from the heat and place on a clean plate and allow it to rest for 20 minutes, remember to keep it covered whilst rest. Then slice and serve.

Ground Black Pepper Lamb Kebabs
Ingredients

- 4 Onions Cut into Quarters
- 1 Jar Maraschino Cherries
- 76gram Butter or Margarine Melted
- ½ Teaspoon Freshly Ground Black Pepper
- ½ Teaspoon Freshly Chopped Rosemary
- ½ Teaspoon Dried Crumbled Sage
- 4 Garlic Cloves Chopped
- 4 Green Bell Peppers Cut into Large Chunks
- 2.26Kg Boneless Lamb Shoulder Cut Into 1 Inch Chunks
- 6 Tablespoons Dijon Mustard
- 4 Tablespoons White Wine Vinegar
- 4 Tablespoons Olive Oil
- ½ Teaspoon Salt
- 1 Packet Fresh Whole Mushrooms
- 1 Can Pineapple Chunks
- 256gram Cherry Tomatoes

Instructions

- In a large bowl put the chunks of lamb ready for the marinade to be added to them. To make the marinade place the mustard, vinegar, olive oil, salt, pepper, sage, rosemary and garlic and mix well together before then pour over the lamb.

- Use your hands and mix all these Ingredients together to make sure that all parts of the lamb are then coated in the marinade. Once you have done this cover the bowl over and place in the refrigerator overnight. Whilst the barbecue is heat up you can nonintact to make the kebabs. If you are us wooden skewers make sure that they have been soak in some water for at least 30 minutes.
- To make each kebab thread on pieces of meat along with some of the mushrooms, tomatoes, pineapple and cherries and then place on the lightly oiled barbecue Traeger Grill to cook. Each kebab should remain on the barbecue for around 12 minutes and you should be turn them over frequently to prevent them from burn. It is important that whilst cook the kebabs that you baste them with a sauce made from the melted butter, pineapple and cherry juice. This will help to enhance the flavor not only of the lamb but the other Ingredients on the kebabs.

Herb Marinated Soy Sauce Lamb Chops
Ingredients

- ½ Teaspoon Freshly Ground Pepper
- 2 Tablespoons Sodium Reduced Soy Sauce
- 1 ½ Teaspoons Fresh Minced Basil
- 1 Minced Garlic Clove
- 4 Lamb Loin Chops Bone In (1 Inch Thick)
- 60ml Dry Red Wine

Instructions

- In a large plastic resealable bag mix together the wine, soy sauce, basil, mint, garlic and pepper. Once thoroughly mixed together pop the chops into the bag and shake the bag so that all parts of the chops are coated in the refrigerator. Meningeal the back up and place in the refrigerator for at least 8 hours. However, if you have enough time available leave them in the refrigerator overnight.
- Whilst the barbecue is heat up remove the lamb chops from the refrigerator and from the bag. Any marinade left in the bag should be discarded. Once the barbecue is at the right temperature you need to be cook the lamb chops over a medium heat with the cover up. To cook the chops on a medium heat the Traeger Grill, which has been lightly oiled, should sit about 4 to 6 inches above the heat source.
- Now cook each side of the chop for between 5 and 7 minutes or until the meat has reached the way you like lamb to be cooked. When the lamb chops are cooked remove from heat and let them rest for a short while before serve. A good accompaniment to serve with this particular recipe would be some couscous.

Grilled Asian Lamb Chops
Ingredients

- 2 Teaspoons Onion Powder
- 1 Teaspoon Garlic Powder
- 1 Teaspoon Garam Masala
- 12 Lamb Rib Chops
- 60ml Water
- 3 Tablespoons Vegetable Oil
- 2 Tablespoons Curry Powder
- 1 Tablespoon White Vinegar
- ¼ Teaspoon Salt

Instructions

- Place the 12 lamb rib chops into a shallow dish. Now in a bowl mix together the oil, curry powder, white vinegar, onion and garlic powder, the garam masala and salt and then pour this over the lamb chops. It is a good to pour ½ the marinade over first then turn the chops over and pour the rest of the marinade over them. You now need to place the dish, which you have covered over, in the refrigerator for 1 to 3 hours. Remove them from the refrigerator at least 15 minutes before required in order to the meat back up to room temperature.
- Whilst wait for the chops to comeback up to room temperature now is when you should light the barbecue so it will be hot enough for you to then cook the lamb rib chops on it very quickly. In fact, you need to cook the lamb chops on the barbecue on a medium heat so the Traeger Grill should sit around 4 to 6 inches above the heat source.
- When it comes to cook the lamb chops, they should be cooked on each side for 4 minutes. However, before you place them on the Traeger Grill make sure that you have oiled it well. Once the chops are cooked, they can be served immediately with either some chutney or a yogurt sauce.

Chopped Cilantro Moroccan Leg of Lamb
Ingredients

- 60ml Olive Oil
- 2 Minced Garlic Cloves
- 2 Teaspoons Ground Coriander
- 1.36 to 1.81Kg Boneless Leg of Lamb
- 43gram Freshly Chopped Cilantro
- 32gram Freshly Chopped Mint
- 1 Teaspoon Salt
- ½ Teaspoon Chili Powder

Instructions

- In a small mix together the oil, cilantro, mint, garlic, coriander, Ginger, salt and chili powder. Place the boneless leg of lamb into a shallow dish and then pour over the marinade you have just made. Cover the dish with some aluminum foil and place in the refrigerator for it to then marinate for between 2 and 4 hours.
- When the time comes to remove the lamb from the refrigerator you should nonintact heat up the barbecue. Make sure that it is heated up to a temperature that allows you to cook the lamb on a medium to low heat. As soon as the barbecue is ready place the leg of lamb on to the Traeger Grill, which has been oiled before, and cook directly above the heat source for 20 to 30 minutes or until it has cooked to the way you like it. Once the lamb has cooked remove from the barbecue and place on a clean plate to rest for 10 minutes before you then carve and serve it.
- A nice accompaniment to this particular dish would be a fresh green bean salad and some couscous or rice.

Traeger Grilled Lamb and Apricot Sosa ties
Ingredients

- 1 Dessertspoon Curry Powder
- 1 Tablespoon Caster Sugar

- 1 Tablespoon Vegetable Oil
- 200gram Diced Lamb
- 225gram Low Fat Natural Yogurt
- 350gram Dried Apricots
- 1 Large Onion

Instructions

- In a bowl combine together the yogurt; curry powder, sugar and oil to make a sauce. Add as much salt and pepper to this to season. Take the onion and cut this in 1 ¼ inch pieces which you will then thread on to the skewers alternately with the diced lamb and the dried apricots. If you are going to be us wooden skewers then make sure that you soak them in some water for around 30 minutes before you make the Sosa ties.
- Once you have threaded all the lamb, apricot and onions on to the skewers place them in a large plastic resealable bag or a container then pour the sauce you made previously all over them. If you need to do turn the kebabs over to ensure that they are well coated with the sauce that you are now go to marinate them in. You can either leave them to marinate in the sauce for 8 hours.
- However, if you want the Sosa ties to become infused with lots of the marinade's flavor it is best to leave them in it in a refrigerator overnight. When it comes to cook the Sosa, ties preheat the barbecue to a medium heat and just before you lay the Sosa ties on the Traeger Grill brush it with some oil. Cook the Sosa ties on the Traeger Grill for 8 to 10 minutes on each side. Then remove from the heat and serve immediately to your guests.

Garlic Minced Lamb Chops

Ingredients

- 32gram Freshly Chopped Mint
- 3 Cloves Garlic Minced
- 1 Teaspoon Salt
- 8 Lamb Chops
- 120ml Olive Oil
- 120ml Red Wine Vinegar
- 1 Teaspoon Freshly Ground Black Pepper

Instructions

- In a bowl combine together the olive oil, red wine vinegar, freshly chopped mint and minced garlic cloves. Now pour this mixture (marinade) into a bag that is resealable and to this add the lamb chops. Move the chops around inside the bag to ensure that they are well coated in the marinade and place in the refrigerator. Leave them there for 2 hours. After remove the lamb chops from the refrigerator you should pre heat the barbecue in readiness for when they will need cook. Before place the lamb chops on the Traeger Grill you should season with a little salt and pepper.
- Then after make sure that the Traeger Grill of the barbecue is about 3 inches above the heat source you should oil it lightly before place the chops on it. You should cook each chop for 5 to 6 minutes on each side. It is a good idea to turn them over regularly to prevent them from burn rather than just charr. Once the cook time has elapsed remove from heat and place on a clean plate to rest for a few minutes. Then serve them with some pitta bread, yogurt dip and a Greek salad.

Traeger Grilled Beef Tenderloin

Ingredients

- 1 Sweet Onion (Cut Into ½ Inch Slices)
- 2 Plum Tomatoes (Chopped)
- 2 Tablespoons Kalamata Olives (Pipped and Chopped)
- 2 Tablespoons Olive Oil
- 1.3to1.8Kg Center Cut Beef Tenderloin
- 2 Japanese Eggplants
- 2 Red or Yellowing sweet Peppers
- 1 Tablespoon Balsamic Vinegar
- ¼ to ½ Teaspoon Salt
- 1/8 Teaspoon Ground Black Pepper
- 2 Teaspoons Crushed Dried Oregano
- 2 Teaspoons Cracked Black Pepper
- 1 ½ Teaspoons Freshly Shredded Lemon Peel
- 3 Cloves Garlic (Minced)
- 2 Tablespoons Freshly Snipped Basil

Instructions

- In a small bowl combine together the cracked black pepper, lemon peel, oregano, and 2 of the minced garlic cloves. Once thoroughly combined together rub this all over the meat. To cook the meat, you need to place a drip tray in the bottom of the barbecue and around it places the hot charcoal.
- Once the temperature has reached the right level place the meat on the Traeger Grill above the drip tray. As for the vegetables these should be placed around the meat directly over the coals, brush them with olive oil first. Close the lid on the Traeger Grill and allow it to remain closed for 10 to 12 minutes. By this time the vegetables should be tender and need to be removed from the Traeger Grill.
- Once the vegetables have been removed and placed on a clean plate and covered close the lid on the barbecue once more and allow the meat to continue cook for between 25 and 30 minutes or until the internal temperature of the meat has reached 135 degrees Fahrenheit when a meat thermometer is inserted. If this temperature has been reached remove meat from barbecue place on a clean plate and cover leave it to rest for 15 minutes before you slice it. Now the vegetables have had sufficient time to cool down you can make the relish to go with the beef. Simply put all the vegetables into a bowl after coarsely chop them and add to them the olives, basil, tomatoes, and garlic clove, vinegar, salt and ground black pepper.

Traeger Grilled Rack of Lamb

Ingredients

- 240ml White Wine (Dry or Medium Would Be Best)
- 64gram Butter
- 64gram Minced Shallots
- 1 Rack of Lamb
- 240ml Red Currant Jelly
- 240ml Dijon Mustard
- 2 Tablespoons Fresh Crushed Rosemary

Instructions

- In a saucepan place the red currant jelly and mustard and simmer on a low heat for about 5 minutes or until the jelly has melted. Then allow the sauce to cool completely. Cut the rack of lamb into chops and then French cut. If you are not able to do this then get your butcher to do it for you. It is important if you decide to do this yourself that you don't remove any of the fat from the eye of the chop.
- This fat actually helps to prevent the meat from burn when you place it on the barbecue Traeger Grill. Once the rack of lamb is ready you of it completely in the sauce you made earlier and leave it in it to marinade overnight. Cover the dish in which the lamb has been placed and put in the refrigerator. When it comes to cook the lamb, it should be done over a medium to high heat and with some hickory coals added to the barbecue beforehand. Also make sure that the Traeger Grill has been oiled before the lamb is placed on it. Cook on the barbecue for 4 to 5 minutes on each side and bast each side regularly with more of the marinade sauce. Whilst the lamb is rest you can now prepare the garnish to go with them.
- In a saucepan place the butter and allow it to melt over a low heat then add the minced shallots to it. Allow the shallots to brown before then add the crushed rosemary and white wine. As soon as the garnish is ready place the lamb on clean plates and serve with the garnish poured over it and with Traeger Grill ed vegetables and potatoes.

Greek Yogurt Lamb Burgers

Ingredients

- 1 Teaspoon Freshly Minced Ginger Root
- 1 Teaspoon Minced Garlic
- 1 Teaspoon Salt
- ½ Teaspoon Freshly Ground Black Pepper
- Yogurt Sauce
- 450gram Greek Yogurt
- Zest Of ½ Lemon
- 450gram Ground Lamb
- 225gram Ground Beef
- 3 Tablespoons Freshly Chopped Mint
- 1 Minced Garlic Clove
- ½ Teaspoon Salt

Instructions

- To make the burgers you place the ground lamb and beef in to a bowl with the mint, Ginger root, garlic, salt and pepper and stir together until just about combined. Now divide the mixture up into four portions then shape them into four patties.

- Set them aside. It is best if you cover them up and place in the refrigerator until you are ready to cook them. After make the burgers you are now ready to make the sauce. To do this place the yogurt, lemon zest, garlic and salt into a bowl and mix well. Place the mixture, which you have covered over, into the refrigerator until it is needed. When it comes to cook the lamb, the barbecue should be at a medium heat and will need to be cooked on both sides for between 3 and 4 minutes each.
- The best way to test to see if they are cooked through is to insert a meat thermometer and see if the temperature inside them has reached 160 degrees Fahrenheit. Once the burgers are ready you need to prepare the buns in which the burgers will be served. The first then you should do is place a slice of onion and tomato on the Traeger Grill and cook them until they are lightly charred on each side. Then spread some of the yogurt sauce over the burger or ciabatta roll and then place the burger on top of this. Then place on top of this the onion and tomato slices before some leaves of lettuce. Then top it all off with some slices of feta cheese and the top part of the roll.

Lemon Oil Sliced Over Arugula with Garlic
Ingredients

- Kosher or Sea Salt
- Freshly Ground Pepper
- 6 Ounces Baby Arugula Leaves
- 2¼ Cups Lemon-Infused Extra-Virgin Olive Oil
- 1 Flank Steak, 1¼ to 1½ Pounds, Trimmed of Fat
- 2 Tablespoons Extra-Virgin Olive Oil
- 1 Teaspoon Minced Garlic
- Other Finish Salt for Sprinkle

Instructions

- Prepare a hot fire in a charcoal Traeger Grill or preheat a gas Traeger Grill on high. Remove the flank steak from the refrigerator 20 to 30 minutes before Traeger Grill and place it on a large, rimmed back sheet. In a small bowl, combine the 2 tablespoons olive oil and the garlic. Rub the steak on both sides with the mixture and season with salt and pepper. Oil the Traeger Grill grate. Place the flank steak directly over the hot fire.
- Cover the Traeger Grill and sear the steak on one side, 4 minutes for rare or 6 minutes for medium-rare. Turn, re-cover, and cook for 4 minutes more, or until an instant-read thermometer registers 120°F for rare or 130° to 135°F for medium-rare. Transfer the steak to a car board and let rest for 5 minutes. Cut the meat across the grain into ¼-inch-thick slices. Scatter an equal amount of arugula on each dinner plate. Arrange overlap slices of steak over the greens and spoon any accumulated juices over the top. Drizzle 1 tablespoon of the lemon olive oil over each portion of steak and sprinkle with fleur de sel. Serve immediately.

Chapter 3: Pork Recipes

Barbecued Pork Steaks with Worcestershire Sauce
Ingredients

- 1 Tablespoon Worcestershire Sauce
- 1 Teaspoon Garlic Salt
- 4 Pork Blade Steaks that are between 1 and 1 ¼ Inches Thick
- 120ml Bottle Barbecue Sauce
- 80ml Honey
- ½ Teaspoon Dijon Mustard

instructions

- In a bowl combine together the barbecue sauce, honey, Worcestershire sauce, garlic salt and mustard. This you will then use to baste the pork steaks as they cook. To cook the pork steaks, you need to place them on an oiled Traeger Grill about 4 inches above the heat source. This will provide them with a medium heat to cook and will also ensure that they cook slowly so more of the moisture is retained.
- You should cook each steak for around 8 minutes on each side before you then cook them for a further five minutes. But the last five minutes is when the pork should be brushed with the sauce. It is important that you turn the steaks over regularly during this last five minutes to ensure that they are both well coated in the sauce and to help it adhere to the surface of them. Once the steaks are cooked place onto clean plates and serve with a crispy green salad and some nice crusty bread.

Traeger Grilled Pork Chops with Minced Garlic
Ingredients

- 2 Teaspoons Minced Garlic
- 4 Bone-In, Center-Cut Pork Loin Chops, ¾ to 1 Inch Thick (10 To 12 Ounces Each)
- ½ Cup Red Miso
- 2 Tablespoons Asian Sesame Oil
- ½ Teaspoon Sambal Oelek

Instructions

- Prepare a medium-hot fire in a charcoal Traeger Grill or preheat a gas Traeger Grill on medium high. Remove the pork chops from the refrigerator 20 to 30 minutes before Traeger Grill and place them on a rimmed back sheet. In a small bowl, combine the miso, sesame oil, garlic, and sambal Oelek and stir until creamy. Brush the chops on both sides with the paste. To create a cool zone, bank the coals to one side of the Traeger Grill or turn off one of the burners. Oil the Traeger Grill grate.
- Place the pork chops directly over the medium-hot fire. Traeger Grill the pork on one side until nicely seared, about 4 minutes. Turn and cook until seared, 3 to 4 minutes longer. Move the chops to the cooler part of the Traeger Grill, cover, and Traeger Grill until the meat is slightly pink in the center, or an instant read thermometer registers 145°F, 10 to 12 minutes longer. Remove the chops from the Traeger Grill and let rest for 5 minutes before serve.

Traeger Grilled Pork Chops
Ingredients

- Salt
- Freshly Ground Black Pepper

- 1 Tablespoon Olive Oil
- ½ Teaspoon Brown Sugar
- ¼ Teaspoon Freshly Chopped Rosemary
- 4 Pork Rib Chops About 1 Inch Thick
- 60ml Lemon Juice
- 3 Tablespoons Soy Sauce

Instructions

- The first then you need to do is make the marinade for the chops. To do this in a bowl place the lemon juice, soy sauce, olive oil, brown sugar, rosemary, salt and pepper. Then mix to ensure that they are combined together well. Next you need to place the pork chops in a shallow dish or a resealable plastic bag and then pour over the chops the marinade made just now. Make sure that you toss the pork chops in this mix to ensure that all sides of them are coated in it. Once this has been done either cover the dish over or seal up the bag and place in the refrigerator for 30 minutes.
- After the 30 minutes has elapsed remove the chops from the refrigerator and leave to one side to come up to room temperature. Also, after take the chops out of the refrigerator now is when you should be heating the barbecue up. As soon as the barbecue is ready you can nonintact cook the chops. The Traeger Grill, which has been lightly oiled, should be placed quite close to the heat source as this will then help to sear the meat and ensure plenty of the meat's juices are retained whilst you then cook them on a medium heat for 6 to 8 minutes. To reduce the heat, you simply move the Traeger Grill up away from the heat source. Also, when cook the chops remember to turn them over regularly to prevent them from burn. As soon as the chops are cooked you should serve them immediately to your guests on a nice clean plate with say a jacket potato and coleslaw.

Traeger Grilled Barbecued Pork Ribs
Ingredients

- 240ml Ready Made Barbecue Sauce
- 1.36 Kg Pork Spare Ribs

Instructions

- Take the ribs and place them over a low heat on the barbecue and cook for between 1 and 1 ½ hours. You could of course cut down the cook time if you wish by initially cook them in the oven. About 15 minutes before you then remove the pork spare ribs from the barbecue you nonintact to brush them with the barbecue sauce.
- It is important that during these last minutes of cook is that you turn the ribs over and baste them with the sauce regularly. This will then help to ensure that all sides of the ribs get a good coat of the sauce and also will help to prevent the sauce from burn. As soon as the ribs are cooked remove from the barbecue and cut up into portions that people will find easy to eat. Also, it is a good idea to serve them with freshly made coleslaw and some crusty bread.

Southern Pulled Pork with Ground Cumin
Ingredients

- 1 Teaspoon Ground Red Pepper
- 1 Tablespoon Chili Powder
- 1 Tablespoon Ground Cumin
- 1 Tablespoon White Sugar
- 1 ½ Teaspoons Ground Black Pepper
- 2 Teaspoons Salt
- 1.8 to 2.2 Kg Pork Shoulder Roast
- 2 Tablespoons Paprika
- 1 Tablespoon Brown Sugar

Instructions

- Into a bowl place all the spices to form a dry rub and then press it well into all the pork's surfaces. Whilst you are do this you should get the barbecue heated up ready for cook. As soon as the barbecue has heated and you have placed the Traeger Grill high above the heat source you can now put the pork on to cook.
- When placed on the Traeger Grill it will now require between 2.5 and 3 hours to cook. Whilst cook it is important that you turn the meat regularly to prevent it from burn. Also, to make sure that the meat is cook properly insert a meat thermometer into the center of it. The right temperature inside the meat, which will ensure it is cooked through, should be 170 degrees Fahrenheit. After the cook time has elapsed you now need to remove the pork from the barbecue and leave it to rest for around 10 minutes. Then it is ready to be shredded. You do this by us two forks to pull the meat apart and it is this action, which has given this recipe its name. As soon as you have done this place the meat on a clean plate and allow your guests to take a bun and pile it on it before add some hot sauce if they want.

Traeger Grilled Pork Tenderloin with Pineapple
Ingredients

- 1 Tablespoon Packed Dark Brown Sugar
- ¼ Teaspoon Freshly Ground Pepper

- 1 Ripe Pineapple, Peeled, Halved Lengthwise, And Cut Crosswise Into ½-Inchthick
- Slices
- 2 Pork Tenderloins, about 1 Pound Each, Trimmed of Excess Fat and Silver Skin
- ½ Cup Jerk Paste
- 3 Tablespoons Unsalted Butter, Melted

Instructions

- Prepare a medium-hot fire in a charcoal Traeger Grill or preheat a gas Traeger Grill on medium high. Remove the tenderloins from the refrigerator 20 to 30 minutes before Traeger Grill and place them on a large, rimmed back sheet. Liberally rub the pork on all sides with the spice paste. In a small bowl, combine the butter, sugar, and pepper.
- Stir to dissolve the sugar. Arrange the pineapple slices in a s le layer on a rimmed back sheet, and brush both sides of each slice with the butter mixture. Set aside. Oil the Traeger Grill grate. Place the pineapple directly over the medium-hot fire. Cover and Traeger Grill, turn once, until Traeger Grill marks appear on both sides of the slices and the pineapple is golden and tender when pierced with a knife, about 3 minutes per side. Transfer to a plate and keep warm while you Traeger Grill the pork. To create a cool zone, bank the coals to one side of the Traeger Grill or turn off one of the burners. Oil the Traeger Grill grate. Place the tenderloins directly over the medium-hot fire. Traeger Grill the pork, turn to sear on all sides, for about 8 minutes.
- Move the tenderloins to the cooler part of the Traeger Grill, cover, and Traeger Grill until the meat is slightly pink in the center, or an instant-read thermometer inserted into the thickest part of a tenderloin registers 145°F, 8 to 10 minutes longer. Transfer the pork to a cut board and let rest for 5 minutes. Cut the pork on the diagonal, across the grain, into ½-inch-thick slices and divide among warmed dinner plates. Divide the pineapple slices among the plates. Serve immediately.

Teriyaki Kebabs with Cherry Tomatoes

- **Ingredients**
- 2 Tablespoons Vegetable Oil
- 1 20 Ounce Can Pineapple Chunks Drained
- 500gram Cherry Tomatoes
- 900gram Pork Tenderloin - Trimmed and Cut Into 1 Inch Cubes
- 240ml Ready Prepared Teriyaki Sauce
- 2 Red or Green Bell Peppers – Cut Into 1 ½ Inch Pieces

Instructions

- Piece the cubes of pork tenderloin so that the meat can absorb the sauce and oil you are us to marinate them in. To make the marinade simply pour the sauce and oil into a bowl and whisk. However before pour it over the pork make sure that you keep at least 2 tablespoons to one side in a separate bowl.
- Once poured over the meat cover and place in a refrigerator and leave for at least 1 hour. Whilst it is in the fridge make sure that you turn the meat occasionally this will then help to ensure that as much of the teriyaki sauce is absorbed by the meat. After 1 hour remove the meat from the fridge then thread on to skewers. After each piece of meat thread on a piece of pineapple, a tomato and some pepper.
- Continue do this until all Ingredients have been used up. It is important that whilst you are do this that the barbecue should be heat up. To cook the kebabs, you place them on the lightly oiled Traeger Grill about 4 or 5 inches above the heat source and cook them on the barbecue for 15 minutes. It is important that when cook these kebabs you turn them over frequently and brush with the marinade placed to one side earlier. As soon as the kebabs are cooked served with a noodle or rice salad.

Grilled Back Barbecued Ribs
Ingredients

- 2 Teaspoons Garlic Powder
- 1 ½ Teaspoons Ground Black Pepper
- 120ml Water
- 1.36Kg Baby Back Pork Ribs
- 1 Tablespoon Brown Sugar
- 1 Tablespoon Paprika
- 350ml Ready Made Barbecue Sauce

Instructions

- Before wrap the baby back pork ribs in aluminum foil combine together the sugar, paprika, garlic powder and pepper and rub all other them. Remember to turn them over and coat all sides with this season. Now wrap in the aluminum foil, but leave one end open, as into this you will then pour the water. Now fold up the open end to seal the meat inside. It is a good idea to leave some room around the meat to allow heat inside to then circulate when the ribs are cook.
- When it comes to cook these on the barbecue you place them on the Traeger Grill and pull the lid down and leave them there for between 45 minutes and an hour. Once the time has elapsed remove the ribs from the tin foil and then replace them on the Traeger Grill, which has been lightly oiled. After place the ribs on the Traeger Grill you can nonintact bast them with the barbecue sauce. You should allow them to remain on the Traeger Grill for a further 10 to 15 minutes. During this final cook time you should be turn them over every 5 minutes and brush them with the sauce each time they are turned.

Maple Garlic Pork Tenderloin Ground Black Pepper
Ingredients

- 3 Garlic Cloves Minced
- 240ml Maple Syrup
- 680gram Pork Tenderloin
- 2 Tablespoons Dijon Mustard
- 1 Teaspoon Sesame Oil
- Freshly Ground Black Pepper

Instructions

- In a bowl mix together the maple syrup, mustard, sesame oil, garlic and pepper. Whisk thoroughly to ensure that all these Ingredients are combined together well. In a shallow dish place the pork tenderloin and then coat it thoroughly with the marinade that you have just made. Cover the meat over and place in the refrigerator to chill for at least 8 hours. However, if you really want the meat to absorb as much of the flavor of the marinade as possible then it is best to leave it in the refrigerator overnight.
- Whilst the barbecue is heat up remove the pork from the refrigerator so that it can come up to room temperature. Once the barbecue is hot enough remove the meat from the dish and set over to one side.
- As for any sauce left in the dish pour this into a small saucepan. Now before you place the meat on the Traeger Grill make sure you have brushed it with some oil first to prevent the meat from stick to it. Cook the pork on the particular for between 15 and 25 minutes make sure that you baste it regularly with the reserved marinade, which you have heated up in the saucepan for five minutes first. Make

sure that you cook the meat on a medium heat otherwise the marinade will burn. Plus of course remember to turn the meat regularly to ensure that it is cooked through evenly. As soon as the meat is cooked the inside no longer looks pink place to one side for a few minutes before car and serve to your guests.

Maple Glazed Ribs Cider Vinegar
Ingredients

- 1 Tablespoon Cider Vinegar
- 1 Tablespoon Worcestershire Sauce
- ½ Teaspoon Salt
- 1.5kg Baby Back Pork Ribs
- 180ml Maple Syrup
- 2 Tablespoons Brown Sugar
- 2 Tablespoons Ketchup
- ½ Teaspoon Mustard Powder

Instructions

- Place the ribs into a large saucepan or pot and cover with water. Then cook on a low heat so the water is simmer for at least an hour or until the meat has become tender. Once the meat is cooked remove the ribs from the water and place them in a shallow dish and set aside whilst you make the marinade.
- To make the marinade place the maple syrup, sugar, ketchup, vinegar, Worcestershire sauce, salt and mustard into a saucepan. Place on the hob and bra to the Ingredients to the boil before then reduce the heat down and cook for five minutes.
- Make sure that you stir the sauce frequently then allow to cool slightly before then pour it over the ribs. Now place the ribs in the dish covered in the sauce in the refrigerator for 2 hours to marinate. You will be cooking the ribs on an indirect heat on the Traeger Grill so make sure that it is hot enough. Once the barbecue has heated up sufficiently remove the ribs from the marinade and place them on the lightly oiled barbecue Traeger Grill. Any marinade left over should be put into a saucepan and boiled for a few minutes. The ribs should only need to remain on the barbecue for around 20 minutes. During this time, they should be turned frequently and brushed with the cooked marinade often until the ribs have become nicely glazed. Divide up the ribs into manageable portions and serve to your guests.

Rubbed Pork Chops with Bourbon
Ingredients

- ¼ Cup Espresso-Cardamom Rub Bourbon-And-Maple-Traeger Grill Ed Acorn
- Squash
- 4 Bone-In, Center-Cut Pork Loin Chops, ¾ to 1 Inch Thick (10 To 12 Ounces Each)
- Extra-Virgin Olive Oil

Instructions

- Prepare a medium-hot fire in a charcoal Traeger Grill or preheat a gas Traeger Grill on medium high. Remove the pork chops from the refrigerator 20 to 30 minutes before Traeger Grill and place them on a rimmed back sheet. Rub the pork on both sides with the olive oil; then with the spice rub. While the Traeger Grill is heat, prepare the acorn squash for Traeger Grill, and make the bourbon-butter sauce.

- To create a cool zone, bank the coals to one side of the Traeger Grill or turn off one of the burners. Oil the Traeger Grill grate. Place the squash on the cool side of the Traeger Grill and Traeger Grill. Place the pork chops directly over the medium-hot fire. Traeger Grill the chops on one side until nicely seared, about 4 minutes. Turn and cook until seared, 3 to 4 minutes longer. Move the chops to the cooler part of the Traeger Grill, cover, and Traeger Grill until the pork is slightly pink in the center, or an instant-read thermometer registers 145°F, 10 to 12 minutes longer. Remove the chops from the Traeger Grill and let rest for 5 minutes. Transfer the chops to warmed dinner plates and accompany with the acorn squash. Serve immediately.

Traeger Grilled Pork Tenderloin
Ingredients

- 60ml Water
- 3 Tablespoons Reduced Sodium Soy Sauce
- 2 Tablespoons Reduced Fat Creamy Peanut Butter
- 4 ½ Teaspoons Canola Oil
- 450gram Pork Tenderloin
- 1 Small Chopped Onion
- 32gram Brown Sugar
- 2 Garlic Cloves Minced

Instructions

- In a small saucepan put the onion, sugar, water, soy sauce, peanut butter, canola oil, garlic and Ginger. Then over a medium heat bra these Ingredients to a boil before turn the heat down so that they start simmer and leave uncovered for 10 to 12 minutes or until the sauce has started to thicken. To prevent the sauce from stick to the base of the saucepan and burn you need to be stirred it regularly. As soon as the sauce has become thick remove from heat and place about 120ml to one side.
- Take the pork tenderloin and cut in half width wise before then cut   each half into thin strips than you then thread on to eight wooden or metal skewers. If you are us   wooden skewers remember to soak them in water for ½ hour. To cook place, them on a lightly oiled Traeger Grill on the barbecue over a medium to hot heat and cook on each side for 2 to 3 minutes. It is important whilst the kebabs are cook that you baste them regularly with the sauce you made earlier. The meat will be cooked when it no longer looks pink.
- To serve these kebabs simply place them on a clean plate along with the reserved sauce and allow guests to pick them up and then dip in the sauce.

Traeger Grilled Chorizo Quesadillas
Ingredients

- 1½ Cups (6 Ounces) Grated Monterey Jack Cheese
- 1 Cup Loosely Packed Fresh Cilantro Leaves
- 12 Ounces Fresh Chorizo Sausages
- 1 Can (16 Ounces) Refried Black Beans
- 8 8-Inch Flour Tortillas
- 1¼ Cups Store-Bought Tomatillo Salsa (See Cook's Note) ½ Cup Sour

Instructions

- Prepare a medium-hot fire in a charcoal Traeger Grill or preheat a gas Traeger Grill on medium high. Remove the sausages from the refrigerator 20 to 30 minutes before Traeger Grill. Oil the Traeger Grill grate.
- Place the sausages directly over the medium-hot fire. Traeger Grill the sausages, turn several times, until seared on all sides and fully cooked, 6 to 8 minutes total. Transfer the sausages to a cut board and cut on the diagonal into ¼-inch-thick slices. Spread 2 rounded tablespoons of the refried beans evenly over one-half of each tortilla, leave a ½-inch border at the edges. Scatter the chorizo slices evenly over the beans. Scatter the cheese and cilantro over the sausages. Fold the tortillas over to form half-circles.
- Oil the Traeger Grill grate again. Us a wide spatula, carefully transfer the quesadillas to the Traeger Grill. Traeger Grill on one side for about 1 minute, slide and turn the quesadillas 90 degrees, and Traeger Grill until nice crosshatch Traeger Grill marks appear, about 1 minute longer. Slide the spatula underneath the quesadillas and flip them.
- Traeger Grill until the tortillas are toasted and the cheese begins to melt, 1 to 2 minutes longer. Transfer the quesadillas to a cut board and cut into wedges. Serve hot with the tomatillo salsa and sour cream.

Smoked Grilled Pork Ribs
Ingredients

- 1 Teaspoon Cayenne Pepper
- 1 Teaspoon Jalapeno Season Salt (Optional)
- 2 Tablespoons Fresh Lemon Juice
- 1 Finely Chopped Jalapeno Pepper (Optional)
- 3 Tablespoons Hot Pepper Sauce
- 240ml Apple Cider
- 180ml Apple Cider Vinegar
- 1 Tablespoon Onion Powder
- 1 Tablespoon Paprika
- 1 Tablespoon Freshly Ground Black Pepper
- 2 Tablespoons Garlic Powder
- 2 Teaspoons Onion Powder
- 2 Teaspoons Salt
- 3Kg Pork Spareribs
- Dry Rub Mixture
- 64gram Brown Sugar
- 2 Tablespoons Chili Powder
- 2 Teaspoons Ground Cumin
- 1 Teaspoon Ground Cinnamon
- 1 Tablespoon Garlic Powder

Instructions

- In a bowl place the brown sugar, chili powder, paprika, black pepper, garlic powder, onion powder, salt, cumin, cinnamon, jalapeno season and cayenne pepper and mix well together. Then rub all over the spareribs, cover and put in the refrigerator for at least 4 hours to allow the rub to become infused in to the meat. However, leave them overnight would prove even better. Whilst the barbecue is heat up you should now remove the spareribs from the refrigerator and start prepare the sauce. In a bowl you need to place all the Ingredients mentioned above and stir together.

- Once the barbecue is ready before you place the spareribs on the lightly oiled Traeger Grill you must first place some of the soaked wood chips on to the barbecue itself. Once you have done this you can now place the spareribs on the Traeger Grill with the bone at the bottom. Now close the lid and allow the ribs to cook for between 3 ½ to 4 hours. If you need to add more coals then do so. Every hour you will need to baste the ribs with the sauce and also make sure at this time you also add some more of the soaked wood chips to the barbecue. It is important that the temperature within the remains at a constant 225 degrees Fahrenheit to ensure that the pork spareribs cook properly. You can tell when the ribs are ready to eat as the rub will have help to create a crispy blackened bark on the meat and it pulls away from the bone easily. Simply separate into portions that your guests can enjoy and discard any sauce that may be left over.

Grilled Pork Ribs with Dark Brown Sugar
Ingredients

- 240ml Light Soy Sauce
- 150ml Bourbon
- 1.36Kg Pork Ribs
- 128gram Dark Brown Sugar
- 4 Garlic Cloves Minced

Instructions

- In a food processor or blender place the sugar, soy sauce, garlic and bourbon and turn on until all Ingredients are thoroughly combined. Now pour this mixture over the ribs, which have been placed in a shallow dish. Cover the ribs and place them in a refrigerator to marinate for several hours. The longer you leave them in the refrigerator then the more the marinate will infuse into the rib meat.
- Whilst the barbecue is heat up you should remove the ribs from the refrigerator to allow them to come up to room temperature. But before you place them on the barbecue grate make sure it has been brushed with oil. Once the ribs are on the grate you now need to close the lid and cook them for between 45 minutes and an hour. How long you cook them for will depend on how thick the ribs are. The best way to test if they are ready to eat is to insert a meat thermometer into the thickest part of the rib. If the internal temperature measures 160 degrees Fahrenheit they are ready to serve up on to plates after be   separated with the salad and potatoes.

Boneless Glazed Pork Chops
Ingredients

- 1 Jalapeno Pepper Seeded and Finely Chopped
- 2 Tablespoons Lime Juice or Tequila
- 4 Boneless Pork Loin Chops That Are About 1 Inch Thick
- 160ml Orange Marmalade

Instructions

- In a bowl mix together the marmalade, jalapeno pepper, lime juice or tequila and the Ginger. This is what will be used to glaze the pork chops. Before you place the chops on the Traeger Grill make sure that they cook over a medium heat you trim off the fat.
- Allow the chops to cook on the barbecue for between 12- and 15-minutes dependent on the thickness of them. The best way of test to see if they are ready to eat is to insert a skewer into the thickest part and see if the juices from inside that come out run clear. It is also important that you turn the chops over regularly when cook them. During the last five minutes of the chops cook this is when the glaze you made earlier must be applied. During this time the chops should only be turned once, but you must apply the glaze often. Once the chops are ready to eat remove from the barbecue and place on clean plates then sprinkle with a little chopped fresh cilantro and some orange and lime wedges.

Ham Steaks with Fresh Lime
Ingredients

- 1 Tablespoon Packed Light Brown Sugar
- 1 Teaspoon Chopped Fresh Thyme
- ½ Teaspoon Kosher or Sea Salt
- ½ Pineapple, Peeled, Halved Lengthwise, Cored, And Cut Into ¼-Inch Dice
- 1 Small Red Bell Pepper, Seeded, Defibbed, And Cut Into ¼-Inch Dice
- 2 Green Onions, Include Green Tops, Halved Lengthwise and Thinly Sliced
- 1 Jalapeño Chile, Include Seeds and Ribs, Finely Minced
- 2 Tablespoons Fresh Lime Juice
- 4 Bone-In Ham Steaks, About ¼ Inch Thick (About 12 Ounces Each) 2 Tablespoons
- Extra-Virgin Olive Oil
- Freshly Ground Pepper
- Pineapple-Jalapeño Salsa

Instructions

- Prepare a medium-hot fire in a charcoal Traeger Grill or preheat a gas Traeger Grill on medium high. Remove the ham steaks from the refrigerator 20 to 30 minutes before Traeger Grill and place them on a large, rimmed back sheet. Blot the steaks with paper towels if they are moist. Brush the steaks on both sides with olive oil and lightly season on both sides with pepper. While the Traeger Grill is heat, make the salsa: In a bowl, combine the pineapple, bell pepper, green onions, jalapeño, lime juice, sugar, thyme, and salt and mix thoroughly. Set aside.
- Oil the Traeger Grill grate. Place the ham steaks directly over the medium-hot fire. Traeger Grill the steaks on one side until nicely seared, 2 to 3 minutes. Turn and sear on the other side, 2 to 3 minutes longer. Transfer the ham steaks to warmed dinner plates. Put a large spoonful of salsa on each plate. Serve immediately.

Leaf Parsley Baby Back Ribs
Ingredients

- ¼ Teaspoon Freshly Ground Pepper; Plus, More for Season

- 3 Red Bell Peppers, Quartered, Seeded, And Defibbed
- 1 Cup Cergol Or Sicilian Green Olives, Pitted and Halved
- 2 Porterhouse Steaks, 1½ Inches Thick (About 1½ Pounds Each) 1 Tablespoon
- Extra-Virgin Olive Oil; Plus, More for The Rub
- Kosher or Sea Salt
- ¼ Cup Capers, Rinsed and Drained
- 1 Tablespoon Minced Fresh Flat-Leaf Parsley

Instructions

- Prepare a hot fire in a charcoal Traeger Grill or preheat a gas Traeger Grill on high. Remove the steaks from the refrigerator 20 to 30 minutes before Traeger Grill and place them on a large, rimmed back sheet. Rub the steaks on both sides with olive oil.
- Liberally season the steaks on both sides with salt and pepper. Place the bell peppers in a bowl and toss with just enough olive oil to coat them lightly. In another bowl, combine the olives, capers, parsley, and ¼ teaspoon freshly ground pepper. Set aside. Oil the Traeger Grill grate. Place the peppers directly over the hot fire. Cover the Traeger Grill and cook, turn once, until dark brown Traeger Grill marks appear and the peppers are crisp-tender, 4 to 5 minutes. Transfer the peppers to a cut board. Oil the Traeger Grill grate again and place the steaks directly over the hot fire.
- Traeger Grill the steaks on one side, 5 minutes for rare or 6 minutes for medium-rare. Turn and cook for 5 minutes more, or until an instant-read thermometer registers 120°F for rare or 130° to 135°F for medium-rare. Transfer the steaks to a car board and let rest for 5 minutes. While the steaks are rest, cut the Traeger Grill ed peppers lengthwise into ½-inch-wide strips and add to the bowl with the olives. Add 1 tablespoon olive oil and toss gently to combine. Us a sharp knife, cut along the bone of each steak, separate it from the meat. Cut the meat across the grain into ½-inch-thick slices. Arrange overlap slices of steak on warmed dinner plates or a platter, and spoon the bell pepper mixture over the top. Serve immediately.

Indian Pork Satay with Lemongrass
Ingredients

- 6 Quarter-Size Slices Peeled Fresh Ginger
- 1 Shallot, Quartered
- 1 Teaspoon Red Pepper Flakes
- 5 Tablespoons Vegetable Oil
- 1 Tablespoon Sugar
- 1½ Teaspoons Kosher or Sea Salt
- 12 10-Inch Bamboo Skewers, Soaked in Water For 15 Minutes, Then Drained
- 2 Pork Tenderloins, 10 To 12 Ounces Each, Trimmed of Excess Fat and Silver Skin
- 1 Stalk Lemongrass
- 1 Teaspoon Ground Cumin
- 1 Teaspoon Ground Coriander

Instructions

- Immerse the skewers before light the Traeger Grill, so they have plenty of time to soak. Prepare a medium-hot fire in a charcoal Traeger Grill or preheat a gas Traeger Grill on medium high. Remove the tenderloins from the refrigerator 20 to 30 minutes before Traeger Grill. Cut the pork on a sharp diagonal, across the grain, into -inch-thick slices and place in a large bowl. Cut off and discard the dried, grass like top half of the lemongrass.

- Trim the base from the bulb end and remove and discard the tough outer leaves. Us only the white and light green parts, cut in half lengthwise, and then cut crosswise into ½- inch pieces. In a food processor fitted with the metal blade, combine the lemongrass, Ginger, shallot, sugar, salt, cumin, coriander, and red pepper flakes and process until finely minced. With the machine run, add the vegetable oil through the feed tube and process until a paste form. Transfer the paste to the bowl with the pork and brush or rub the paste evenly over the meat. Thread the pork onto the skewers, divide it evenly and weave each slice to pierce it 2 or 3 times. Bunch the meat a bit, so it covers about 8 inches of each skewer. Oil the Traeger Grill grate. Fold a footlong piece of aluminum foil in half lengthwise and lay it on the Traeger Grill grate. Arrange the skewers so the exposed bamboo is protected from the flame by the foil and the meat is directly over the fire. Use 2 pieces of foil if necessary. Traeger Grill the skewers, turn them once, until the pork is cooked through and the edges are slightly caramelized and charred, about 3 minutes per side. Serve immediately.

Pork Tenderloin in Olive Oil
Ingredients

- Extra-Virgin Olive Oil
- 2 Pork Tenderloins, about 1 Pound Each, Trimmed of Excess Fat and Silver Skin
- ¼ Cup Latin Spice Rub

Instructions

- Prepare a medium-hot fire in a charcoal Traeger Grill or preheat a gas Traeger Grill on medium high. Remove the tenderloins from the refrigerator 20 to 30 minutes before Traeger Grill and place them on a large, rimmed back sheet. Rub the pork on all sides with olive oil. Liberally season the tenderloins on all sides with the spice rub.
- To create a cool zone, bank the coals to one side of the Traeger Grill or turn off one of the burners. Oil the Traeger Grill grate. Place the tenderloins directly over the medium-hot fire. Traeger Grill the pork, turn to sear on all sides, for about 8 minutes. Move the tenderloins to the cooler part of the Traeger Grill, cover, and Traeger Grill until the meat is slightly pink in the center, or an instant-read thermometer inserted into the thickest part of a tenderloin registers 145°F, 8 to 10 minutes longer. Transfer the pork to a car board and let rest for 5 minutes. Cut the pork on the diagonal, across the grain, into ½-inch-thick slices and divide among warmed dinner plates. Serve immediately.

Pork Kebabs with marinated Mushrooms
Ingredients

- 2 Garlic Cloves Crushed
- 24 Button Mushrooms
- 24 Fresh Sage Leaves
- Salt
- 450gram Pork Fillet Cut Into 1 Inch Chunks
- 4 Tablespoon Olive Oil
- Freshly Ground Black Pepper

Instructions

- The first then you need to do if you are going to be us wooden skewers for make the kebabs is to soak them in some water for at least half an hour. This will then help to ensure that they don't burn when placed on the barbecue. Now you need to prepare the pork. To do this you need to place in a bowl the olive oil, garlic, salt and pepper and mix together thoroughly. Once this has been done now

you need to put the chunks of pork in to the mixture and toss them around thoroughly so each piece of meat is thoroughly coated.
- Then you can leave the meat in the refrigerator or to one side for 20 minutes or more. It is best to let the meat stay in the sauce for at least 20 minutes to help it absorb some of it. Whilst the barbecue is heat up now you are ready to start make the kebabs on to each skewer thread pieces of pork with the mushrooms and sage leaves. Ideally you should thread on one piece of meat and then one mushroom and sage leave and continue do this until all skewers have these Ingredients on them. Once the kebabs are ready you should cook them over a high heat on the barbecue for 15 to 20 minutes remember to turn them often to prevent them from burn. Plus baste them regularly with any of the sauce that remains. As soon as the meat is cooked through then they are ready to serve.

Chili-Rubbed Pork with Salsa
Ingredients

- 4 Nectarines, Halved, Pitted, And Cut Into ½-Inch Cubes
- ½ Cup Diced Red Onion
- ½ Cup Loosely Packed Chopped Fresh Cilantro
- 1 Small Jalapeño Chile, Include Seeds and Ribs, Minced
- 2 Tablespoons Fresh Lime Juice
- ¼ Cup Traeger Grill Every Day Spice Rub
- Nectarine Salsa
- 1 Tablespoon Honey
- ½ Teaspoon Kosher or Sea Salt
- ¼ Teaspoon Red Pepper Flakes
- 2 Pork Tenderloins, about 1 Pound Each, Trimmed of Excess Fat and Silver Skin
- Extra-Virgin Olive Oil

Instructions

- Prepare a medium-hot fire in a charcoal Traeger Grill or preheat a gas Traeger Grill on medium high. Remove the tenderloins from the refrigerator 20 to 30 minutes before Traeger Grill and place them on a large, rimmed back sheet. Rub the pork on all sides with olive oil. Liberally season the tenderloins on all sides with the spice rub. While the Traeger Grill is heat, make the salsa: In a bowl, combine the nectarines, onion, cilantro, jalapeño chile, lime juice, honey, salt, and red pepper flakes. Stir to combine. Set aside until ready to serve. To create a cool zone, bank the coals to one side of the Traeger Grill or turn off one of the burners. Oil the Traeger Grill grate.
-
- Place the tenderloins directly over the medium-hot fire. Traeger Grill the pork, turn to sear on all sides, for about 8 minutes. Move the tenderloins to the cooler part of the Traeger Grill, cover, and Traeger Grill until the meat is slightly pink in the center, or an instant-read thermometer inserted into the thickest part of a tenderloin registers 145°F, 8 to 10 minutes longer. Transfer the pork to a cut board and let rest for 5 minutes. Cut the pork on the diagonal, across the grain, into ½-inch-thick slices and divide among warmed dinner plates. Put a large spoonful of salsa alongside the pork. Serve immediately.

Pork Tenderloin in Ground Pepper
Ingredients

- 2 Tablespoons Extra-Virgin Olive Oil
- 2 Large Cloves Garlic, Minced

- 2 Pork Tenderloins, about 1 Pound Each, Trimmed of Excess Fat and Silver Skin
- ¼ Cup Plus 1 Tablespoon Dijon Mustard
- ¼ Cup Apricot Jam, Warmed
- 2 Teaspoons Freshly Ground Pepper

Instructions

- Prepare a medium-hot fire in a charcoal Traeger Grill or preheat a gas Traeger Grill on medium high. Remove the tenderloins from the refrigerator 20 to 30 minutes before Traeger Grill and place them on a large, rimmed back sheet. In a small bowl, whisk together the mustard, jam, olive oil, garlic, and pepper until smooth to make the glaze.
- Set aside half the glaze and brush the pork on all sides with the rest. To create a cool zone, bank the coals to one side of the Traeger Grill or turn off one of the burners. Oil the Traeger Grill grate. Place the tenderloins directly over the medium-hot fire. Traeger Grill the pork, turn to sear on all sides, for about 6 minutes. Move the tenderloins to the cooler part of the Traeger Grill and brush liberally with half of the reserved glaze. Cover and Traeger Grill until the meat is slightly pink in the center, or an instant-read thermometer registers 145°F when inserted into the tenderloins' thickest part, 10 to 12 minutes longer. Brush with the reserved glaze about 2 minutes before the pork is done. Transfer the pork to a car board and let rest for 5 minutes. Cut the pork on the diagonal, across the grain, into ½-inch-thick slices and divide among warmed dinner plates. Serve immediately.

Spicy Asian Rubbed Pork Chops
Ingredients

- ¼ Cup Latin Spice Rub
- 4 Bone-In, Center-Cut Pork Loin Chops, ¾ to 1 Inch Thick (10 To 12 Ounces Each)
- Extra-Virgin Olive Oil
- 1 Cup Chimichurri

Instructions

- Prepare a medium-hot fire in a charcoal Traeger Grill or preheat a gas Traeger Grill on medium high. Remove the pork chops from the refrigerator 20 to 30 minutes before Traeger Grill and place them on a rimmed back sheet.
- Rub the chops on both sides with olive oil. Liberally season the chops on both sides with the spice rub. While the Traeger Grill is heat, make the sauce. To create a cool zone, bank the coals to one side of the Traeger Grill or turn off one of the burners. Oil the Traeger Grill grate. Place the pork chops directly over the medium-hot fire.
- Traeger Grill on one side until nicely seared, about 4 minutes. Turn and cook until seared, 3 to 4 minutes longer. Move the chops to the cooler part of the Traeger Grill, cover, and Traeger Grill until the meat is slightly pink in the center, or an instant-read thermometer registers 145°F, 10 to 12 minutes longer. Remove the chops from the Traeger Grill and let rest for 5 minutes. Transfer the chops to warmed dinner plates and spoon some of the sauce over the top. Place the rest of the sauce in a bowl for pass. Serve immediately.

Traeger Grilled Tomatoes and Green Onions
Ingredients

- 1 Tablespoon Ground Cumin
- 1½ Teaspoons Kosher or Sea Salt
- 1½ Teaspoons Freshly Ground Pepper

- 4 Bone-In, Center-Cut Pork Loin Chops, ¾ to 1 Inch Thick (10 To 12 Ounces Each)
- 1 Tablespoon Ground Coriander
- 2 Tablespoons Extra-Virgin Olive Oil
- Bulgur Salad with Smoky Traeger Grill Ed Tomatoes and Green Onions

Instructions

- Prepare a medium-hot fire in a charcoal Traeger Grill or preheat a gas Traeger Grill on medium high. Remove the pork chops from the refrigerator 20 to 30 minutes before Traeger Grill and place them on a rimmed back sheet. In a small bowl, stir together the coriander, cumin, salt, pepper, and olive oil. Rub the chops on both sides with the spice paste.
- While the Traeger Grill is heat, soak the bulgur for the salad, prepare the tomatoes for Traeger Grill, and chop and measure the Ingredients for the salad. To create a cool zone, bank the coals to one side of the Traeger Grill or turn off one of the burners. Oil the Traeger Grill grate. Place the pork chops directly over the medium-hot fire. Traeger Grill the pork on one side until nicely seared, about 4 minutes. Turn and cook until seared, 3 to 4 minutes longer. Move the chops to the cooler part of the Traeger Grill, cover, and Traeger Grill until the meat is slightly pink in the center, or an instant read thermometer registers 145°F, 10 to 12 minutes longer. While the pork is cook, make the salad. Remove the chops from the Traeger Grill and let rest for 5 minutes. Transfer the chops to warmed dinner plates and accompany with the bulgur salad. Serve immediately.

Grilled Cider Vinegar Pork Chops
Ingredients

- 1 Tablespoon White Wine
- 2 Teaspoon Worcestershire Sauce
- 2 Teaspoon Onion Powder
- 4 Pork Chops (3/4-Inch-Thick Ones Are Best)
- 90ml Honey
- 3 Tablespoon Fresh Orange Juice
- 1 Tablespoon Cider Vinegar
- ½ Teaspoon Dried Tarragon
- 3 Tablespoon Dijon Mustard

Instructions

- Into a small bowl place, the honey, orange, vinegar, wine, Worcestershire sauce, onion powder, tarragon and mustard and mix together. Now place to one side. Next take the pork chops and make some cuts into the fatty edge of each one. This will then prevent the meat from actually curl whilst it is cook on the barbecue. However, make sure that you don't cut into the fat too far.
- Once this has been done place in a shallow dish and pour some of the marinade over them before then turn the chops over and pour the rest of the marinade over them. Cover and place in the refrigerator for at least 2 hours. Whilst the barbecue is heat up remove the chops from the refrigerator to allow them to come up to room temperature. Once the barbecue is hot enough and you have lightly oiled the Traeger Grill you can place the chops on it. Cook each side of the chop for about 12 to 15 minutes and during this time turn them over at least 3 or 4 times. Each time you turn the chops over remember to brush on any of the marinade that is left over. Once cooked you can nonservice them on a clean plate with say a fresh green salad and a jacket potato.

Parisian Traeger Grilled Pork Chops
Ingredients

- Kosher or Sea Salt
- Freshly Ground Pepper
- 4 Bone-In, Center-Cut Pork Loin Chops, ¾ to 1 Inch Thick (10 To 12 Ounces Each)
- Extra-Virgin Olive Oil
- 1¼ Cups Hoisin-Ginger Bast Sauce

Instructions

- Prepare a medium-hot fire in a charcoal Traeger Grill or preheat a gas Traeger Grill on medium high. Remove the pork chops from the refrigerator 20 to 30 minutes before Traeger Grill and place them on a rimmed back sheet. Rub the pork on both sides with olive oil. Season generously on both sides with salt and pepper. Have the bast sauce in a bowl with a brush next to the Traeger Grill. To create a cool zone, bank the coals to one side of the Traeger Grill or turn off one of the burners. Oil the Traeger Grill grate.
- Place the pork chops directly over the medium-hot fire. Traeger Grill the pork on one side until nicely seared, about 4 minutes. Turn, baste with some of the sauce, and cook until seared, 3 to 4 minutes longer. Move the chops to the cooler part of the Traeger Grill, baste with more sauce, cover, and Traeger Grill, bast a couple more times with the remain sauce, until the meat is slightly pink in the center, or an instant-read thermometer registers 145°F, 10 to 12 minutes longer. Remove the chops from the Traeger Grill and let rest for 5 minutes before serve.

Chorizo Burgers and Traeger Grilled Red Onions
Ingredients

- 1 Large Egg, Beaten
- 1 Teaspoon Kosher or Sea Salt
- 1 Red Onion, Cut Into ½-Inch-Thick Slices
- ¼ Cup Olive Oil
- 4 Slices Monterey Jack Cheese
- 1 Pound Freshly Ground Chuck
- 8 Ounces Fresh Bulk Chorizo Sausage
- 2 Green Onions, include 2 Inches of Green Tops, Very Thinly Sliced
- ¼ Cup Loosely Packed Chopped Fresh Cilantro
- 4 Sesame-Seed Hamburger Buns, Split
- 4 Lettuce Leaves
- Mayonnaise

Instructions

- Prepare a hot fire in a charcoal Traeger Grill or preheat a gas Traeger Grill on high. In a large bowl, combine the ground chuck, sausage, green onions, cilantro, egg, and salt and mix thoroughly. Divide into 4 equal portions, and shape each portion into a patty 1 inch thick. Refrigerate the patties while the Traeger Grill heats.
- Arrange the onion slices in a s le layer on a rimmed back sheet and brush on both sides with 2 tablespoons of the olive oil. Oil the Traeger Grill grate. Place the onion slices directly over the hot fire and Traeger Grill, turn once, until Traeger Grill marks appear on both sides and the onions are crisp tender when pierced with a knife, about 4 minutes per side. (If you have room, Traeger Grill the burgers at the same time.) Brush the burgers on both sides with the remain 2 tablespoons olive oil. Place the burgers directly over the hot fire and sear on one side, 3 to 4 minutes. Turn and sear on the other side until juicy and cooked through, about 4 minutes longer. Place a slice of cheese on each burger, cover the Traeger Grill, and cook until the cheese is melted, about 1 minute longer. Place the

buns, cut side down, on the Traeger Grill to toast during the last minute while the burgers are Traeger Grill. Serve the burgers on the toasted buns with the Traeger Grill ed onion slices, lettuce, and mayonnaise.

Grilled Sausage Hoagies with Bell Pepper

Ingredients

- 4 Large Sweet or Hot Fresh Italian Sausages, Slit Lengthwise Without Cut in Half
- 1 Large Walla Walla Or Other Sweet Onion, Cut Into ½-Inch-Thick Slices
- 1 Large Red Bell Pepper, Quartered Lengthwise, Seeded, And Defibbed
- ¼ Cup Extra-Virgin Olive Oil, Plus More for Brush
- 1 Large Clove Garlic, Minced
- 2 Teaspoons Dried Oregano, Crushed
- 4 (8-Inch-Long) Crusty Italian Submarine Sandwich Rolls, Split
- 4 To 6 Large Pepperoncini, Cored, Seeded, And Thinly Sliced

Instructions

- Prepare a medium-hot fire in a charcoal Traeger Grill or preheat a gas Traeger Grill on medium high. In a small bowl, stir together the ¼ cup olive oil, the garlic, and oregano. Set aside. Arrange the sausages on a plate and brush on all sides with olive oil.
- Arrange the onion slices and bell pepper pieces in a s le layer on a large, rimmed back sheet and brush on both sides with olive oil. Oil the Traeger Grill grate. Place the onion and bell pepper directly over the medium-hot fire and Traeger Grill, turn once, until dark brown Traeger Grill marks appear on both sides and the vegetables are crisp-tender when pierced with a knife, about 3 minutes per side. If you have room, without crowd, Traeger Grill the sausages at the same time.
- Place the sausages, skin side down, directly over the medium-hot fire. Traeger Grill the sausages, turn once, until Traeger Grill marks are etched across the sausages on both sides and they are fully cooked through, 6 to 8 minutes total. Place the rolls, cut side down, on the Traeger Grill to toast during the last 30 to 60 seconds the sausages are Traeger Grill. Transfer the Traeger Grill ed vegetables to a cut board. Cut the onion slices in half and the pepper quarters lengthwise into narrowing strips. Brush the toasted sides of each roll with some of the garlic oil. Place a Traeger Grill ed sausage on each roll bottom. Scatter the onion and pepper pieces and the pepperoncini over the sausages. Put the roll tops in place and serve immediately.

Yellow Mustard Baby Back Ribs

Ingredients

- 1 tablespoon Worcestershire sauce
- Traeger Pork and Poultry Rub, or your favorite barbecue rub
- 1/2 cup packed dark brown sugar
- 1/3 cup honey, warmed
- 2 racks baby back pork ribs (about 5 pounds total), trimmed
- 1/3 cup yellow mustard
- 1/2 cup apple juice (divided use), plus more if needed
- Traeger BBQ Sauce, or your favorite barbecue sauce

Instructions

- If your butcher has not already done so, remove the thin papery membrane from the bone-side of the ribs by work the tip of a butter knife or a screwdriver underneath the membrane over a middle bone. Use paper towels to get a firm grip, then tear the membrane off. In a small bowl, combine the mustard, 1/4 cup of apple juice (reserve the rest), and the Worcestershire sauce. Spread thinly on both sides of the ribs; season with Traeger Pork and Poultry Rub. When ready to cook, start the Traeger Grill on Smoke with the lid open until the fire is established (4 to 5 minutes).
- Smoke the ribs, meat-side up, for 3 hours. Transfer the ribs to a rimmed back sheet but leave the Traeger Grill on. Set the temperature to 225 degrees F. Tear off four long sheets of heavy-duty aluminum foil. Top with a rack of ribs; pull up the sides to keep the liquid enclosed. Sprinkle half the brown sugar on the rack, then top with half the honey and half of the remain apple juice. (Use a bit more apple juice if you want.) Lay another piece of foil on top and tightly crimp the edges so there's no leakage. Repeat with the remaining rack of ribs.

Chapter 4: Poultry Recipes

Shish Tao Traeger Grilled Chicken
Ingredients

- 180ml Plain Yogurt
- ¼ Teaspoon Ground All Spice
- ¼ Teaspoon Ground Cinnamon
- ¼ Teaspoon Ground Cardamom
- 4 Cloves Garlic (Minced)
- 2 Teaspoons Tomato Paste
- 1 ½ Teaspoons Salt
- 1 Teaspoon Dried Oregano
- 907gram Chicken Breast (Cut Into 2 Inch Pieces)
- 2 Onions (Cut into Large Chunks)
- 1 Large Green Bell Pepper (Cut into Large Chunks and Seeds Removed)
- 60ml Fresh Lemon Juice
- 60ml Vegetable Oil
- ¼ Teaspoon Ground Black Pepper

Instructions

- In a bowl whisk together the lemon juice, oil, yogurt, garlic, tomato paste, oregano, all spice, cinnamon, cardamom, oregano, pepper and salt. Then add the chicken and toss it through the mixture to make sure that all pieces are well coated. Then transfer to a large plastic bag (resealable kind is best) and place in the refrigerator for 4 hours.
- Whilst you are thread the chicken, onions and bell pepper on to skewers start up the barbecue so it has reached the required temperature to cook these chicken kebabs. It is important that you cook the chicken over a medium to high heat for 5 minutes on each side. The exterior of the meat should be golden in color, whilst when you make an insertion in to the meat it should look white inside. Once they have been cooked through properly remove kebabs from heat then sprinkle over some of the flat leaf parsley before serve.

Traeger Grilled Pizza with Barbecued Chicken with Cheddar Cheese
Ingredients

- ¾ Cup Thinly Sliced White Onion
- 1 Tablespoon Minced Garlic
- 1 Red Bell Pepper, Halved Lengthwise, Seeded, Defibbed, And Cut into Long,
- Narrowing strips
- 2 Cups (8 Ounces) Coarsely Shredded Medium or Sharp Cheddar Cheese
- Vegetable-Oil Cook Spray
- 1 16-To 18-Ounce Package Fresh or Frozen Pizza Dough
- 2 Cups Shredded Roast Chicken Breast
- ¾ Cup Store-Bought Barbecue Sauce
- All-Purpose Flour for Dust
- ¼ Cup Lightly Packed Fresh Cilantro Leaves

Instructions

- If using fresh dough, remove it from the refrigerator 30 minutes before you roll it out. If us frozen dough, transfer it to the refrigerator a day before you plan to make pizza, so it can thawing slowly, and then let it sit at room temperature for 30 minutes before you roll it out. Prepare a hot fire in a charcoal Traeger Grill or preheat a gas Traeger Grill on high.
- If the Traeger Grill has a built-in thermometer, it should register between 500° and 600°F. Have ready a 14-inch, non-perforated pizza pan, preferably an inexpensive aluminum one. While the Traeger Grill heats, prepare the top s: In a bowl, toss the chicken with ¼ cup of the barbecue sauce. Set aside. Have all the other top s—onion, garlic, bell pepper, cheese—ready for assembly. Coat the pizza pan with the vegetable-oil spray. Remove the dough from the plastic bag and place on a lightly floured work surface.
- Lightly dust the dough with flour. Us a roll pin, roll the dough into a 10-inch round without roll over the edges. Lift the dough occasionally to make sure it isn't stick to the work surface. Shake the excess flour from the dough. Lay the dough on the prepared pizza pan and gently stretch it into a 14-inch round. To top the pizza: Spread the remain ½ cup barbecue sauce over the dough, leave a 1-inch border. Evenly scatter the onion, garlic, and red pepper over the sauce. Distribute the chicken over the vegetables, then top with the cheese. Place the pizza in the center of the Traeger Grill directly over the hot fire and cover. (Work quickly so the Traeger Grill temperature doesn't drop too much.) Traeger Grill the pizza until the crust is crisp and golden brown, and the cheese is bubbly and melted, about 10 minutes. Us a pizza peel or thick oven mitts, remove the pizza from the Traeger Grill. Scatter the cilantro over the top. Cut the pizza into wedges and serve immediately.

Traeger Grilled Butter Chicken

Ingredients

- 120ml Melted Butter or Clarified Butter (Ghee)
- 4 to 5 Cloves of Garlic (Minced)
- 1 Serrano Chili (Seeds Removed and Minced)
- 2 ½ Tablespoons Ground Ginger
- 1.3 to 1.8 kg Whole Chicken (Cut into Quarters and Skin Removed)
- 114gram of Pureed Onion
- 120ml Plain Yogurt
- 1 Tablespoon Ground Coriander Seeds
- 1 Tablespoon Oil
- 1 ½ Teaspoons Salt

Instructions

- Combine together the onion, yogurt, garlic, chili, Ginger, coriander, oil and salt in a bowl. When combined together thoroughly now pour of the chicken pieces that have been placed in a shallow glass bowl. Now cover the chicken and allow it to marinate in the sauce for between 8 and 12 hours.
- Next remove the chicken from the refrigerator and let it stand for 20 to 30 minutes. Whilst this is happening take half of the butter and melt it in saucepan and let it cook for 3 to 5 minutes. Whilst the chicken is come back up to room temperature turn on the barbecue so that you are able to then Traeger Grill the meat on it at a medium to high heat. Make sure that the Traeger Grill on which you place the meat has been lightly oiled first and then cook each piece of chicken for 25 to 30 minutes. You must make sure that you turn the chicken over regularly and baste it with the melted butter often. Once the chicken has cooked through remove from the Traeger Grill. Now place on to a clean plate and pour over the rest of the butter.

Maple Barbecued Chicken with Hot Chili Sauce
Ingredients

- 3 Tablespoons Hot Chili Sauce (Optional)
- 1 Tablespoon Cider Vinegar
- 1 Tablespoon Canola Oil
- 4 Skinless Chicken Thighs
- 3 Tablespoons Maple Syrup
- 2 Teaspoon Dijon Mustard
- Salt
- Freshly Ground Pepper

Instructions

- Whilst the barbecue is heat up in a saucepan combine together the maple syrup, cider vinegar and mustard. Plus of course the hot chili sauce if you are look to give this recipe an extra kick. After mix the Ingredients together place saucepan on a medium heat and let the mixture simmer for 5 minutes.
- Next you need to brush the chicken with the oil before then sprinkle on some salt and pepper to season. Then place them on to the Traeger Grill and cook for between 10 and 15 minutes. As you cook them turn them regularly and each time that you turn them brush a generous amount of the sauce over them. Once cooked place on a clean plate and serve immediately. Any sauce left over can either be poured over the chicken thighs or placed a bowl, which the thighs can then be dipped into.

Traeger Grilled Chicken with Sweet Red Chili
Ingredients

- 1 Teaspoon Fresh Lime Juice
- 1 Tablespoon Fresh Cilantro (Minced)
- 1.13Kg Chicken Wings
- 350ml Jar of Peach Jam
- 240ml Thai Sweet Red Chili Sauce

Instructions

- In a bowl mix together the peach jam, the chili sauce, the lime juice and cilantro. Take half of this mixture and pour into a bowl, as you will use this a dip sauce to serve with the cooked chicken wings. After your barbecue has reached the right temperature and you have sprayed the Traeger Grill with oil to prevent the chicken wings from stick place them on it.
- Traeger Grill the wings for between 20 and 25 minutes, remember to turn them over frequently to ensure that they are cooked through evenly. Only when the juices are run clear from the chickens can you then apply the remain half of the sauce to glaze them. After apply the glaze make sure that you cook them for a further 3 to 5 minutes. Again, you need to turn them over once during this time to make sure that they are well coated with the glaze.

Cornish Lemon and Thyme Game Hens
Ingredients

- 3 Cloves Garlic
- Kosher or Sea Salt
- Freshly Ground Pepper
- ½ Cup (1 Stick) Unsalted Butter, At Room Temperature, Cut into Chunks

- 4 Cornish Game Hens
- Zest Of 1 Lemon, Removed In ½-Inch-Wide Strips
- 1 Tablespoon Fresh Thyme Leaves

Instructions

- Prepare a medium fire in a charcoal Traeger Grill or preheat a gas Traeger Grill on medium. In a mini-chop or small food processor fitted with the metal blade, combine the garlic, lemon zest, thyme, and ½ teaspoon each salt and pepper and process until minced. Add the butter and process until well combined.
- To butterfly the hens, place a hen, breast down, on a cut board. Us poultry shears, sharp, sturdy kitchen scissors, or a chef's knife, cut through the hen from one end to the other on each side of the backbone to remove it. Turn the hen breast side up, pull the body open, and use the heel of your hand to press down firmly, crack the rib bones so the hen rests flat. Repeat with the other hens. Transfer to a large, rimmed back sheet. Us your f errs, loosen the skin from the breast of a hen to create a pocket. Then, us about 2 tablespoons of the prepared butter, smear the butter all over the breast meat with your f errs, push some butter over the thigh meat. Repeat with the other hens. Rub all over with any remain butter and season with salt and pepper. To create a cool zone, bank the coals to one side of the Traeger Grill or turn off one of the burners.
- Oil the Traeger Grill grate. Place the hens, skin side down, directly over the medium fire, cover, and sear on one side, about 5 minutes. Turn, re-cover, and sear on the other side for about 5 minutes. Move the hens to the cooler part of the Traeger Grill, re-cover, and Traeger Grill until the juices run clear when the thickest part of the thigh is pierced with a knife, or an instant-read thermometer registers 165°F, 5 to 7 minutes longer. Transfer the hens to warmed dinner plates and let rest for 5 minutes before serve.

Barbecue Mustard Grilled Chicken Breasts
Ingredients

- 1 ½ Teaspoons Dijon or English Mustard
- 3 Tablespoons Honey
- 3 Tablespoons Tomato Ketchup
- 1 Teaspoon Olive Oil
- 4 x 250gram Skinless Chicken Breasts
- Zest Of 1 Orange
- 1 Dried Chili
- 1 ½ Teaspoons (Heaped) Smoked Paprika
- 1/16 Teaspoon Sea Salt
- Freshly Ground Black Pepper to Taste

Instructions

- Into a bowl put the finely grated zest of the orange, along with the dried chili (crumbled), the paprika, mustard, honey, tomato ketchup and the olive oil. Then after combine all these Ingredients together add a pinch of salt along with some pepper then stir again. Take out a couple of spoonsful of the mixture made and put to one side. To the rest of the marinade in the bowl you add the chicken breasts.
- Turn them over so that they are completed coated by the marinade made and cover with plastic wrap before leave to one side for 5 to 10 minutes. Once the barbecue has heated up correctly you need to put the chicken on the Traeger Grill but before you do make sure that you lightly oil it. When you place them on the Traeger Grill make sure that the heat underneath isn't too high. If you notice the outer part of the chicken is start to char quickly then move them over to a cooler part of the barbecue

and reduce the heat if possible. You should be aim to cook the chickens on each side for about 5 minutes, turn them every minute and bast them with some more of the marinade left in the bowl.
- You should only remove them from the heat when they have turned a golden brown and are cooked all the way through. The best way of test to see that they are cooked all the way through is to push a skewer in to. If the juices that flow out are clear then you know the chicken is properly cooked. Remove from heat, then place on clean plates and spoon some of the sauce that you put aside earlier over them.

Traeger Grilled Chicken Koftas
Ingredients

- 2 Cloves Garlic (Minced)
- 1 Tablespoon Cilantro (Finely Chopped)
- 1 Teaspoon Hot Sauce
- 450gram Ground Chicken Breast
- 229gram Bread Crumbs
- 1 Egg (Lightly Beaten)
- 1 Teaspoon Salt
- ¼ Teaspoon Freshly Ground Black Pepper

Instructions

- In a large mix bowl combine together the ground chicken breast, bread crumbs, egg, garlic, cilantro, hot sauce, salt and pepper.
- Then cover and allow to rest in the refrigerator as this will make it much easier to then form the Koftas (sausage shape patties), which you form around a metal skewer. As soon as you have formed the Koftas around the skewer they are now ready to cook. Place them about 3 inches above the barbecue and allow them to cook for around 10 minutes. During this time make sure that you turn them frequently to ensure that they don't burn and that the meat cooks evenly. As soon as they are cooked you can then serve them.

Thai Traeger Grilled Chicken with White Pepper
Ingredients

- ½ Teaspoon Minced Birds Eye Chili

- 1 Teaspoon Garlic (Minced)
- ¼ Teaspoon Salt
- 2 Tablespoons Fresh Chopped Cilantro
- 1 Teaspoon Ground Turmeric
- 1 Teaspoon Curry Powder
- ½ Teaspoon White Pepper
- 6 Tablespoons Rice Vinegar
- 1.36Kg Chicken Breast (Cut into Pieces)
- 120ml Coconut Milk
- 2 Tablespoons Fish Sauce
- 2 Tablespoons Garlic (Minced)
- 4 Tablespoons Water
- 4 Tablespoons Sugar

Instructions

- In a shallow dish mix the coconut milk, fish sauce, garlic, cilantro, turmeric, curry powder and white pepper. Then when thoroughly combined add the chicken pieces and turn them over in the sauce so that they are completely coated. Cover and place in the refrigerator for 4 hours or overnight to let the chicken pieces marinate in the sauce. Whilst the chicken is marina you can now make the sauce.
- To do this you place the vinegar, water, sugar, garlic, chili and salt in to a saucepan and bra this mixture to the boil. Now lower the heat and let the mixture simmer for about 5 minutes. It is important you stir the sauce from time to time to prevent it stick to the base of the saucepan and burn. Remove from heat and allow to cool before place into a serve bowl. When cook the chicken on the barbecue make sure that the Traeger Grill has been lightly oiled first. Cook each piece of chicken for 10 minutes on each side or until the juices start to run out of them clear. Brush them with a little of the sauce you made earlier before serve, whilst the rest remains in the serve dish and which people can then dip the chicken wings into if they wish.

Garlic-Traeger Tomato Grilled Chicken
Ingredients

- 1 Teaspoon Garlic Powder
- Extra-Virgin Olive Oil
- 1 Lime, Quartered
- 1½ Cups (6 Ounces) Grated Monterey Jack Cheese
- 2 Cups Shredded Iceberg Lettuce
- 1½ Cups Store-Bought Tomatillo Salsa) 8 8-Inch Flour
- Tortillas
- 1 Cup Loosely Packed Fresh Cilantro Leaves
- 4 Boneless, Skinless Chicken Breast Halves
- 1½ Tablespoons Chili Powder
- 1½ Teaspoons Ground Turmeric
- 1½ Teaspoons Kosher or Sea Salt
- 2 Large Hass Avocados, Halved, Pitted, Peeled, And Cut into Thin Wedges

Instructions

- Prepare a medium-hot fire in a charcoal Traeger Grill or preheat a gas Traeger Grill on medium high. Remove any clumps to the chicken breasts and place the breasts in a shallow back dish or bowl. In a

small bowl, combine the chili powder, turmeric, salt, and garlic powder. Rub the chicken breasts on both sides with olive oil and then rub them with the spice rub. Set aside until the Traeger Grill is ready.
- Arrange the lime, cilantro, avocados, cheese, lettuce, and salsa in separate small bowls and have them ready for assemble the tacos. Oil the Traeger Grill grate. Place the chicken breasts directly over the medium-hot fire and sear on one side, about 4 minutes. Turn and sear on the other side until the juices run clear when the thickest part of a breast is pierced with a knife, or an instant read thermometer registers 165°F, about 4 minutes longer. While the chicken is cook, Traeger Grill the tortillas.
- Depend on the size of the Traeger Grill, lay 1 or 2 tortillas on the Traeger Grill at a time, warm them over direct heat for about 15 seconds per side. Stack them on a plate and keep warm. Transfer the chicken to a cut board and cut across the grain into ½-inch-thick strips. Arrange on a warmed serve plate. Let diners assemble their own tacos. To assemble, place 2 chicken slices in a tortilla, squeeze a bit of lime juice over the chicken, and mound with cilantro, avocado, cheese, and lettuce. Spoon some salsa on top. Serve with plenty of napkins!

Catalan Cinnamon Chicken Quarters
Ingredients

- 120ml Red Wine
- ¼ Teaspoon Freshly Ground Black Pepper
- 114gram Olives (Pitted and Chopped)
- 5 Cloves of Garlic (Minced)
- 2 Tablespoons Olive Oil
- 1 Teaspoon Salt
- ½ Teaspoon Cumin
- 4 Chicken Leg Quarters
- 1 Onion (Chopped)
- 172gram Chorizo (Spicy Sausage Chopped)
- 1 Can Whole Tomatoes (Drained and Chopped)
- ½ Teaspoon Cinnamon
- ¼ Teaspoon Cayenne Pepper

Instructions

- In a bowl combine together the salt, cumin, black pepper and cayenne pepper and rub over the surface of the chicken, make sure you get as much of this rub under the skin of the chicken as well. Allow the chicken to rest in the refrigerator for a while (covered) whilst you start prepare the sauce to go with them.
- To make the sauce sauté the onions and garlic in the olive oil before add the sausage, tomatoes and red wine. Allow this to simmer on a low heat whilst you are then cook the chicken quarters on the barbecue. You should cook the chicken quarters until the juice runs clear from them, remember to turn them over often to prevent the skin from burn. Whilst the chicken is cook you should now add the olives to the sauce and continue simmer it for a further 20 minutes. To serve simply place one of the chicken quarters on to a plate and then pour over some of the sauce.

Thai Grilled Chicken Satay with Soy Sauce
Ingredients

- 2 Cloves Garlic (Crushed)
- 1 Teaspoon Ground Cumin

- 2 Teaspoon Red Thai Curry Paste
- 1 Tablespoon Fish Sauce
- 1 Teaspoon Tomato Paste
- 1 Tablespoon Brown Sugar
- 1 Teaspoon Ground Coriander
- 1 Tablespoon Fresh Lime Juice
- 1 Teaspoon Muscovado Sugar
- 907gram Chicken Breasts Without the Skin (Cut into Strips)
- 2 Tablespoons Vegetable Oil
- 2 Tablespoons Soy Sauce
- 2 Teaspoons Tamarind Paste
- 1 Stalk Lemon Grass (Chopped)
- ½ Teaspoon Chili Powder
- 2 Tablespoons Peanut Butter (Crunchy)
- 2 Tablespoons Peanuts (Chopped)
- 1 Can Coconut Milk

Instructions

- You first need to make up the sauce in which the chicken pieces will be marinated. To do it get a large bowl and into place the vegetable oil, soy sauce, tamarind paste, lemon grass, garlic, cumin, coriander, lime juice, sugar and chili powder. Make sure that you combine these Ingredients well before add the chicken and stir round until you know all the chicken pieces have been coated in the marinade. Cover the bowl and place in the refrigerator for one hour. Whilst the chicken is marina you can make the satay (peanut) sauce.
- To do this into a small saucepan put the peanut butter, peanuts, coconut milk, red Thai curry paste, fish sauce, tomato paste and sugar. Cook the Ingredients on a medium to low heat, make sure that you stir it frequently and until it looks smooth. It is important that you keep the sauce warm after it has been made so turn the heat down as low as possible and cover. To cook the chicken pieces, you first need to thread them onto skewers and when this is turn place them on to the lightly oiled barbecue Traeger Grill and allow them to cook on each side for around 3 to 5 minutes. Once the chicken is thoroughly cooked remove from the heat and either pour the satay sauce over them or provide it in a bowl which guests can then dip their chicken kebabs if they wish.

Spicy Plum Chutney Grilled Chicken Thighs
Ingredients

- 1 Small Coarsely Chopped Onion
- 60ml Honey
- 60ml Soy Sauce
- 2 Tablespoons Fresh Lime Juice
- 1 Tablespoon Granulated Sugar
- 4 Cloves Garlic (Coarsely Chopped)
- 1 Tablespoon Fresh Coarsely Chopped Ginger
- 1 Coarsely Chopped Thai Chili
- ¼ Teaspoon Ground Cinnamon
- ¼ Teaspoon Ground Cloves
- 8 Chicken Thighs (Skin on And Bone In)
- Salt and Freshly Ground Black Pepper
- Plum Sauce

- 2 Tablespoons Peanut Oil
- 680gram Red or Purple Plums (Pitted and Coarsely Chopped)

Instructions

- Before you do anything else you need to make the plum sauce. To do this in a medium size saucepan place the oil and heat it up. When it is hot enough add the onions and garlic and cook until they are soft. Then add to these the Ginger, cinnamon, Thai chili and cloves and cook for 2 minutes.
- Now you need to add the rest of the Ingredients listed above and cook until the plums have softened and the sauce has started to thicken. Then place the mixture into a food processor or blender and mix them until smooth. Pour into a bowl and allow to cool. After make the sauce you need to heat the barbecue up to a medium low indirect heat for cook the chicken thighs. Just before you place the chicken thighs on to the Traeger Grill lightly oil it first and season the thighs with salt and pepper.
- Cook on either side until they turn a light golden brown between 1 and 5 minutes. Now brush one side of the chicken with the plum sauce made earlier and turn the thighs over and continue cook for 3 to 4 minutes. Once this time has elapsed brush the sides of the thighs fac you with more sauce and again turn them over to cook for another 3 to 4 minutes. You should continue turn and bast the thighs with the plum sauce until they are cooked through. You will find that they will be cooked through properly after 15 to 20 minutes. However, if you are unsure just insert a skewer in to the thickest part of the thigh. If you notice the juices run out are clear then the chicken is cooked. Please don't forget to keep the thighs at a good height above the heat to prevent them and the sauce from burn.

Chicken Tikka Skewers with Cherry Tomatoes
Ingredients

- Handful Coriander Leaves Chopped
- 4 Skinless Boneless Chicken Breasts Cut into Cubes
- 150gram Low Fat Natural Yogurt
- 2 Tablespoon Hot Curry Paste
- 4 Whole meal Chapattis
- 50gram Lamb's Lettuce or Pea Shoots
- ½ Cucumber Cut in Half Lengthways, Deseeded and then Sliced
- 1 Red Onion Thinly Sliced
- 250gram Cherry Tomatoes
- Juice 1 Lemon

Instructions

- Place the wooden skewers (8 in all) in some water in a bowl to soak. After do this you need to place the yogurt and curry paste in a bowl and mix together then to this you add the cubes of chicken.
- Make sure that you stir the chicken into the mixture well to ensure all pieces are coated. Now cover the top of the bowl and place in the refrigerator to marinate for an hour or so. Next in another bowl place the cucumber, red onion, coriander and lemon and toss them altogether. Again, place this bowl in the refrigerator (covered over) and leave there until you are ready to serve the chicken. Whilst the barbecue is heated up now you need to start prepare the skewers. You must make sure that you shake off any excess marinade before then thread the pieces of chicken on to the skewers.
- After thread on a piece of chicken now thread on a cherry tomato and do this until all skewers have been used. Once the Chicken Tikka skewers are ready and the barbecue has heated up you are now ready to start cook. You should keep the skewers on the barbecue for between 15 and 20 minutes, make sure that you turn them regularly so that they get cooked through and become a nice brown

color. When it comes to serve the skewers place them to one side on a clean plate to rest for a few minutes whilst you prepare the salad. Into the salad before serve mix the lettuce and pea shoots and divide this equally between four plates and on top of which you then place two of the skewers.
- Serve them with chapattis that have been warmed through on the barbecue. The best way to warm the chapattis on the barbecue is to wrap them in some aluminum foil.

Sweet & Spicy Grilled Chicken
Ingredients

- 1kg Chicken Wings
- 4 Tablespoon Curry Paste
- 3 Tablespoon Mango Chutney
- 200g Sliced Radishes
- 1 Cucumber Halved Lengthways and Sliced
- 1 Small Bunch Roughly Chopped Mint
- Juice Of 1 Lemon

Instructions

- Start get the barbecue heated up. Now in to a large bowl place the curry pastes and 2 tablespoons of the mango chutney with a little salt and pepper to season, then stir well. Place the chicken wings in the mixture and toss around so that they are all well coated and then leave to marinate for a short while.
- Now place on to the barbecue griddle make sure that the surface has been lightly oiled first to prevent the chicken stick to it. Now cook for between 40 and 45 minutes, turn occasionally until all sides are golden brown and the wings are cooked through. The quickest way to determine if the wings have been cooked through is to stick a skewer into the thickest part and when removed do the juices run clear.
- Finally, just before you are about to serve the chicken wings in another bowl place the radishes, cucumber, mint, the rest of the mango chutney and the lemon juice and stir thoroughly. Now place the chicken wings on a clean plate and then beside it places the freshly made coleslaw.

Mustard Chicken Drumsticks
Ingredients

- 8 Chicken Drumsticks
- 1 Tablespoon Olive Oil
- 1 Tablespoon Tomato Puree
- 2 Tablespoon Soy Sauce
- 1 Tablespoon Honey
- 1 Tablespoon Dijon Mustard

Instructions

- You need to make 3 slashes into each chicken drumstick as this will then help the meat to absorb quite a bit of the marinade you are about to make. Then place the drumsticks into a shallow dish. To make the marinade you need to place the soy sauce, honey, olive oil, mustard and tomato puree into a bowl and whisk together thoroughly.
- Once all these Ingredients have been combined pour some over the drumsticks before turn them over and pour the remainder of the marinade over them. Once this has been done you must place them in the refrigerator overnight (remember to cover them). Whilst the barbecue is heat up ready

for you to cook the drumsticks remove them from the refrigerator and allow them to come up to room temperature. When the barbecue is heated up sufficiently you can now place the drumsticks on to the Traeger Grill.
- Although there is oil in the marinade don't forget to brush some over the Traeger Grill to prevent the chicken drumsticks from stick to them. It is important that you cook these for around 35 minutes or until the juice inside them starts to run clear. Also, it is important to remember to turn them over regularly to prevent the exterior from become burnt and also to ensure that they cook right through. Once they are cooked now place them on a clean plate and serve to your wait guests.

Grilled Chicken Tikka Kebabs
Ingredients

- 2 Kg Boneless Chicken Loin Cut Into 1 ½ Inch Cubes
- 128gram White Sugar
- 240ml Soy Sauce
- 1 Onion Diced
- 5 Garlic Cloves Chopped
- 1 Teaspoon Ground Black Pepper

Instructions

- Into a bowl place the sugar, soy sauce, onion, garlic and black pepper and whisk together well. Then to this you add the diced-up pork and toss to ensure that all pieces are thoroughly coated in the marinade. Now cover the bowl over and place in the refrigerator for at least 2 hours. However, if you really want the meat to taste even much sweeter then allow the chicken to remain in the marinade overnight. Whilst you are preparing the kebabs you should get the barbecue ready.
- Place the Traeger Grill at a level so that the heat is very hot and make sure that it has been lightly oiled before you place the kebabs on it. On to each wooden skewer, which has been soak in water for 30 minutes, you thread on some of the pork. Once all the skewers have pork on them, they are ready to cook. Ideally you should cook each side of the kebab for between 3 and 5 minutes or until the center of the meat is no longer pink. As soon as the kebabs have cooked you can serve them up to your guests with such accompaniments as coleslaw, rice or potato salad.

Grilled Chicken & Chorizo Kebabs
Ingredients

- 5 Tablespoon Olive Oil
- 2 Tablespoon Red Wine Vinegar
- 4 Tablespoon Freshly Chopped Parsley
- 1 Red Chili Chopped
- 1 Garlic Clove Chopped
- 2 Teaspoon Dried Oregano
- 250g Chicken Breast Cut into Chunks
- 250g Chorizo Cut into Chunks
- Olive Oil for Brush the Kebabs
- 2 Teaspoon Smoked Paprika

Instructions

- On to several skewers you need to place chunks of the chicken and chorizo sausage and then lightly season with some salt and pepper before then brush with some olive oil before place on to the barbecue. It is important that whilst cook these for around 10 minutes you turn them regularly to prevent them from become burnt. Whilst the kebabs are cook you can now make the Chimichurri sauce.
- This is very simple to do simply place all the Ingredients above in a bowl and then whisk thoroughly. By the time you have done this the kebabs should have cooked and will be ready to serve. Simply place two kebabs on each clean plate and serve a small bowl of the Chimichurri beside them.

Barbecued Grilled Chicken Tikka Burgers
Ingredients

- 4 Tablespoon Brown Sauce
- 2 Teaspoon Clear Honey
- 2 Garlic Cloves Crushed
- 4 Skinless Chicken Breasts
- 4 Tablespoon Tomato Ketchup
- Splash of Chili Sauce (Optional)

Instructions

- In a large bowl combine together the tomato ketchup, brown sauce, honey and garlic cloves. It is at this time you also add the chili sauce if you wish this will give this sweet recipe a little kick. Once this has been done put take some of the mixture out as this you can then use as a sauce that people can put on to the chicken burgers after they have cooked. Next you need to cut halfway into the thickest part of the chicken breast and then open it up in the same way you would a book.
- You should flatten the breasts down slightly us the palm of your hand then place them in the bowl with the marinade and toss to ensure all parts of the breast are coated with it. Now place in the refrigerator for around 20 minutes (remember to cover the breasts over). Whilst the barbecue is heat up you now need to remove the chicken from the refrigerator to bra it back up to room temperature. Once the barbecue is heated up sufficiently you can now place the chicken breasts on the Traeger Grill, remember to brush it lightly with oil first. You should cook each chicken breast for around 10 minutes or until they are cooked through. Also, whilst cook the breasts remember to turn them over regularly to help the marinade to become sticky and also to help prevent the meat from burn. Once they are cooked you can place them in buns with slices of bacon (cooked) and some lettuce and slices of tomato and onion. Plus, don't forget to add a dollop of the sauce you put to one side earlier.

Rotisserie Melted Butter Chicken

Ingredients

- 1 Tablespoon Salt
- 1 Tablespoon Paprika
- 1.36 Kg Whole Chicken
- 57gram Butter (Melted)
- ¼ Tablespoon Ground Black Pepper

Instructions

- Season the inside of the chicken us a pinch of salt. Then spear it with the rotisserie skewer before then place on your preheated barbecue. Make sure that the heat is as hot as possible and then allow the chicken to cook for 10 minutes. Whilst the chicken is cook in a bowl mix together the melted butter, salt, paprika and pepper. Once the mixture is ready and the 10 minutes have elapsed reduce the heat and baste the chicken with the mixture you have just prepared. Once all the chicken has been basted you can close the lid and cook the chicken for 1 to 1 ½ hours.
- Whilst it is cook don't forget to regularly baste it with the mixture as this will help to prevent the meat from dry out. You know when the meat is ready when the juices run clear after insert a skewer into the thickest part of the chicken body or when you insert a meat thermometer the internal temperature of the chicken has reached 180 degrees Fahrenheit. After the meat has cooked you now remove it from the barbecue and allow it to rest for 10 to 15 minutes before then car it up and serve. Whilst it is rest make sure that you keep the meat covered up.

Traeger Grilled Chicken Breasts Tikka

Ingredients

- Extra-Virgin Olive Oil
- Freshly Ground Pepper
- 2 Tablespoons Minced Canned Chipotle Chiles In Adobo Sauce
- 1 Teaspoon Kosher or Sea Salt, Plus More for Season
- 4 Boneless, Skin-On Chicken Breast Halves
- 4 Tablespoons (½ Stick) Unsalted Butter
- ¼ Cup Honey

Instructions

- Prepare a medium-hot fire in a charcoal Traeger Grill or preheat a gas Traeger Grill on medium high. In a small saucepan or microwave-safe bowl, melt the butter. Add the honey, chiles, and 1 teaspoon salt and stir to mix thoroughly. Keep warm. Generously brush the chicken breasts on both sides with olive oil and season with salt and pepper.
- To create a cool zone, bank the coals to one side of the Traeger Grill or turn off one of the burners. Oil the Traeger Grill grate. Place the chicken breasts, skin side down, directly over the medium-hot fire and sear on one side, about 3 minutes. Turn and sear on the other side for 3 to 4 minutes. Move the chicken to the cooler part of the Traeger Grill, and brush generously on both sides with the chipotle butter.
- Cover and Traeger Grill, bast once or twice with more chipotle butter, until the juices run clear when the thickest part of a breast is pierced with a knife, or an instant-read thermometer registers 165°F, 6 to 8 minutes longer. Baste the chicken once or twice while it is Traeger Grill. Divide the breasts among warmed dinner plates and serve immediately.

Chicken Breasts Tikka with Mustard Paste
Ingredients

- ½ Teaspoon Freshly Ground Pepper
- 2 Tablespoons Extra-Virgin Olive Oil
- 1 Tablespoon Dried Tarragon Leaves, Crushed
- 4 Boneless, Skin-On Chicken Breast Halves

Instructions

- Prepare a medium-hot fire in a charcoal Traeger Grill or preheat a gas Traeger Grill on medium high. In a bowl or back dish large enough to hold the chicken, combine the mustard, olive oil, tarragon, and pepper. Stir to mix thoroughly. Add the chicken breasts and turn to coat on both sides. Set aside until the Traeger Grill is ready. To create a cool zone, bank the coals to one side of the Traeger Grill or turn off one of the burners. Oil the Traeger Grill grate. Place the chicken breasts, skin side down, directly over the medium-hot fire and sear on one side, about 5 minutes.
- Turn and sear on the other side for 5 minutes. Move the chicken breasts to the cooler part of the Traeger Grill, cover, and Traeger Grill until the juices run clear when the thickest part of a chicken breast is pierced with a knife, or an instant-read thermometer registers 165°F, 5 to 7 minutes longer. Divide the chicken breasts among warmed plates. Serve immediately.

Chicken Breasts with Pesto
Ingredients

- 1½ Teaspoons Kosher or Sea Salt
- 1½ Teaspoons Freshly Ground Pepper
- 4 Boneless, Skinless Chicken Breast Halves
- 2 Teaspoons Ground Cumin
- Extra-Virgin Olive Oil
- ½ Cup Moroccan Pesto

Instructions

- Prepare a medium-hot fire in a charcoal Traeger Grill or preheat a gas Traeger Grill on medium high. Remove any pieces of the chicken breasts and place the breasts in a shallow back dish or bowl. In a small bowl, combine the cumin, salt, and pepper.

- Rub the chicken breasts on both sides with olive oil and then rub them with the spice rub. Set aside until the Traeger Grill is ready. Oil the Traeger Grill grate. Place the chicken breasts directly over the medium-hot fire and sear on one side, about 4 minutes. Turn and sear on the other side until the juices run clear when the thickest part of a breast is pierced with a knife, or an instant read thermometer registers 165°F, about 4 minutes longer. Divide the chicken breasts among warmed plates and drizzle with the pesto. Serve immediately.

Grilled Chicken Breasts Tikka Lemon-Marinated

Ingredients

- 2 Large Cloves Garlic, Minced
- ¼ Teaspoon Kosher or Sea Salt
- ¼ Cup Extra-Virgin Olive Oil
- 2 Tablespoons Fresh Lemon Juice
- Freshly Ground Pepper
- 4 Boneless, Skinless Chicken Breast Halves

Instructions

- Prepare a medium-hot fire in a charcoal Traeger Grill or preheat a gas Traeger Grill on medium high. In a bowl or back dish large enough to hold the chicken, combine the olive oil, lemon juice, garlic, salt, and a few grinds of pepper, and stir to mix thoroughly. Add the chicken breasts and turn to coat on both sides.
- Let the chicken marinate while the Traeger Grill heats. Oil the Traeger Grill grate. Place the chicken breasts directly over the medium-hot fire and sear on one side, about 4 minutes. Turn and sear on the other side until the juices run clear when the thickest part of a breast is pierced with a knife, or an instant read thermometer registers 165°F, about 4 minutes longer. Divide the chicken breasts among warmed dinner plates. Serve immediately.

Boneless Grilled Garlic Chicken

Ingredients

- 4 Teaspoons Sugar (Divided)
- 1 ½ Teaspoons Salt
- 320ml Mayonnaise
- 2 Tablespoons Water
- 2 Tablespoons Cider Vinegar
- 1 Teaspoon Garlic Powder
- 1 Teaspoon Dried Thyme
- 1 Teaspoon Lemon Pepper Season
- 1 Teaspoon Cayenne Pepper
- 4 Boneless and Skinless Chicken Breasts Halved
- 1 Tablespoon Paprika
- 1 ½ Teaspoons Pepper (Divided)

Instructions

- In a small bowl place, the paprika, 1 teaspoon sugar, 1 teaspoon salt, the garlic powder, lemon pepper, thyme, cayenne pepper, and ½ to 1 teaspoon of pepper. Mix well together then sprinkle over all sides of the chicken and set the meat to one side. In another bowl you place the mayonnaise, water, vinegar and the rest of the sugar, salt and pepper.

- Once all Ingredients have been combined together you put around 240ml of this to one side, which you place in the refrigerator to chill. The rest of the mixture is what you will be bast the chicken in. To cook the chicken place over indirect medium heat on the barbecue. Remember to oil the Traeger Grill first to ensure that the chicken doesn't stick to it then cook on each side for 4 to 6 minutes or until the juices that are released by the chicken as it cooks run clear. Don't forget as you are cook the chicken on the Traeger Grill to baste it regularly with the sauce made us the mayonnaise. After cook serve with the sauce in the refrigerator.

Salted Rubbed Chicken Breasts
Ingredients

- 2 Large Cloves Garlic, Minced
- ½ Teaspoon Kosher or Sea Salt
- ½ Teaspoon Freshly Ground Pepper
- ¼ Cup Fresh Orange Juice
- 3 Tablespoons Extra-Virgin Olive Oil
- 2 Tablespoons Minced Canned Chipotle Chiles In Adobo Sauce
- 4 Boneless, Skin-On Chicken Breast Halves

Instructions

- Prepare a medium-hot fire in a charcoal Traeger Grill or preheat a gas Traeger Grill on medium high. In a bowl or back dish large enough to hold the chicken, combine the orange juice, olive oil, chiles, garlic, salt, and pepper. Stir to mix thoroughly. Add the chicken breasts and turn to coat on both sides. Let the chicken marinate while the Traeger Grill heats.
- To create a cool zone, bank the coals to one side of the Traeger Grill or turn off one of the burners. Oil the Traeger Grill grate. Place the chicken breasts, skin side down, directly over the medium-hot fire and sear on one side, about 3 minutes. Turn and sear on the other side for 3 to 4 minutes.
- Move the chicken to the cooler part of the Traeger Grill, cover, and Traeger Grill until the juices run clear when the thickest part of a breast is pierced with a knife, or an instant-read thermometer registers 165°F, 6 to 8 minutes longer. Divide the chicken breasts among warmed dinner plates. Serve immediately.

Olive Oil Chicken Tenders Basted
Ingredients

- 2 Tablespoons Extra-Virgin Olive Oil, Plus More for Brush
- 1½ Pounds Chicken Breast Tenders (About 16 Tenders) Kosher or Sea Salt
- 16 7-Inch Bamboo Skewers, Soaked in Water For 15 Minutes, Then Drained
- ¼ Cup Store-Bought Basil Pesto, At Room Temperature
- Freshly Ground Pepper

Instructions

- Immerse the skewers before light the Traeger Grill, so they have plenty of time to soak. Prepare a medium-hot fire in a charcoal Traeger Grill or preheat a gas Traeger Grill on medium high. In a small bowl, combine the pesto and 2 tablespoons olive oil and mix well; set aside. Place the chicken breast tenders in a bowl, drizzle olive oil over the top, and brush or rub the chicken on both sides with the oil.
- Season generously with salt and pepper. Thread 1 chicken tender onto each skewer, unless there are small pieces to combine together. Weave the tenders so the skewers pierce each piece 2 or 3 times.

Bunch the meat a bit, so it covers about 5 inches of the skewer. Oil the Traeger Grill grate. Fold a footlong piece of aluminum foil in half lengthwise and lay it on the Traeger Grill grate. Arrange the skewers so the exposed bamboo is protected from the flame by the foil and the meat is directly over the fire.
- Use 2 pieces of foil if necessary. Traeger Grill the chicken, turn once and bast frequently with the pesto oil, until the meat is firm and the juices run clear when a tender is pierced with a knife, about 2½ minutes per side. Divide the skewers among warmed dinner plates. Serve immediately.

Traeger Grilled Herb Chicken Burgers
Ingredients

- 2 Cloves Garlic (Minced)
- 1 Teaspoon Dried Parsley
- 1 Teaspoon Dried Basil
- 450gram Ground Chicken Breast
- 1 Small Carrot (Grated)
- 2 Green Onions (Minced)
- ¼ Teaspoon Salt
- ¼ Teaspoon Freshly Ground Black Pepper

Instructions

- Into a large mix bowl put the ground chicken meat, the carrot, onions, garlic, herbs, salt and pepper. Mix thoroughly together. It is best if you use your hands to do this. Whilst you are mix these Ingredients together then you should have the barbecue turned on or you should have lit the charcoal. So, by the time the burgers are made you can then start cook them.
- After mix the Ingredients together, you should make between 4 and 6 burgers from it. Before you cook them however place them on a sheet of wax paper and let them rest in the refrigerator for a few minutes.
- Once the barbecue has heated up you must first lightly oil the Traeger Grill before then place the burgers on to it. To make sure that the chicken is cooked properly they should remain on the Traeger Grill for between 12 and 15 minutes. It is important that during this time you turn them over at least once. You will know when they are cooked through, as the juices run out of them will run clear.

Grilled-Glazed Chicken Leg Piece
Ingredients

- Kosher or Sea Salt
- Freshly Ground Pepper
- 8 Bone-In, Skin-On Chicken Thighs
- Extra-Virgin Olive Oil

Instructions

- Prepare a medium-hot fire in a charcoal Traeger Grill or preheat a gas Traeger Grill on medium high. Trim the chicken thighs of any excess skin and fat. Place the thighs in a large bowl, drizzle olive oil over the top, and brush or rub the thighs all over with the oil. Season generously with salt and pepper. Have the bast sauce in a bowl with a brush next to the Traeger Grill. To create a cool zone, bank the coals to one side of the Traeger Grill or turn off one of the burners. Oil the Traeger Grill grate.
- Place the chicken thighs, skin side down, directly over the medium-hot fire and sear on one side, about 3 minutes. Turn, baste with some of the sauce, and sear on the other side, about 7 minutes. Move the

chicken to the cooler part of the Traeger Grill, baste with more sauce, cover, and Traeger Grill, bast the thighs twice more as they cook, until the juices run clear when the thickest part of a thigh is pierced with a knife, or an instant-read thermometer registers 165°F, 10 to 15 minutes longer. Divide the chicken thighs among warmed dinner plates. Serve immediately.

Lemon Barbecue Chicken Tikka
Ingredients

- 2 Lemons Quartered
- 1 Garlic Clove Crushed
- Juice and Zest Of 1 Lemon
- A Little Water or Beer to Taste
- Salt
- 1.3kg Spatchcock Chicken
- 3 Tablespoon Olive Oil
- 1 Teaspoon Paprika
- Freshly Ground Pepper

Instructions

- Whilst the barbecue is heat up in a bowl mix together the oil, garlic, paprika, lemon zest, salt and pepper. Once all these Ingredients have been mixed together you brush it all over the skin of the chicken before then place it covered in the fridge for 30 minutes to allow it to marinate. When it comes to cook the chicken on the barbecue you should cook it initially for 5 minutes on each side in the middle of the barbecue. Then move over to the side so that the heat cook it is much gentler. It is important whilst the chicken is cook that you turn it regularly and baste in between each turn with either beer or water.
- The best way of determine when the chicken is cooked through is to pierce between the thigh and breast bone with a sharp knife. When you do the flesh should feel firm and should look white. You should be cooking each side of the chicken for between 20 and 30 minutes. Plus, place smooth over the top, as the steam produced will help the chicken to cook through. Once the chicken has cooked you now need to remove it from the heat and leave it to rest. Make sure that you cover it with foil and leave it to rest for around 10 to 15 minutes. Once this time has passed cut it up into pieces and drizzle some lemon juice, oil, salt, pepper and paprika over them. Then serve on a fresh plate with the lemon quarters.

Grilled Chicken Thighs with Olive Oil
Ingredients

- 8 Bone-In, Skin-On Chicken Thighs
- Cup Espresso-Cardamom Rub
- Extra-Virgin Olive Oil

Instructions

- Prepare a medium-hot fire in a charcoal Traeger Grill or preheat a gas Traeger Grill on medium high. Trim the chicken thighs of any excess skin and fat. Place the thighs in a large bowl, drizzle olive oil over the top, and brush or rub the thighs all over with the oil. Rub the thighs all over with the spice rub.
- To create a cool zone, bank the coals to one side of the Traeger Grill or turn off one of the burners. Oil the Traeger Grill grate. Place the chicken thighs, skin side down, directly over the medium-hot fire

and sear on one side, about 3 minutes. Turn and sear on the other side, about 7 minutes. Move the chicken to the cooler part of the Traeger Grill, cover, and Traeger Grill until the juices run clear when the thickest part of a thigh is pierced with a knife, or an instant-read thermometer registers 165°F, 10 to 15 minutes longer. Divide the chicken thighs among warmed dinner plates. Serve immediately.

Grilled Hens with Lemon Slices
Ingredients

- Extra-Virgin Olive Oil
- Kosher or Sea Salt
- 4 Cornish Game Hens
- 2 Lemons, Ends Trimmed, Thinly Sliced, And Seeds Removed (8 Slices) 16 Freshes
- Sage Leaves
- Freshly Ground Pepper

Instructions

- Prepare a medium fire in a charcoal Traeger Grill or preheat a gas Traeger Grill on medium. To butterfly the hens, place a hen breast down on a cut board. Us poultry shears, sharp, sturdy kitchen scissors, or a chef's knife, cut through the hen from one end to the other on each side of the backbone to remove it.
- Turn the hen breast side up, pull the body open, and use the heel of your hand to press down firmly, crack the rib bones so the hen rests flat. Repeat with the other hens. Transfer to a large, rimmed back sheet.
- Slip 2 lemon slices under the skin, place 1 slice over each breast half. Place 2 sage leaves on top of each lemon slice. Repeat with the other hens. Rub the hens generously on all sides with olive oil and season on all sides with salt and pepper. To create a cool zone, bank the coals to one side of the Traeger Grill or turn off one of the burners. Oil the Traeger Grill grate. Place the hens, skin side down, directly over the medium fire, cover, and sear on one side, about 5 minutes. Turn, re-cover, and sear on the other side for about 5 minutes. Move the hens to the cooler part of the Traeger Grill, cover, and Traeger Grill until the juices run clear when the thickest part of the thigh is pierced with a knife, or an instant-read thermometer registers 165°F, 5 to 7 minutes longer. Transfer to warmed dinner plates and let rest for 5 minutes before serve.

Chicken Thighs with Smashed Traeger Grilled Potatoes
Ingredients

- Traeger Grill -Roasted and Smashed Baby White Potatoes
- Cup Chopped Fresh Cilantro (Optional)
- ¼ Cup Store-Bought Mole
- 1 Cup Canned Low-Sodium Chicken Broth
- ¼ Teaspoon Ground Cinnamon
- Teaspoon Kosher or Sea Salt
- 8 Bone-In, Skin-On Chicken Thighs
- Extra-Virgin Olive Oil
- Cup Traeger Grill Every Day Spice Rub
- Teaspoon Sugar

Instructions

Prepare a medium-hot fire in a charcoal Traeger Grill or preheat a gas Traeger Grill on medium high. Trim the chicken thighs of any excess skin and fat. Place the thighs in a large bowl, drizzle olive oil over the top, and brush or rub the thighs all over with the oil. Rub the thighs all over with the spice rub. To create a cool zone, bank the coals to one side of the Traeger Grill or turn off one of the burners. Oil the Traeger Grill grate. Place the chicken thighs, skin side down, directly over the medium-hot fire and sear on one side, about 3 minutes.

Turn and sear on the other side, about 7 minutes. Move the chicken to the cooler part of the Traeger Grill, cover, and Traeger Grill until the juices run clear when the thickest part of a thigh is pierced with a knife, or an instant-read thermometer registers 165°F, 10 to 15 minutes longer. While the chicken is Traeger Grill, prepare the mole sauce. In a small saucepan, combine the mole, chicken broth, cinnamon, salt, and sugar and place over medium-low heat. Simmer, stir occasionally, until the sauce is smooth and thickened, about 5 minutes. Keep warm. To serve, spoon enough mole sauce on each dinner plate to cover the surface lightly. Arrange 2 or 3 smashed potatoes in the center of each plate, and set 2 chicken thighs on top. Garnish each plate with a generous sprinkle of cilantro. Serve immediately.

Grilled Chicken with Blood Orange Oil

Ingredients

- 1 Tablespoon Minced Garlic
- ½ Teaspoon Kosher or Sea Salt, Plus More for Season
- 3 Tablespoons Extra-Virgin Olive Oil, Plus More for Rub
- 1 Tablespoon Minced Fresh Thyme
- 1 Tablespoon Minced Fresh Sage
- ½ Teaspoon Freshly Ground Pepper, Plus More for Season
- 1 Whole Chicken, 3½ to 4 Pounds

Instructions

- Prepare a medium fire in a charcoal Traeger Grill or preheat a gas Traeger Grill on medium. In a small bowl, combine the 3 tablespoons olive oil, the thyme, sage, garlic, and ½ teaspoon each kosher salt and pepper. Set aside.
- To spatchcock the chicken, place the bird, breast down, on a cut board. Us poultry shears, sharp sturdy kitchen scissors, or a chef's knife, cut through the chicken from one end to the other on each side of the backbone to remove it. Turn the chicken breast up, pull the body open, and use the heel of your hand to press down firmly, crack the rib bones so the chicken rests flat. Transfer to a large, rimmed back sheet.
- Spoon the herb mixture under the skin, spread it evenly over both sides of the breast. Rub the chicken generously on all sides with olive oil and season on all sides with kosher salt and pepper. To create a cool zone, bank the coals to one side of the Traeger Grill or turn off one of the burners. Oil the Traeger Grill grate. Place the chicken, skin side down, directly over the medium fire, cover, and sear on one side, about 7 minutes. (Check halfway through the cook time to make sure the skin isn't brown too quickly, and watch for flare-ups. Have a spray bottle of water near the Traeger Grill to tame flare-ups.) Us long tongs or a spatula, turn the chicken and re-cover.
- Sear on the other side for 7 to 10 minutes. Move the chicken to the cooler part of the Traeger Grill, re-cover, and Traeger Grill until the juices run clear when the thickest part of the thigh is pierced with a knife, or an instant-read thermometer registers 165°F, about 15 minutes longer. Transfer the chicken to a car board and let rest for 5 to 10 minutes. Cut the chicken into parts for serve, slice the breast meat, if desired. Drizzle the chicken with the blood orange olive oil and sprinkle with fleur de sel. Serve immediately.

Honey Grilled Chicken Wings with Mustard

Ingredients

- 1 Tablespoon Dried Tarragon, Crushed
- ½ Teaspoon Freshly Ground Pepper, Plus More for Season
- ½ Cup Honey Mustard
- ¼ Cup Plus 3 Tablespoons Extra-Virgin Olive Oil
- 16 Chicken WINGS (About 3¾ Pounds) Kosher or Sea Salt

Instructions

- Prepare a medium-hot fire in a charcoal Traeger Grill or preheat a gas Traeger Grill on medium high. In a small bowl, combine the mustard, ¼ cup of the olive oil, the tarragon, and ½ teaspoon pepper and mix well. Set aside. Place the in a large bowl. Rub the wings all over with the 3 tablespoons olive oil and then season them lightly with salt and pepper. Oil the Traeger Grill grate.
- Place the chicken wings directly over the medium-hot fire and cover. Sear on one side, about 5 minutes. Turn, re-cover, and sear on the other side, about 5 minutes longer. Brush the wings all over with the mustard sauce and continue to Traeger Grill, bast and turn the wings, until they are bronzed and the juices run clear when the thickest part is pierced with a knife, about 10 minutes longer. Pile the wings on a warmed serve plate. Serve immediately.

Lime Grilled Chicken Kebabs

Ingredients

- 1 Tablespoon Olive Oil
- Bunch Spry Onions Finely Chopped
- 1 Red Chili Chopped (This Is Optional)
- Juice of 1 Lime
- 1 Large Yellow Pepper Cut Into 2cm Cubes
- Mango Salsa
- 320g Mango Diced
- Jerk Chicken
- 4 Skinless Chicken Breasts Cut into Chunks
- 2 Teaspoon Jerk Season
- 1 Large Red Pepper Deseeded and Diced

Instructions

- In a bowl place the jerk season, olive oil and lime juice and then mix thoroughly together. A whisk would be best to do this. Then once all these Ingredients have been thoroughly combined toss the chunks of chicken in it and place in the refrigerator for at least 20 minutes. However, if you really want the meat to absorb as much of the marinade as possible then it is best to leave it in the refrigerator for at least 24 hours. Once the meat has time to marinade you are now ready to start cook it. But whilst the barbecue is heat up you can nonintact make the salsa. To do this you simply place all the Ingredients mentioned above in a bowl and stir together.
- Add a little salt and pepper to season then place in the refrigerator until you are ready to serve it with the kebabs. To make the kebabs you need some wooden skewers, which have been left in some water for at least 30 minutes. Remember do this will prevent them from burn. Now on to each skewer you thread a piece of chicken followed by a piece of the yellow pepper. You should be aim to put on each of the 8 skewers 3 pieces of meat and 3 pieces of pepper. Once the kebabs have been made and the barbecue is hot enough you can start cook them. Each side of the kebab should be cooked for around 8 minutes. This will not only ensure that they are cooked through but also helps to create a little charr on them. Once they are cooked place two kebabs on a plate and add some salsa

Asian Turkey Grilled Tikka Burgers
Ingredients

- 2 Tablespoons Peeled and Minced Fresh Ginger
- 1 Tablespoon Minced Garlic
- 4 Slices Provolone Cheese
- 4 Sesame-Seed Hamburger Buns, Split
- 4 Lettuce Leaves
- Soy Sauce Mayonnaise
- 3 Tablespoons Low-Sodium Soy Sauce
- 2 Teaspoons Fresh Lemon Juice
- 1½ Pounds Ground Turkey
- 3 Tablespoons Chopped Fresh Cilantro
- 2 Green Onions, include 2 Inches of Green Tops, Very Thinly Sliced
- ½ Teaspoon Kosher or Sea Salt
- 2 Tablespoons Canola Oil

Instructions

- Prepare a hot fire in a charcoal Traeger Grill or preheat a gas Traeger Grill on high. In a large bowl, combine the turkey, cilantro, green onions, Ginger, garlic, soy sauce, lemon juice, and salt and mix well. Divide into 4 equal portions, and shape each portion into a patty 1 inch thick. Refrigerate the patties while the Traeger Grill heats. Oil the Traeger Grill grate. Brush the burgers on both sides with the canola oil.
- Place the burgers directly over the hot fire and sear on one side, about 5 minutes. Turn and sear on the other side until almost cooked through, about 4 minutes longer. Place a slice of cheese on each burger, cover the Traeger Grill, and cook until the cheese is melted, about 1 minute longer. Place the buns, cut side down, on the Traeger Grill to toast while the cheese is melting. Serve the turkey burgers on the toasted buns with the lettuce and mayonnaise, if desired.

Salted Grilled Chicken Wings with Jalapeno
Ingredients:

- 1 Tsp. Celery Seed
- 8 Tbsp. Butter, Unsalted
- 2 - 4 Jalapeno Peppers, Thinly Sliced Crosswise
- 1/2 Cup Cilantro Leaves
- 1 Tsp. Black Pepper, Freshly Ground
- 1 Tsp. Cayenne Pepper
- 1 Tsp. Onion Powder
- 1 Tsp. Granulated Garlic
- 1/2 Cup Hot Sauce

Instructions:

- Cut the wings into three bits throughout the joints. Discard the w ideas, or store for poultry stock. Transfer the rest of the chicken drumettes and apartments into a large resealable plastic bag or a bowl. Br to a boil, then lower the heat and simmer for 10 minutes. Seal the bag and refrigerate for many hours, or even overnight.
- When ready to cook, place the temperature to 350°F and preheat, lid shut for 15 minutes. Cook for 45 to 50 minutes, or until the skin is brown and crispy and the beef is no longer pink in the bone. Turn once during the cook period to prevent the wings from stick to the Traeger Grill grate.

Spicy Chicken Tacos with Garlic
Ingredients:

- 2 Lbs. Boneless Skinless Chicken Thighs
- 1 Tbsp Olive Oil
- 1 Tsp Salt
- 1 Tsp Black Pepper
- 1/2 Yellow Onion, Small Dice
- 2 Cups Shredded Red Cabbage
- 1/2 Cup White Wine Vinegar
- 1 Tbsp Salt
- 1 Tbsp Sugar
- Braised Chicken
- 4 Tbsp Adobo Sauce
- 1 Ea. Chipotle Chile In Adobo
- Juice Of 2 Limes
- 1 (12 Oz) Can Model Beer
- 1 Jalapeño, Deseeded and Chopped
- 1 Clove Garlic, Minced
- 1 Tsp Chili Powder
- 1 Tsp Garlic Powder

Instructions:

- When ready to cook, place the temperature to 375°F and preheat, lid shut for 15 minutes. While Traeger Grill is preheating, dry chicken a paper towel. Put wings in a large bowl and sprinkle with cornstarch, Traeger Chicken Scrub and salt to taste. Mix to coat each side of the chicken wings. After the Traeger Grill has heated, then put the wings on the Traeger Grill and cook for 35 minutes total, turn halfway through cook time.

- Check the internal temperature of these wings in 35 minutes. The internal temperature should be 165°F. However, an inner temperature of 175-180°F will give a much better feel. For your Buffalo Sauce: In a different pot include the Franks Red Hot, butter and mustard. Whisk to blend and heat through to the stove.
- Keep sauce warm while the wings are still cook. When wings are done, pour the skillet on the wings, turn with tongs to coat. Cook for an additional 10-15 minutes on the Traeger Grill to get the sauce to place!

Roasted Shawarma with Tomatoes
Ingredients:

- 5.5 Lbs. Top Sirloin
- Pita Bread
- Top Options: Cucumber, Tomatoes, Tahini, Pickles, Fries, Israeli Salad
- A Double Skewer
- A Cast Iron Griddle
- 5.5 Lbs. Boneless Skinless Chicken Thighs
- 4.5 Lbs. Lamb Fat
- 4 Tbsp Traeger Rub
- 2 Large Yellow Onions

Instructions:

- When ready to cook, set temperature to Top and preheat, lid shut for 15 minutes. · If you purchased entire chicken wings, then remove the trick and different the drumettes and tails from one another. Discard the w tips or store them for poultry stock. Combine all the dry rub Ingredients at a skillet. Add the oil and whisk to blend.
- For the Glaze: Blend glaze Ingredients in a small saucepan. Br to a boil over moderate heat. Cook till mixture is decreased by roughly 1/3 and starts to thicken, about 3 minutes. Keep the syrup hot when await glaze. Put the wings right on the Traeger Grill grate and cook, turn once, until the internal temperature of these wings reaches 155-160°F, about 20 minutes. Brush the wings together with the glaze and continue to cook until the internal temperature reaches 165-175°F, about 5-10 minutes more.

Chicken Grilled Mayonnaise Salad
Ingredients:

- 1/2 Red Bell Pepper, Finely Diced
- 1/2 Green Bell, Finely Diced
- 2 Scallions, Thinly Sliced
- 1 To 2 Tbsp. Pickled Jalapeno Peppers, Minced
- 1 Cup Mayonnaise
- 1 Tbsp. Fresh Lime Juice
- 1 Tsp. Ground Cumin
- 1 Tsp. Black Pepper, Freshly Ground
- 1/2 Tsp. Garlic Salt
- 1 Qt. Cold Water
- 1/4 Cup Kosher Salt
- 4 Large Chicken Breasts, Boneless
- 4 Chicken Thighs, Bone-In
- 2 Tbsp. Fresh Cilantro Leaves, Minced

Instructions:

- For your brine, in a large saucepan or mix bowl, combine the salt and water and stir until the salt crystals glow. Add the chicken breasts and breasts. Cover and simmer for two to four hours.
- When ready to cook, then begin the Traeger Grill on Smoke us the lid open before the flame is set (4 to 5 minutes). Arrange the chicken on the Traeger Grill grate and smoke for half an hour. Increase the temperature to 350F and continue to cook the chicken until the juices run clear and the internal temperature when read in an instant-read beef thermometer is 165F, 25 to half an hour. Dice the chicken, discard any bones, skin, or gobbets of fat. Transfer to a mix bowl. Add the green and red bell peppers, the scallions, and pickled jalapenos. Stir lightly to disperse the Ingredients set aside. In a mix bowl whisk together the mayonnaise, lime juice, cumin, black pepper, and garlic salt. Stir in the cilantro. Add the dress into the chicken mixture and stir lightly until well-combined. Transfer to a serve bowl. Dust with paprika. Serve immediately, or cover and chill for up to 3 times.

BBQ Chicken Mexican Blend
Ingredients:

- 24 Large Tortilla Chips
- 3 Cups Mexican Blend Shredded Cheese
- 1/2 Cup Black Olives, Sliced and Drained
- Pickled Jalapenos, Sliced
- 3 Scallions, Thinly Sliced
- 1-1/4 Lbs. Chicken Breasts, Boneless, Skinless
- Traeger Pork & Poultry Rub, As Needed
- 1/2 To 3/4 Cup Traeger Qu BBQ Sauce
- 1 Cup Sour Cream

Instructions:

- Prepare the spice mix by mix the Ginger, garlic and all of the spices in a small bowl. For the Marinade: In a big bowl combine the chopped chicken breast, yogurt, 1/2 the spice mix, and kosher salt. Mix well. Cover with plastic wrap and chill in the refrigerator overnight for marinated chicken perfection. When ready to cook, then place the temperature to Top and preheat with the lid shut for 15 minutes.
- For the Sauce: Heat a high-sided, oven-safe pan above medium-heat and melt the ghee. Add the onion, cilantro stalks, cardamom, and a pinch of salt, and cook until the onion softens, about 5

minutes. Add the tomato paste and remain spice mix, and cook for two minutes. Br the sauce to a simmer and cook for approximately 8 minutes, until thickened. While the sauce is cook, add the carrot pieces into the Traeger Grill and cook 2 minutes each side, until just begin to turn into attractively golden brown. Remove and put aside. Stir the cream to the sauce mix, then fold in the chicken. Transfer the curry into the Traeger Grill and cook lid shut, for 35 to 40 minutes, until the chicken is cooked through and the curry is thick and magnificent. Divide the cooked basmati rice on plates, then top with curry. Enjoy!!

Chili Bonnet Chicken

Ingredients:

- 1 Whole Chicken
- 6 Thai Chiles
- 2 Tbsp Sweet Paprika
- 1 Scotch Bonnet
- 2 Tbsp Sugar
- 3 Tbsp Salt
- 1 White Onion
- 5 Garlic Cloves
- 4 Cups Grape Seed Oil

Instructions:

- For the Marinade: In a medium bowl combine the olive oil, juice from the oranges (approximately 1/4 cup of freshly squeezed juice), the orange zest, Dijon mustard, rosemary leaves and salt. Whisk to blend. Put the chicken into a shallow back dish big enough to be opened in 1 piece. Pour the marinade over the chicken make sure that it is coated with the marinade.
- Cover with plastic wrap and refrigerate for at least two hours or up to overnight, turn once throughout the procedure. When ready to cook, set temperature to 350°F and preheat, lid shut for 15 minutes. Cook for 25-30 minutes until your skin is well-browned, then reverse. Proceed to Traeger Grill chicken until the internal temperature of the breast reaches 165°F along with the thigh reaches 175°F, about 5-15 minutes more.

Traeger Grilled Thai Chicken Burgers

Ingredients:

- 1/2 Cup Mayonnaise
- 1 1/2 Tsp Curry Powder
- 1 Tbsp Vegetable Oil
- 8 Big Leaves Butter Lettuce Or 4 Hamburger Buns
- 1 Lb. Ground Chicken Thigh Meat
- 1/2 Cup Panko or Gluten Free Bread Crumbs
- 1/4 Cup Coconut Cream (Thick Milk Solids From 1 May Chilled Coconut Milk)
- 1/2 Cup Chopped Fresh Cilantro
- 2 Garlic Cloves, Minced
- 2 Tsp Kosher Salt
- 6 Oz Shredded Green Papaya (From 1 Moderate Papaya)
- 1/2 Red Onion, Thinly Sliced
- 2 Tsp Grated Lime Zest

- 3 Tbsp Plus 2 Tsp Fresh Lime Juice
- 1 Tbsp Fish Sauce
- 1 Tbsp Brown Sugar
- 1 Tsp Ground Cumin
- 1 Tsp Freshly Ground Black Pepper

Instructions:

- For your Papaya Slaw: In a medium bowl, combine the papaya, 1, 3 Tbsp of the carrot juice, fish sauce along with the brown sugar. Cover and refrigerate until ready to use up to 3 hours. In a large bowl stir together the chicken, breadcrumbs, coconut cream, cilantro, Ginger, garlic, pepper, salt, cumin, lime zest, and remain 2 tsp lime juice till thoroughly blended. Refrigerate for 20 minutes. If the mixture appears too dry or wet correct with breadcrumbs or coconut milk till it remains together. In a small bowl, stir together the mayonnaise and curry powder. Put aside.
- When ready to cook, set temperature to Top and preheat, lid shut for 15 minutes. With your hands, shape the chicken mixture into four equal patties. Brush each bean with all the vegetable oil on each side. Cook for 4-5 minutes each side, or before the hamburgers reach 165°F internally. Remove from the Traeger Grill and allow to rest for a couple minutes before serve. Place each burger on a leaf of lettuce top with curry mayonnaise and pickled papaya slaw. Top with another lettuce leaf and serve. Alternately, use routine hamburger buns and stack high with all the hamburgers, curry mayonnaise and papaya slaw!

Mayonnaise Chicken Cheese Dip
Ingredients:

- 1 Tsp Kosher Salt
- 1/2 Cup Franks Red Hot Sauce
- 2 Cups Chicken, Cooked and Shredded
- 1 Cup Cheddar Cheese, Shredded
- 1 Cup Mozzarella Cheese, Shredded
- 1 (8 Oz) Package Cream Cheese, Softened
- 1/2 Cup Sour Cream
- 1/2 Cup Mayonnaise
- 2 Tbsp Dry Ranch Season
- Blue Cheese, To Taste
- Crumbled Bacon, To Taste

Instructions:

- When ready to cook begin the Traeger Grill on Smoke us the lid open until flame is created (4-5 minutes). Place the temperature to 350 degrees F and F, lid shut for 10-15 minutes. From the bowl of a stand mixer, combine cream cheese, sour cream, mayonnaise, ranch, salt, and hot sauce and combine together with the paddle attachment until blended. Twist together the cheddar and mozzarella cheese and shredded chicken. Transfer to an oven proof dish and top with blue cheese and crumbled bacon.
- Put directly on the Traeger Grill grate and cook for 20-30 minutes until the top is golden brown and dip is bubbly. Serve with crackers, chips, Crostini, or chopped vegetables.

Smokey Chicken with Garlic
Ingredients:

- Traeger Big Game Rub
- 1 Tsp Garlic, Minced
- 1 (3 To 3 1/2 Lb.) Whole Chicken
- 1 Lemon, Halved
- Brine
- 1/2 Cup Kosher Salt
- 1 Cup Brown Sugar
- 1 Gallon Water
- Whole Chicken
- 1 Medium Yellow Onion, Quartered
- 3 Whole Garlic Cloves
- 4-5 Sprigs Thyme

Instructions:

- Begin with segment the wings to three bits, cut through the joints. Discard the w tips or save them to earn a stock. · Lay out the remain pieces on a rimmed back sheet lined with nonstick foil or parchment paper. When ready to cook, set temperature to 350°F and preheat, lid shut for 15 minutes.
- Put the back sheet with wings right on the Traeger Grill grate and cook for 45-50 minutes until they're no longer pink in the bone. Add the honey and hot sauce and cook for a couple of minutes until fully blended. Keep sauce warm while the wings are still cook. When wings are done, pour the hot honey-garlic sauce on the wings, turn with tongs to coat. Place back wings to the Traeger Grill and cook for an extra 10-15 minutes to place the sauce. Serve together with the ranch or blue cheese dress table!

Grilled Honey Wings with Blue Cheese
Ingredients:

- 1/2 Cup Hot Sauce
- 1/4 Cup Honey
- 2-1/2 Lbs. Chicken Wings
- Traeger Pork & Poultry Rub, As Needed
- 4 Tbsp Butter
- 2-3 Cloves Minced Garlic
- 1 1/2 Cups Blue Cheese or Ranch Dress

Instructions:

- Season chicken generously with Traeger Chicken Rub, for example, cavity. Open the can of beer and then place the chicken on top of the beer. Make certain all but the base 1-1/2" of this beer is from the cavity of the chicken.
- When ready to cook, then place the Traeger into 350°F and preheat, lid shut for 15 minutes. Put chicken onto a sheet tray and set directly on the Traeger Grill grate. Cook for 60-75 minutes or until the internal temperature registers 165°F from the thickest portion of their breast!

Grilled Chicken Tikka with Beer Marinated
Ingredients:

- 1 (3-5 Lb.) Whole Chicken
- 1 Can Beer

- Traeger Chicken Rub, As Needed

Instructions:

- With kitchen shears eliminate the fat on either side of the chicken thighs. Reduce 1/4" off the underside and upper bone knuckle of the chicken thighs. Reduce skin to match now trimmed thighs. Put the back skin to the thighs. After done with all thighs, then inject 1/2 ounces of lowing sodium chicken broth to all sides of the thigh and then let rest for 60 minutes. While rest, season the surface of the chicken thighs us Traeger Big Game Rub. Put in a refrigerator or cold cooler until ready to cook. Place thighs in a sizable skillet and then add the melted butter into the pan for a brays liquid.
- When ready to cook, set temperature to 250°F and preheat, lid shut for 15 minutes. Slide the entire disposable pan of chicken on the grate and cook for one hour. After one hour, then wrap on the top of this skillet in aluminum foil and cook for another hour or until the internal temperature reaches 165°F. Once thighs reach inner temperature of 165°F, use tongs to remove each chicken thigh and dip it in to heated Traeger Apricot BBQ sauce. Put back in a fresh skillet and cook for another 20 minutes. Remove from Traeger Grill and let rest for 10 minutes prior to serve!

Buffalo March Masala Chicken BBQ

Ingredients:

- Traeger Pork & Poultry Rub, As Needed
- Bleu Cheese Crumbles, For Serve
- 4-6 Boneless, Skinless Chicken Thighs
- 1 Cup Buffalo W Sauce
- 4 Tbsp. Butter
- Ranch Dress, For Serve

Instructions:

- For your Brine: To some stockpot, add 1 gallon of water, salt, and sugar and stir well. Cover and simmer for two to four hours. When ready to cook, place the temperature to 375°F and preheat, together with the lid shut for 15 minutes. Remove the wings from the brine and wash them thoroughly with paper towel. Discard brine.
- Toss the wings together with the olive oil coat them completely. Put the wings right on the Traeger Grill grate and cook to an internal temperature of 165°F, about 45 to 60 minutes. For the Sauce: In a bowl, combine all of the sauce Ingredients: and simmer till smooth. Heat over medium-heat till the sauce just comes to a simmer, then remove from heat and set aside. Toss the cooked wings with 2/3 of this sauce, the green onions, celery, peanuts, and sesame seeds. Serve wings with fresh cilantro, lime wedges, and additional sauce for dip. Enjoy!

Traeger Grilled Lowing sodium BBQ Chicken

Ingredients:

- 6 Oz Traeger Big Game Rub
- 20 Oz Lowing sodium Chicken Broth
- 20 Bone in Chicken Thighs (Approximately 1/2 Lb. Each)
- 3 Sticks Melted Butter
- 24 Oz Traeger Apricot BBQ Sauce

Instructions:

- For your Thai Chili Sauce: Put Ingredients except the cornstarch in a sauce pan and whisk to blend. Br the mixture to a small boil and then simmer for 10 minutes. Reduce heat and add the cornstarch and water mix. Remove sauce from heat while fires cook. When ready to cook, set temperature to Top and preheat, lid shut for 15 minutes. This fever can help capture the wings crisper compared to a decrease temperature cooks that may result in rubbery skin. If you purchased the entire w, then remove the tip and then divide the drumette and w from one another. Season the wings fairly on either side with Meat Church Holy Gospel Rub. This is a combination of our Holy Cow and our Gospel All-Purpose rubs. It's amaze as the foundation for poultry.
- Place wings right on the Traeger Grill grate and cook for an entire period of 20 minutes. Twist the wings halfway through the cook. I love to have as many yummy snacks of char in my wings and Place them can help attain this on an extra side. Employ a quick thermometer to check the internal temperature of chicken wings. The final temperature must be between 165 -180°F after about 20 minutes. While chicken is safe to consume at 165°F, it's fine to carry wings even further as it's difficult to wash them out. To complete the wings, throw wings from the sweet Thai chili sauce. Put them back Traeger for 5 minutes to permit sauce to place. This will keep the sauce from run around you when seek to consume!

Salted and Black Pepper BBQ Chicken Thighs
Ingredients:

- Traeger Big Game Rub
- 6 Bone-In Chicken Thighs, Skin On
- Salt and Ground Black Pepper, To Taste

Instructions:

- When ready to cook, set the Traeger to 350°F and preheat, lid closed for 15 minutes.
- While Traeger Grill is heat, trim excess fat and skin from chicken thighs. Season with a light layer of salt and pepper and a layer of Traeger Big Game rub.
- Place chicken thighs on the Traeger Grill grate and cook for 35 minutes. Check internal temperature, chicken is done at 165°F, but there is enough fat that they will stay moist at an internal temperature of 180°F and the texture is better.
- Remove from the Traeger Grill and let rest for 5 minutes before serve. Enjoy!

Olive Chicken Leg with Spices
Ingredients:

- 3 Tbsp Olive Oil
- Traeger Pork & Poultry Rub, To Taste
- 8 Connected Chicken Leg and Thigh Pieces

Instructions:

- Put the chicken pieces in a large mix bowl. Pour oil on the chicken to coat each slice, then season to taste with all the beverage. Heal the chicken pieces to promote the oil and season s get beneath skin.
- Cover and simmer for 1 to 2 hours. When ready to cook, set temperature to 180°F and preheat, lid shut for 15 minutes. Remove the chicken in the fridge, allow any excess oil drip back into the bowl.
- Boost Traeger Grill temperatures to 350°F and continue to shake the chicken before the internal temperature at the thickest portion of a thigh is 165°F, or so the chicken is golden brown and the juices run clear, about 50 to 60 minutes. Permit the chicken to rest for 8-10 minutes and function!

Grilled Chicken Wings with Chili Barbecue Sauce

Ingredients:

- 3 Oz Traeger Chicken Rub
- 24 Wings (Sectioned)
- 12 Oz Italian Dress
- 8 Oz Traeger Chili Barbecue Sauce

Instructions:

- Wash all wings and set into resealable bag. Insert Italian Dress into the resealable bag comprise the wings. Put in refrigerator and let it marinate for 6-12 hours. When ready to cook, then place the Traeger into 225°F and preheat, lid shut for 15 minutes. Season all sides of their wings with Traeger Chicken Scrub and let sit 15 minutes before putting wings on the Traeger. Cook wings into an internal temperature of 160°F. Remove the wings and throw in Chili Barbecue Sauce.
- After at temperatures, put the wings on the Traeger and sear both sides obtain the inner temperature of the chicken wings to 165°F. Serve with your favorite side dress or sauce

Chicken Arugula Leaves with Mayonnaise

Ingredients:

- 2 Lbs. Ground Chicken
- 1 Cup Parmesan Cheese, Shredded
- 1 Tbsp. Worcestershire Sauce
- A Few Grinds Black Pepper, Freshly Ground
- 1 Cup Mayonnaise
- 2 Tbsp. Prepared Pesto Sauce
- 12 Slider Buns, Split
- 3 Roma Tomatoes, Thinly Sliced
- 1 Small Red Onion, Thinly Sliced
- For Serve Fresh Spinach or Arugula Leaves, Washed, And Dried

Instructions:

- In a large mix bowl combine the chicken, the Parmesan, the Worcestershire, along with several grinds of black pepper. Wet your hands with warm water, and utilize them to combine the Ingredients. Divide the meat mixture in half, then form six 2-inch patties from each half. Place the patties on the back sheet, then cover with another sheet of plastic wrap, and refrigerate for at least 1 hour. Blend the mayonnaise and pesto in a small bowl and whisk together. When ready to cook, then begin the Traeger Grill on Smoke us the lid open before the flame is set (4 to 5 minutes).
- Place the temperature to 300F and preheat, lid shut, for 10 to 15 minutes. Arrange the chicken patties on the Traeger Grill grate and Traeger Grill, turn once, until the patties are cooked through (165F), about half an hour. To serve, place a chicken patty onto the base of a slider bun and top with a dollop of this pesto mayonnaise. Add onion, tomato, and lettuce as wanted. Replace the cover of the bun and skewer with a frilled toothpick, if needed.

Indian Sweet and Spicy Chicken Wings

Ingredients

- 1/2 Tbsp To 1 Tbsp Dried Crushed Chili Pepper, Depend on Desired Heat Level

- 1 1/2 Tbsp Cornstarch, Dissolved In 4 Tbsp Water
- Sweet Thai Chili Sauce
- 1/2 Cup Sugar
- 1/2 Cup Rice Vinegar
- 1/4 Cup Water
- 3 To 4 Lbs. Chicken Wings, Drumettes And Flappers Preferred, Separated Over the Entire W
- Meat Church Holy Gospel Season, As Needed
- Toasted Sesame Seeds, To Garnish
- Sliced Green Onions, To Garnish
- 3 Tbsp Fish Sauce
- 2 Tbsp Cook Sherry
- 4 Cloves Garlic, Minced Fine

Instructions:

- When ready to cook, then place the Traeger into 350°F and preheat, lid shut for 15 minutes. While Traeger Grill is heat, cut excess skin and fat from chicken thighs. Season with a light layer of pepper and salt along with a coat of Traeger Big Game rub. Place chicken thighs onto the Traeger Grill grate and cook for 35 minutes.
- Assess internal temperature, chicken is performed at 165°F, however there's enough fat they will remain moist at an internal temperature of 180°F and the feel is better. Remove from the Traeger Grill and let rest for 5 minutes prior to serve!

Chicken Bouillon with Vegetable Oil

Ingredients:

- 1 Tsp Chicken Bouillon
- 1 Small Can Tomato Juice
- 1 Egg, Scrambled
- 2 Rolls Pie Crust
- 1 Lb. Chicken, Shredded
- 2 Carrots
- 2 Stalks Celery
- 1 Tbsp Vegetable Oil
- Salt and Pepper
- 1/4 Cup Water
- 1 Large Oven Safe Pan

Instructions:

- Begin the Traeger on Smoke us the lid open before a flame is set (4-5 minutes). Then turn temperature to 450 degrees F and F, lid shut, for 10 to 15 minutes. Chop celery and carrots. Decide on a huge oven safe skillet in to your Traeger, heat oil in skillet and cook celery and carrots. Add pepper and salt.
- Cook until celery and carrots soften, about 5 to 10 minutes, stir periodically. After vegetables soften, add chicken, tomato juice, water and chicken bouillon. Cook another 5-10 minutes or until sauce begins to thicken. Turn down the heat to 350 degrees F. Roll out pie crusts and cut circles around 4" in diameter. Put some fill in the center of the dough and then rub on just a small egg wash onto one half of the circle's border. This will guarantee a fantastic seal when you fold it on and person. Fold

dough over and press to produce half-moon pastries. Brush top of the sweater us a small egg wash and a dash of salad.

Chapter 5: Seafood Recipes

Marinated Lemon Grilled Barbecued Swordfish
Ingredients

- 2 Tablespoons Soy Sauce
- 2 Tablespoons Olive Oil
- 1 Tablespoon Savory Season
- ¼ Teaspoon Salt
- 4 Swordfish Steaks
- 4 Garlic Cloves
- 75ml White Wine
- 4 Tablespoons Lemon Juice
- 1/8 Teaspoon Freshly Ground Black Pepper

Instructions

- In a shallow dish you whisk together the garlic, white wine, soy sauce, lemon juice, olive oil, salt and pepper and savory season. Now place the swordfish steaks into the dish and turn them over so that they are coated in the marinade you have just made fully. Then place in the refrigerator for one hour make sure that turn the steaks over frequently during this time. After one hour remove the steaks from the refrigerator and turn on the barbecue.
- Whilst the barbecue is heat up this will provide the steaks with sufficient time to reach room temperature and so will help to ensure that they then cook properly. As soon as the barbecue has heated up it needs to be as hot as possible you lightly oil the grate and then place the swordfish steaks on to it. Cook for 5 to 6 minutes on each side before then remove to a clean plate and garnish them with some freshly chopped parsley and wedges of lemon.

Barbecued Salmon with Vegetable Oil
Ingredients

- 5 Tablespoons Soy Sauce
- 4 Tablespoons Dark Brown Soft Sugar
- 5 Tablespoons Water
- 4 Tablespoons Vegetable Oil
- 700grams Salmon Fillet
- 1 Tablespoon Lemon Zest
- 1 Tablespoon Minced Garlic Clove
- Freshly Ground Black Pepper to Taste

Instructions

- In a bowl place the sugar, water, vegetable oil, lemon zest, minced garlic, pepper and soy sauce and mix together until as much of the sugar has dissolved as possible. Once you have made the marinade you now place the salmon fillet into a large resealable plastic bag and pour the marinade over it.
- Close the bag up and then turn it over several times to ensure that the fillet of salmon is completely covered in the marinade. Place in the refrigerator for at least 2 hours. Once the two hours has passed removed the salmon from the refrigerator and start heat up the barbecue. By the time the barbecue

has heated up the salmon fillet should have come up to room temperature and will be ready to start cook. To cook the salmon fillet on the barbecue you can either place it directly on to the grate that has been lightly oiled or directly on to a piece of aluminum foil that has been lightly oiled. Any marinade that remains should now be discarded. You should cook each side of the salmon for between 5 and 6 minutes or when you use a fork to separate the flesh it flakes easily. Once cooked simply place on a clean plate and then allow your guests to help themselves.

Traeger Grilled Squid with Soy Sauce
Ingredients

- 1 Tablespoon Soy Sauce
- 1 Tablespoon Oyster Sauce
- 2 Teaspoons Freshly Grated Ginger
- 1 ½ Teaspoons Cider Vinegar
- Juice of 1 Lime
- 8 Squid Bodies (Rinsed and Dried)
- 2 Teaspoons Mirin
- 110grams Sunflower Sprouts
- 1 Serrano Chili Halved Lengthways, Seeds Removed and Thinly Sliced Crosswise
- 1 Teaspoon Black Sesame Seeds
- Coarse Salt to Taste
- ½ Teaspoon Sugar
- 3 Tablespoons Vegetable or Canola Oil
- 5 Stalks of Celery Halved Lengthways Then Sliced Diagonally into 2 ½ inch pieces
- 1 Tart Apple Size Pieces
- 1 Garlic Clove Minced
- 3 Tablespoons White or Light Miso Paste
- 3 Tablespoons Sake
- 2 Green Onions Halved Lengthways Then Slice Into 2 ½ inch Matchsticks

Instructions

- In a saucepan mix together the garlic, white or light miso paste, sake, mirin, soy sauce and oyster sauce to make a marinade. You need to cook this sauce over a medium to high heat for around 3 minutes, make sure that you stir it continuously. After the 3 minutes have elapsed remove from heat and place in a bowl to cool slightly.
- You now need to tenderize the squid to do this you need to pound both sides of it with a kitchen mallet a few times. Then cut along the seam of the squid with a sharp knife so you can open it up and lightly score the inside at ¼ inch intervals. After do this add the squid to the marinade and leave it to stand for 20 minutes. Whilst the squid is marina in the sauce you can now make the dress to go with the salad that you will serve with the Traeger Grill ed squid. First of all, you need to whisk together the Ginger, lime juice, vinegar, sugar and salt and add the oil to it very slowly until the liquid becomes emulsified. 4. To cook the squid on the barbecue you need to make sure that it is preheated to a medium to high heat. When the barbecue is heated up you can now cook the squid. You will need to use smooth to put on top of the squid as it is cook line a skillet with aluminum foil and put smooth like bricks in it should help.
- Before you place the squid on the Traeger Grill sprinkle the scored sides of the squid with salt and then place them fac down on to the Traeger Grill. It is a good idea to lightly oil the Traeger Grill first before place the squid on it to prevent them from stick. Once you have placed the squid on the Traeger Grill place the weighted skillet on top and let them cook for about 1 ½ minutes. Once the squid is

cooked remove and cut into ¾ inch pieces. To finish off take the apple, celery, green onions, sprouts and chilly into a bowl and pour over 3 tablespoons of the dress made earlier. Toss the Ingredients so that they are all coated in the dress then place some on to a clean plate with some of the squid on top before then sprinkle over this some sesame seeds.

Traeger Grilled Fillets in Butter
Ingredients

- 4 Cod Fillets
- ½ Teaspoon Salt
- ½ Teaspoon Freshly Ground Black Pepper
- 1 Small Finely Chopped Onion
- 60ml White Wine
- 45gram Butter
- 1 Tablespoon Extra Virgin Olive Oil
- 1 Sliced Lemon

Instructions

- Whilst the barbecue is heat up you should be preparing the onion butter. To do this into a small fry pan (skillet) place the better and once it is melted to it add the finely chopped onion and allow it to cook for about 1 to 2 minutes. Then to this you add the wine and leave to simmer for 3 minutes. When this time has elapsed remove from the heat and let it cool slightly. As soon as the barbecue has reached the right temperature you should now lightly brush the cod fillets with the olive oil and sprinkle on some salt and black pepper before then place on to the lightly oiled barbecue Traeger Grill.
- Cook the fish on one side for about 8 minutes before then turn it over and bast with some of the butter sauce you made earlier. Now allow the fish to cook for a further 6 to 7 minutes or until you notice the flesh has begun to turn opaque. During this cook time it is important that you baste the fish with the butter sauce a further 2 or 3 times before then remove from the heat and place on a clean plate and serve with the wedges of lemon.

Traeger Grilled Thai Red Packets
Ingredients

- 2 Garlic Cloves Minced
- 1 Tablespoon Fish Sauce
- 1 Tablespoon Olive Oil
- 4 Red Snapper Fillets (140 to 170grams)
- 1 Carrot Julienne
- 1 Green Onion Minced
- 32grams Fresh Cilantro
- 3 Tablespoons Fresh Lime Juice
- Aluminum Foil

Instructions

- Start the barbecue is up so it is ready for place the packets contain the red snapper on to cook. Whilst the barbecue is heat up in a small bowl mix together the fish sauce, olive oil, Ginger, lime juice, sugar and garlic.
- On to four separate pieces of aluminum foil you place one of the four red snapper fillets (skin side down) and pour over some of the mixture you have just made. Then sprinkle over the top of this some

of the carrots, cilantro and green onion. Then bra up the sides of the aluminum to seal the fish inside. But don't secure the packets too tightly as you need to allowing some of the steam produced as the fish cooks to escape.
- As soon as the barbecue has heated up place the Thai red snapper packets on the Traeger Grill and cook for between 8 and 10 minutes. Once this time has elapsed remove from the barbecue and then cut open the packets with a pair of scissors and serve without remove them from the aluminum foil on a clean plate.

Barbecued Lemon Halibut Steaks with Soy Sauce
Ingredients

- 1 Tablespoon Lemon Juice
- 2 Teaspoons Soy Sauce
- ½ Teaspoon Freshly Ground Black Pepper
- 450grams Halibut Steak
- 30grams Butter
- 2 Tablespoons Dark Brown Soft Sugar

Instructions

- Place in a small saucepan over a medium heat the butter, sugar, garlic, lemon juice, soy sauce and pepper. Stir this mixture occasionally and remove from heat as soon as all the sugar has dissolved. Lightly oil your preheated barbecue with some oil and just before you place the halibut steaks on to it lightly brush each side with the sauce you made earlier.
- Cook each side of the fish for about 5 minutes or until the flesh of the fish can be flaked easily with a fork. Whilst the fish is cook make sure that you keep bast with the sauce. Once the fish is cooked serve to your guests on a plate with some warm new potatoes and a crisp green salad. Otherwise you may want to consider serve the fish with some rice.

Traeger Grilled Salty Trout with Parsley
Ingredients

- 2 Tablespoons Freshly Minced Basil
- 1 Tablespoon Freshly Minced Rosemary
- 2 Freshly Minced Cloves of Garlic
- ½ Teaspoon Salt
- 2 x 450gram Trout (Whole Is Best)
- 2 Tablespoons Freshly Minced Parsley
- 2 Tablespoons Olive Oil
- ½ Teaspoon Freshly Ground Black Pepper

Instructions

- In a small bowl combine together the parsley, olive oil, basil, rosemary and garlic and then spread this evenly over the inside of the fish. Now place the fish in a shallow dish, cover and place in a refrigerator for 2 hours. After 2 hours have elapsed remove the trout from the refrigerator and start heat up the barbecue.
- Just before place the trout on to the barbecue Traeger Grill brush it with some oil and sprinkle both sides of the trout with salt and pepper. Cook the trout on a medium heat for 4 to 5 minutes on each side before carefully remove it and serve the trout on a clean plate.

Barbecued Olive Oil Teriyaki Tuna Steaks

Ingredients

- 180ml Olive Oil
- 2 Garlic Cloves Minced
- 4 Tuna Steaks
- 225ml Teriyaki Sauce
- 1 Teaspoon Freshly Ground Black Pepper

Instructions

- Into a large resealable plastic bag pour the teriyaki sauce, olive oil, minced garlic and freshly ground black pepper. Seal the bag up and the shake vigorously to ensure that all these   Ingredients combine well together.
- Now place the tuna steaks in the bag and make sure that it is tightly sealed before turn it over several times to ensure that all the marinade coats the steaks well. Now place in the refrigerator to allow the marinade to infuse into the stakes for 30 minutes. Whilst the tuna is in the refrigerator marina you should now heat up the barbecue.
- As soon as the barbecue is ready for cook   on take the tuna steaks out of the bag and place them on the oiled barbecue Traeger Grill and cook until done. If there is any marinade remain in the bag this should be discarded. As soon as the tuna steaks are cooked remove from barbecue place on clean plates and serve with a fresh crispy green salad.

Grilled Tuna with Honey Glaze

Ingredients

- 1 Tablespoon Freshly Minced Ginger Root
- 1 Small Bunch Freshly Chopped Coriander
- Honey Glaze
- 4 Tablespoons Honey
- 450grams Tuna Fillets
- 4 Tablespoons Olive Oil
- 4 Tablespoons Lime Juice (Fresh Would Be Best)
- 2 Tablespoons Balsamic Vinegar
- 2 Cloves Garlic Minced
- 2 Tablespoons Olive Oil
- 2 Tablespoons Freshly Chopped Coriander

Instructions

- Into a medium size bowl mix together the olive oil, lime juice, minced garlic, balsamic vinegar, freshly minced Ginger root and freshly chopped coriander. Once all these   Ingredients have been combined well together you add the tuna fillets and turn them over several times to ensure that each one is evenly coated in the marinade. Now cover the bowl over and place in a refrigerator and leave for several hours.
- After several hours now is the time to start heat up the barbecue. It is important that when cook the tuna on the barbecue you do so on a high heat. Whilst the barbecue is heat up this is the time when you should be making   the honey glaze.
- To make the honey glaze place the honey, olive oil and freshly chopped coriander in a bowl and whisk. Then set it to one side. By the time you have finished make   the honey glaze the barbecue should have

reached the desired temperature for cook the tuna fillets. However, before you place the tuna fillets on the Traeger Grill make sure that you lightly oil it first.
- Once you have placed the tuna on the Traeger Grill close the lid and allow the fillets to cook for 1 to 2 minutes before open the lid and then turn the fillets over. Now close the lid for a further minute then open the lid and continue to cook the tuna until it is barely done. It is important that whilst the tuna fillets are cook you baste them regularly with the marinade. As soon as the tuna fillets are nearly cooked through you should brush both sides of them with the honey glaze and then remove from the barbecue and serve.

Grilled Blackened Fish in Melted Butter
Ingredients

- 339grams Unsalted Butter Melted
- 6 Firm Fish Fillets
- 3 Tablespoons Cajun Blacken Spices

Instructions

- Heat up the barbecue until it is good and hot. Once the barbecue has reached the desired temperature now you can begin cook the fish fillets. Pour most of the melted butter into a shallow dish (leave around 12 tablespoons of the butter to one side as you will use this later when serve the fish). After pour the melted butter into the dish dip each fillet (both sides) in it before then sprinkle some of the Cajun blacken spices over them. Once this has been done place the fillets on the oiled barbecue Traeger Grill and cook for about 2 minutes before then turn them over and cook the other side for a further 2 minutes.
- As soon as this time has elapsed or when you feel the fillets are cooked through remove from heat and place on clean plates along with a small bowl in which some of the remain butter has been placed that your guests can then dip the fish fillets into.

Marinated Halibut Steak in Grapefruit Juice
Ingredients

- 1 Dessertspoon Freshly Chopped Marjoram
- ½ Teaspoon Salt
- 1/8 Teaspoon Freshly Ground Black Pepper
- 800grams Halibut Steaks
- 7 Tablespoons Fresh Grapefruit Juice

- 4 Tablespoons Olive Oil
- 4 Spry s Fresh Marjoram to Use as Garnish

Instructions

- In a shallow dish mix together the grapefruit juice, olive oil, freshly chopped marjoram, salt and pepper. To this mixture add the fish make sure you turn it over so both sides are coated in the marinade.
- Now cover and place in the refrigerator for 1 to 2 hours. Whilst it is marina make sure that you turn the fish over once or twice. After the marina time has elapsed you should start heat up the barbecue, with the Traeger Grill placed 4 to 6 inches above the heat source. Whilst the barbecue is heat up take the fish out of the refrigerator so that they come up to room temperature.
- When the barbecue has heated up now place the halibut steaks into a fish basket that has been lightly oiled and place on the barbecue Traeger Grill. You should cook these steaks for between 10 and 12 minutes turn them once and brush with any marinade you have left over. Serve once the steaks have become barely opaque in the thickest part on a clean plate with the sprigs of fresh marjoram.

Traeger Grilled Sea Bass with Butter
Ingredients

- 2 Garlic Cloves Minced
- ¼ Teaspoon Garlic Powder
- ¼ Teaspoon Paprika
- 907grams Sea Bass
- 3 Tablespoons Butter
- 1 ½ Tablespoons Extra Virgin Olive Oil
- 1 Tablespoon Freshly Finely Chopped Italian Parsley
- ¼ Teaspoon Onion Powder
- Lemon Pepper and Salt to Taste

Instructions

- In a bowl combine together the garlic powder, onion powder, paprika, lemon pepper and salt and then sprinkle this over both sides of the sea bass. Then place in the refrigerator to rest whilst you go ahead and prepare the garlic sauce. To make the garlic sauce into a small saucepan place the butter minced garlic cloves and parsley and heat on a low heat until all the butter has melted. Then place to one side ready to use later on.
- When it comes to cook the sea bass on the barbecue you need to do so on a medium high heat and ensure that the grate has been oiled first.
- Now place the sea bass on the barbecue and cook it for 7 minutes before then turn it over. After you have turned the fish over brush some of the garlic sauce over the top and then allow the sea bass to cook for a further 7 minutes. As soon as the necessary cook time has elapsed the fish should flake easily and this is the right time to remove from the heat. Place the fish on a clean plate and then drizzle over some olive oil and some more of the garlic sauce.

Grilled Swordfish with Sesame Oil
Ingredients

- 8 Garlic Cloves Freshly Minced
- 6 Swordfish Steaks

- 175ml Teriyaki Sauce
- 150ml Dry Sherry
- 1 Teaspoon Sesame Oil

Instructions

- Into a saucepan (large) place the teriyaki sauce, dry sherry, garlic, Ginger and sesame oil, mix and bra up to the boil. Once boil remove the pan from the heat and set to one side to cool for 10 minutes. In a shallow dish place the swordfish steaks and pour some of the marinade over the top that you made earlier. Then turn the steaks over and pour the rest of the marinade over them.
- Cover the dish up and place in the refrigerator for 1 ½ hours. During this time, you should make sure that you turn the Swordfish steaks over frequently. About 15 minutes before you remove the fish from the refrigerator you should get the barbecue started and place the Traeger Grill about 4 to 6 inches above the heat source. This type of fish should be cooked on a medium to high heat.
- Once the barbecue has heated up you can now place the steaks on the lightly oiled Traeger Grill and cook them on each side for 4 minutes. The best way of tell that the Swordfish steaks are cooked is that when prodded with a fork the meat should easily flake. Serve to your guests immediately after remove from the barbecue.

Traeger Grilled Catfish in Asian Style
Ingredients

- 2 Tablespoons Rice Wine Vinegar
- 2 Tablespoons Sesame Seeds
- 1 Tablespoon Sesame Oil
- 2 to 4 Catfish Fillets
- 80ml Vegetable Oil
- 60ml Lowing sodium Soy Sauce
- 2 Garlic Cloves Freshly Minced
- ¼ Teaspoon Freshly Ground Black Pepper
- ¼ Teaspoon Pepper Flakes

Instructions

- In to a resealable plastic bag place the catfish fillets. In a small bowl now combine together the vegetable oil, soy sauce, garlic, rice wine vinegar, sesame seeds, sesame oil, black pepper and pepper flakes.
- Then pour over the fillets in the bag and seal it. Turn the bag over several times to ensure that the catfish fillets have been well coated in the marinade before then place the bag in the refrigerator and leave there for 1 to 8 hours. The longer you let the fish remain in the marinade the more of its flavor will be absorbed by the fish. As soon as you are ready to cook the fish then heat up the barbecue and make sure that you place the Traeger Grill at a height that allows you to cook the catfish fillets on a medium to high heat.
- Once the barbecue has heated up remove the catfish fillets from the marinade, which can now be discarded and place the fillets on the Traeger Grill, which you have lightly oiled first and cook for between 12 and 13 minutes. During this time, you must turn the fillets over at least once. The fish will be cooked when it easily flakes with a fork. As soon as the fish is cooked remove from heat and serve to your guests.

Barbecued Sea Bass with Lemon Juice
Ingredients

- 1 Teaspoon Olive Oil
- Salt & Freshly Ground Black Pepper to Taste
- 500gram Fresh Sea Bass
- 1 Tablespoon Fresh Lemon Juice
- 1 Bay Leaf

Instructions

- In a bowl mix together the lemon juice, olive oil, salt, pepper and bay leaf. Then rub the sea bass both inside and out with this. You should be do this whilst the barbecue is heat up. As soon as the barbecue has heated up place the fish on the lightly oiled Traeger Grill ed about 4 to 6 inches above the heat source and cook for around 8 to 10 minutes.
- Halfway through the cook time you should turn the fish over and finish off cook. You will know when the fish is cooked as it flakes easily with a fork.

Traeger Grilled Salted Trout
Ingredients

- 20grams Unsalted Butter
- ½ Teaspoon Freshly Ground Black Pepper
- Kitchen Twine
- 4 Trout Fillets
- 4 Fresh Corn Husks
- 8 Strips Bacon

Instructions

- Check the fish over to make sure that there are no bones in the fillets. Whilst you are do this now is the time to get the barbecue heated up. Once you have checked to make sure there are no more bones in the fish you can nonintact make up the little corn husk packets. Place a fillet on each corn husk and then over these places two of the slices of bacon along with 5 grams of the butter.
- Now close the husks up and secure them in place by wrap some of the kitchen twine around them. Once you have placed the twine around the corn husks you can place the packets on to the barbecue

Traeger Grill and cook for between 15 and 18 minutes or until the fish is cooked through. As soon as the fish is ready remove from heat and serve to your guests with barbecued corn on the cob and some fresh new potatoes.

Traeger Grilled Tandoori with Ground Cumin
Ingredients

- 2 Teaspoons Ground Cumin
- 2 Teaspoons Ground Coriander
- 1 Teaspoon Red Pepper
- 4 to 6 Cod Fillets Cut Into ½ Inch Chunks
- 240ml Plain Yogurt
- 60ml Olive Oil
- 4 Garlic Cloves Minced
- 1 Teaspoon Turmeric
- 1 Teaspoon Salt

Instructions

- In a medium size bowl combine together the yogurt, olive oil, garlic, Ginger, cumin, coriander, red pepper, turmeric and salt. Once combined together well add the chunks of cod and mix again. It is important to make sure that every piece of cod is coated well in the marinade you have just made. Now cover the bowl over and place in a refrigerator for 1 hour to let the fish absorb as much of the marinade as possible.
- About 15 minutes before you remove the fish from the refrigerator you should nonintact heat up your barbecue. Put the Traeger Grill at a height of about 4 to 6 inches above the heat source so that the fish will then cook on a medium to high heat.
- As soon as the barbecue has heated up sufficiently you are now ready to start cook the fish. Remove the fish from the marinade and thread on to wooden skewers that have been soak in water for around 30 minutes and then place them on to the lightly oiled Traeger Grill. Cook for around 17 to 19 minutes turn frequently to ensure that the fish doesn't get burnt. When the flesh of the code turns opaque you can now remove from the heat and serve.

Traeger Grilled Bass with Rice Wine
Ingredients

- 2 Tablespoons Toasted Sesame Seeds
- 3 Teaspoons Sugar
- 2 Teaspoons Water
- 1 Garlic Clove Minced
- 1 Teaspoon Dijon Mustard
- 4 Sea Bass Fillets each weigh About 140 to 170grams
- 6 Green Onions Trimmed
- 80ml White Miso Paste
- 3 Tablespoons Rice Vinegar
- 2 Tablespoons Japanese Rice Wine (Mirin)
- 1 Teaspoon Soy Sauce
- Olive Oil
- Salt
- Freshly Ground Black Pepper

Instructions

- Whilst the barbecue is heat up in to a bowl mix together the water and mustard until they are mixed thoroughly. Now into a small saucepan place the miso, vinegar, mirin, soy sauce, garlic, sugar and mustard mixture and place pan on to a medium heat.
- Whisk the mixture whilst heat until it turns smooth, this should take between 3 to 5 minutes to happen. Once the mixture has turned smooth remove from heat and brush the sauce over the fish and also brush the green onions with some olive oil. Sprinkle the fish and onions with salt and pepper to taste.
- Now place the fish on to the barbecue Traeger Grill which has been lightly oiled and cook on either side for 4 to 5 minutes or the flesh inside turns opaque in color. Next you need to cook the fish for a further 2 minutes on either side and whilst this is happening you should place the green onions on the Traeger Grill to cook as well. You are now ready to remove the fish and onions from the barbecue to serve to your guests. Place each fish on a clean plate with the onions and a small amount of the miso sauce you have left over and sprinkle over some of the toasted sesame seeds.

Lime & Basil Tilapia
Ingredients

- 2 Teaspoons Bourbon
- 1 Teaspoon Salt
- Freshly Ground Pepper to Taste
- 4 Tilapia Fillets (Each Weigh Around 115grams)
- 60ml Olive Oil
- 2 Tablespoons Lime Juice
- Zest of 2 Limes
- 1 Tablespoon Freshly Minced Basil

Instructions

- In a resealable plastic bag put the olive oil, lime juice and zest, freshly minced basil, bourbon, salt and pepper. Now close the bag up ensure it is tightly sealed and shake the contents inside vigorously to make sure that they are all mixed together properly.
- Once the marinade is prepared you now need to open the bag up and put the tilapia fillets in and seal the bag once more. After do this turn the bag over several times to ensure that all of the fillets have

been coated in the marinade and then place in a refrigerator for 30 minutes. When the 30 minutes have elapsed remove the fillets from the bag and pour any marinade left in the bag into a saucepan.
- Whilst the barbecue is heat up you now need to heat the marinade up in the saucepan and then bra it to a low boil. As soon as the marinade starts to boil remove from the heat and place to one side. Next you need to cook the Tilapia fillets. It is important that you cook this fish on a high heat and each side should be cooked for at least 3 minutes. As soon as the fish has turned opaque you should remove it from the heat and serve with some of the marinade in the saucepan drizzled over the top.

Sea Bass Kebabs with Dried Oregano
Ingredients

- 680grams Sea Bass Cut Into ½ Inch Chunks
- 60ml Fresh Lemon Juice
- 60ml Olive Oil
- 2 Garlic Cloves Minced
- 1 Teaspoon Dried Oregano
- ¼ Teaspoon Salt
- ¼ Teaspoon Freshly Ground Black Pepper

Instructions

- In a large bowl mix together the lemon juice, olive oil, garlic, oregano, salt and pepper. Once thoroughly combined together add in the chunks of sea bass and then cover the bowl and place in the refrigerator to marinate for 1 to 2 hours. About 15 minutes before you remove the sea bass from the refrigerator you should start warm up the barbecue.
- You will need to cook the kebabs on a very high heat. If you are going to be us wooden skewers then make sure that these have been soak in water for no less than an hour, as this will then prevent them from burn when placed on the barbecue. As you remove each piece of fish from the marinade thread them on to the skewers and place to one side ready for cook. Don't discard any leftover marinade, as you will be us this later on when cook the fish. As soon as the barbecue is hot enough you can place the kebabs on the Traeger Grill.
- Make sure that you have lightly oiled the Traeger Grill first to prevent the fish kebabs from stick to it and cook them for between 5 and 7 minutes. As well as turn the kebabs over frequently to prevent them from burn also baste them with any marinade that is left over. As soon as the kebabs are ready serve.

Moroccan Traeger Grilled Fish Kebabs
Ingredients

- ½ Teaspoon Paprika
- ½ Teaspoon Salt
- ¼ Teaspoon Freshly Ground Black Pepper
- ¼ Teaspoon Chili Powder
- 2 Garlic Cloves Minced
- 680grams White Fish Fillets Cut into Chunks
- 32grams Red Onion Chopped
- 80ml Olive Oil
- 2 Tablespoons Fresh Cilantro Finely Chopped
- 3 Tablespoons Fresh Lemon Juice

Instructions

- Cut the fillets of fish into chunks measure an inch each and place them in a resealable plastic bag. Now in to a bowl place the onion, olive oil, cilantro, lemon juice, paprika, salt, pepper, chili powder and minced garlic and stir well to ensure that the Ingredients are mixed thoroughly together.
- Now pour this mixture into the same bag as the fish. Then close the bag and turn it over or shake until all pieces of fish have been coated in the marinade you have just made. Once you have done this place the sealed bag in to a refrigerator and leave there for between 2 and 4 hours.
- When it comes to cook the fish remove from the bag discard any marinade that remains and thread each chunk of fish on to the skewers you have been soak in water. Once you have thread each skewer with fish you should now lightly oil the Traeger Grill on your preheated barbecue and place the skewers on to it. You should be cooking the fish kebabs on a medium to high heat for between 8 and 10 minutes make sure that you turn them over occasionally to prevent them from burn. As soon as they have cooked you should remove them from the barbecue and serve to your guests immediately.

Traeger Grilled Fish Cakes
Ingredients

- 1 Tablespoon Freshly Chopped Lemon Grass
- 1 Teaspoon Freshly Chopped Mint
- ½ Teaspoon Freshly Grated Black Pepper
- 1 Tablespoon Sugar
- 120ml Coconut Milk
- 1 Tablespoon Coriander
- 450grams White Fish Fillets
- 1 Onion Chopped
- 6 Cashew Nuts
- 1 Teaspoon Chili Powder
- ½ Teaspoon Turmeric
- Salt to Taste
- Banana Leaf's for Cook the Fish Cakes In

Instructions

- The first then you should do before you cut the fish fillets into small pieces is to make sure that there no bones inside them. After cut the fish fillets into small pieces mix them together with the onion, nuts, chili powder, turmeric, lemon grass, mint, black pepper, sugar, coconut milk, coriander and salt in a food processor until they form a smooth mixture. Before you can place any of the fish cake mixture on to a piece of banana leaf measure 6 inches square, they leave need to be boiled in water for about a minute as this will help to soften them up and make them more pliable to use.
- As soon as the banana leaves are ready place 2 tablespoons of the fish cake mixture on to each one and then fold the leaves over. To keep the leaves securely in place pierce through the areas where they come together with a toothpick.
- You should be do this whilst the barbecue is heat up. As soon as the barbecue has heated place the banana leaves with the fish cake mixture inside on to the barbecue and cook on a high heat for 5 minutes. It is important that halfway through this time you turn the fish cakes over to ensure that they are cooked evenly. Once the fish cakes are ready serve to your guests still encased in the banana leaves.

Grilled Tarragon Fish with Canola Oil
Ingredients

- 1 Carrot Cut into Julienne Strips
- 1 Tablespoon Canola Oil
- 2 x 170grams Fish Fillets (You May Want to Give Orange Roughie A Try)
- ½ Zucchini Cut into Julienne Strips
- ½ Small Red Bell Pepper Cut into Thin Strips
- 32grams Sliced Red Onion
- 2 Tablespoons Freshly Chopped Tarragon (If you cannot get hold of fresh tarragon use ¾ Teaspoon of Dried Tarragon Instead)
- 1 Tablespoon Butter

Instructions

- Whilst the barbecue is heat up in a fry pan place the oil and cook the vegetables for about 2 to 3 minutes on a medium to high heat. Then place to one side, as you will need them in a minute.
- Next take too large pieces of aluminum foil and on to these places the fish fillets then on top of these place ½ tablespoon of the butter, half the vegetables and half of the tarragon. Then tightly wrap the foil around each piece and place on the Traeger Grill of the barbecue. Traeger Grill each piece of fish on a medium heat for between 12 and 18 minutes. How long you cook them for will depend on how thick each fish fillet is.
- The thicker the fillet then the longer they will need to remain on the barbecue. It is important that after remove the packets from the barbecue that you open them carefully as the steam released can be extremely hot and can cause burns.

Indian Style Trout with Olive Oil
Ingredients

- 1 Tablespoon Freshly Chopped Parsley
- 1 Small Chopped Shallot
- 1 Teaspoon Salt
- 1 Teaspoon Freshly Chopped Chives
- ½ Teaspoon Freshly Ground Black Pepper
- 4 Trout (Heads Removed, Boned and Butterflied)
- 4 Tablespoons Butter
- 32grams Black Olives Which Have Been Coarsely Chopped
- 2 Tablespoons Pernod (Or Other Liquor Ice Flavored Liqueur)
- 2 Tablespoons Olive Oil
- 1/8 Teaspoon Freshly Ground Black Pepper

Instructions

- Sprinkle both sides of the fish with the salt, ½ teaspoon black pepper and Pernod. Now cover and leave the fish to stand for around 30 minutes at room temperature. Whilst this is happening now would be a good time to get the barbecue started. Whilst the fish is left to one side you now need to make up the mixture, which you will then stuff the fish fillets with. In a food processor place the shallots and olives and process them until they are finely chopped.
- Now to this mixture add the butter, chives, parsley and the 1/8 teaspoon freshly ground black pepper and again turn the food processor on to blend all these Ingredients together well. Once the mixture is ready stuff it inside the fillets of trout and fold the open closed. If you want you can prevent the fillet from open again by secure it with a toothpick. As soon as the barbecue has heated up place the trout fillets on to the Traeger Grill and cook on a medium to high heat for 8 minutes on each side. As

soon as the cook time has been completed remove from heat and serve to your guests on clean plates with a crisp fresh green salad.

Perch with Sage with Zucchini

Ingredients

- 3 Roma Tomatoes
- 1 Tablespoon Olive Oil
- 2 x 340grams Perch (Scaled)
- 2 Slices of Zucchini
- 10 Sprigs of Fresh Sage

Instructions

- Whilst the barbecue is heat up make around 4 slits into the flesh of the perch on each side. Now coat them with oil and insert sprigs of sage into them.
- Once the barbecue has heated up place the perch on to the oiled Traeger Grill and cook for around 4 minutes on each side. As you are about to turn the fish over you should now add the zucchini and tomatoes on to the Traeger Grill and cook these.
- As soon as everything has cooked remove everything from the barbecue. To serve the fish remove the sprigs of sage and then stuff them with the tomatoes and zucchini.

Traeger Grilled Jamaican Jerk Catfish

Ingredients

- 1 Tablespoon Freshly Minced Ginger
- 1 Garlic Clove Minced
- 1 Teaspoon Allspice
- ½ Teaspoon Dried Thyme
- 4 Catfish Fillets
- 2 Green Onions Finely Chopped
- 1 Jalapeno Pepper Seeded and Chopped
- 2 Tablespoons Brown Sugar
- 2 Tablespoons Worcestershire Sauce
- 2 Tablespoons White Wine Vinegar
- ¼ Teaspoon Salt
- 1/8 Teaspoon Freshly Ground Black Pepper

Instructions

- Preheat heat the barbecue to a medium heat. Whilst the barbecue is heat up in to a bowl (large) place the onions, jalapeno pepper, brown sugar, Worcestershire sauce, white wine vinegar, Ginger, garlic, allspice, dried thyme, salt and pepper and mix thoroughly. Now into the bowl add the fish and coat well before then cover the bowl and leave the fish to marinate in the sauce for 5 to 10 minutes at room temperature.
- After the relevant amount of time has elapsed remove the catfish fillets from the marinade and place them to one side. Don't throw away the marinade as you are going to need this. Place the catfish fillets on the barbecue Traeger Grill that has been lightly oiled and brush with some of the remain marinade.

- Now cook for about 5 minutes before then turn the fish over. After turn the fish over you need to again brush with the marinade that is remain and cook for a further 7 to 9 minutes. As soon as the fillets are cooked remove from the barbecue and serve with a crisp fresh green salad.

Sweet & Sour Halibut with Cider Vinegar
Ingredients

- 3 Tablespoons Cider Vinegar
- 3 Tablespoons Tomato Ketchup
- 1 Tablespoon Soy Sauce
- 1 Red and Green Bell Pepper
- 2 Green Onions Cut Into 2 Inch Strips
- 60ml Water
- 55grams Brown Sugar
- ¾ Teaspoon Freshly Grated Ginger
- 2 Garlic Cloves Minced
- 4 x Halibut Steaks (Weigh About 340grams Each)

Instructions

- Coat the Traeger Grill on your barbecue with oil and then turn it on so it can start heat up. Take the bell peppers and cut them in half and remove the seeds then set to one side for use later on. In to bowl place the brown sugar, water, cider vinegar, tomato ketchup, soy sauce, garlic and Ginger and mix well together. Remove around 60ml of the sauce you have just made and set aside for later. With the rest of the sauce you have just made dip each of the halibut steaks into it make sure that both sides of the fish have been evenly coated in it and again set to one side. By now the Traeger Grill should have heated up and you should place the bell peppers on them to cook.
- Place the peppers on the Traeger Grill with the skin side down and cook until the skin begins to blacken. Remove once the skin starts to blacken and peel it away from the rest of the pepper. Once the skin has been removed cut them peppers into thin strips. Now place the halibut steaks on the Traeger Grill and cook until they are done the flesh should start to turn opaque in color.
- Once the steaks are cooked place each one on a clean plate then top with some of the slices of the bell peppers and the green onions before then pour over equal amounts of the sauce that you put aside earlier.

Grilled Halibut & Red Pepper Kebabs
Ingredients

- 1 ½ Teaspoons Serrano Pepper Minced
- 680grams Halibut Steaks Cut Into 1 Inch Chunks
- 1 Large Bell Pepper Cut Into 1 Inch Squares
- 4 Tablespoons Olive Oil
- 3 Tablespoons Fresh Finely Chopped Cilantro
- 2 Tablespoons Sugar
- 1 Large Red Onion Cut Into 1 Inch Squares
- 120ml Fresh Lime Juice

Instructions

- In a small bowl place, the lime juice, 2 tablespoons of olive oil, sugar, Serrano pepper and the sugar and combine well together until all the sugar has dissolved. Now leave this to one side for around an

hour so that all the flavors blend together. Whilst the sauce is blend you should now be turning the barbecue on so that it can heat up ready to start cook the halibut, pepper and onion kebabs. To make the kebabs you should thread on to each one alternate pieces of the halibut, pepper and onion until they are all used up.
- Metal skewers can be used however if you intend to use wooden ones make sure that they have been soak in some water for at least an hour to ensure that they don't burn when placed on the barbecue. Before you place the kebabs on the Traeger Grill brush them all over with the remain olive oil and cook on a high heat for about 1 ½ minutes on all sides so you should be cook them for a total of around 6 minutes. You will know that the halibut is cooked as it will have turned opaque and will be flaky through the middle. After remove the kebabs from the Traeger Grill onto a clean plate nonservice them with the sauce you made earlier alongside.

Fish Grilled Roll Ups with Worcestershire Sauce
Ingredients

- 3 Tablespoons Flour
- 1 Teaspoon Lemon Juice (Fresh Is Best)
- 1 Teaspoon Freshly Chopped Parsley
- ½ Teaspoon Worcestershire Sauce
- ¼ Teaspoon Salt
- 100grams Smoked Fish
- 240ml Milk
- 6 Slices of Buttered Bread
- 22grams Grated Cheese
- 3 Tablespoons Butter
- ¼ Teaspoon Freshly Ground Black Pepper

Instructions

- Whilst the barbecue is heat up flake the smoked fish and melt the butter in a saucepan to which you then add the flour, pepper, salt and parsley. Cook this mixture until it begins to boil then very slowly add the milk and then continue cook for a further two minutes. Now add the Worcestershire sauce, cheese, lemon juice and the flaked smoked fish. Mix all the Ingredients together well. Now take this mixture and spread it over the unbuttered side of the bread and roll each one up and secure them us a toothpick.
- Once you have made up each fish roll place them on the barbecue Traeger Grill, which you can lightly oil, and cook for around 2 to 3 minutes. During this time make sure that you turn them over once and then serve immediately to your wait guests.

Traeger Grilled Catfish with Lemon Juice
Ingredients

- 2 Sprigs Fresh Rosemary
- 1 Teaspoon Cayenne Pepper
- 450grams Catfish Fillet
- 3 Garlic Cloves Crushed
- 2 Tablespoons Lemon Juice (Fresh If Possible)
- 1 Tablespoon Balsamic Vinegar
- 1 Teaspoon Soy Sauce

Instructions

- Whilst the barbecue is heat up place the catfish fillet on to a piece of aluminum foil that is large enough that when you fold the edges up it turns into a makeshift pan. Now place the fish in the aluminum foil on to the barbecue and then pour over the other Ingredients and let the catfish fillet cook them until it is done.
- On average the fish should be cooked in about 4 to 9 minutes depend on how hot the barbecue is and what the weather is like. It is important that you watch the fish carefully whilst it is cook otherwise it could become over cooked very easily. You will know when the fish is cooked because the edges of it start to turn up and become crispy. But don't rely on this solely for tell you that the fish is cooked you should check to see if the middle of the catfish fillet has turned opaque.

Asian Jerk Red Snapper with Soy Sauce
Ingredients

- 60ml Lemon Juice
- Zest of Two Lemons
- 2 Tablespoons Jerk Rub
- 2 Whole Red Snapper
- 4 Green Onions Diced
- 4 Garlic Cloves Minced
- 2 Tablespoons Olive Oil
- 2 Tablespoons Soy Sauce

Instructions

- In a small bowl combine together 2 minced garlic cloves, scallions, lemon zest and 1 tablespoon Jerk rub. Then rub it all over the insides of the cleaned out red snapper. Now into another bowl you should combine together the other 1 tablespoon jerk rub along with the rest of the garlic, the lemon juice, the soy sauce and olive oil and place to one side. It is important that before you start make up the above you actually turn the barbecue on so it will then be ready for cook the fish on.
- As soon as the barbecue has heated up place the red snapper on to the Traeger Grill about 4 to 6 inches above the heat source so it cooks on a medium to high heat. Let the fish cook on each side for 8 to 10 minutes and whilst this is happening baste frequently with the lemon, soy sauce and jerk rub sauce.

Traeger Grilled Fresh Sardines
Ingredients

- 1 Garlic Clove Peeled
- 6 Inch Baguette Cut Into 16 Thin Slices Diagonally
- 8 Medium Sized Whole Fresh Sardines
- 1 ½ Tablespoons Extra Virgin Olive Oil
- ¾ Teaspoon Coarse Salt
- ¼ Teaspoon Freshly Ground Black Pepper

Instructions

- Brush both sides of the sardines with 1 tablespoon of the extra virgin olive oil and thin sprinkle over them 1/2 teaspoon of salt and 1/8 teaspoon of the freshly ground black pepper.
- Whilst you are do this heat up the barbecue. Once the barbecue is hot enough lightly oil the surface of the Traeger Grill and them place the sardines on to it and cook them on a medium to high heat.
- Cook each sardine for 2 minutes on each side. Halfway through cook the sardines you should also be cook the slices of baguette that you will be serve with the fish. But before place the baguette

slices on the barbecue first rub each side of them with the garlic and brush them with the rest of the olive oil. Then sprinkle with the salt and pepper that is left over.
- Cook each side of the bread for 1 minute or until they turn crisp. As soon as everything is cooked place the sardines and bread on to a clean plate and serve with some lemon wedges to your guests.

Marinated with Plum Tomatoes Monkfish
Ingredients

- 1 Teaspoon Ginger Puree or Freshly Grated Ginger
- 1 Green Chili (Deseeded and Finely Chopped)
- 1 Tablespoon Sunflower or Ground Nut Oil
- Salt and Freshly Ground Black Pepper to Taste
- 700grams Monkfish Tail
- 100grams about 4 Large Raw Tiger Prawns or 8 to 12 Smaller Ones
- 1 Garlic Clove Crushed
- 500grams Plum Tomatoes
- 1 Stalk Lemongrass (Outer Leaves Removed Then Finely Sliced)
- Juice of 1 Lime
- Wedges of Lime to Serve with Dish
- 2 Teaspoons Coriander Seeds
- 1 Green Chili (Deseeded and Finely Chopped)
- 1 Garlic Clove Crushed

Instructions

- Rinse the monkfish in cold water and then pat dry with paper towels. Remove any grey membrane and then cut the flesh away from the backbone cartilage so you have two long pieces. Then cut each piece into equal size chunks. You should aim to get between 8 and 12 chunks from each piece.
- Next you need to peel the prawns if you can leave the tails on and just remove the legs and heads.
- Now run a sharp knife along the back of each prawn and pull out the dark thread run through him or her. Then rinse them in cold water then pat dry and put to one side for use later as with the monkfish. Now you are ready to start make the marinade for the kebabs. To do this mix the garlic, chili, Ginger and oil in a bowl and then to this add the monkfish and prawns and mix all Ingredients together well.

- Whilst the fish and prawns are marina take your wooden skewers and place them in some water to soak. Whilst the monkfish and prawns are marina you can begin make the salsa. First off you need to cover the tomatoes with boil water and then leave them like this for one minute. After a minute has passed remove the tomatoes from the water and peel away the skin and cut in half so that you can remove the seeds. Now cut each half of the tomato into chunky puree.
- Unfortunately, you will have to do this by hand rather than us a food processor. Now place the chunks of tomato into a bowl and into this mix the chilly, garlic, lime juice and lemongrass. Then add a little salt and pepper to taste. Cover the bowl over and place in the refrigerator ready for when you want to serve the kebabs. To cook the kebabs, you need to place them on the barbecue Traeger Grill on a medium to high heat and cook each one for between 3 to 4 minutes on both sides. You can tell when the kebabs are ready, as the prawns will have turned a pink color and feel much firmer. You should have threaded onto each skewer chunks of monkfish and 1, 2 or 3 prawns.

Grilled Shrimp and Pineapple Skewers
Ingredients

- 1½ Tablespoons Fresh Lime Juice
- 2 Cloves Garlic, Minced
- 1½ Tablespoons Minced Fresh Cilantro
- 8 (10-Inch) Bamboo Skewers, Soaked in Water For 15 Minutes, Then Drained
- 1 Pound Large Shrimp (26/30 Count), Peeled and Deveined, Tails Removed
- 2 Red Bell Peppers, Seeded, Defibbed, And Cut Into 1-Inch Squares
- ½ Pineapple, Peeled, Halved, Cored, And Cut Into 1-Inch Cubes (About 24 Pieces)
- 6 Tablespoons Extra-Virgin Olive Oil, Plus More for Brush
- ½ Teaspoon Kosher or Sea Salt
- ½ Teaspoon Sugar
- ½ Teaspoon Freshly Ground Pepper

Instructions

- Immerse the skewers before light the Traeger Grill so they have plenty of time to soak. Prepare a medium-hot fire in a charcoal Traeger Grill or preheat a gas Traeger Grill on medium high. To assemble the skewers, pinch a shrimp into a horseshoe shape and thread it onto a skewer, pierce it once near the tail end and again near the head end.
- Follow with a square of red pepper and a cube of pineapple. Repeat the lineup three more times, then load the remain 7 skewers the same way.
- Arrange the skewers on a rimmed back sheet and brush them with olive oil. Set aside.
- While the Traeger Grill is heat, prepare the sauce: In a small bowl, combine the 6 tablespoons olive oil, the lime juice, garlic, cilantro, salt, sugar, and pepper. Stir to mix, and set aside. Oil the Traeger Grill grate. Fold a footlong piece of aluminum foil in half lengthwise and lay it on the Traeger Grill grate. Arrange the skewers so the exposed bamboo is protected from the flame by the foil and the food is directly over the medium-hot fire. Use 2 pieces of foil if necessary.
- Traeger Grill on one side until light Traeger Grill marks appear on the shrimp and the pineapple begins to caramelize, about 3 minutes. Turn and Traeger Grill until the shrimp turn pink on the outside and are just opaque on the inside, about 3 minutes longer. Arrange 2 skewers on each warmed dinner plate, and drizzle the garlic and cilantro sauce over the skewers. Serve immediately.

Traeger Grilled Red Snapper
Ingredients

- 3 Tablespoons Lime Juice
- 970grams Whole Red Snapper (Split and Butterflied)
- 60ml Achiote Paste
- 60ml Orange Juice
- 3 Tablespoons Lemon Juice

Instructions

- In a bowl mix together the achiote paste with the orange, lemon and lime juice and spread over all surfaces of the Red Snapper. Place into a shallow dish which you then cover before putt in the refrigerator to rest for at least 2 hours.
- Just before the fish comes out of the refrigerator start up the barbecue and place the Traeger Grill about 6 inches above the heat source as you want to cook this fish on a medium heat. Once the barbecue has heated up lightly oil the Traeger Grill and then place the Red Snapper on it skin side down and leave it there for about 5 minutes.
- Then after this time turn the fish over and let it cook for a further 3 minutes. You will notice that the fish is done when the juices begin boil and also you will find remove the central bone is easy because it simply lifts out when the fish is cooked. If you would like to cook the fish in the same way that Mexican people do then try and get a banana leaf on which to place it when cook.
- If you can make sure that the leaf is still wet when you place it on the Traeger Grill first before add the fish. Not only will this prevent the fish from stick to the Traeger Grill but also help to stop it from fall apart as you turn it over.

Charred Courgettis Skewered Swordfish
Ingredients

- 1 Garlic Clove Crushed
- 15grams Fresh Basil Chopped
- 500grams Swordfish Steaks Cut Into 2cm Chunks

- 3 Lemons
- 3 Tablespoon Olive Oil
- 500grams Small Courgettis Trimmed

Instructions

- Whilst four long wooden skewers are soak in water you need to cut the swordfish up into 2cm chunks. To do this you first need to cut away the skin. As the skin is quite thick you need to use a very sharp knife. In a bowl grate the zest from one of the lemons and add to this the juice of it along with the olive oil and garlic and then add to it the finely chopped up basil leaves then mix well together. As for the other two lemons you now need to cut these into 8 wedges.
- Next cut the courgettis in half lengthways and then score the white flesh with the tip of a sharp knife so a Criss cross pattern is formed on them.
- Then lightly brush with some of the marinade you have just made and set to one side for cook on the barbecue later. Now into the marinade you need to put the chunks of swordfish and mix well together before then place to one side for them to marinate in the sauce for between 5 and 10 minutes. Whilst the swordfish is marina in the sauce now is the time to turn on or light your barbecue. As soon as the marina time has elapsed you are now ready to make up the kebabs on to each skewer thread chunks of swordfish along with the lemon wedges in an alternate pattern.
- Then sprinkle both the kebabs and courgettis with some coarsely ground black pepper and place all items on to the barbecue Traeger Grill, which has been lightly oiled. Cook both the kebabs and courgettis for between 10 and 15 minutes, make sure that you turn the kebabs over occasionally to ensure that the fish is cooked right through. The same also goes for the courgettis. It is important that whilst the kebabs are cook that you also baste them regularly with any marinade you have left over. Once the kebabs and courgettis are cooked serve to guests on clean plates along with the warm focaccia bread.

Mango Salsa Marinated Scallop Brochettes
Ingredients

- ¼ Teaspoon Kosher or Sea Salt
- 8 10-Inch Bamboo Skewers, Soaked in Water For 15 Minutes, Then Drained
- 24 Large Sea Scallops (1¼ to 1½ Pounds)
- ¼ Cup Extra-Virgin Olive Oil, Plus More for Brush
- 2 Tablespoons Fresh Lemon Juice
- 1 Large Clove Garlic, Minced
- 1 Tablespoon Minced Fresh Cilantro
- ¼ Teaspoon Freshly Ground Pepper
- 2 Red Bell Peppers, Seeded, Defibbed, And Cut Into 1-Inch Squares (About 24 Pieces)
- 1 To 1½ Cups Mango Salsa, Homemade or Store-Bought

Instructions

- Immerse the skewers before light the Traeger Grill so they have plenty of time to soak. Prepare a medium-hot fire in a charcoal Traeger Grill or preheat a gas Traeger Grill on medium high. Rinse the scallops under cold water to remove any small particles of grit. Remove any tough muscle on the side of each scallop.
- Pat the scallops dry with paper towels. While the Traeger Grill is heat, prepare the sauce: In a small bowl, combine the ¼ cup olive oil, the lemon juice, garlic, cilantro, salt, and pepper. Stir to mix thoroughly. Set aside until ready to serve. To assemble the skewers, thread a scallop through its side

onto a skewer. Follow with a square of red pepper and piece of green onion. Repeat the lineup three more times, then load the remain 7 skewers the same way.

- Arrange the skewers on a rimmed back sheet and brush generously on all sides with olive oil. Oil the Traeger Grill grate. Fold a footlong piece of aluminum foil in half lengthwise and lay it on the Traeger Grill grate.
- Arrange the skewers so the exposed bamboo is protected from the flame by the foil and the food is directly over the medium-hot fire. Use 2 pieces of foil if necessary. Traeger Grill on one side until light Traeger Grill marks appear on the scallops, about 3 minutes. Turn and Traeger Grill until the scallops are etched with Traeger Grill marks on the second side and are just opaque and cooked through in the center when tested with a knife, about 3 minutes longer. Arrange 2 skewers on each warmed dinner plate, and drizzle the olive oil sauce over the skewers. Mound a spoonful of mango salsa alongside each pair of skewers. Serve immediately.

Dijon Mustard Salmon Burgers
Ingredients

- 2 Eggs (That Have Been Lightly Beaten)
- 1 Tablespoon Fresh Rosemary Minced
- ½ Teaspoon Salt
- 1Kg Salmon Fillet (Skinned and Bones Removed)
- 100grams Dried Breadcrumbs
- 80grams Minced Red Onion
- 1 Tablespoon Dijon Mustard
- 2 Teaspoons Horseradish (Freshly Grated If Possible)
- ½ Teaspoon Freshly Ground Black Pepper
- 2 Tablespoons Olive Oil

Instructions

- You need to cut the salmon into strips crossways and then chop these up until the fish has become well minced. As you do chop the fish up look out for any bones and remove these. Now into a large bowl place the minced salmon, breadcrumbs, red onion, mustard, horseradish and eggs. Then season this mixture with the salt and pepper and rosemary and combine them all together.
- Now place the mixture in the refrigerator to chill for at least 30 minutes. Whilst the salmon mixture is chill you should now get your barbecue go and place the Traeger Grill which you will have oiled just before you start cook around 4 to 6 inches above the heat source. This is because you will be cooking the burgers on a medium to high heat. After remove the salmon mixture from the refrigerator form it into 8 burger patter and then lightly coat each one with some olive oil.
- Then place each patty on the barbecue and cook for between 4 and 5 minutes on each side. As soon as the burgers are cooked serve on a bun with lettuce and tomato and pot of mustard and horseradish beside them.

Grilled Ground Cumin Fish Kebabs
Ingredients

- 1 Teaspoon Ground Cumin
- 1 Teaspoon Lemon Juice (Fresh If Possible)
- Salt and Freshly Ground Black Pepper to Taste
- 750grams Firm Fish Fillets
- 2 Tablespoons Olive Oil

- 1 Garlic Clove Finely Chopped
- 1 Tablespoon Fresh Coriander Chopped

Instructions

- In a bowl combine together the olive oil, garlic, coriander, cumin, lemon juice, salt and pepper, then place to one side, as this is the marinade for the fish. Now take the fish fillets and cut these in to 3cm size cubes and combine with the sauce you made earlier. Now place the covered bowl into a refrigerator for several hours.
- Whilst the fish is marina make sure that you stir it occasionally. Just before you are about to start thread the fish cubes on to wooden skewers that have been soak in water for at least 30 minutes you should get the barbecue go. It is important that before you thread the cubes of fish on to the skewers you drain them well first and also make sure that the Traeger Grill on the barbecue has been oiled.
- Now place the skewers on the barbecue and cook each kebab for between 6 and 8 minutes turn them occasionally and also bast them with any leftover marinade. The fish is cooked through when the flesh has turned opaque and the exterior is a light brown color. Once the kebabs are cooked serve them with a crisp green salad and some lemon wedges.

Grilled Salmon with Lemon Marinated
Ingredients

- 2 Tablespoons Fresh Lemon Juice
- 2 Tablespoons Chopped Fresh Dill
- ½ Teaspoon Kosher or Sea Salt
- ½ Teaspoon Freshly Ground Pepper
- 1 Untreated Alder Plank, About 15 By 7 By Inches
- ¼ Cup Extra-Virgin Olive Oil
- 2 Tablespoons Vodka
- Freshly Grated Zest Of 1 Lemon

Instructions

- Rinse the alder plank and place it in a pan, sink, or large leakproof plastic bag filled with water. Soak the plank for at least 20 minutes. (The plank can be submerged in water and left to soak all day, so plan ahead and soak the plank before you leave for work.) Prepare a medium fire in a charcoal Traeger Grill or preheat a gas Traeger Grill on medium. In a small bowl, combine the olive oil, vodka, lemon zest, lemon juice, dill, salt, and pepper and mix thoroughly. Place the whole salmon fillet on a large, rimmed back sheet and pour the marinade evenly over the top. Set aside while the Traeger Grill heats.
- When ready to Traeger Grill, place the soaked plank on the Traeger Grill grate directly over the medium fire and cover. After a few minutes, the plank will begin to smoke and crackle. Turn the plank over, re-cover, and "toast" the other side for about 2 minutes. Uncover the Traeger Grill, transfer the salmon fillet to the plank, and then recover the Traeger Grill. Cook the salmon until it is almost opaque throughout but still very moist when tested with a knife, or an instant-read thermometer inserted in the center registers 125° to 130°F, 15 to 25 minutes, depend on the thickness of the fillet. (Keep a spray bottle with water nearby in case the plank gets too hot and begins to flame.
- Ext wish the flame and continue Traeger Grill the salmon, adjust the heat level if necessary.) Us 2 long spatulas, transfer the salmon to a warmed platter. Use tongs, heatproof gloves, or the spatulas to remove the plank from the heat and set it aside to cool. Cut the salmon into individual serve s and serve immediately. Alternatively, for a rustic presentation, leave the salmon on the plank and place the plank on a large heatproof platter.

Grilled Salmon with Fresh Herbs

Ingredients

- Kosher or Sea Salt
- Freshly Ground Pepper
- Leaves From 4 Sprigs Fresh Thyme
- 1 Untreated Alder Plank, about 15 By 7 By Inches (See Cook's Note) 1 Whole
- Side of Salmon (About 3 Pounds), Skin on And Scaled, Pin Bones Removed
- Extra-Virgin Olive Oil
- Leaves From 4 Sprigs Fresh Rosemary
- ½ Lemon

Instructions

- Rinse the alder plank and place it in a pan, sink, or large leakproof plastic bag filled with water. Soak the plank for at least 20 minutes. (The plank can be submerged in water and left to soak all day, so plan ahead and soak the plank before you leave for work.)
- Prepare a medium fire in a charcoal Traeger Grill or preheat a gas Traeger Grill on medium. Rub the salmon with olive oil and sprinkle lightly on both sides with salt and pepper.
- Scatter the thyme and rosemary leaves over the flesh, press them lightly so they adhere to the flesh. Set aside while the Traeger Grill heats. When ready to Traeger Grill, place the soaked plank on the Traeger Grill grate directly over the medium fire and cover. After a few minutes, the plank will begin to smoke and crackle. Turn the plank over, re-cover, and "toast" the other side for about 2 minutes.
- Uncover the Traeger Grill, transfer the whole salmon fillet to the plank, and then re-cover the Traeger Grill. Cook the salmon until it is almost opaque throughout but still very moist when tested with a knife, or an instant-read thermometer inserted in the center registers 125° to 130°F, 15 to 25 minutes, depend on the thickness of the fillet. (Keep a spray bottle with water nearby in case the plank gets too hot and begins to flame. Ext wish the flame and continue Traeger Grill the salmon, adjust the heat level if necessary.) Us 2 long spatulas, transfer the salmon to a warmed platter.
- Use tongs, heatproof gloves, or the spatulas to remove the plank from the heat and set it aside to cool. Squeeze the lemon half over the salmon, cut into individual serve s, and serve immediately. Alternatively, for a rustic presentation, leave the salmon on the plank and place the plank on a large heatproof platter.

Traeger Grilled Snapper with Soy Sauce

Ingredients

- 1 Tablespoon Freshly Crushed Ginger
- 2 Garlic Cloves Minced
- 1 Teaspoon Freshly Ground Black Pepper
- 900grams Snapper
- 2 Tablespoons Freshly Chopped Coriander Root
- 1 ½ Tablespoons Soy Sauce
- Vegetable Oil
- Banana Leaf

Instructions

- Into a food processor place the garlic, Ginger, black pepper and coriander root and blend together so that it forms a paste. Then add the soy sauce and continue to blend until all the Ingredients become well combined. Nonwinged this mixture to one side. Next you should rinse the snapper and then pat it dry with some paper towels. Once you have done this take the sauce you made earlier and rub it all over the surface of the fish and place the fish to one side for 30 minutes. It is now that you should be start your barbecue up so that it has reached the required temperature for cook the fish on. Once the 30 minutes have elapsed take the snapper and place it on to the banana leaf.

- It is important that the leaves you use are large enough to completely cover the fish. However, if you cannot get large ones then it is perfectly to cut the fish into pieces that will fit easily inside the leaves you do have. But before you do wrap the fish in the leaves make sure that you have washed them thoroughly. Also, they need to be blanched in hot water for a number of seconds as this will help to make the soft and so much easier to wrap around the fish. After the banana leaves have been blanched you should remove the thick spine from them with a pair of kitchen scissors. Then place them on a work surface shiny side fac downwards. Then you must brush vegetable oil all over the leaf fac towards you, which will then come into contact with the fish. Once you have done this you can place the fish on to and then wrap the leaf around it. To help keep the leaf around the fish when cook secure it in place either with a skewer or toothpicks.
- After wrap the snapper in the banana leaf you can now place it on the barbecue to cook. Cook it on a medium heat so place the Traeger Grill around 4 to 6 inches above the heat source and cook on each side for between 8 and 10 minutes. You need to keep an eye on the fish as it is cook to ensure that the banana leaf doesn't become burnt. Although it may start to blacken in areas you don't want the heat to burn right through the leaf. After 16 minutes remove the packages from the barbecue and very gently open them to see whether the fish is cooked or not. You will know when the fish is cooked because it is opaque in appearance and flakes easily with a fork. If you notice that the fish isn't cooked then securely wrap back in the banana leaf and place on the barbecue again for another couple of minutes.

Traeger Grilled Shark with Ketchup
Ingredients

- 40grams Freshly Chopped Parsley
- 2 Tablespoons Fresh Lemon Juice
- 2 Garlic Cloves Minced
- 6 Shark Steaks
- 120ml Soy Sauce
- 60ml Tomato Ketchup
- 120ml Fresh Orange Juice
- 1/3 Tablespoon Freshly Ground Pepper

Instructions

- In a bowl combine together the garlic, pepper, soy sauce, orange juice, tomato ketchup, chopped parsley and lemon juice. Take the shark steaks and place them in a shallow back dish and pour the sauce you have just made over them. It is important that you turn the steaks over to ensure that all sides of them are coated in the sauce, which you are go to be marina them in. Now cover the dish and place in the refrigerator for 2 hours. When it comes time to cook the shark steaks make sure that the Traeger Grill on the barbecue has been lightly oiled first to prevent them from stick to the surface.
- As soon as the barbecue has heated up remove the steaks from the marinate and place them on the Traeger Grill keep any leftover marinate in the dish for use later. Traeger Grill the shark steaks over a high heat for 6 minutes on each side or until when tested with a fork the fish flakes easily. Throughout the time the shark steaks are cook make sure that you baste them regularly with the remainder of the sauce you marinated them in earlier.

Grilled Lacquered Salmon with Lemon Juice

Ingredients

- Kosher or Sea Salt
- ½ Teaspoon Freshly Ground Pepper; Plus, More for Sprinkle
- 5 Tablespoons Soy Sauce
- 3 Tablespoons Honey
- ½ Cup Packed Fresh Cilantro Leaves, Coarsely Chopped
- 2 Tablespoons Black Sesame Seeds
- 3 Packages (2 Ounces Each) Bean Thread Noodles
- 4 Center-Cut Salmon Fillets (About 6 Ounces Each), Skin on And Scaled, Pin
- Bones Removed
- Extra-Virgin Olive Oil
- 3 Tablespoons Asian Sesame Oil
- 2 Teaspoons Fresh Lemon Juice

Instructions

- Prepare a medium-hot fire in a charcoal Traeger Grill or preheat a gas Traeger Grill on medium high. In a large bowl, soak the noodles in hot water to cover until softened, about 20 minutes. Generously brush the salmon fillets on both sides with olive oil and sprinkle lightly with salt and pepper. To make the glaze, in a small bowl, combine 1 tablespoon of the soy sauce, 2 tablespoons of the honey, and ½ teaspoon pepper and mix thoroughly. Set aside. To make the dress, in a small bowl, combine the remain 4 tablespoons soy sauce and 1 tablespoon honey, the sesame oil, and the lemon juice, mix well.
- Drain the noodles well in a colander, shake the colander a few times to make sure all the water is removed. Pat the noodles dry with paper towels. Toss the noodles with the dress, cilantro, and sesame seeds. Set aside. Oil the Traeger Grill grate. Use tongs to arrange the salmon fillets, flesh side down, directly over the medium-hot fire.
- Traeger Grill the salmon until Traeger Grill marks are etched across the fillets, about 3 minutes. Turn the fillets, skin side down, and brush the salmon flesh generously with the glaze. Cover the Traeger Grill and continue Traeger Grill the salmon until it is almost opaque throughout but still very moist when tested with a knife, or an instant-read thermometer inserted in the center registers 125° to 130°F, 3 to 4 minutes longer.
- Divide the noodles among dinner plates. Us a wide spatula, place a salmon fillet in the center of each plate, on top of the noodles. Serve immediately.

Traeger Grilled Salmon with Herbs

Ingredients

- Kosher or Sea Salt
- Freshly Ground Pepper
- 8 Sprigs Fresh Thyme
- 4 Center-Cut Salmon Fillets (About 6 Ounces Each), Skin on And Scaled, Pin
- Bones Removed
- Extra-Virgin Olive Oil
- 8 Sprigs Fresh Rosemary
- 1 Lemon, Cut Into 8 Thin Slices

Instructions

- Prepare a medium fire in a charcoal Traeger Grill or preheat a gas Traeger Grill on medium. Generously brush the salmon fillets on both sides with olive oil and sprinkle lightly with salt and pepper. Lay 2 thyme sprigs and 2 rosemary sprigs on the flesh side of each fillet, press them lightly so they adhere to the flesh.
- Oil the Traeger Grill grate. Use tongs to arrange the salmon fillets, herb side down, directly over the medium fire and cover. Traeger Grill the salmon until Traeger Grill marks are etched across the fillets, about 3 minutes. Turn the fillets, re-cover, and cook until the salmon is almost opaque throughout but still very moist when tested with a knife, or an instant-read thermometer inserted in the center registers 125° to 130°F, 3 to 4 minutes longer.
- Using tongs or a wide spatula, transfer the fillets to warmed dinner plates. Remove the herbs from the salmon, arrange 2 slices of lemon on each plate, and serve immediately.

Asian Mahi Grilled Marks
Ingredients

- 2 Tablespoons Olive Oil
- 1 Tablespoon Honey
- 3 Garlic Cloves Minced
- 6 x 170grams Mahi Grill marks Fish Fillets
- 40grams Freshly Chopped Cilantro
- 60ml Fresh Lemon Juice
- 1 Teaspoon Hot Chili Powder (Optional)
- Salt and Freshly Ground Black Pepper to Taste

Instructions

In a bowl combine well together the cilantro, lemon juice, olive oil, honey, garlic, salt and pepper. Plus, the hot chili powder if you want to add a little kick to this dish. Then set to one side. Now into a resealable bag or on a shallow back dish place the fish fillets and pour over the sauce you made earlier. Remember to turn the fish over so that all sides are coated in the marinade and leave if the refrigerator to marinate for 30 minutes. Whilst the fish is marina in the refrigerator you should be light your barbecue so that it is ready then for cook the fish once you take it out of the refrigerator. To cook the fish, remove from the marinade and place on the barbecue directly over the heat sauce and then cook on each side for 3 to 4 minutes or until the fish is cooked through. To check to see if it is done see if the fish flakes easily with a fork and has turned opaque throughout.

Salmon Wrapped with Fresh Thyme
Ingredients

- Kosher or Sea Salt
- Freshly Ground Pepper
- 8 Sprigs Fresh Thyme
- 8 Sprigs Fresh Rosemary
- 4 Sheets Cedar Paper, each 6 Inches Square 4 Center cut
- Salmon Fillets (About 5 Inches Long And 2 Inches Wide), Skin and Pin Bones
- Removed
- Extra-Virgin Olive Oil
- 1 Lemon, Cut Into 8 Paper-Thin Slices
- 4 Green Onions with Long Green Tops

Instructions

- Prepare a medium fire in a charcoal Traeger Grill or preheat a gas Traeger Grill on medium. Soak the cedar paper sheets in warm water until pliable, 5 to 10 minutes.
- Generously brush the salmon fillets on both sides with olive oil and sprinkle lightly with salt and pepper. Lay 2 thyme sprigs and 2 rosemary sprigs on each fillet, press them lightly so they adhere to the flesh. Arrange 2 lemon slices, overlap them slightly, over the top of the herbs on each fillet. Place the 4 sheets of soaked cedar on a work surface. Place a salmon fillet in the center of each sheet, parallel to the grain of the wood. Cut 8 long strips from the green tops of the onions to use as ties. Work with 1 cedar sheet at a time, bra up the sides to encase the piece of salmon, form a tube and overlap the edges if possible. Wrap a long strip of green onion around the tube about one-third of the way down from the top edge, and tie it gently to secure the tube.
- Wrap another strip of green onion about one-third of the way up from the bottom edge and tie it. Repeat to secure the other packets. Oil the Traeger Grill grate. Use tongs to arrange the cedar packets, edge side up, directly over the medium fire and cover. Traeger Grill until the packets begin to smoke and crackle, about 4 minutes.
- Turn the packets over, re-cover the Traeger Grill, and "toast" the other side until the salmon is almost opaque throughout but still very moist when tested with a knife, or an instant-read thermometer inserted in the center registers 125° to 130°F, 3 to 4 minutes longer.
- Using tongs, transfer the salmon packets to warmed dinner plates. Snip the onions with a knife and use the tongs to open the packets and unroll the wood sheets. Serve immediately.

Traeger Grilled Halibut with Oregano
Ingredients

- ¾ Teaspoon Freshly Ground Pepper
- ½ Teaspoon Kosher or Sea Salt
- 4 10-Inch Bamboo Skewers, Soaked in Water For 15 Minutes, Then Drained
- Cup Extra-Virgin Olive Oil, Plus More for Brush
- 2 Tablespoons Fresh Lemon Juice
- 2 Tablespoons Finely Minced Shallots
- 2 Tablespoons Finely Minced Fresh Oregano
- Teaspoon Garlic Powder
- 1½ Pounds Halibut Fillets, Skin Removed, Cut Into 1½-Inch Chunks

Instructions

- Immerse the skewers before light the Traeger Grill so they have plenty of time to soak. Prepare a medium-hot fire in a charcoal Traeger Grill or preheat a gas Traeger Grill on medium high. In a bowl, combine the cup olive oil, the lemon juice, shallots, oregano, pepper, salt, and garlic powder and mix well.
- Reserve 2 tablespoons of the marinade. Put the halibut chunks in the marinade and toss to coat all sides.
- Set aside while the Traeger Grill heats. Thread the halibut onto skewers, divide it evenly and cover about 8 inches of each skewer. Just before Traeger Grill, brush the halibut with olive oil to keep it from stick to the Traeger Grill grate. Oil the Traeger Grill grate. Fold a footlong piece of aluminum foil in half lengthwise and lay it on the Traeger Grill grate. Arrange the skewers so the exposed bamboo is protected from the flame by the foil and the meat is directly over the fire.

- Traeger Grill the skewers, turn them as each side browns, until the fish is just opaque in the center when tested with a knife, about 5 minutes total. Arrange the skewers on warmed dinner plates and brush with the reserved marinade. Serve immediately.

Halibut Marinated with Red Wine
Ingredients

- 1 Large Clove Garlic
- 2 Teaspoons Red Wine Vinegar
- ½ Cup Extra-Virgin Olive Oil
- ¼ Teaspoon Red Pepper Flakes
- 4 Halibut Fillets, 1 To 1¼ Inches Thick (About 6 Ounces Each), Skin Removed
- Salsa Verde
- ¼ Cup Extra-Virgin Olive Oil
- 2 Teaspoons Freshly Grated Lemon Zest
- ½ Teaspoon Kosher or Sea Salt
- 1 Cup Loosely Packed Fresh Flat-Leaf Parsley Leaves
- 2 Tablespoons Capers, Rinsed and Drained
- 2 Oil-Packed Anchovy Fillets, Patted Dry and Minced

Instructions

- Prepare a medium-hot fire in a charcoal Traeger Grill or preheat a gas Traeger Grill on medium high. In a back dish large enough to hold the halibut in a s le layer, combine the ¼ cup olive oil, the lemon zest, salt, and red pepper flakes.
- Stir to blend thoroughly. Add the halibut fillets and turn to coat both sides. Set aside. While the Traeger Grill is heat, make the salsa: In a food processor fitted with the metal blade, combine the parsley, capers, anchovies, garlic, and vinegar and process until minced.
- With the machine run, add the ½ cup olive oil through the feed tube and process until emulsified. Transfer the salsa to a bowl and set aside. Oil the Traeger Grill grate. Use tongs to arrange the halibut fillets, flesh side down, directly over the medium-hot fire and cover.
- Traeger Grill the halibut until Traeger Grill marks are etched across the fillets, about 3 minutes.
- Turn the fillets and re-cover the Traeger Grill. Cook until the halibut is almost opaque throughout but still very moist when tested with a knife, or an instant-read thermometer inserted in the center registers 125° to 130°F, 2 to 3 minutes longer. Us tongs or a wide spatula, transfer the fillets to warmed dinner plates, and accompany each fillet with a spoonful of the salsa. Serve immediately.

Black Pepper Salmon with Orange Juice
Ingredients

- 1 Large Lime
- 100ml Freshly Squeezed Lemon Juice
- 100ml Freshly Squeezed Orange Juice
- Olive Oil
- 4 Tablespoons Balsamic Vinegar
- 2 Teaspoons Freshly Chopped Dill
- 2 Large Garlic Cloves Divided
- Freshly Ground Black Pepper
- 4 Salmon Fillets with Skin Left On

- 2 Small Lemons
- 2 Medium Oranges
- Sea Salt
- 50ml Freshly Squeezed Lime Juice

Instructions

- Wash the salmon fillets thoroughly before then pat dry and drizzle them with some olive oil and sprinkle over them some sea salt and pepper on the skin side and rub it in. Then place in the refrigerator for 30 minutes. Cut the lemon, lime and oranges into segments make sure that you retain as much of their juices as possible. Then mix these segments with some olive oil and ½ crushed garlic clove.
- Now place in the refrigerator. Next you need to combine the freshly cut dill with 1 garlic clove that has been crushed, the lime, lemon and orange juice and a little olive oil, salt and pepper. Once you have done this you remove the salmon fillets from the refrigerator and place them in a shallow dish and pour over this marinade. Cover the dish and replace in the refrigerator and leave the salmon to marinate in the dill for at least 2 hours. Once two hours is up removing the salmon fillets from the refrigerator and as the barbecue warms up this will allow them to come up to room temperature. Allow the salmon to be out of the refrigerator for 20 minutes before you then place on the barbecue.
- Before you place the salmon on the barbecue rub the grate with a clove of garlic and then place the fish on it skin side down. After two minutes you must turn the salmon over and allow it to cook for a further two minutes.
- Also, it is important to place some sort of cover over the salmon such as saucepan lid that is well ventilated. Once cooked let the salmon fillets rest for 3 minutes before serve. When you serve the salmon place on the plate a small salad made up of lettuce, cherry tomatoes and drizzle some balsamic vinegar around the plate.

Crusted Halibut Chile-and-Peanut
Ingredients

- Cup Thai Lime and Chile Peanuts
- 4 Halibut Fillets, 1 To 1¼ Inches Thick (About 6 Ounces Each), Skin Removed
- 2 To 3 Tablespoons Extra-Virgin Olive Oil
- 1 Lime, Quartered

Instructions

- Prepare a medium-hot fire in a charcoal Traeger Grill or preheat a gas Traeger Grill on medium high. Arrange the halibut fillets on a rimmed back sheet and brush or rub on both sides with the olive oil. Put the peanuts in a heavy-duty lock-top plastic bag. Use a roll pin or the bottom of a small, heavy saucepan to crush the nuts finely. Crush them just enough to create small pieces without turn them to meal. Divide the nuts into 4 equal portions, and press a portion into the top, or flesh side, of each fillet, create a crust.
- To create a cool zone, bank the coals to one side of the Traeger Grill or turn off one of the burners. Oil the Traeger Grill grate. Us a spatula, transfer the halibut fillets, untrusted side up, directly over the medium-hot fire and cover.
- Traeger Grill the halibut until Traeger Grill marks are etched across the fillets, about 3 minutes. Use a spatula to move the fillets to the cool side of the Traeger Grill. Re-cover and Traeger Grill until the halibut is almost opaque throughout but still very moist when tested with a knife, or an instant-read thermometer inserted in the center registers 125° to 130°F, 4 to 5 minutes longer. Us a spatula, transfer the fillets to warmed dinner plates, and place a lime wedge on each plate. Serve immediately.

Salted Halibut with Chipotle Sauce and Mayonnaise
Ingredients

- 2 Tablespoons Minced Fresh Cilantro
- ¼ Teaspoon Kosher or Sea Salt
- 4 Halibut Fillets, 1 To 1¼ Inches Thick (About 6 Ounces Each), Skin Removed
- Chipotle Sauce
- 1 Cup Mayonnaise
- ¼ Cup Extra-Virgin Olive Oil
- ½ Teaspoon Kosher or Sea Salt
- ¼ Teaspoon Freshly Ground Pepper
- ¼ Teaspoon Red Pepper Flakes
- 3 Tablespoons Buttermilk or Sour Cream
- 2 Canned Chipotle Chiles In Adobo Sauce, Minced

Instructions

- Prepare a medium-hot fire in a charcoal Traeger Grill or preheat a gas Traeger Grill on medium high. In a back dish large enough to hold the halibut in a s le layer, combine the olive oil, ½ teaspoon salt, the pepper, and red pepper flakes. Stir to blend thoroughly. Add the halibut fillets and turn to coat on both sides. Set aside. While the Traeger Grill is heat, make the sauce: In a small bowl, combine the mayonnaise, buttermilk, chiles, cilantro, and ¼ teaspoon salt and mix well. Set aside. Oil the Traeger Grill grate.
- Use tongs to arrange the halibut fillets, flesh side down, directly over the medium-hot fire and cover. Traeger Grill the halibut until Traeger Grill marks are etched across the fillets, about 3 minutes. Turn the fillets and re-cover the Traeger Grill.
- Cook until the halibut is almost opaque throughout but still very moist when tested with a knife, or an instant-read thermometer inserted in the center registers 125° to 130°F, 2 to 3 minutes longer. Us tongs or a spatula, transfer the fillets to warmed dinner plates, and accompany each fillet with a spoonful of the sauce. Serve immediately.

Tuna with a Black Tapenade Sauce
Ingredients

- 2 Tablespoons Kosher or Sea Salt

- Cup Coarsely Crushed Peppercorns
- 2 Tablespoons Extra-Virgin Olive Oil
- Cup Store-Bought Black Olive Tapenade
- 4 Ahi Tuna Steaks, 1¼ Inches Thick (About 5 Ounces Each)

Instructions

- Prepare a hot fire in a charcoal Traeger Grill or preheat a gas Traeger Grill on high. In a small bowl, combine the olive oil and tapenade and mix well. Set aside. On a dinner plate, mix together the salt and peppercorns and spread the mixture out on the plate.
- Press each tuna steak into the mixture, coat it heavily on both sides. Set aside on a separate plate. Oil the Traeger Grill grate. Use tongs to arrange the steaks directly over the hot fire. Traeger Grill the tuna until Traeger Grill marks are etched across the steaks, about 2 minutes. Turn the steaks and Traeger Grill until red-rare in the center when tested with a knife, or an instant read thermometer inserted in the center registers 120°F, about 2 minutes longer.
- Use tongs to transfer the steaks to a cut board and cut across the grain into ¼- inch-thick slices. Arrange the slices, overlap them, on warmed dinner plates, and accompany with a spoonful of the sauce. Serve immediately.

Spicy Tuna Steaks with Cayenne Pepper
Ingredients

- 3 Garlic Cloves Minced
- 3 Shallots Minced
- 2 Teaspoons Cayenne Pepper
- 2 Teaspoons Ground Cumin
- 6 Small Tuna Steaks (Weigh Around 170grams Each)
- 80ml Olive Oil
- 80ml Lemon Juice (Fresh Would Be Best)
- 4 Tablespoons Chopped Cilantro Leaves
- 1 Teaspoon Salt

Instructions

- In a bowl combine together well the lemon juice, olive oil, and 3 tablespoons of the cilantro leaves, garlic, shallots, cumin, cayenne pepper and salt. Now into a large resealable bag you place the tuna steaks and then pour the sauce you have just made over them.
- Make sure that you turn the bag over several times to ensure the sauce coats the steaks evenly then place in the refrigerator for 1 hour to allow them to marinate in the sauce. About 15 minutes before you remove the tuna steaks from the refrigerator you should start up your barbecue so it is heated up correctly for cook the steaks on it. Just before you take the steaks out of the marinade after remove from the refrigerator lightly oil the Traeger Grill on your barbecue and then place the tuna steaks on them.
- Make sure the Traeger Grill is placed as close to the heat source as possible as you need to cook the steaks on a high heat. You should cook each side of the tuna steaks for around 4 to 5 minutes or until you feel they are cooked to the way people enjoy eat this type of fish. Once they are cooked remove from the barbecue place on clean plates and sprinkle with the remain cilantro and then serve.

Swordfish with Traeger Grilled Peppers and Olives
Ingredients

- Freshly Ground Pepper
- 2 Red Bell Peppers, Seeded, Defibbed, And Cut Lengthwise Into 6 Strips Each
- 2 Yellow Bell Peppers, Seeded, Defibbed, And Cut Lengthwise Into 6 Strips Each
- 4 Swordfish Fillets (6 To 7 Ounces Each), Skin Removed
- Tuscan Extra-Virgin Olive Oil
- Kosher or Sea Salt
- 1 Cup Pitted Sicilian-Style Green Olives, Quartered

Instructions

- Prepare a medium-hot fire in a charcoal Traeger Grill or preheat a gas Traeger Grill on medium high. Arrange the fillets on a rimmed back sheet and rub generously on both sides with olive oil. Sprinkle lightly on both sides with salt and pepper.
- Set aside. In a bowl, toss the peppers with olive oil to coat. Set aside. Oil the Traeger Grill grate. Use tongs to arrange the bell peppers directly over the medium hot fire and cook, turn once, until light Traeger Grill marks appear, about 2 minutes per side.
- Transfer to a warmed platter or rimmed back sheet and keep warm. Oil the Traeger Grill grate again. Use tongs to arrange the swordfish fillets directly over the medium-hot fire and cook, bast frequently with olive oil, until Traeger Grill marks are etched across the fillets, about 3 minutes.
- Turn the fillets and cook, continue to baste frequently, until almost opaque throughout but still very moist when tested with a knife, or an instant-read thermometer inserted in the center registers 125° to 130°F, about 3 minutes longer. Arrange a mixture of yellow and red peppers on each warmed dinner plate. Place a fillet on top, and scatter some olives over the fish. Serve immediately, with a drizzle of olive oil, if desired.

Grilled Shrimp with Soft Tacos and Salsa
Ingredients

- ¾ Cup Loosely Packed Fresh Cilantro Leaves
- 1 Large, Ripe Tomato, Cored, Halved Crosswise, Seeded, And Chopped
- 2 Cups Shredded Iceberg Lettuce
- 1 To 1½ Cups Store-Bought Salsa 8 8-Inch Flour Tortillas
- 2 Large Hass Avocados, Halved, Pitted, Peeled, And Cut into Thin Wedges
- 1 Pound Large Shrimp (26/30 Count), Peeled and Deveined, Tails Removed
- 2 Tablespoons Traeger Grill Every Day Spice Rub 1 Lime, Quartered

Instructions

- Prepare a medium-hot fire in a charcoal Traeger Grill or preheat a gas Traeger Grill on medium high. In a bowl, toss the shrimp with the spice rub until well coated. Arrange the lime, lettuce, cilantro, tomato, avocados, and salsa in separate small serve bowls and have them ready for assemble the tacos. Oil the Traeger Grill grate.
- Arrange the shrimp directly over the medium-hot fire and Traeger Grill, turn once, until the shrimp turn pink on the outside and are just opaque on the inside, about 2 minutes per side. While the shrimp are cook, Traeger Grill the tortillas.
- Depend on the size of the Traeger Grill, lay 1 or 2 tortillas on the Traeger Grill at a time, warm them over direct heat for about 15 seconds per side. Stack them on a plate and keep warm. Transfer the shrimp to a serve bowl. Let diners assemble their own tacos. To assemble, place 2 or 3 shrimp in a tortilla, squeeze a bit of lime juice over the shrimp, and mound lettuce, cilantro, tomato, and avocado on top. Finally, add a spoonful of salsa. Serve with plenty of napkins!

Grilled Salted Shrimp with Olive Oil

Ingredients

- ¼ Cup Loosely Packed Fresh Oregano Leaves
- ½ Cup Extra-Virgin Olive Oil
- 3 Large Cloves Garlic
- 1 Tablespoon Sea Salt
- 2 Pounds Large Shrimp (26/30 Count) In the Shell, Deveined

Instructions

- Prepare a medium-hot fire in a charcoal Traeger Grill or preheat a gas Traeger Grill on medium high. In a small food processor fitted with the metal blade, combine the garlic, salt, and oregano and process until minced. With the machine run, pour the olive oil through the feed tube and process until the marinade is well blended. Reserve 2 tablespoons of the marinade for bast. In a bowl, toss the shrimp with the remain marinade until well coated.
- Set aside while the Traeger Grill heats. Oil the Traeger Grill grate. Remove the shrimp from the marinade and arrange them directly over the medium-hot fire. Traeger Grill, turn once, until the shrimp turn pink on the outside and are just opaque on the inside, about 2 minutes per side. Baste the shrimp with the reserved marinade as they Traeger Grill. Transfer the shrimp to a serve bowl. Let diners peel their own shrimp and enjoy the fun of eat with their f errs. Serve with plenty of napkins!

Traeger Grilled Sliced Calamari

Ingredients

- 1 Garlic Clove Thinly Sliced
- 2 Sprigs of Fresh Oregano or ½ Teaspoon Dried Oregano
- ½ Teaspoon Coarse Salt
- 450grams Fresh Calamari (Cleaned, Rinsed & Well Dried)
- 60ml Extra Virgin Olive Oil
- 1 ½ Tablespoons Fresh Lemon Juice (About 1 Small Lemon)
- Freshly Ground Black Pepper

Instructions

- In a bowl place the olive oil; lemon juice and salt then stir until they combined together. Then into this mix the garlic and the whole sprigs or dried oregano. Whilst you are making up this sauce you should be get the barbecue heated up and place the Traeger Grill down as low as possible in order to cook the calamari quick on a very high heat.
- When the barbecue has heated up place the squid on the oiled Traeger Grill and char each side of it for 1 minute. Now remove from the barbecue and slice all parts of the calamari include the tendrils cross wise into ¼ inch r s.
- Then add the calamari to the lemon sauce made earlier and then place on a serve plate. Just before you serve this dish to your guests make sure that you sprinkle over some freshly ground black pepper.

Large Grilled Shrimp Skewers

Ingredients

- 1 Teaspoon Soy Sauce
- 1 Teaspoon Vegetable Oil

- 2 Tablespoons Jamaican Jerk Season
- 3 Dashes Hot Pepper Sauce
- 900grams Large Shrimps (Peeled and Deveined)
- 80ml Fresh Lime Juice
- 80ml Honey
- Salt and Freshly Ground Black Pepper to Taste
- 12 Wooden Skewers That Have Been Soaked in Water for 1 Hour

Instructions

- In a bowl combine together the lime juice, honey, soy sauce and oil. Then to this add the Jamaican jerk season, hot pepper sauce, salt and pepper. Now add to the sauce you have just made the shrimps make sure that you mix everything well together so that the shrimps are completely coated in the sauce.
- Cover the bowl and place in the refrigerator and leave there for one hour to allow the shrimps to marinate in the sauce. This is the time when the skewers should have been placed in the water to soak. About 30 minutes before the shrimps are due to come out the refrigerator you should now get your barbecue go.
- The shrimps will need to be cooked on a medium to high heat so place the Traeger Grill of the barbecue about 4 to 6 inches above the heat source. After remove the shrimps from the refrigerator now remove the skewers from the water, then pat them dry before then spray or brush with some nonstick cook spray or oil.
- Now thread on to each skewer the shrimps until all 12 skewers have been used and place on the Traeger Grill and cook each kebab for 5 minutes on each side or until the shrimps have turned pink in color. Once the shrimps are cooked place on clean plates and serve with the seasoned rice and frozen margaritas.

Tangy Shrimp with Garlic and Paprika
Ingredients

- 7 Tablespoons Lemon Juice (Fresh Would Be Ideal)
- 5 Tablespoons Worcestershire Sauce
- 28 Large Shrimps (Peeled & Deveined)
- 28 Large Sea Scallops
- 113grams Butter or Margarine
- 1 Teaspoon Garlic Powder
- 1 Teaspoon Paprika

Instructions

- In a large resealable bag place the scallops and shrimps. Now into a bowl (that can be used safely in a microwave) place the butter or margarine, the lemon juice, Worcestershire sauce, garlic powder and paprika. Cook on 50% power for about 1 to 1 ½ minutes or until the butter/margarine is melted then stir to ensure that all these Ingredients are blended together.
- Once the sauce is made set aside about a third of it as this you will then use to baste the shrimps and scallops in whilst they are cook. As for the rest of the sauce this must be poured over the scallops and shrimps in the bag. Meningeal the bag and turn it over several times to ensure that every scallop and shrimp is coated in the sauce and place in the refrigerator for one hour. Whilst in the refrigerator make sure that you turn the back over occasionally. Whilst the barbecue is heat up you can now prepare the kebabs.

- Take some wooden skewers that have been soak in water and thread alternately on to them the scallops and shrimps. Once all the kebabs are made place them on the preheated barbecue and cook them on a medium to hot heat for 6 minutes turn once during this time. Both before and during this cook time baste them occasionally with the sauce you set to one side earlier. Then cook them for a further 8 to 10 minutes or longer until the shrimps have turned pink and the scallops opaque.

Traeger Grilled Oysters
Ingredients

- Hot Sauce
- 12 to 18 Oysters for Each Person
- Melted Butter
- Worcestershire Sauce

Instructions

- Once the barbecue has heated up place the oysters on to the Traeger Grill on a medium to high heat. If you want to prevent any flare ups whilst the oysters are cook as juices drip out of them then cover the Traeger Grill with some aluminum foil first.
- After place the oysters on the Traeger Grill close the lid of the barbecue and let them cook. It is important that you keep a close eye on the oysters as they are cook. So, check them every 3 to 4 minutes.
- Once you notice the shells start to open then remove them from the Traeger Grill. After remove the oysters from the Traeger Grill open the shells and then loosen the meat and place on a plate so your guests can then help themselves. Beside the plate of oysters put some bowls with the melted butter, hot sauce and Worcestershire sauce in them and which the guests can then spoon on top of the oysters if they wish. Then simply pop in the mouth and enjoy.

Thai Spiced Prawns
Ingredients

- 1 Tablespoon Dijon Mustard
- 2 Garlic Cloves Minced
- 1 Tablespoon Brown Sugar
- 450grams Medium Size Prawns (Peeled and Deveined)
- 3 Tablespoons Fresh Lemon Juice
- 1 Tablespoon Soy Sauce
- 2 Teaspoons Curry Paste

Instructions

- In either a resealable plastic bag or a shallow back dish mixes together the lemon juice, soy sauce, mustard, garlic, sugar and curry paste. Then add the prawns and mix all these Ingredients together thoroughly. Meningeal up the bag or cover the dish with some cl film and place in the refrigerator to marinate for 1 hour.
- Next heat up the barbecue and place the Traeger Grill down low as you will be cooking these prawns on a high heat. Once the barbecue is ready lightly oil the Traeger Grill and place the prawns that have been threaded onto skewers and cook on each side for 3 minutes each. If you want to make turn them over easier place the kebabs inside a fish basket. You will know when the prawns are ready, as they will turn a pink opaque color.

- As for the remain sauce, which you marinated the prawns in initially, transfer this to a small saucepan and heat up until it starts to boil. Allow it to boil for a few minutes before then transfer to a bowl which your guests can then dip the kebabs in and which you have also used to baste the prawns in whilst cook.

Garlic Traeger Grilled Shrimps
Ingredients

- Salt to Taste
- 30ml Olive Oil
- 450grams Large Size Shrimps (Peeled and Deveined)
- 4 Garlic Cloves
- ¼ Teaspoon Freshly Ground Black Pepper to Taste

Instructions

- Start the barbecue up and lightly oil the Traeger Grill. Now take the four garlic cloves and chop them up then sprinkle with some salt and us the back of a large knife smash the garlic up until it forms a paste. Then place the garlic with some olive oil in a fry pan (skillet) and cook over a medium to low heat until the garlic starts to turn brown.
- This should take around 5 minutes then once the garlic has turned brown remove from heat. Next you take the shrimps and thread them onto wooden skewers and sprinkle over them some salt and pepper to season.
- Then brush one side of the shrimps with the garlic and olive oil mixture you made earlier and place this side down on to the barbecue. Cook the shrimps until they start to turn pink in color and they begin to curl. This should take around 4 minutes and then turn them over. But before place back down on the barbecue brush with more of the garlic oil and then cook for a further 4 minutes until the flesh has turned opaque and the shrimps are pink all over.

Traeger Grilled Oysters
Ingredients

- 1 Tablespoon Minced Shallots
- 1 Tablespoon Chopped Fennel Greens
- 24 Fresh Live Unopened Medium Size Oysters
- 1 Teaspoon Grounded Fennel Seed
- 226grams Softened Butter
- 1 Teaspoon Freshly Ground Black Pepper
- ½ Teaspoon Salt

Instructions

- Get the barbecue go so and place the Traeger Grill down low as possible as you will be cooking the oysters on a very high heat. In a bowl mix together the butter, fennel seeds, shallots, fennel greens, pepper and salt.
- Then put to one side for use later. If you want place in the refrigerator to keep the butter from melt completely and remove about 10 minutes before needed. Place the oysters on the Traeger Grill of the barbecue and close the lid and leave it closed for between 3 and 5 minutes or until you start to hear them hiss or they start to open.
- Take an oyster knife and pry each one of the oysters open at the h e and loosen the oyster inside. Discard the flat part of the shell and then top each of the open oysters with ½ teaspoon of the butter

you made earlier and then return them back to the barbecue once more. Then cook them once more until the butter has melted and is hot.

Traeger Grilled Crab with Minced Cilantro
Ingredients

- 1 Tablespoon Freshly Minced Ginger
- 1 Jalapeno Chili Seeds Removed Then Minced
- 1 Tablespoon Minced Cilantro
- 2 Large Live Crabs
- 60ml White Wine Vinegar
- 2 ½ Teaspoons Sugar
- 2 Tablespoons Olive Oil
- 1 Medium Tomato Chopped

Instructions

- In a bowl mix together the chopped tomato, vinegar, oil, Ginger, chili, garlic and cilantro. Then place to one side for use later. Now into a large pot of boil water place the crabs one at the time head first. Reduce the heat and allow the crabs to sit in simmer water for 5 minutes before then remove. If, however you find the thought of cook live crabs a little too much then you can use frozen ones instead. Of course, you need to allow them sufficient time to thaw out before you can start cook with them.
- After remove the crabs from the water turn over and pull the triangular tab from the belly and lift of the shell. Remove the entrails and gills from the crab before then wash and drain. Now place on the barbecue that you have preheated and close the lid. But before clos the lid brush with the mixture you made earlier and do this regularly throughout the time the crabs are Traeger Grill on the barbecue.
- About halfway through the cook time (around about 5minutes) you need to turn the crabs over and repeat the same process again for a further 5 minutes or until the meat in the legs of the crabs has turned opaque.
- Now place the crabs on to a plate to serve them but before you do serve spoon over any remain sauce you have that you used to baste the crabs in when cook. If you wish you can put the meat back in the shells before serve.

Sesame Scallops with Vegetable Oil
Ingredients

- 2 Tablespoons Soy Sauce
- 2 Tablespoons Dry Sherry
- 1 Tablespoon Freshly Minced Ginger
- 1 Teaspoon Sesame Oil
- 1 Garlic Clove Minced
- 1 Green Onion Minced
- Sesame Seeds
- 900grams Fresh Sea Scallops
- 60ml Vegetable Oil
- 60ml Distilled White Vinegar
- 2 Tablespoons Hoisin Sauce

Instructions

- First off wash and then pat dry with some paper towels the scallops. Now into a bowl mix together the oil, vinegar, hoisin and soy sauce, dry sherry, Ginger, sesame oil, garlic and onion. Then pour this mixture into a resealable bag and then add to these the scallops. Turn the bag over several times to ensure that all the scallops are covered in the marinade and place in the refrigerator overnight.
- Whilst the barbecue is heat up you can now remove the scallops from the refrigerator and thread them on to skewers ready for cook. Once placed on the skewers then sprinkle over some of the sesame seeds and cook over a medium heat (so place the Traeger Grill about 4 to 6 inches above the heat source) and cook for 6 to 8 minutes. You will know the scallops are ready to eat when they have turned opaque.

Margarita Shrimps with Olive Oil
Ingredients

- 3 Tablespoons Olive Oil
- ¼ Teaspoon Ground Red Pepper
- ¼ Teaspoon Salt
- 2 Teaspoons Tequila
- 3 Tablespoons Freshly Chopped Cilantro
- 450grams Shrimps (Peeled and Deveined)
- 2 Garlic Cloves Minced
- 2 Tablespoons Fresh Lime Juice

Instructions

- In a bowl place the lime juice, olive oil, tequila, garlic, cilantro, pepper and salt and combine well together before then add the shrimps. Toss the mixture about lightly to ensure that the shrimps are covered in the sauce then cover the bowl and place in the refrigerator for between 30 minutes and 3 hours to marinate.
- Turn on or light the barbecue about 30 minutes prior to when you want to start cook the shrimps. You need to place the Traeger Grill down low in the barbecue, as you will be cook these on a high heat for a very short space of time. Whilst the barbecue is heat up take the shrimps out of the fridge and thread them on to either metal or wooden skewers. Put about 3 or 4 on each skewer and place to one side. If there is any marinade left over in the bowl discard this. Before you place the shrimps on to the barbecue Traeger Grill lightly oil it first to prevent the shrimps from stick to it.
- Now cook the shrimps for between 2 and 3 minutes on each side or until they have turned pink. Then serve.

Scallops with An Oregano Leaves
Ingredients

- 32grams Fresh Thyme Leaves
- 3 Garlic Cloves Chopped
- 2 Teaspoons Chicken Flavored Bouillon Granules
- 1 Teaspoon Freshly Shredded Lemon Peel
- 450grams Scallops (About 12 to 15 Scallops)
- 64grams Toasted Pecan Pieces
- 43grams Fresh Oregano Leaves
- ¼ Teaspoon Freshly Ground Black Pepper
- 3 Tablespoons Olive Oil

Instructions

- In a food processor place the pecan pieces, oregano, thyme, garlic, bouillon granules, lemon peel and black pepper. Turn machine on until they form a paste then very slowly and gradually add the olive oil. Once you have formed a paste now rub it onto the scallops and then thread three of each on to a skewer. If you are us wooden ones remember to soak in water for at least 30 minutes to prevent them from burn when on the barbecue.
- Once the scallops are ready on the skewers place on the preheated barbecue over a medium heat so set the Traeger Grill about 6 inches above the heat source and cook them for between 5 and 8 minutes.
- The best way of know when the scallops are ready to serve is to see if they have turned opaque in color. As soon as the scallops are cooked serve to your guests on clean plates with some crusty bread and a crisp green salad that has been drizzled with lemon juice and olive oil.

Grilled Scallops & Tomato Kebabs
Ingredients

- 2 Tablespoons Olive Oil
- 2 Tablespoons Dijon Mustard
- 1/8 Teaspoon Salt
- 16 Large Sea Scallops
- 24 Cherry Tomatoes
- 1 Lemon

Instructions

- Start prepare the barbecue for cook this dish on a medium heat. This means putt the Traeger Grill of the barbecue about 6 inches above the main heat source. Also place the wooden skewers in some water. Whilst the barbecue is heat up you can now prepare the sauce for the kebabs. In a bowl place 1 tablespoon of lemon juice along with ½ teaspoon of its peel. To this then add the olive oil, Dijon mustard and salt and mix well together. Then put to one side ready for use later.
- Now on to each of the wooden skewers you need to thread 3 tomatoes and 2 scallops alternately. You should start and finish with the tomatoes. Next brush the kebabs you have just made with some of the sauce you made earlier and place on the barbecue to cook. Each kebab will need to cook for between 7 and 9 minutes and should be turned over several times. After this time has elapsed brush the kebabs with the remainder of the sauce and then cook for another 5 minutes or more remember to turn them over frequently. The kebabs will be ready to consume when the scallops have turned opaque right through.
- Once the kebabs are cooked served to your guests immediately with a little green salad and some crusty bread.

Traeger Grilled Lobster with Butter
Ingredients

- 60ml Fresh Lime Juice
- ½ Teaspoon Crushed Bay Leaf
- ¼ Teaspoon Freshly Ground Black Pepper
- 3 x 680grams Fresh Lobsters
- 113grams Butter
- ¼ Teaspoon Salt

Instructions

- To parboil the lobsters, you need to bra around 3 inches of water to boil in an 8-quart saucepan. Once the water begins boil add the lobsters, then cover the pan and cook for 10 minutes. Once the 10 minutes has elapsed remove the lobsters from the pan and leave them to one side to cool. Whilst the barbecue is heat up in another saucepan place the butter, lime juice, bay leaf, salt and pepper and cook for 10 minutes over a low heat. Then put to one side to use later on.
- By now the lobsters should have cooled down sufficiently to enable you to cut them in half lengthwise and brush them with the butter mixture you have just made. After brush the cut side of the lobster with the butter mixture you place them cut side down onto the Traeger Grill of the barbecue which you have placed about 4 inches above the heat source and cook them for 5 minutes.
- Now turn the lobsters over carefully brush them with some more of the butter mixture and continue cook them on the barbecue until the meat is cooked through. This should take about another 5 minutes. As soon as the meat is cooked through remove the lobsters from the barbecue place on a clean plate and garnish them with lime wedges and bay leaves if you want. Each of your guests should be given ½ lobster each.

Traeger Grilled Prawns & Garlic Chili Sauce
Ingredients

- 5 Fresh Thai Chili's Thinly Sliced
- 1 Shallot Thinly Sliced
- 2 Kaffir Lime Leaves
- 1 Tablespoon Fish Sauce
- 450grams Jumbo Size Prawns (Devein Them)
- 2 Tablespoons Cook Oil
- 2 Tablespoons Minced Garlic
- 2 Tablespoons Thinly Sliced Lemon Grass
- Juice Of 1 Lime
- 1 Tablespoon Thai Roasted Chili Paste
- 1 Tablespoon Torn Fresh Mint Leaves

Instructions

- Turn on or light your barbecue ready for cook the prawns on. Place the Traeger Grill which has been lightly oiled about 6 inches above the heat sauce allow you to cook the prawns on a medium heat. Once the barbecue is heated up now place the prawns on to the Traeger Grill and cook until the outside starts to turn pink and the meat inside no longer looks transparent. They will need to cook for between 5 and 10 minutes and should be turned over frequently. Whilst they are cook you should now be making the sauce, which the prawns can then be dipped into. To make the sauce heat some oil over a medium heat in a skillet and to this then add the garlic until it turns brown, which should take around 7 to 10 minutes.
- Now remove from the heat and to the oil and garlic add the lemon grass, chilies, shallot, lime leaves, fish sauce, lime juice and chili paste. Toss to combine all these Ingredients together then spoon some of them over the prawns, which you have removed from the barbecue and placed on a serve dish and the rest you pour into a bowl. Garnish with the freshly torn mint leaves.

Traeger Grilled New England Seafood
Ingredients

- 225grams Red New Potatoes (Skins Scrubbed then Thinly Sliced)
- 2 Ears of Corn Quartered

- 2 Tablespoons Butter (Room Temperature)
- 2 Tablespoons Finely Chopped Fresh Dill
- 1 Small Garlic Clove Minced
- 450grams Skinless Cod Fillet (Cut into Four Equal Pieces)
- 225grams Frozen Uncooked Prawns (Peeled and Deveined and Thawed)
- Coarse Salt and Freshly Ground Black Pepper to Taste
- 1 Lemon Thinly Sliced

Instructions

- Start by get your barbecue go and place the Traeger Grill 6 inches above the heat source to allow the packets you are about to make to cook on a medium heat. Whilst the barbecue is heat up in a bowl mix together the butter, dill, garlic, salt and pepper and place to one side for now. Take four squares of aluminum foil measure 14 inches square each. On to each of these four pieces of foil first place the thinly sliced potatoes before then place on top of them a piece of the cod.
- Next lay on some of the prawns and alongside the potatoes; cod and prawns place two pieces of the corn. Season each parcel with salt and pepper before add a spoonful of the butter mixture on top. Then place on top of these two slices of the lemon. Now bra up the sides of the foil and crimp the edges to seal the Ingredients inside them tightly. Place each parcel on to the Traeger Grill make sure that the potato is on the bottom and cook for about 12 to 14 minutes or until the fish is just cooked through and the potatoes are tender. You should make sure that you rotate not flip the parcels occasionally as this will help to ensure that everything inside is cooked properly. Once the cook time has passed remove the parcels from the heat and slit open the top of each one and transfer the contents to plates. If you want garnish the food with some more dill sprigs and serve some warm crusty rolls with them.

Honey Traeger Grilled Shrimps
Ingredients

- 80ml Worcestershire Sauce
- 2 Tablespoons Dry White Wine
- 57grams Melted Butter
- 2 Tablespoons Worcestershire Sauce
- 2 Tablespoons Italian Style Salad Dress
- Honey Sauce
- 450grams Large Shrimps
- ½ Teaspoon Garlic Powder
- ¼ Tablespoon Freshly Ground Black Pepper
- 60ml Honey

Instructions

- Into a large bowl mix together the garlic powder, black pepper, Worcestershire sauce, dry white wine and the salad dress. Then add the shrimp and toss them to coat them evenly in the marinade. Now cover the bowl over and place in the refrigerator to let the shrimp marinate in the sauce for 1 hour.
- Start the barbecue up and place the Traeger Grill, which needs to be lightly, oiled about 4 inches above the heat source to allow the shrimps to cook on a high heat. Remove the shrimps from the marinade and thread onto skewers. Pierce one through the head then the next one through the tail. Any marinade left over can now be discarded. Then set the shrimps to one side for a moment whilst you make the honey sauce. To make the honey sauce in a small bowl mix together the honey melted butter

and the other 2 tablespoons of Worcestershire sauce. This is what you will be bast the shrimps in as they cook.
- Take the shrimps and place on the lightly oiled Traeger Grill and cook for 2 to 3 minutes on each side, make sure you baste them occasionally with the honey sauce you have just made. You will know when the shrimps are ready to serve because the flesh will have turned opaque throughout. Serve to your guests immediately once cooked.

Grilled Scallops Wrapped in Prosciutto
Ingredients

- 2 Lemons Halved
- Freshly Ground Black Pepper
- Extra Virgin Olive Oil (For Drizzle)
- 900grams (40) Medium Sized Scallops
- 450grams Paper Thin Slices Prosciutto

Instructions

- Turn your gas barbecue on to high and allow to heat up whilst you are preparing the scallops for cook. If you are us a charcoal barbecue you will know when it is hot enough when you can only hold your hand over it about 5 inches above the Traeger Grill for 2 seconds. Take one slice of the prosciutto and cut in half lengthwise then fold in half and wrap it around the sides of a scallop. You need to make sure that the ends of the prosciutto overlap and then thread it on to a skewer. Do the same for the other pieces of prosciutto and the scallops. Next take the olive oil and drizzle it lightly over the scallops and then squeeze some lemon juice over them. Then season with the freshly ground black pepper.
- Then place on the barbecue to cook. Cook on each side for about 3 minutes or until you see the flesh of the scallops has turned opaque. Remove from barbecue place on a clean plate with some lemon wedges and serve to your guests.

Shrimp & Scallop Kebabs
Ingredients

- ½ Teaspoon Salt
- ½ Teaspoon Freshly Ground Black Pepper
- 120ml Tomato Ketchup

- 60ml Orange Juice
- 60ml Maple Syrup
- ½ Teaspoon Paprika
- 3 Garlic Cloves Minced
- 12 Jumbo Shrimps (Peeled and Deveined)
- 12 Large Sea Scallops
- 3 Tablespoons Vegetable Oil
- 1 Tablespoon Worcestershire Sauce
- 1 Tablespoon Apple Cider Vinegar

Instructions

- Onto a skewer thread 3 scallops and 3 shrimps alternately. Then brush with the vegetable before season with the salt and pepper. Then place to one side for cook later. In to bowl put the ketchup, orange juice, maple syrup, Worcestershire sauce, apple cider vinegar, paprika and garlic and combine well together.
- This you will then be used for bast the scallops and shrimps as they cook on the barbecue. So, set to onside until you start cook. Whilst you are do the various tasks above you should be get your barbecue started with the Traeger Grill be set about 4 to 6 inches above the heat source so the food can cook on a medium to high heat.
- As soon as your barbecue is ready lightly oil the Traeger Grill and then place the shrimp and scallop kebabs on it. But just before you do brush the kebabs all over with the maple orange sauce and then baste them with it regularly. Each side of these kebabs should be allowed to cook for 2 to 3 minutes or until the flesh of the scallops and shrimps have turned opaque.

Black Pepper Ginger Shrimp
- **Ingredients**
- 3 Tablespoons Vegetable Oil
- 4 Ripe Plum Tomatoes (Cut in Half Lengthwise)
- 1 Teaspoon Sugar
- 1 Tablespoon Freshly Chopped Cilantro
- 1 Tablespoon Freshly Chopped Basil
- 2 Medium Green Tomatoes (Cut in Half Lengthwise)
- Coarse Salt
- Freshly Ground Black Pepper
- 2 Tablespoons Fresh Lime Juice
- 20 Extra Large Shrimps (Peeled, Deveined but Tails Left On)
- 2 Garlic Cloves Minced
- 1 ½ Tablespoons Grated Peeled Ginger
- 1 Tablespoon Freshly Minced Jalapeno Chili (With Seeds)

Instructions

- In to a bowl mix together the garlic and Ginger. Now take half of this and transfer to another bowl and add to these 2 tablespoons of the oil before then add the shrimps and toss them in the mixture to make sure that they are evenly coated in it.
- Now cover this bowl over and place in the refrigerator for 30 minutes to allow the shrimps to marinate. As for the rest of the Ginger and garlic mixture this should be covered and placed in the refrigerator as well. Now heat up the barbecue and whilst this is happening into another bowl put

- the tomatoes and toss them in the last tablespoon of oil along with some salt and pepper to season. Now Traeger Grill the tomatoes on the barbecue the cut sides fac upwards until the skins become charred and the flesh inside becomes tender.
- The plum tomatoes will take around 4 to 6 minutes to cook and the green tomatoes will take about 8 to 10 minutes to cook. If the green tomatoes are especially hard, they may need a little longer than 10 minutes.
- Also be careful when cook the tomatoes as both the juices from them and the oil in which they are coated may cause flare ups to occur. Once the skins have become charred on the tomatoes and the flesh soft remove from heat and set to one side to allow them to cool down a little. As soon as they have cooled down enough peel away and discard the skins and seeds then finely chop them up and add to the garlic and Ginger mixture from earlier. Also add to this mixture the lime juice, jalapeno chili, sugar cilantro and basil then well combined together pour into a serve dish and set to one side for later.
- Remove shrimps from refrigerator and just before place on to the barbecue thread one shrimp on to a skewer through both the top and tail and sprinkle with some salt and pepper. Place on the barbecue and cook for about 2 minutes on each side or until the flesh has turned opaque throughout. Once cooked place the skewers on to a clean plate along with the bowl of tomato relish you made earlier.

Traeger Grilled Crab Legs
Ingredients

- 2 Tablespoons Olive Oil
- 450grams K Crab Legs per Person
- 2 Tablespoons Melted Butter

Instructions

- Preheat the barbecue and place the Traeger Grill around 6 inches above the heat source as the crab's legs will need to be cooked on a medium heat. Whilst the barbecue is heat up in a bowl mix together the olive oil and butter and then brush this over the crab legs. Now place the crab legs on the Traeger Grill, which you may want to lightly oil as well and close the lid on your barbecue.
- Now let the legs cook on the barbecue for between 4 and 5 minutes make sure that halfway through you turn them over.
- Once the crab legs are cooked remove from the barbecue and serve them with some fresh crusty bread along with a cocktail or garlic butter sauce. To make the garlic butter sauce in a sauce pan place 50grams of melted butter with 1 tablespoon of freshly chopped garlic and heat gently. Do this will then allow the flavor of the garlic to become infused in the butter.

Grilled Shrimp & Broccoli Florets
Ingredients

- 225grams Medium Size Shrimps (Peeled and Deveined)
- 175grams Instant Rice
- 2 Teaspoons Seafood Season
- 2 Garlic Cloves Minced
- 220grams Broccoli Florets
- 2 Tablespoons Butter (Cut into Pieces)
- 8 Ice Cubes
- 120ml Water

Instructions

- Preheat the barbecue and place the Traeger Grill about 4 to 6 inches above the heat source so you can cook these parcels on a medium to high heat. Whilst the barbecue is heat up place half the shrimps on a piece of aluminum foil with the nonstick (dull) side fac up towards the food.
- Then around this arrange half the rice and sprinkle it and the shrimps with some of the seafood season before then top off the shrimps with half the minced garlic. Then place half the broccoli on top of the shrimp and sprinkle with garlic and butter. Do the same for the other parcel and then top each one off with 4 ice cubes. Now bra the sides of the aluminum foil up and double fold over the top and at one end. At the end, which is still open, pour in half the water and then fold this end over so that the Ingredients are congealed inside.
- Make sure that you use a large enough piece of foil to allow room for heat and steam to circulate inside. Once the parcels are ready place on the barbecue and let them cook for 9 to 13 minutes. It is important that you close the lid whilst the parcels are cook to ensure that the s cook evenly. After remove from the Traeger Grill snip open the parcels and stir the rice before you then serve as they are to your guests. It is also a good idea to squeeze some fresh lemon juice over the shrimps, rice and broccoli just before serve.

Barbecued Oysters Served with Rice Vinegar
Ingredients

- 2 Finely Chopped Shallots
- 3 Tablespoons Freshly Squeezed (Strained) Lime Juice
- 1 Small Jalapeno Chili (Seeded and Finely Chopped)
- 48 Oysters (Scrubbed)
- Hogwash
- 120ml Natural Rice Vinegar
- 120ml Seasoned Rice Vinegar
- Fresh Roughly Chopped Cilantro

Instructions

- Heat up the barbecue until it is very hot then place the unopened fresh oysters on to the lightly oiled Traeger Grill and close the lid. After about 3 minutes check to see if the oysters are open. If the oysters are open then detach the oysters from the top shell us an oyster knife.
- Then loosen the top shells and discard these. Then you simply need to place a spoonful of the Hogwash sauce you have made over each one before serve them. In order to make the Hogwash place the seasoned and natural rice vinegar into a bowl with the shallots, lime juice, jalapeno chili and cilantro and mix well together.
- You should make this before you actually begin cook the oysters, as it needs to go into the refrigerator for at least an hour.

Black Pepper Scallops, Orange & Cucumber Kebabs
Ingredients

- 120ml Fresh Orange Juice
- 8 Very Thin Slices Peeled Fresh Ginger
- 2 Tablespoons Honey
- Freshly Ground Black Pepper
- ½ Navel Orange Cut into Wedges
- ½ Cucumber Cut in Half Lengthways Then Cut Into ½ Inch Slices
- Coarse Salt

- 450grams Large Scallops

Instructions

- Start by get the barbecue heated up. You will need to place the lightly oiled Traeger Grill about 6 inches above the heat source as you want to cook these kebabs on a medium heat to ensure that north burns.
- Whilst the barbecue is heat up in a small bowl mix together the honey and orange juice and set to one side for later. Next take four skewers (wooden ones will do but you can use metal ones if you want). On to these threads an orange wedge followed by a slice of Ginger, cucumber and scallop until each skewer is full.
- Also make sure that you end with another wedge of orange on the kebabs. Nonseason each kebab with salt and pepper before then brush with the orange and honey sauce made earlier. Place each kebab on to the Traeger Grill of the barbecue and cook for between 4 and 6 minutes or until the scallop flesh has turned opaque.
- Make sure that you turn the kebabs frequently and baste regularly with the sauce. Once the kebabs are cooked serve with some rice or a crisp green salad.

Prawns with Pictou Virgin Olive Oil
Ingredients

- 12 Anchovy Fillets (Rinsed)
- 2 Garlic Cloves (Peeled)
- 60ml Extra Virgin Olive Oil
- Coarse Salt
- Freshly Ground Black Pepper
- 12 Prawns (Shelled and Deveined but With Heads Left On)
- 27.5grams Whole Raw Almonds
- 128grams Loose Packed Fresh Flat Leaf Parsley
- 2 Tablespoons Extra Virgin Olive Oil
- Zest of 1 Lemon

Instructions

- Take the whole raw almonds and place in the oven on a back tray for 10 minutes at 350 degrees Fahrenheit. Stir the almonds occasionally and remove from oven when golden brown and fragrant. Then allow to cool down completely before coarsely chop them. Now take the coarsely chopped almonds and place them in food processor with the basil, parsley, anchovies and garlic and process until all have been combined together. Then to this paste add the oil very slowly in a steady stream and continue process until a smooth paste is formed. Now transfer this mixture to a large bowl and mix in the lemon zest, salt and pepper. Put around a ¼ of this mixture to one side, as this is what your guests will then dip the shrimps in after they are cooked.
- Whilst you are preparing the Pictou you should be allow the barbecue to heat up ready for cook. Place the Traeger Grill about 5 inches above the heat source, as you will want to cook the shrimps on a medium to high heat. As soon as the barbecue is ready toss the shrimps in the rest of the Pictou and place them o
- n the barbecue and cook for about 2 ½ minutes on each side. Plus, before place on the barbecue season with some salt and pepper. You should only turn the shrimps over once during the cook time and to make sure that they are cooked through the flesh should be firm and they should have turned pink. As soon as the shrimps are cooked place onto a clean plate with some lemon wedges and the bowl of Pictou you put to one side earlier. Your guests can then dip the shrimps into this.

Grilled Black & White Pepper Shrimps

Ingredients

- 1 ½ Tablespoons Maldon Sea Salt
- 3 Tablespoons Safflower Oil
- 8 Sprigs Fresh Cilantro for Garnish
- 450grams Jumbo Shrimps (Heads Still on But Peeled & Deveined)
- 1 Tablespoon Black Peppercorns
- 2 Teaspoons White Peppercorns

Instructions

- In a shallow dish place 8 wooden skewers measure 10 inches in cold water for at least 10 minutes. Nienstedt the barbecue up putts the Traeger Grill about 6 inches above the heat source so that the shrimps can cook on a medium to high heat. Whilst the barbecue is heat up thread the shrimps on to the skewers start with at the tail and thread through the body until it comes out of the head. Now put each one of these on to a back tray for now. In a mortar place the peppercorns and coarsely grind them together with a pestle.
- Then transfer these to a small bowl and mix into them the sea salt. Just before you place the shrimps on the barbecue drizzle them with the oil (both sides) and then sprinkle with the peppercorn and salt mixture. Now place the shrimps on the lightly oiled barbecue Traeger Grill and cook until the prawns become a light pink color and slightly charred. This should take around 2 minutes to occur then turn the shrimps over and cook for about the same amount of time again. To serve place the shrimps on a place and sprinkle with the sprigs of cilantro and a dip sauce in a bowl.

Traeger Grilled Prawns

Ingredients

- ¼ Tablespoon Freshly Chopped Cilantro
- 1 Thai or Serrano Chili Minced
- 180ml Peanut or Canola Oil
- Vinaigrette
- 60ml Lime Juice
- 900grams (16-20) Extra Large Shrimps
- 32grams Minced Lemon Grass (White Part Only)
- 2 Tablespoons Cold Water
- 3 Tablespoons Grated Lime Zest
- 1 Tablespoon Freshly Minced Ginger Root
- 32grams Fresh Minced Ginger Root
- 2 Tablespoons Minced Garlic
- 60ml Rice Wine Vinegar
- 120ml Japanese Sweet Wine (Mirin)
- 2 Tablespoons Dark Soy Sauce
- 2 Teaspoons Fish Sauce
- 2 Fresh Thai or Serrano Chili's (Seeds Removed)
- 2 Teaspoons Minced Garlic
- 113grams Unsalted Smooth Peanut Butter

Instructions

- In a bowl (large) combine together the Ginger, lemon grass, garlic, cilantro, chili and oil. Then add the shrimps and let them marinate in the sauce made for 20 to 30 minutes at room temperature. Whilst the shrimps are marina in the sauce you can nonintact heat up the barbecue place the Traeger Grill about 6 inches above the heat source.
- This will then enable you to cook the shrimps that you will thread on to skewers on a medium to high heat. Now into a food processor place the lime juice, rice vinegar, mirin, soy sauce and water and blend.
- Then add to this the lime zest, Ginger, fish sauce, chilies, garlic and peanut butter and process until the mixture becomes smooth.
- Whilst these Ingredients are combining together slowly pour in the peanut oil until the mixture looks smooth and creamy. Pour this mixture into a bowl and then stir into it the mint, cilantro and chopped peanuts. Add some salt if needed. To cook the shrimps remove them from the marinade, shake off any excess and thread them on to skewers then cook them on either side for about 2 minutes or until they have turned pink and firm. Once cooked serve on a plate immediately with the sauce beside them.

Traeger Grilled Rock Lobster
Ingredients

- 1 Tablespoon Freshly Squeezed Lemon Juice
- 1 Tablespoon Olive Oil
- ½ Teaspoon Dried Oregano
- ¼ Teaspoon Salt
- 6 x 226gram Rock or Spiny Lobster Tails
- 12 Green Onions
- 1 Tablespoon Grated Orange Rind
- 2 Tablespoons Freshly Squeezed Orange Juice
- Dash of Hot Sauce (Such as Cholula)
- 1 Garlic Clove Minced
- 2 Tablespoons Melted Butter

Instructions

- Get the barbecue go so it is ready in time for cook to begin. Now you need to start prepare the lobster. To do this cut each lobster tail in half lengthwise and then coat each one along with the onions with some cook spray. Next place the tails on to the Traeger Grill of the barbecue cut side fac downwards and after you have oiled the Traeger Grill lightly.
- Traeger Grill the tails for 3 minutes and then turn them over. Now Traeger Grill them for a further five minutes.
- About 2 minutes after turn over the tails now place the green onions on the Traeger Grill to cook. These will require about 3 minutes and should be turned over at least once during this cook time.
- Remove from barbecue once they have become tender. To make the sauce which you will serve with the lobster tails in to a bowl place the orange rind, orange juice, lime juice, olive oil, oregano, salt, hot sauce and garlic and whisk well.
- Then very gradually add to this mixture the melted butter makes sure that you whisk the Ingredients continuously then drizzle it over the cut side of the tails. Transfer to a clean plate and serve alongside them some warm tortillas and some lime wedges.

Grilled Bacon Wrapped Shrimps

Ingredients

- Barbecue Seasoning to Taste
- 16 Large Shrimps (Peeled and Deveined)
- 8 Slices of Bacons

Instructions

- Preheat the barbecue and place the Traeger Grill about 4 to 6 inches above the heat. Take each shrimp and wrap them in half of each slice of bacon and then secure with a toothpick or thread two of them on to a wooden skewer that has been soak in water for 30 minutes. Nonwinged some of the season over them and then place each one on to the lightly oiled barbecue Traeger Grill and cook for around 10 to 15 minutes.
- It is important that you turn the shrimps over frequently to prevent the bacon from burn and also to ensure that the shrimps are cooked through evenly. Once cooked place on a clean plate and allow your guests to help themselves.

Chapter 6: Vegetables Recipes

Salted Asparagus Spears
Ingredients

- Kosher or Sea Salt
- 28 Thick Asparagus Spears
- 1 To 2 Tablespoons Extra-Virgin Olive Oil
- Freshly Ground Pepper

Instructions

- Preheat a gas Traeger Grill on top. Snap off the fibrous bottom end of every and every spear, or cut the entire bunch into a uniform length. If wanted, us a vegetable peeler or sharp level knife, peel off the thick spears from marginally under the tip to the foundation. (This is not an important thing; many cooks prefer their own asparagus peeled, whereas some others enjoy them) Put the spears at a back dish, then toss them together with the olive oil, and season lightly with salt and pepper. Oil that the Traeger Grill grate.
- Put the asparagus straight over the hot flame and Traeger Grill, flip a couple days, till Traeger Grill marks show up on either side and the spears are crisp-tender, about 4 minutes. (Tim will change depend on the depth of their spears.) Transfer to a heated platter and serve immediately.

Grilled Corn in the Husk
Ingredients

- Unsalted Butter, At Room Temperature
- 4 Ears of Corn, Husks Intact
- Kosher or Sea Salt (Optional) Freshly Ground Pepper (Optional)

Instructions

- Preheat a gas Traeger Grill on top. Pull back the husk from every ear of corn with no really remove it. Eliminate the silk, then re-cover the corn with the husk. Run water into the ears of corn, then drain the surplus, then twist on the husks in the very top to close. Oil that the Traeger Grill grate.
- Set the corn straight over the hot flame and Traeger Grill, flip the ears a couple occasions to Traeger Grill on all sides, until the husks are charred and the kernels are tender and gently burnished, about 20 minutes. Eliminate from the Traeger Grill and pull and drop the husks, or knot the dragged back husks to get a rustic-chic appearance. Generously brush the corn with butter and season with pepper and salt, if needed. Transfer to a heated platter and serve hot.

Grilled Walla Walla Sweet Onions
Ingredients

- Cup Canola or Grapeseed Oil
- ¾ Teaspoon Ground Chipotle Chile
- 2 Large Walla Walla Or Other Sweet Onions, Cut Crosswise Into ½-Inch-Thick Slices
- ½ Teaspoon Kosher or Sea Salt

Instructions

- Preheat a gas Traeger Grill on top. Arrange the onion slices at a le coating on a large, rimmed rear sheet. In a small bowl, combine the oil, chile, and salt and blend well. Brush both sides of each onion piece with the oil. O
- il that the Traeger Grill grate. Set the onions right over the hot flame and Traeger Grill, turn after, till Traeger Grill marks look on either side along with the onions are crisp-tender, about 4 minutes each side. (Use a combo of tongs and a long-handled spatula to flip the onion pieces in order that they remain intact.) Transfer to a heated platter and serve hot, or keep warm until ready to serve.

Traeger Grilled Roma Tomatoes
Ingredients

- 1 Teaspoon Minced Garlic
- ¼ Teaspoon Kosher or Sea Salt
- 8 4-Inch-Long Sprigs Fresh Rosemary
- 2 Tablespoons Roasted Garlic-Flavored Olive Oil, Plus More for Brush
- 2 Teaspoons Minced Fresh Basil
- ¼ Teaspoon Freshly Ground Pepper
- 4 Roma Tomatoes, Halved Crosswise

Instructions

- Run water on the rosemary sprigs to soften them. Put aside. In a small bowl, combine the 2 tablespoons garlic-flavored olive oil, basil, salt, garlic, and pepper. Put aside. Arrange the tomatoes, cut side up, on a rimmed back sheet or a plate and brush the cut side of each tomato with the olive oil mix.
- Oil that the Traeger Grill grate. Organize the lavender sprigs in a row, then vertical to the pubs of this Traeger Grill grate and marginally split, directly above the moderate flame. Put the tomatoes, cut side down, on top of the rosemary. Us tongs, gently turn the tomatoes cut side up, and brush off some of those charred rosemary leaves. Brush the tomatoes liberally using the olive oil mix. Cover and Traeger Grill till the berries are hot and tender but still hold their shape, about two minutes more. Transfer to a heated serve platter or dinner plates and serve immediately, or keep warm until ready to serve.

Traeger Grilled of Zucchini
Ingredients

- 3 Pattypan Or Other Yellowing Summer Squashes, Ends Trimmed and Cut into Thick
- Slices (See Headnote) 3 Zucchini, Ends Trimmed and Cut on The Diagonal Into
- Thick Slices
- 2 Tablespoons Store-Bought Basil Pesto
- 3 Tablespoons Extra-Virgin Olive Oil, Plus More for Brush
- Kosher or Sea Salt
- Freshly Ground Pepper

Instructions

- Run water on the rosemary sprigs to soften them. Put aside. In a small bowl, combine the 2 tablespoons garlic-flavored olive oil, basil, salt, garlic, and pepper. Put aside. Arrange the tomatoes, cut side up, on a rimmed back sheet or a plate and brush the cut side of each tomato with the olive oil mix. Oil that the Traeger Grill grate. Organize the lavender sprigs in a row, then vertical to the pubs of this Traeger Grill grate and marginally split, directly above the moderate flame.

- Put the tomatoes, cut side down, on top of the rosemary. Us tongs, gently turn the tomatoes cut side up, and brush off some of those charred rosemary leaves. Brush the tomatoes liberally using the olive oil mix. Cover and Traeger Grill till the berries are hot and tender but still hold their shape, about two minutes more. Transfer to a heated serve platter or dinner plates and serve immediately, or keep warm until ready to serve.

Grilled Cherry Tomato Skewers
Ingredients

- 3 Tablespoons Extra-Virgin Olive Oil
- 8 7-Inch Bamboo Skewers, Soaked in Water For 15 Minutes, Then Drained
- 40 Cherry Tomatoes (About 1 Pint) 32 Large Fresh Basil Leave
- Kosher or Sea Salt
- Freshly Ground Pepper

Instructions

- Ditch the skewers before mild the Traeger Grill, so that they have loads of time. To build the skewers, thread 5 berries on each skewer, put a basil leaf, folded in half crosswise, involving the berries. Arrange the skewers at a le layer on a rimmed back sheet and brush the berries liberally on all sides with olive oil. To make a trendy zone, then bank the coals to one side of this Traeger Grill or turn off one of those burners.
- Oil that the Traeger Grill grate. Put the skewers straight over the medium-hot flame and Traeger Grill, turn once, till light Traeger Grill marks show up on either side, about 30 seconds each side. Transfer the skewers into the cooler section of this Traeger Grill, pay, and Traeger Grill till the berries are warm but the skin has not blistered, 1 to 2 minutes more. Transfer the skewers into a function dish and season with pepper and salt. Serve hot or at room temperature.

Grilled Choy with Sesame Oil
Ingredients

- 2 Teaspoons Asian Sesame Oil
- Kosher or Sea Salt
- 8 Heads Baby Bok Choy, Halved Lengthwise
- 2 Tablespoons Canola or Grapeseed Oil
- Store-Bought Thai Peanut Sauce for Drizzle

Instructions

- Organize the bok choy in a le layer on a large, rimmed rear sheet. In a small bowl, combine the canola and sesame oils and blend well. Brush both sides of their crispy white stalks (not the green leaves) of this bok choy with the petroleum mix.
- Oil that the Traeger Grill grate. Put a very long strip of transparency about 6 inches wide, across the duration of this Traeger Grill. Organize the bok choy, cut down, and so the white stalks are straight above the medium-hot fire along with also the delicate green leaves are all remainder on the transparency, shielded from the flame.
- Switch and Traeger Grill until light brown Traeger Grill marks seem and the bok choy is crisp-tender when pierced with a knife, about two minutes more. Organize the bok choy halves, cut side up, on a heated platter and garnish with the skillet. Drink immediately.

Salted Grilled Eggplant with Herbs

Ingredients

- ½ Cup Extra-Virgin Olive Oil
- Purple Globe Eggplants (About 12 Ounces Each), Cut Crosswise Into ½-Inchthick Slices
- 1 Tablespoon Herbs De Provence, Crushed
- 1 Teaspoon Kosher or Sea Salt

Instructions

- Arrange the eggplant slices in a le coating on a large, rimmed back sheet. In a small bowl, combine the olive oil, herbs de Provence, and salt and blend well. Generously brush the eggplant slices on both sides with the oil mix.
- Oil that the Traeger Grill grate. Put the eggplant slices straight over the medium-hot flame, pay, and Traeger Grill until dark brownish Traeger Grill marks seem, 2-3 minutes. Turn, recuperate, and Traeger Grill until dim Traeger Grill marks seem and the pieces are tender when pierced with a knife, about 3 minutes more. Transfer to a heated serve plate and serve immediately, or keep warm until ready to serve.

Asian Grilled Eggplant with Mayonnaise

Ingredients

- ¼ Teaspoon Freshly Ground White Pepper
- 4 Purple Asian Eggplants (About 8 Inches Long), Stem Ends Trimmed, Halved Lengthwise
- ¼ Cup Mayonnaise
- 1 Tablespoon White Miso 1½ Teaspoons Asian Sesame Oil
- 1 Teaspoon Soy Sauce
- 5 Tablespoons Canola or Grapeseed Oil
- 2 Tablespoons Asian Sesame Oil
- Kosher or Sea Salt

Instructions

- Create the miso mayonnaise: In a small bowl whisk together the mayonnaise, miso, sesame oil, soy sauce, and pepper until well mixed. Set aside. Arrange the eggplant halves in a le coating on a large, rimmed back sheet. Generously brush both sides of each eggplant half together with the oil mix. Oil that the Traeger Grill grate.
- Put the eggplants, flesh side down, right above the medium hot flame. Cover and Traeger Grill till dark brownish Traeger Grill marks appear, about 3 minutes. Twist, re-cover, and Traeger Grill on the skin side until the eggplants are tender when pierced with a knife, about 3 minutes more. Arrange the eggplant halves, flesh side up, on a heated platter. Drizzle the sauce over the top, or pass the sauce in the table.

Traeger Grilled Acorn Squash

Ingredients

- ¼ Cup Packed Dark Brown Sugar
- 1 Teaspoon Kosher or Sea Salt, Plus More for Sprinkles
- 1 Teaspoon Freshly Ground Pepper
- ¾ Cup (1½ Sticks) Unsalted Butter

- ¼ Cup Pure Maple Syrup
- ¼ Cup Good-Quality Bourbon Whiskey Such as Maker's Mark
- 2 Acorn Squashes

Instructions

- Grill or preheat a gas Traeger Grill on medium high. In a small saucepan, melt butter over moderate heat. Pour or ladle 1/4 cup of the egg into a heatproof bowl or quantify cup and put aside. Add the maple syrup, brown sugar, 1 tsp salt, and the pepper into the butter from the pan and simmer until the sugar is melted.
- Remove from the heat, add the bourbon, and stir till smooth. Set aside and keep warm. Cut each squash in half lengthwise. Scoop out and discard the seeds and str s. Cut each half into thick wedges, either quarters or thirds, are contingent on the size of the skillet. Order the skillet into a s le coating on a rimmed back sheet and brush the wedges liberally onto the flesh side using all the reserved melted butter.
- Sprinkle with salt. To make a trendy zone, then bank the coals to one side of this Traeger Grill or turn off one of those burners. Oil that the Traeger Grill grate. Put the skillet on the trendy side of this Traeger Grill, pay, and Traeger Grill until only start to caramelize in the borders and simmer, 15 minutes. Brush the wedges together with the bourbon-butter mix, re-cover, and Traeger Grill another five minutes. Brush the pliers, re-cover, and Traeger Grill until tender when pierced with a knife, about 5 minutes more. Transfer the skillet into a function dish and serve immediately, or keep warm until ready to serve.

Traeger Grilled Ratatouille
Ingredients

- 1 Large Purple Globe Eggplant (About 1 Pound), Stem End Trimmed, Cut
- Lengthwise Into ¾-Inch-Thick Slices
- 10 Large Fresh Basil Leaves, Coarsely Chopped
- 1 Tablespoon Tomato Paste
- Freshly Ground Pepper
- 2 Zucchinis, Ends Trimmed, Halved Lengthwise
- 1 Large Red Bell Pepper, Quartered Lengthwise, Seeded, And Defibbed

- 2 10-Inch Bamboo Skewers, Soaked in Water For 15 Minutes, Then Drained
- Cup Roasted Garlic-Flavored Olive Oil
- 1½ Tablespoons Herbs De Provence, Crushed
- ½ Teaspoon Kosher or Sea Salt, Plus More for Season
- ½ Pint Cherry Tomatoes
- 1 Walla Walla Or Other Sweet Onion, Cut Crosswise Into ½-Inch-Thick Slices

Instructions

- Ditch the skewers before mild the Traeger Grill, so that they have loads of time. Prepare a medium-hot fire in a charcoal Traeger Grill or preheat a gas Traeger Grill on medium high. In a small bowl combine the olive oil, herbs de Provence, and 1/2 tsp salt and blend well. Thread the berries on the skewers and arrange on a plate. Brush the tomatoes lightly with the oil mix. Organize the stay vegetables at a le layer on a large, rimmed back sheet and brush liberally on both sides with the oil mix. Oil that the Traeger Grill grate.
- Put all of the vegetables except the tomatoes right above the medium-hot flame, and Traeger Grill, flip once, till dark brown Traeger Grill marks look on either side along with the veggies are crisp-tender when pierced with a knife, 2-3 minutes each side. Tim will change slightly for every vegetable; observe carefully and flip the veggies as needed.
- Traeger Grill the skewered tomatoes in precisely the exact same time, turn them until their skin blisters, about two minutes total. Transfer the Traeger Grill ed vegetables except the tomatoes to some cut plank, and cut to 1/2-inch balls. Put into a large bowl. Twist the berries off the skewers and add to the vegetables in the bowl, together with the basil.
- Mix the tomato paste with 2 tbsp water to cut it, and then fold the diluted paste evenly to the vegetable mix. Season to taste with pepper and salt. Serve hot or at room temperature.

Grilled Eggplant Stacks with Fresh Mozzarella
Ingredients

- 2 Large Balls (8 Ounces Total) Fresh Mozzarella Cheese, Each Cut Into 4 Slices
- 4 Ounces Arugula
- 6 Large Fresh Basil Leaves, Stacked, Rolled Like A Cigar, And Cut Crosswise Into
- 1 Large Purple Globe Eggplant (About 1 Pound), Cut Crosswise Into 8 Thick Slices
- 3 Tablespoons Tuscan Extra-Virgin Olive Oil, Plus More for Drizzle
- Kosher or Sea Salt
- Freshly Ground Pepper

Instructions

- Prepare a medium-hot fire in a charcoal Traeger Grill or preheat a gas Traeger Grill on medium high. Arrange the eggplant Pieces in a le layer on a large, rimmed back Sheet and brush the pieces on Either side together with the 3 tbsp olive oil. Sprinkle with salt. Oil the Traeger Grill grate. Arrange the eggplant straight above the medium-hot fire, pay, and Traeger Grill till dark brownish Traeger Grill marks seem, 2-3 minutes. Twist, re-cover, and Traeger Grill until shadowy Traeger Grill marks appear, about 2 minutes more.
- Put a slice of mozzarella on top of each eggplant slice, re-cover, and Traeger Grill until the eggplant is tender when pierced with a Knife along with the cheese is melted and hot, about 3 minutes more. To serve, put One-fourth of the arugula in the middle of each warmed meal. Top with two Eggplant pieces, overlap them slightly.
- Scatter the beer threads over the top. Drizzle about 1 tablespoon olive oil on the top of every function, and Garnish with honey. Drink immediately.

Potatoes Tossed with Extra-Virgin Olive Oil
Ingredients

- Kosher or Sea Salt
- Freshly Ground Pepper
- 1 To 1¼ Pounds New Red Potatoes, Halved
- 2 Tablespoons Tuscan Extra-Virgin Olive Oil, Plus More for Drizzle

Instructions

- Poke the potato wedges once together with the tines of a fork. Put the potatoes into a bowl and toss them with the two tbsp olive oil. To make a trendy zone, then bank the coals to one side of this Traeger Grill or turn off one of those burners. Oil that the Traeger Grill grate. Arrange the potatoes, cut side down, right over the medium-hot flame, pay, and Traeger Grill until dark brown Traeger Grill marks appear, about 4 minutes.
- Turn cut side up, re-cover, and Traeger Grill for 4 minutes more. Transfer the potatoes into the cooler section of this Traeger Grill, pay, and Traeger Grill until tender when pierced with a knife, about 10 minutes more. Transfer the potatoes to a bowl that is serve. Drizzle with olive oil, sprinkle with fleur de promote, and throw.

Traeger Grilled Yukon Gold Potatoes
Ingredients

- Kosher or Sea Salt
- Freshly Ground Pepper
- 4 Yukon Gold Potatoes (About 2 Pounds), Cut Into ½-Inch-Thick Slices
- ¼ Cup Extra-Virgin Olive Oil, Plus More for Drizzle
- Fleur De Sell or Other Finish   Salt for Sprinkle

Instructions

- Arrange the potato slices in a le coating on a large, rimmed back sheet and brush both sides of each piece generously with the 1/4 cup olive oil. Oil that the Traeger Grill grate.
- Set the potatoes straight over the moderate flame, pay, and Traeger Grill until dark brown Traeger Grill marks appear, about 4 minutes. Switch, re-cover, and Traeger Grill until dark Traeger Grill marks look as well as the potatoes are tender when pierced with a knife, about 4 minutes more. Transfer to a function dish, drizzle with a little olive oil, and sprinkle with fleur.

Traeger Grilled Potatoes with Blue Cheese
Ingredients

- Freshly Ground Pepper
- Blue Cheese Sauce
- ½ Teaspoon Freshly Ground Pepper
- 3 Tablespoons Minced Fresh Flat-Leaf Parsley
- 2 Tablespoons Snipped Fresh Chives
- ½ Cup Plain Low-Fat Yogurt or Sour Cream
- ½ Cup Mayonnaise
- 2 Teaspoons Dijon Mustard
- 1 To 1¼ Pounds F Erle   Potatoes

- 2 Tablespoons Extra-Virgin Olive Oil
- Kosher or Sea Salt
- 1 Tablespoon Sugar
- 3 Ounces Blue Cheese, Crumbled

Instructions

- Poke the sausage in many places with the tines of a fork. Put the potatoes into a bowl and toss with the olive oil. Season with pepper and salt. To make a trendy zone, then bank the coals to one side of this Traeger Grill or turn off one of those burners. Oil that the Traeger Grill grate. Arrange the potatoes in a coating on the trendy side of this Traeger Grill, pay, and Traeger Grill till they're tender when pierced with a knife, 18 to 20 minutes.
- While the potatoes are Traeger Grill, create the sauce: In a bowl whisk together the yogurt, mayonnaise, mustard, sugar, and pepper. Us a rubber spatula, lightly mix in the parsley, chives, and cheese. Serve immediately, or cover and refrigerate for up to 3 times. Remove from the fridge 30 minutes prior function. Serve the potatoes pip hot with the sauce drizzled on the top or served on the other side.

Traeger Grilled Polenta with Onion Wedges

Ingredients

- Kosher or Sea Salt
- ¼ Cup Freshly Grated Parmigiano-Reggiano Cheese
- Freshly Ground Pepper
- 1 Tube (18 Ounces) Precooked Polenta, Such as San Gennaro Brand
- Extra-Virgin Olive Oil
- 2 Red Bell Peppers, Quartered Lengthwise, Seeded, And Defibbed
- 1 Large Walla Walla Or Other Sweet Onion, Cut Into ½-Inch-Thick Slices

Instructions

- Prepare a hot fire in a charcoal Traeger Grill or preheat a gas Traeger Grill on high. Trim off the irregular ends and slice the polenta into ten ½-inch-thick slices. Arrange on a rimmed back sheet. Generously brush the slices on both sides with olive oil and season lightly with salt and pepper. Brush the peppers and onions with olive oil, coat them lightly. Oil the Traeger Grill grate. Arrange the

polenta slices directly over the hot fire and Traeger Grill, turn once, until they have Traeger Grill marks etched across both sides, 8 to 10 minutes total.
- While the polenta is Traeger Grill, arrange the peppers and onions directly over the hot fire and Traeger Grill, turn once, until the edges begin to char and the peppers and onions are tender but still firm, about 5 minutes total. (Use tongs and a spatula to turn the onion slices.) To serve, cut the peppers into thin strips, and slice the onion rounds in half. Arrange 2 polenta slices, slightly overlap them, on each plate and top with some peppers and onions. Sprinkle with the cheese and serve immediately.

Traeger Grilled Tomatoes and Green Onions
Ingredients

- ½ Cup Chopped Fresh Flat-Leaf Parsley
- 3 Tablespoons Extra-Virgin Olive Oil
- 1½ Teaspoons Balsamic Vinegar
- 1 Teaspoon Minced Garlic
- ½ Teaspoon Kosher or Sea Salt
- ½ Teaspoon Freshly Ground Pepper
- 1 Cup Medium-Grind Bulgur (See Cook's Note) 2 Cups Boil Water
- 2 Green Onions, Include Green Tops, Thinly Sliced
- 3 Smoky Traeger Grill -Roasted Roma Tomatoes with Garlic Chopped
- ½ Teaspoon Sugar
- Teaspoon Cayenne Pepper

Instructions

- Preheat a gas Traeger Grill on top. Reduce the ends and slit the polenta to ten 1/2-inch-thick pieces. Arrange onto a rimmed rear sheet. Generously brush the pieces on both sides with olive oil and season lightly with salt and pepper.
- Brush the onions and peppers with olive oil, then coat them gently. Oil that the Traeger Grill grate.
- Arrange the polenta pieces straight over the hot flame and Traeger Grill, flip once, till they possess Traeger Grill marks etched across both sides, 8 to 10 minutes total. While the polenta is Traeger Grill, organize the onions and peppers right over the hot flame and Traeger Grill, flip after, until the edges start to char along with the onions and peppers are tender but still firm, about 5 minutes complete. (Use tongs and a spatula to flip the onion pieces.) Arrange 2 polenta pieces, slightly overlap them on each plate and top with a few onions and peppers.

Lemon Couscous with Apricots
Ingredients

- ½ Teaspoon Freshly Ground Pepper
- 1½ Cups Or 1 Box (10 Ounces) Quick-Cook Couscous Cup Dried
- Cranberries
- Cup Diced Dried Apricots
- 2 Cups Canned Low-Sodium Chicken Broth
- 3 Tablespoons Meyer Lemon-Flavored Extra-Virgin Olive Oil
- ½ Teaspoon Kosher or Sea Salt
- Cup Pine Nuts
- 2 Green Onions, Include Green Tops, Thinly Sliced

Instructions

- Put the bulgur in a large heatproof bowl, Add the boil, and then let stand until softened, 30 to 40 minutes. Drain the bulgur in a large skillet, press out as much water as you can. Dry the bowl and then return the bulgur into the bowl.
- To produce the dress, at a small bowl, whisk together the olive oil, garlic, vinegar, pepper, salt, sugar, and cayenne pepper. Taste and adjust this season. Insert the dress into the salad and toss gently to blend.

Grilled Orzo Salad with Kalamata Olives and Feta
Ingredients

- 1 Large Red Bell Pepper, Seeded, Defibbed, And Cut Into ½-Inch Dice
- 1 Large Yellow or Orange Bell Pepper, Seeded, Defibbed, And Cut Into ½-Inch Dice
- 6 Ounces Feta Cheese, Crumbled
- 1 Teaspoon Kosher or Sea Salt
- 2 Cups (About 12 Ounces) Orzo (Rice-Shaped Pasta) 2 Tablespoons Extra-Virgin
- Olive Oil
- 1 Cup Pitted and Halved Kalamata Olives
- 4 Green Onions, Include Green Tops, Thinly Sliced
- 6 Tablespoons Extra-Virgin Olive Oil
- ¼ Cup Chopped Fresh Flat-Leaf Parsley
- ¾ Teaspoon Kosher or Sea Salt
- 2½ Tablespoons Fresh Lemon Juice
- 2 Cloves Garlic, Minced
- 1 Teaspoon Freshly Ground Pepper

Instructions

- At a 3-quart saucepan, bra that the Stir in the couscous, cranberries, and apricots, cover, and remove from heat. Meanwhile, heat a little, dry skillet over medium-high heat.
- When hot but not smoke, then add the pine nuts and toast them stir constantly, until lightly browned, about 3 minutes. Transfer to a plate. Transfer to a heated function bowl and serve immediately.

Traeger Grilled Sweet Corn
Ingredients

- ¾ Teaspoon Adobo Sauce from Canned Chipotle Chiles
- 1 Teaspoon Kosher or Sea Salt
- 2 Ears Sweet Corn in The Husk 1 Can (15 Ounces) Black Beans, Rinsed and Drained
- 12 Cherry Tomatoes, Quartered
- 5 Slices Cooked Bacon, Crumbled
- 1 Teaspoon Sugar
- ½ Cup Extra-Virgin Olive Oil
- 2 Tablespoons Cider Vinegar
- 2 Teaspoons Whole-Grain Mustard
- ½ Teaspoon Freshly Ground Pepper
- 2 Green Onions, Include Green Tops, Cut on The Diagonal Into ¼-Inch-Thick Slices
- ¼ Cup Coarsely Chopped Fresh Cilantro

Instructions

- Fill out a 4-quart saucepan two-thirds filled with Bra and water to a boil over high heat. Add 1 teaspoon salt to the boil, then add the orzo. Stir and cook the pasta until al dente (cooked but still slightly chewy), 8 to 10 minutes.
- Drain the pasta, rinse with cold water, and drain completely again. Transfer the orzo into a big bowl and toss with olive oil. To produce the dress, at a small bowl, whisk together the olive oil, lemon juice, garlic, parsley, salt, and pepper. Taste and adjust this season. Insert the dress into the salad and toss gently to blend. Remove from the fridge 30 minutes prior function.

Grilled Noodle Salad with Black Sesame Seeds
Ingredients

- 3 Tablespoons Asian Sesame Oil
- 2 Teaspoons Sugar
- ½ Cup Packed Fresh Cilantro Leaves
- 2 Tablespoons Black Sesame Seeds
- 2 Teaspoons Peeled and Minced Fresh Ginger
- 1 Large Carrot, Peeled and Julienned
- 1 Large Stalk Celery, Julienned
- 3 Packages (2 Ounces Each) Bean Thread Noodles (See Cook's Note) ¼ Cup Soy Sauce
- 1 Tablespoon Rice Vinegar
- 2 Green Onions, Include Green Tops, Cut into Matchsticks

Instructions

- To make the dress, at a small bowl, then whisk Collectively the olive oil, mustard, vinegar, adobo sauce, sugar, salt, and pepper. Put aside. In the event the husks are still connected to the ears of corn, then remove and discard them. Function with one ear at a time, stand it upright, stem end down, in a big bowl. Us a sharp knife, cut down across the cob, remove the kernels and rotate the cob per quarter turn after each cut.
- Add the beans, tomatoes, tomatoes, green onions, and cilantro into the corn at the bowl. Insert the apparel and toss gently to coat all of the Ingredients evenly.

Traeger Grilled with Walnut Vinaigrette
Ingredients

- ½ Teaspoon Kosher or Sea Salt
- 1 Tablespoon Plus ¼ Teaspoon Kosher or Sea Salt
- 1 Pound Young, Tender Green Beans, Stem Ends Trimmed
- Cup Walnut Oil (See Cook's Note) 2 Tablespoons Rice Vinegar
- 1 Tablespoon Minced Shallot
- 1 Teaspoon Sugar
- 12 Ripe Black Mission Figs, Halved Lengthwise
- Extra-Virgin Olive Oil
- 3 Ounces Fresh Goat Cheese
- ½ Cup Chopped Walnuts
- 2 Teaspoons Walnut Oil

Instructions

- In a large bowl, soak the bean ribbon Noodles in warm water to cover until softened, about 20 minutes. Drain well in a colander, shake the colander several times to make sure all the water has been eliminated. Pat the noodles dry with paper towels. To make the Saladin a big bowl whisk together the soy sauce, ginger, sesame oil, sugar and Ginger. Add the noodles and toss until well coated with the apparel.
- Add the carrot, celery, green onions, cilantro, and sesame seeds and toss to disperse all of the Ingredients evenly. Serve immediately, or cover and refrigerate until ready to serve or to get as much as two days. Remove from the fridge 30 minutes prior function.

Grilled Bruschetta in Olive Oil
Ingredients

- Extra-Virgin Olive Oil
- 1 1-Pound Loaf Country-Style Bread or Large, Crusty Baguette
- 2 Cloves Garlic, Halved

Instructions

- Prepare a hot fire in a charcoal Traeger Grill Or preheat a gas Traeger Grill on top. Cut the bread crosswise into pieces about 1 inch thick.
- Arrange the pieces in a le coating on a large, rimmed back sheet and liberally brush the pieces on both sides with olive oil. Arrange the pieces on the Traeger Grill grate directly over the hot flame, and Traeger Grill, flip once, till they have appealing Traeger Grill marks on either side and are golden brown at the edges, 4 to 5 minutes complete.
- Eliminate from the Traeger Grill and rub each slice with the cut side of the garlic. Drizzle with a bit more olive oil, if desired.

Israeli Couscous with Zucchini and Parsley
Ingredients

- 2 Tablespoons Minced Fresh Flat-Leaf Parsley
- 1¼ Cups Toasted (Israeli) Couscous
- 2 Cups Canned Low-Sodium Chicken Broth
- ½ Teaspoon Freshly Ground Pepper
- 1 Zucchini, Ends Trimmed, Cut Into ¼-Inch Dice
- 2 Tablespoons Extra-Virgin Olive Oil
- 1 Small Yellow Onion, Diced
- 1 Teaspoon Minced Garlic
- 1 Small Red Bell Pepper, Seeded, Defibbed, And Cut Into ¼-Inch Dice

Instructions

- In a sauté pan with a tight-fit lid, heat the olive oil over moderate heat. Swirl to coat the pan, then add the garlic and onion, and sauté, stir continuously, until just start to soften, about two minutes. Add the couscous and stir till lightly browned, 2-3 minutes. Add the chicken broth and pepper and bra to a simmer.
- Turn the heat to low, cover, and simmer until virtually all the liquid is absorbed, about 8 minutes. Stir in the zucchini and bell pepper, cover, and cook until the zucchini is bright green and tender, 3 minutes more. Stir in the skillet, move to a heated serve bowl, and serve immediately.

Grilled Carrot Salad

Ingredients

- 4 Teaspoons Fresh Lemon Juice
- 1 Tablespoon Honey
- 2 Teaspoons Ground Cumin
- 1 Fennel Bulb, Halved Lengthwise, Cored, And Thinly Sliced Lengthwise
- ¾ Teaspoon Kosher or Sea Salt
- Teaspoon Cayenne Pepper
- Freshly Ground Pepper
- 1 Package (10 Ounces) Shredded Carrots
- ½ Cup Coarsely Chopped Fresh Mint

Instructions

- To make the dress, at a small bowl, then whisk Collectively the olive oil, lemon juice, honey, cumin, salt, cayenne pepper, and pepper to taste.
- In a bowl, combine the carrots, fennel, and mint. Insert the apparel and toss gently to coat all of the Ingredients evenly. Serve immediately, or cover and refrigerate until ready to serve or to get up to 8 hours. Remove from the fridge 30 minutes prior function.

Grilled Eastern Chickpea Salad

Ingredients

- 1 Teaspoon Kosher or Sea Salt
- 1 Cup Loosely Packed Fresh Flat-Leaf Parsley Leaves
- 4 Ounces Feta Cheese, Crumbled Cayenne Pepper
- ½ Teaspoon Freshly Ground Pepper
- Teaspoon2 Cans (15.5 Ounces Each) Chickpeas, Rinsed and Drained
- 1 Can (6 Ounces Drained Weight) Pitted Ripe Olives, Halved
- 6 Tablespoons Extra-Virgin Olive Oil
- Freshly Grated Zest Of 1 Lemon
- 2 Tablespoons Fresh Lemon Juice
- 1 Large Clove Garlic, Minced
- 1 Pint Cherry Tomatoes, Halved

Instructions

- To make the dress, at a small bowl, then whisk Collectively the olive oil, lemon zest, lemon juice, garlic, pepper, salt, and Cayenne pepper. In a large bowl, combine the chickpeas, olives, tomatoes, parsley, and feta.
- Insert the apparel and toss gently to blend. Put aside at room Temperature for 30 minutes to permit the flavors to develop. Alternatively, Cover and refrigerate until ready to serve or to get as many as two days. Eliminate from the Refrigerator 30 minutes before function.

Chapter 7: Starters, Salads & Appetizers Recipes

Salted Jalapeno Poppers
Ingredients

- 4 ounces grated Mexican four-cheese blend or Cheddar cheese
- 1 teaspoon chili powder, or more to taste
- 18 media to large jalapeno peppers
- 8 ounces cream cheese, at room temperature
- 1/2 teaspoon garlic salt
- 2 scallions (green onions), trimmed, white and green parts minced
- 8 to 10 slices of thin-cut bacon

Instructions

- Eliminate the seeds and ribs. A baby spoon or demitasse spoon works nicely for this. (You might choose to use latex gloves) In a mixture bowl combine the cream cheese, Mexican cheese, chili powder, and garlic salt till well-blended. Transfer the mix to a quart-size resealable plastic bag. Using a scissors, clip roughly 1/2-inch off among the corners to produce a pastry bag. Squeeze the cheese mix into the jalapeno pepper halves. (Leftover cheese mix is fantastic on baked potatoes.)
- Cut the bacon crosswise into bits long enough to wrap round the center of every jalapeno, seam-side down. Arrange on a rear sheet covered with foil or parchment paper. When ready to cook, then begin the Traeger Grill on Smoke using the lid open before the flame is set (4 to 5 minutes). Place the temperature to 350 degrees F and F, lid shut, for 10 to 15 minutes. Let cool for a couple moments before function.

Traeger Grilled Baguette with Herbs
Ingredients

- Salt
- ½ cup (1 stick or 4 ounces) salted butter, at room temperature 1
- baguette, cut into ½-inch slices
- 3 tablespoons fresh mixed herbs

Instructions

- Get the Traeger Grill for guide Traeger Grill. Preheat to moderate heat. In a small bowl, then stir the herbs, garlic, and salt to flavor in the butter, mix well to incorporate.
- Spread the butter mixture on each side of the chopped bread and set in a le layer in a long-handled Traeger Grill basket. Serve.

Traeger Grilled Spicy Trout
Ingredients

- 1-quart cold water
- 1-1/2 pounds trout (3 to 4), cleaned and butterflied, skin-on
- 1/2 cup brown sugar
- 1/4 cup kosher salt
- • 1 tablespoon pickle spice

Instructions

- Create the brine: Combine the brown sugar Stir until the salt and sugar dissolve. Open the hens. Run your f errs within the flesh to find bones remove any you find with kitchen tweezers or even needle-nose pliers.
- Submerge the hens at the brine; simmer for 2-3 hours, but no more. When ready to cook, then begin the Traeger Grill on Smoke using the lid open before the flame is set (4 to 5 minutes). Eliminate the trout out of the brine, knock off some large parts of these pickle spices, and then dry the fish on paper towels. Organize the trout skin-side Back on the Traeger Grill grate. Transfer into a cool stand. When cool, cover with plastic wrap and refrigerate till function time. Smoked trout can keep, refrigerated, for 2-3 days.

Teriyaki Wings with Soy Sauce
Ingredients

- 1/4 cup brown sugar
- 2 tablespoons rice wine vinegar or balsamic vinegar
- Vegetable oil for oil   the Traeger Grill grate
- 1 tablespoon sesame seeds, lightly toasted in a dry nonstick skillet
- 2 scallions (green onions), trimmed, white and green parts thinly sliced
- 1 clove garlic, minced
- 2-1/2 pounds large chicken wings
- 1/2 cup soy sauce
- 1/4 cup water
- 2 teaspoons sesame oil
- 2 nickel-sized pieces of fresh Ginger, smashed

Instructions

- Using a sharp knife, then cut on the wings Three pieces throughout the joints. Discard the w hints, or store for poultry stock. Transfer the stay "drumettes" and "apartments" into a large resealable plastic bag or a bowl. Br into a boil, and then lower the heat and simmer for 10 minutes.
- Seal the bag and refrigerate for many hours, or even overnight. When ready to cook, then begin the Traeger Grill on Smoke using the lid open before the flame is set (4 to 5 minutes). Place the temperature to 350 degrees F and F, lid closed, for 10 to 15 minutes. Oil that the Traeger Grill grate. Cook for 45 to 50 minutes, or until the skin is brown and crispy and the beef is no longer pink in the bone. Turn once through the cook time to stop the wings from adhere into the Traeger Grill grate. Transfer to a bowl or bowl and sprinkle with the sesame seeds.

Antipasto Crostini with Basil Leaves
Ingredients

- ½ bunch fresh basil leaves, divided
- 1 zucchini, cut lengthwise into ½-inch slices 2 red bell peppers,
- cored, seeded, and cut into 2-inch strips 8 green onions, tops and
- 1 tablespoon salted butter, melted
- 1 garlic clove, crushed
- 1 tablespoon fresh parsley, finely chopped Coarse salt
- Freshly ground black pepper
- bottoms trimmed Coarse salt
- ¼ cup good-quality olive oil
- 2 tablespoons balsamic vinegar

- Freshly ground black pepper
- 2 tablespoons good-quality olive oil
- 4 large slices sourdough or peasant bread

Instructions

- Get the Traeger Grill for guide Traeger Grill. Preheat to heat. In a small bowl, whisk olive oil and balsamic vinegar together. Finely chop four or three basil leaves and increase the olive oil mixture, mix until well mixed.
- When ready to cook, then brush the sexy Traeger Grill grate lightly with petroleum. Season with salt and honey to taste. Organize the Traeger Grill ed vegetables onto a function platter or individual plates. In a small bowl, whisk together the olive oil, garlic, butter, parsley, and salt and pepper to taste until mixed. Gently add the oils, stir till well mixed.

Traeger Barbecue Sausage
Ingredients

- Traeger Pork and Poultry Rub, or your favorite barbecue rub
- 1 1-pound uncooked sausage chub, such as Bob Evans or Jimmy Dean brands, any flavor
- 1 tablespoon fine- to medium-grind coffee

Instructions

- The sausage therefore the sausage stays log-shaped, about 2-1/2 to 3 inches in diameter. Season evenly with all the Traeger Pork and Poultry Rub, then piled with all the java. When ready to cook, then begin the Traeger Grill on Smoke using the lid open before the flame is set (4 to 5 minutes). Increase the heat to 225 degrees F.
- Continue to cook the sausage before an instant-read meat thermometer inserted through the finish reads 160 degrees F, about 45 minutes to 1 hour. Let rest for 15 minutes prior slit!

Smoked Grilled Salmon with Green Herbs
Ingredients

- 1 cup brown sugar or brown sugar substitute
- 1/2 cup coarse (kosher) salt
- 1 salmon fillet (1-1/2 to 2 pounds), preferably wild-caught
- 1 cup vodka or apple juice
- 1 tablespoon coarse black pepper

Instructions

- Eliminate any pin bones that you locate with kitchen tweezers or needle-nose pliers. Set the salmon fillet into a large resealable plastic bag and pour the vodka over it. Heal the bag to ensure that the salmon is chilled, then simmer for 1 to 2 hours. Make the remedy: Blend the salt, sugar, and black pepper into a different large resealable plastic bag.
- Drain fish. Insert the noodle into the sugar mix, be certain that the salmon is completely coated. Rinse off the cure the salmon and dry with paper towels. When ready to cook, then begin the Traeger Grill on Smoke using the lid open before the flame is set (4 to 5 minutes). Arrange the salmon (skin-side down, in case it's skin) about the Traeger Grill grate. Smoke for half an hour. (The specific time will be dependent on the depth of the fillet.)
- There's not any need to flip the fish. Cover the fish with plastic wrap and refrigerate till function time. Can be made two to three times beforehand.

Chicken Quesadillas Tortillas
Ingredients

- Jack or pepper Jack cheese
- 2 cups shredded or chopped cooked chicken
- 1 small bunch fresh cilantro, leaves pulled off stems
- 2 medium tomatoes, seeded and diced
- 4 10-inch flour tortillas
- Vegetable oil
- 2 cups grated Monterey
- 4 scallions (green onions), trimmed, green and white parts thinly sliced
- 1/4 cup pickled jalapeno slices, chopped (optional)
- Salt
- Salsa and/or sour cream for serve

Instructions

- Lay a tortilla Back on a money-back sheet Leave one-half of this tortilla bare. Top another half with a number of the poultry, cheese, cilantro leaves, tomatoes, scallions, and pickled jalapenos, if desired. Finish with a bit more grated cheese. (This may "paste" another Ingredients collectively as it stinks.) Twist the bare half of the tortilla over the full half and set aside. Repeat the procedure with the stay tortillas. When ready to cook, then begin the Traeger Grill on Smoke using the lid open before the flame is set (4 to 5 minutes).
- Place the temperature to 375 degrees F and F, lid shut, for 10 to 15 minutes. Using a large spatula, carefully move the quesadillas into the Traeger Grill grate. Cook until the cheese is melted and the exterior is starting to brown (8 to 10 minutes total). Us that the spatula, turn half-way through the cook time. Cut each quesadilla into three wedges using a scissors or sharp knife. Serve with salsa or sour lotion.

Barbecued Chicken Breasts
Ingredients

- 3 cups (12 ounces) grated Mexican four cheese blend
- 1/2 cup sliced black olives, drained
- Sliced pickled jalapenos (optional)
- 1-1/4 pounds boneless skinless chicken breasts
- Traeger Pork and Poultry Rub, or taco season
- 1/2 to 3/4 cup Traeger Regular Barbecue Sauce
- 24 large tortilla chips (not broken)
- 3 scallions (green onions), trimmed, white and green parts thinly sliced
- 1 cup sour cream, for serve

Instructions

- Season the chicken breasts with all the Traeger When ready to cook, then begin the Traeger Grill on Smoke using the lid open before the flame is set (4 to 5 minutes). Place the temperature to 350 degrees F and F, lid shut, for 10 to 15 minutes. Arrange the chicken breasts on the Traeger Grill grate and cook turn once halfway through the cook time, for 25 to 30 minutes, or until the internal temperature when read in an instant-read beef thermometer is 170 degrees F. Transfer into some cut board and let rest for 3 minutes.

- Leave the Traeger Grill on in the event that you're making the nachos immediately. Dice the chicken into little cubes, 1/2-inch or not. Transfer into a mixture bowl and then pour 1/2 cup of Traeger Regular Barbecue Sauce within the diced chicken. Stir lightly to coat each slice. (Add more sauce if necessary, but not too much that the mix sloppy".) Put aside, or cover and refrigerate or even create the nachos immediately. Lay the tortilla chips at a le layer on a rimmed back sheet or pizza pan.
- Sprinkle evenly with half of the cheese. Spoon a bit of this barbecued chicken mixture on each processor. Sprinkle the stay half of the cheese evenly over the chips. Scatter the chopped onions over the chips. Set the back sheet onto the Traeger Grill grate. Bake till the chips are crispy and the cheese is melted, 12 to 15 minutes. Using a spatula, move the nachos into a plate or plate.

Pepperoni-Provolone Bread with Dried Parsley
Ingredients

- 1 teaspoon dried basil
- 1 teaspoon dried parsley
- 4 ounces thinly sliced pepperoni
- 1 loaf frozen bread dough, such as Rhodes
- Extra-virgin olive oil
- 1 teaspoon dried oregano
- 4 ounces thinly sliced provolone cheese, or mozzarella
- Cornmeal for dust the back sheet

Instructions

- Thaw the bread dough and let it rise accord into the Package instructions. On a lightly floured kitchen counter or other horizontal surface, roll up and stretch the dough to a 12- by 18- inch rectangle. (It takes a Little patience when the dough is quite elastic. Allow it to rest for a Couple of Minutes and Brush with olive oil, and sprinkle evenly with half the oregano, Organize the pepperoni at a le layer on the dough, make a 1-inch border on either side. Lay the cheese in addition to the pepperoni.
- Start on the Long side, roll up the dough equally jelly roll-style. Pinch the extended seam Together along its span. enclosed. Lay the bread, then seam-side down, in an oiled back sheet Scatter the stay dried herbs evenly within it. Us a Bread, slit shallow vents at top onto a diagonal. Cover with oiled Plastic wrap and let rise in a warm place for half an hour. Begin the Traeger Grill on Smoke using the lid open before the flame is Place the temperature to 350 degrees F and F, Lid shut, for 10 to 15 minutes. Remove the plastic wrap in the bread. Transfer the trunk sheet together with the bread into your Traeger Grill. Bake for 40 to 50 minutes, or until the bread is baked through. (It is Better to overbake compared to underbake, in this circumstance.) Allow the bread cool completely on a stand before serve and slice.

Traeger Grilled Corn Salsa
Ingredients

- 3 ears sweet corn, husked
- 1 teaspoon cumin
- 1/4 cup fresh cilantro leaves, chopped
- 2 cloves garlic, finely minced
- 1 to 2 tablespoons vegetable oil
- 4 tomatoes, such as Roma, halved
- 1 medium-size onion, peeled and quartered through the root end
- 1/2 to 2 jalapeno peppers, or more to taste, halved

- Fresh lime juice to taste
- 1-1/2 teaspoons Traeger Veggie Shake, or salt and freshly ground pepper to taste

Instructions

- When ready to cook, begin the Traeger Grill on Smoke using the lid open before the flame is set (4 to 5 minutes). Place the temperature to 450 degrees F (High) and preheat, lid shut, for 10 to 15 minutes. Traeger Grill till the veggies have fine char marks on the cut sides. Traeger Grill the corn in precisely the exact same time, turn often, until a few of those kernels are deeply browned.
- Transfer the vegetables to a cut plank and let cool. Using a sharp knife, cut the corn kernels off the cob (in case you operate on a moist towel that the kernels will not scatter so much). Seed the jalapenos (or leave the seeds for a clearly hotter salsa), and mince. Transfer the Traeger Grill ed vegetables to some mixture bowl. Drink room temperature to the very best taste. The salsa can be made a few hours beforehand, but is best the day it's mad.

Grilled Honey Wings
Ingredients

- Shake, Sweet Rub, or your favorite barbecue rub
- 2-1/2 pounds large chicken wings
- Traeger Pork and Poultry
- 12.8-ounce bottle Traeger Honey-Bourbon Barbecue Sauce

Instructions

- Using a sharp knife, then cut on the wings Three pieces throughout the joints. Discard the w hints, or store for poultry stock. Transfer the stay "drumettes" and "apartments" into a large resealable plastic bag or a bowl. When ready to cook, then begin the Traeger Grill on Smoke using the lid open before the flame is set (4 to 5 minutes). Place the temperature to 350 degrees F and F, lid shut, for 10 to 15 minutes.
- Cook for 45 to 50 minutes, or till the chicken is no longer pink in the bone. Baste the wings on either side with an Traeger Honey-Bourbon Sauce. Cook for 5 to 10 minutes longer to "place" the sauce. Drink immediately.

Grilled Potato Salad with Sour Cream

Ingredients

- 1 red onion, diced
- 1 tablespoon dried dill
- ¼ cup sour cream
- ½ cup mayonnaise
- ¾ teaspoon dry mustard
- 2½ pounds Red Bliss potatoes, halved
- 3 hard-boiled eggs, peeled and diced
- 4 green onions, finely chopped
- 2 celery ribs, trimmed and diced
- 1½ tablespoons white distilled vinegar 2 teaspoons sugar
- Salt
- Freshly ground black pepper
- Paprika (optional)

Instructions

- Put the potatoes into a skillet and Cover with water. Br into a boil, cover, and simmer over low heat till fork-tender, 15 to 20 minutes. Drain cover, and simmer over low heat till fork-tender, 15 to 20 minutes. Roughly cut to bite-size pieces and set in a function bowl. Gently toss. In a small bowl, combine the sour cream, mayonnaise, dry mustard, sugar, vinegar, and pepper and salt to taste.
- Traeger Grill until opaque and firm, 2 to 4 minutes each side. Organize a plate or plate with the sauce and lemon wedges. Drizzle the apparel within the potato mixture and toss to coat. Chill in the fridge for 1 hour before function. Examine the season, dust with paprika, if we and function.

Greek Salad with Olive Oil

Ingredients

- flat-leaf parsley, cut into thin strips ⅓ pound feta cheese, crumbled
- ½ cup pitted kalamata olives
- ¼ cup good-quality olive oil
- Freshly ground black pepper
- Crusty bread, to serve (optional)
- 3 ripe tomatoes, sliced into wedges
- 1 small red onion, sliced into thin strips 1 seedless cucumber, cut into
- bite-size pieces 1 green bell pepper, trimmed and diced 1 cup fresh
- 3 tablespoons red wine vinegar
- ½ teaspoon dried oregano
- Salt

Instructions

- Blend the vegetables, parsley, feta, and Olives in a big bowl. In a small bowl, combine the oil, vinegar, oregano, and salt and pepper to taste, whisk to blend. Traeger Grill until opaque and firm, 2 to 4 minutes each side.
- Organize a plate or plate with the sauce and lemon wedges. Pour on the apparel on the salad.

Grilled Michi Orzo Salad

Ingredients

- 1 tablespoon freshly squeezed lemon juice Salt
- Freshly ground black pepper
- 4 tablespoons good-quality olive oil FOR THE ORZO SALAD
- 16 ounces orzo pasta
- 2 handfuls baby spinach leaves, rinsed and stems trimmed 1
- tablespoon freshly squeezed lemon juice Salt
- Freshly ground black pepper
- ⅓ cup pine nuts
- 8 ounces baby spinach, rinsed and stems trimmed 2 garlic cloves, pressed
- ⅔ cup packed grated Parmesan cheese
- 2 cups cooked chicken breast, cut into bite-size pieces 1-pint cherry
- tomatoes, halved

Instructions

- In a nonstick skillet, dry roast the walnut Nuts over moderate heat, shake the skillet back and forth till the pine nuts are golden brown, 1 to 2 minutes. Put aside to cool. Put the spinach, garlic, toasted pine nuts, Parmesan cheese, and lemon juice in the bowl of a food processor and season with pepper and salt to taste. Drizzle the oil over the surface and purée until the mix is creamy and smooth.
- Traeger Grill until opaque and firm, 2 to 4 minutes each side. Organize a plate or plate with the sauce and lemon wedges. Transfer into a large bowl. In a kettle of salted boil, cook the orzo accord into the package directions until al dente, about 8 minutes. Drain well and instantly combine with the pesto, blend well. Add the cherry tomatoes, spinach, and lemon juice. Stir lightly to combine. Taste and adjust the salt, pepper, or lemon juice as necessary. Chill before function.

Traeger Grilled Radicchio Salad

Ingredients

- 3 tablespoons olive oil
- 4 firm pears, cored and thickly sliced FOR THE SALAD
- 1 tablespoon pine nuts
- 1 head radicchio, cored
- ½ cup black olives, pitted and finely chopped 2 parsley sprigs, finely chopped
- Leaves from 2 rosemary sprigs, finely chopped Leaves from 2 thyme sprigs, finely chopped 4 sage leaves, finely chopped
- 2 garlic cloves, finely chopped
- 2 tablespoons freshly squeezed lemon juice 1 tablespoon lemon zest Coarse salt
- Freshly ground black pepper
- 2 tablespoons freshly squeezed lemon juice Coarse salt
- Freshly ground black pepper

Instructions:

- Set the rosemary, thyme, sage, and garlic in a little bowl. Add the lemon juice and simmer. Season to taste with pepper and salt add olive oil and lightly toss. Arrange the chopped wedges in a large bowl on a rear sheet, garnish with the marinade, cover, and let stand for two hours. When ready to cook, prepare the Traeger Grill for immediate Traeger Grill. Preheat to moderate heat. Traeger Grill for 1 to 2 minutes each side, or until golden. Transfer out of the sexy Traeger Grill into a function tray. In a

large, nonstick skillet over moderate heat, dry roast the pine nuts, stir continuously till they are golden brown, 1 to 2 weeks.
- Add the radicchio leaves, olives, parsley, and lemon juice and cook for another 1 to 2 minutes. Split the radicchio mixture evenly among four plates. Top with all the Traeger Grill ed pears and garnish with the reserved marinade. Season with pepper and salt to taste. Drink hot.

Traeger Grilled Shrimp Cocktail
Ingredients

- 2 tablespoons prepared horseradish, or more to taste
- 1 tablespoon fresh lemon or lime juice
- 1 teaspoon Worcestershire sauce
- Freshly ground black pepper
- 2 pounds jumbo or extra-jumbo shrimp (about 36), peeled and deveined, tail-on
- 1/4 cup extra-virgin olive oil
- Traeger Veggie Shake, or your favorite barbecue rub
- 1 cup Traeger Chili Sauce, or your favorite chili sauce
- Lemon wedges for serve
- 6-inch bamboo skewers

Instructions

- In a medium bowl, toss the fish to coat Using the olive oil and about 2 tsp of Traeger Veggie Shake. Thread the fish on the bamboo skewers, 2 to a skewer. Combine the chili sauce, horseradish, lemon juice, Worcestershire sauce, and Tabasco sauce in a small bowl, then whisk to combine. When ready to cook, then begin the Traeger Grill on Smoke using the lid open before the flame is set (4 to 5 minutes).
- Place the temperature to 450 degrees F (High) and preheat, lid shut, for 10 to 15 minutes. Arrange the fish skewers on the Traeger Grill grate. Traeger Grill until opaque and firm, 2 to 4 minutes each side. Organize a plate or plate with the sauce and lemon wedges.

Traeger Grilled Pineapple
Ingredients

- 1 tablespoon freshly squeezed lemon juice 1 pinch ground cinnamon
- 1 pinch ground cloves
- 1 ripe pineapple
- ¼ cup (½ stick) salted butter
- 4 tablespoons honey
- ⅓ cup warmed gold rum (optional)

Instructions

- Get the Traeger Grill for guide Traeger Grill. Preheat to heat. Cut the lemon in half lengthwise, remove the tough core, and cut each half into 4 wedges, for a total of 5 wedges. In a small saucepan, melt the butter and then stir in the lemon, lemon juice and spices.
- Traeger Grill the lemon, then brush every wedge with all the butter mix. Switch frequently, Traeger Grill until evenly browned, about 4 minutes on each side. Don't overcook and observe attentively, as the sugars in fresh lemon caramelize quickly. Eliminate the lemon out of the Traeger Grill and then place in a shallow dish. Pour the heated rum, if we over the skillet, flambé, and function.

Traeger Grilled Peaches

Ingredients

- 4 ripe peaches
- 1 lemon
- 1 cup ricotta cheese
- 6 ounces flaked almonds
- 6 tablespoons honey, divided
- 1 teaspoon pure almond extract
- 2 tablespoons sugar

Instructions

- Get the Traeger Grill for indirect Traeger Grill. Preheat to medium-high warmth. Toast the almond flakes on moderate heat in a Transfer to a small bowl and blend with 4 Tsp honey along with the almond extract; softly combine. Put aside. Cut the Oil that the Traeger Grill grate and place that the Peach halves, cut side down, on the grill. Traeger Grill for 8 to 10 Minutes, until the peaches are tender, watch them carefully. Meanwhile, rinse the lemon and rub; grate the zest. Squeeze 1 tbsp of juice out of the lemon.
- In a medium bowl combine the ricotta cheese, sugar and lemon juice and Zest and blend until creamy and smooth. Spoon half the ricotta mixture into Four function bowls. Brush each peach half with the stay 2 Tsp honey. Put one peach, cut side up, half with the stay 2 Tsp honey. Put one cherry, cut side up, on top of this ricotta Cheese and top with all the stay peach half, followed with a generous spoonful of the stay ricotta cheese. Spoon the Honey--Almond Sauce On the top and serve immediately.

Chapter 8: Pizza Recipes

Grilled Margherita Pizza
Ingredients

- 1 cup Crushed Tomato Sauce
- 1 large clove garlic, minced
- 8 ounces fresh mozzarella cheese, cut into
- ¼-inch-thick slices (or 1 cup grated if fresh is unavailable)
- ¼ cup uncooked grits or polenta, for roll
- 1 ball prepared pizza dough, at room temperature
- 2 tablespoons olive oil
- 10 fresh basil leaves
- Kosher salt and freshly ground black pepper to taste

Instructions

- Preheat the Traeger Grill, roll out and Shape the dough, and Traeger Grill the initial side of the crust per the master. Use tongs to move it to a peel or rimless back sheet. Flip the crust to reveal the Traeger Grill ed side.
- Distribute the entire surface with the sauce, then sprinkle with the garlic and top with the cheese. Finish Traeger Grill the pizza each the master directions. Remove from the Traeger Grill, garnish with the basil, and season with pepper and salt. Slice and serve immediately.

Italian Sausage & Rapini Pizza
Ingredients

- 2 hot or sweet Italian sausages
- ¼ cup uncooked grits or polenta, for roll
- the dough
- 1 ball prepared pizza dough, at room temperature
- Zest of 1 lemon, finely grated with a
- Microplate or zester
- Kosher salt and freshly ground black pepper to taste
- ½ cup White Bean Purée
- 4 tablespoons olive oil, divided
- 1 bunch rapini (broccoli rabe), ends trimmed
- 2 cloves garlic, minced
- ¼ teaspoon red pepper flakes
- or store-bought
- ¼ cup grated pecorino Romano cheese
- ½ cup grated mozzarella cheese

Instructions

- Preheat a large, heavy sauté pan over medium heat. Add 2 tbsp of the oil and the rapini and cook until it turns bright green and begins to soften, 2-3 minutes. Add the garlic and red pepper stir well to coat.
- Cover and continue to cook until the rapini is cooked through, about 5 minutes. Reserve for best. Preheat the Traeger Grill per the master directions for charcoal or gas. Prick the sausages with a

toothpick several times to stop undesirable explosions. Place the sausages on the cook grate over indirect heat. Traeger Grill, turn occasionally, until cooked through, about 20 minutes.
- Let cool. Cut to 1/4-inch-thick rounds just prior to top. Roll out and form the dough, then Traeger Grill the initial facet of this crust each the master directions. Use tongs to move it from the Traeger Grill to some peel or rimless back sheet. Flip the crust to show the Traeger Grill side. Spread the entire surface with all the bean purée. Top with all the rapini and sausage. End Traeger Grill the pizza each the master directions. Slice and serve immediately.

Meat and Treat Pepperoni Pizza
Ingredients

- 1 cup Five-Minute Amatrice-Style Sauce or cooked tomato sauce of your choice
- 4 ounces pepperoni, thinly sliced (ideally from
- a whole pepperoni)
- 1 cup grated mozzarella cheese
- 1/4 cup uncooked grits or polenta, for roll the dough
- 1 ball prepared pizza dough, at room temperature
- 2 tablespoons olive oil
- 1/4 cup freshly grated Parmigiano-Reggiano cheese
- 1/4 teaspoon red pepper flakes
- Kosher salt and freshly ground black pepper to taste

Instructions

- Shape the dough, and Traeger Grill the first side of this crust per the master. Use tongs to transfer it to a peel or rimless sheet. Flip the crust to show the Traeger Grill side. Spread the whole surface with the sauce.
- Top with the pepperoni and scatter with the cheeses. Finish Traeger Grill the pizza per the master instructions. Eliminate from the Traeger Grill, scatter with the red pepper flakes, and season with salt and black pepper.

Spanish Supreme Mushroom Pizza
Ingredients

- 1/4 cup uncooked grits or polenta, for roll   the dough
- 1 ball prepared pizza dough, at room
- temperature
- 1 cup Crushed Tomato Sauce
- 2 cloves garlic, minced
- Leaves from 3 sprigs fresh thyme (about
- 1 tablespoon) or 2 teaspoons dried
- Freshly ground black pepper to taste
- 1/2 cup grated mozzarella cheese
- 1/2 cup grated Asiago cheese
- 4 tablespoons olive oil, divided
- Pinch of kosher salt
- 10 ounces baby bella (baby portabellas)
- mushrooms, stems trimmed and caps thinly
- sliced (use an egg slicer for speed and consistency)

Instructions

- If you would rather your mushrooms raw, skip this step. Otherwise, preheat a large, heavy sauté pan over medium heat for 1 to 2 minutes. Add 2 tbsp of the oil along with the salt. When the oil is hot, add the mushrooms and cook, stir occasionally, until browned, about 10 minutes. Remove from the heat and book for top. Preheat the Traeger Grill, roll out and form the dough, and Traeger Grill the initial facet of the crust per the master to get charcoal. Use tongs to move into a peel or rimless sheet.
- Flip the crust to show the Traeger Grill side. Distribute the entire surface with the sauce, sprinkle with the garlic and top with the mushrooms. End Traeger Grill the pizza each the master instructions. Remove from the Traeger Grill, sprinkle with the thyme, and season with salt and pepper. Slice and serve immediately.

Crave Special Pizza
Ingredients

- Kosher salt and freshly ground black pepper
- to taste
- ¼ cup uncooked grits or polenta, for roll
- the dough
- 1 ball prepared pizza dough, at room temperature
- ½ cup Roasted Garlic Paste
- red bell pepper
- 1 orange bell pepper
- 1 yellow bell pepper
- 4 tablespoons olive oil, divided
- 2 tablespoons balsamic vinegar
- 8 ounces fresh mozzarella cheese, cut into
- ¼-inch-thick slices (or 1 cup grated if
- fresh is unavailable)
- 3 tablespoons Basil Pesto or
- store-bought

Instructions:

- Roast the peppers as educated on then Peel, seed, and cut into strips. In a medium bowl, combine 2 tablespoons of the oil and the vinegar. Add the pepper strips and throw. Season with pepper and salt and let sit for at least 15 minutes or up per week (refrigerate if longer than two hours). Reserve for best. Preheat the Traeger Grill, roll out and shape the dough, and Traeger Grill the initial facet of this crust per the master to get charcoal. Use tongs to transfer it to a peel or rimless sheet.

- Flip the crust to reveal the Traeger Grill ed side. Spread the whole surface together with the garlic paste. Top with a loaf of carbohydrates. Put the mozzarella slices above everything. Finish Traeger Grill the pizza each the master directions. Remove from the Traeger Grill and complete by place a tiny dollop of pesto on each puddle of mozzarella. Season liberally with pepper and salt. Slice and serve immediately.

Sausages Pepper Pizza
Ingredients

- 1 cup Tuscan Red Sauce or Crushed Tomato Sauce
- ¼ cup pickled sweet and hot peppers, sliced
- 1 ball prepared pizza dough, at room temperature
- 2 tablespoons olive oil
- Kosher salt and freshly ground black pepper to taste
- 1 cup grated mozzarella cheese
- ½ cup grated Monterey Jack cheese
- 1 teaspoon B&E Sprinkle-vicious Spice
- Blend or your favorite spice blend
- 1 pound sweet or hot Italian sausage
- ¼ cup uncooked grits or polenta, for roll the dough

Instructions

- Put the sausage in a large, heavy skillet. Sauté over moderate heat, break up any large pieces, until completely cooked. Alternatively, Traeger Grill the sausage in its case and slice before us. Drain on paper towels and reserve for top. Preheat the Traeger Grill, roll out and form the dough, and Traeger Grill the initial side of this crust per the master to get charcoal. Use tongs to transfer it to a peel or rimless sheet.
- Twist the crust to reveal the Traeger Grill ed side. Distribute the entire surface with the sauce. Top with the sausage and sausage, then sprinkle with the cheeses. End Traeger Grill the pizza each the master instructions. Eliminate from the Traeger Grill, sprinkle with the spice blend, and season with pepper and salt.

Cheddar Cheese Pizza
Ingredients

- ½ cup grated Asiago cheese
- ½ cup grated sharp white Cheddar cheese
- ¼ cup uncooked grits or polenta, for roll
- the dough
- 1 ball prepared pizza dough, at room temperature
- ¼ cup olive oil
- 10 fresh sage leaves (optional)
- ½ cup grated mozzarella cheese
- ½ cup freshly grated Parmigiano-
- R Reggiano cheese
- ½ cup Crushed Tomato Sauce

- Kosher salt and red pepper flakes to taste

Instructions

- If us the sage, warm the oil on your tiniest saucepan over medium heat until it's hot enough to fry the sage. Insert the leaves you at a time, take care they don't overlap, and fry until rigid and dark green, about two minutes. Use a fork to remove them in the oil, set onto a paper towel to drain, and reserve for top. Save 2 tbsp of your sage-infused oil to brush the dough. In a big bowl, combine the four cheeses together.
- Reserve for best. Preheat the Traeger Grill, roll out and shape the dough, and Traeger Grill the first facet of the crust per the master for gasoline. Use tongs to transfer into some peel or rimless sheet. Flip the crust to reveal the Traeger Grill ed side. Distribute the whole surface with the sauce and sprinkle with the cheese mixture. Finish Traeger Grill the pizza each the master instructions. Eliminate from the Traeger Grill, garnish with the fried sage, and season with salt and red pepper.

Basil Base Pesto Pizza
Ingredients

- ½ cup Tomato-Basil Base
- 8 ounces fresh mozzarella cheese, cut into
- ¼-inch-thick slices
- ¼ cup uncooked grits or polenta, for roll the dough
- 1 ball prepared pizza dough, at room temperature
- 2 tablespoons olive oil
- 1 cup Basil Pesto) or store-bought
- 2 tablespoons pine nuts
- Kosher salt and freshly ground black pepper to taste

Instructions

- Preheat the Traeger Grill, roll out and Shape the dough, and Traeger Grill the first side of the crust each the master to get charcoal. Use tongs to transfer it to some peel or rimless sheet. Flip the crust to reveal the Traeger Grill ed side.
- Distribute the entire surface with the pesto. Cover the surface with the tomato-basil base and top with the cheese. Finish Traeger Grill the pizza per the master directions. Remove from the Traeger Grill, garnish with the pine nuts, and season with pepper and salt.

Grilled Tomato & Cabranes Pizza
Ingredients

- 1 cup Onion Marmalade
- 1¼ cups Fire-Roasted Cherry Tomatoes
- 4 ounces Cabranes or your favorite blue cheese, crumbled
- ¼ cup pecan pieces, toasted and chopped
- ¼ cup uncooked grits or polenta, for roll the dough
- 1 ball prepared pizza dough, at room temperature
- 2 tablespoons olive oil
- Freshly ground black pepper to taste

Instructions

- Shape the dough, and Traeger Grill the initial facet of the crust each the master to get charcoal. Use tongs to transfer it to some peel or rimless back sheet. Flip the crust to reveal the Traeger Grilled side. Distribute the entire surface together with the onion marmalade.
- Top with the tomatoes and scatter the cheese. End Traeger Grill the pizza per the master directions. Remove the pizza from the Traeger Grill, garnish with the nuts, and season with pepper. Slice and serve immediately.

Grilled Squash-Palooza Pizza with Fontina Cheese
Ingredients

- ½ cup shredded mozzarella cheese
- 3 tablespoons pumpkin seeds (pepitas)
- 1 small sugar pumpkin, Garnet sweet potato,
- or your favorite squash (try delicate, kombucha, butternut, or acorn)
- 4 tablespoons salted butter
- ¼ cup uncooked grits or polenta, for roll the dough
- 1 ball prepared pizza dough, at room temperature
- 3 tablespoons olive oil
- ½ cup Roasted Garlic Paste
- 1 cup shredded Fontina cheese
- 6 fresh sage leaves
- 1 bunch chard or other greens, such as kale or spinach

Instructions

- Remove the stems from the chard. Fill a Medium pot halfway with bra and water to a boil. Add the greens, then Allow the water return to a boil. Pour off the water, let the greens cool, then squeeze out the surplus water. Reserve. Preheat the Traeger Grill per the master Instructions for gasoline Roll out and form the dough, transfer to your Traeger Grill place, and Traeger Grill the first side of this Crust per the master directions. After the bottom is marked and browned, use Tongs to move the crust to a peel or rimless sheet. Switch the Traeger Grill to indirect heat and close the lid to maintain the Traeger Grill temperature. Twist the crust to reveal the Traeger Grill side.
- Spread The whole surface together with all the garlic paste and then sprinkle with Fontina. Top with spoonsful of this pumpkin-squash mixture. Scatter the cooked greens around, separate them So they're equally distributed. Finish Traeger Grill the pizza each the master instructions. Eliminate from the Traeger Grill. Remove the sage in the egg (or alternately, Crush the leaves and then leave them in), then drizzle on top of this pizza.

Special Vegetable Grilled Pizza
Ingredients

- 4 tablespoons olive oil, divided
- 2 cloves garlic, minced
- 4 oil-packed artichoke hearts (not marinated), cut into eighths
- Leaves from 2 sprigs fresh rosemary or
- 1 teaspoon dried
- 1 tablespoon fresh lemon juice
- ¼ cup uncooked grits or polenta, for roll the dough
- 8 spears white asparagus
- 1 ball prepared pizza dough, at room temperature

- ½ cup White Bean Purée or store-bought
- ¼ cup freshly grated Parmigiano-Reggiano cheese
- ½ cup mascarpone
- ¼ cup walnut halves, toasted and roughly chopped
- Kosher salt and freshly ground white pepper to taste

Instructions

- Heat 2 tbsp of the oil and also the Garlic collectively over medium-low warmth in a medium sauté pan until the garlic just begins to brown, then add the asparagus, artichokes, rosemary, and lemon juice. Reserve for best. Just before us strain and discard the oil. Preheat the Traeger Grill, roll out and form the dough, and Traeger Grill the initial facet of this crust each the master to get charcoal. Use tongs to move into some peel or rimless sheet. Twist the crust to show the Traeger Grill side.
- Distribute the whole surface using all the bean purée. Artfully arrange the artichokes and asparagus at the top. End Traeger Grill the pizza each the master directions. Eliminate from the Traeger Grill, sprinkle the walnuts, and season with pepper and salt.

Forty Olive & Pimiento Pizza
Ingredients

- ½ cup Tuscan Red Sauce or Crushed Tomato Sauce
- Zest of 1 lemon, finely grated with a Microplate or zester
- Kosher salt and freshly ground black pepper to taste
- 1½ cups grated mancheron cheese
- 10 N niçoise olives, pitted
- 10 Kalamata olives, pitted
- 10 picoline olives, pitted
- ¼ cup walnut pieces, toasted
- 1 ball prepared pizza dough, at room temperature
- ¼ cup uncooked grits or polenta, for roll the dough
- 2 tablespoons olive oil
- 10 Cergol olives, pitted
- 1 small shallot, thinly sliced and separated
- ¼ cup pimientos or roasted red bell peppers, diced

Instructions

- Knead the walnuts to the dough, pay with plastic wrap, and place aside. Preheat the Traeger Grill, roll out and form the dough, and Traeger Grill the initial side each the master directions on such as charcoal. Use tongs to move into some peel or rimless sheet. Twist the crust to show the Traeger Grill side.
- Distribute the whole surface with all the sauce. Sprinkle with the cheese and top with the olives, shallot r, and pimientos. End Traeger Grill the pizza each the master directions. Eliminate from the Traeger Grill, sprinkle with the lemon zest, and season with pepper and salt.

Grilled Mushroom Pizza

Ingredients

- 2 tablespoons unsalted butter
- 4 tablespoons olive oil, divided
- Pinch of kosher salt; more to taste
- 6 ounces Camembert cheese, rind removed if preferred, cut into ¼-inch-thick strips
- L eaves from 4 sprigs fresh thyme or
- 2 teaspoons dried
- Freshly ground black pepper to taste
- 1 leek, washed well (be fastidious), cut into
- ¼-inch-thick rounds, and separated
- 10 ounces mixed wild mushrooms, such as morels, chanterelles, hen of the woods, lobster, k   oyster, or other exotic varieties
- 3 ounces cognac
- ¼ cup uncooked grits or polenta, for roll   the dough
- 1 ball prepared pizza dough, at room temperature
- ½ cup Roasted Garlic Paste

Instructions

- Preheat a large sauté pan over moderate heat for 1 to 2 weeks. Add the butter and two tbsp of the oil. When the butter bubbles, add a pinch of salt, stir, and then add the leeks. Cook for 2-3 minutes, then add the mushrooms and cook, stir occasionally, until browned on the edges, about 10 minutes. Add the cognac, let sit for 5 minutes, then light a lengthy game to it.
- Stand back and maintain wayward fabric and shaggy hair from the dancing flames. (If you've got a gas cooker, then bear in mind that spatter particles can cause the alcohol to arouse prematurely.) The fire should burn after about 10 minutes. If it continues to burn, then place it out by put a lid on the pan.
- Remove from the heat and book for top. Preheat the Traeger Grill, roll out and form the dough, and Traeger Grill the initial facet of this crust each the master to get charcoal. Use tongs to move it to some peel or rimless sheet. Twist the crust to show the Traeger Grill side. Distribute the whole surface together with all the garlic paste and then together with the mushroom-leek mix. Artfully arrange the cheese on the top.
- End Traeger Grill the pizza each the master directions. Eliminate from the Traeger Grill, sprinkle with the thyme, and season liberally with pepper and salt.

Grilled Veggie Pizza

Ingredients

- 1 small red onion, cut into 4 slices
- 6 tablespoons olive oil, divided

- Kosher salt to taste
- 1 cup Basil or Sun-Dried Tomato Pesto or store-bought
- 20 Fire-Roasted Cherry Tomatoes
- 6 ounces aged goat cheese (chèvre) or Brie, rind removed if preferred, and cut into ¼-inch-thick slices
- your favorite spice blends
- 2 very large portabella mushrooms, stems
- removed and caps cut into ½-inch-thick slices
- 3 Japanese eggplants, cut into ¼-inch-thick slices
- 1 yellow bell pepper, seeded and quartered
- ¼ cup uncooked grits or polenta, for roll the dough
- 1 ball prepared pizza dough, at room temperature
- Freshly ground black pepper to taste

Instructions

- Instructions for gasoline (Drink 4 bamboo skewers in warm water for 10 minutes. Thread each skewer through the middle of one onion piece so that it looks like a lollipop. Brush them with 1 tbsp of the oil and season with salt. Brush the mushroom and eggplant slices and bell pepper on both sides with 3 tbsp of the oil and season with salt. Put the mushrooms, onions, eggplant, and bell pepper onto the cook directly over the heat and Traeger Grill till well-marked and tender, about 4 minutes each side.
- Reserve on your top. Roll out and form the dough, then Traeger Grill the initial facet of this crust each the master directions. Use tongs to move it in the Traeger Grill into some peel or rimless straight sheet. Twist the crust to show the Traeger Grill side.
- Distribute the surface together with the pesto and Gently arrange the Traeger Grill ed berries and veggies on the top. End Traeger Grill the pizza each the master directions. Eliminate from the Traeger Grill and year using the spice mix, salt, and pepper.

Asparagus with Pizza
Ingredients

- 8 spears asparagus, woody bottoms removed
- 3 tablespoons olive oil, divided
- Kosher salt to taste
- 2 tablespoons chopped mixed fresh herbs,
- such as basil, mint, or tarragon
- Freshly ground black pepper to taste
- ¼ cup uncooked grits or polenta, for roll the dough
- 1 ball prepared pizza dough, at room temperature
- ¼ cup Sun-Dried Tomato Pesto or store-bought
- 1 orange bell pepper, seeded and cut
- 12 yellow cherry tomatoes, cut in half
- 12 cured black olives, pitted
- 12 cloves garlic,
- 8 ounces Brie, rind removed if preferred, and sliced

Instructions

- Brush The spoonful with 1 tbsp of the oil and season with salt, then put it to the cook directly over the heat and Traeger Grill, flip sometimes, until it starts to brown, about 5 minutes. Let cool and book for

top. Roll out and form the dough, then Traeger Grill the initial facet of this crust each the master directions.
- Use tongs to move it in the Traeger Grill into some peel or rimless straight sheet. Twist the crust to show the Traeger Grill side. Distribute the whole surface with the pesto. Top with pepper r, tomatoes, olives, garlic, and asparagus. Artfully set the cheese on top. End Traeger Grill the pizza each the master directions. Eliminate from the Traeger Grill, sprinkle with the herbs, and season with pepper and salt.

Lobster & Corn Pizza
Ingredients

- ¼ cup (½ stick) unsalted butter
- 1 cup Tuscan Red Sauce or
- Crushed Tomato Sauce
- 2 tablespoons crème fraiche or sour cream
- ¼ cup uncooked grits or polenta, for roll   the dough
- 1 ball prepared pizza dough, at room
- 2 ears corn, husked
- 4 fresh chives, thinly sliced
- Freshly ground black pepper to taste
- 3 tablespoons olive oil, divided
- Kosher salt to taste temperature
- 4 ounces St. André cheese (a triple crème cheese)
- 1 cup cooked lobster meat

Instructions

- rush the corn with 1 tbsp of the oil and season with salt, then put on the cook directly over the heat and Traeger Grill, flip sometimes, until it starts to brown, about 5 minutes. Let cool. Reserve for best. Just prior to make the pizza, in a small saucepan over moderate heat (or about the Traeger Grill), melt the butter. Reduce the heat to set it off into the side of this Traeger Grill. In a medium bowl combine the tomato sauce and crème fraiche. Roll out and form the dough, then Traeger Grill the initial facet of this crust each the master directions. Use tongs to move it in the Traeger Grill into some peel or rimless straight sheet. Twist the crust to show the Traeger Grill side.
- Distribute the whole surface with all the sauce. Top with all the cheese and corn. End Traeger Grill the pizza each the master directions. While the pizza completes cook, then add the lobster meat into the butter. Cover and warm for 3 minutes, then remove from heat. After the pizza is hot off the Traeger Grill, organize the freshwater on top. Sprinkle with the chives and season with pepper and salt.

Bacon Casino Pizza
Ingredients

- ½ cup ricotta cheese
- 2 tablespoons olive oil
- 2 tablespoons freshly grated Parmigiano-
- Reggiano cheese
- ½ cup bourse or other soft garlic cheese
- (one 5.2-ounce round)
- 2 slices stale white bread, grated, or
- 1/3 cup plain breadcrumbs

- ¼ cup uncooked grits or polenta, for roll
- 5 strips bacon, chopped
- ¼ cup (½ stick) unsalted butter
- 5 cloves garlic, minced
- ⅓ cup white wine
- 18 fresh clams in the shell the dough
- 1 ball prepared pizza dough, at room temperature
- 2 tablespoons grated pecorino cheese
- Kosher salt and freshly ground black pepper to taste

Instructions

- Preheat a heavy sauté pan over moderate heat for 1 to 2 weeks. Add the bacon and costarred, until the fat starts to leave. Add the garlic and butter; cook only until the butter is melted and bubbly. Eliminate 1 tablespoon of the garlic butter into a bowl. Add the wine into the pan, stir, and simmer for two minutes.
- Remove from heat. Fill a large pot with 3 inches of bra and water into a boil. Just prior to make the pizza, put in the clams and cover. Remove from the heat and take the clams from their cubes. In a medium bowl, use a fork to combine together the ricotta and bourse. Reserve for best. Mix the grated bread to the reserved garlic butter. Put the bread crumbs on a cookie sheet and toast in a preheated 300°F oven for 10 minutes. Preheat the Traeger Grill, roll out and form the dough, and Traeger Grill the initial facet of this crust each the master to get charcoal.
- Transfer into a peel or rimless sheet. Twist the crust to show the Traeger Grill side. Distribute the whole surface with ricotta sauce. Arrange the clams at the top and sprinkle with the bacon mix. End Traeger Grill the pizza each the master directions. Eliminate from the Traeger Grill, sprinkle with the breadcrumbs, and season with pepper and salt.

Black Pepper Salmon Pizza
Ingredients

- 1 small shallot, minced
- 4 slices smoked salmon (about 4 ounces),
- cut into strips
- Zest of 1 lemon, finely grated with a
- Microplate or a zester
- ¼ cup uncooked grits or polenta, for roll the dough
- 1 ball prepared pizza dough, at room temperature
- 2 tablespoons olive oil
- ½ cup bourse or other soft garlic cheese
- 2 tablespoons chopped fresh dill or chives
- Freshly ground black pepper to taste

Instructions

- Form the dough, and Traeger Grill the initial facet of this crust each the master directions on such as charcoal. Flip the crust and Traeger Grill till the next side is nicely browned, 2-3 minutes. (Since you are not melting cheese or hot any high s, you do not have to change to indirect heating for a gasoline Traeger Grill.)
- Eliminate from the Traeger Grill and instantly spread the whole surface with all the bourse. Sprinkle with the shallot and shirt with all the strips of salmon. Finish with all the zest, dill, and pepper.

American Style Puttanesca Pizza

Ingredients

- 2 cloves garlic, minced
- ½ cup Niçoise olives, drained and pitted
- 6 anchovy fillets
- B &E Drizzle-vicious Infused Oiler
- your favorite flavored oil
- 1 tablespoon capers, drained and patted dry
- ¼ cup grated pecorino Romano cheese
- 1 cup grated Asiago cheese
- ¼ cup uncooked grits or polenta, for roll   the dough
- 1 ball prepared pizza dough, at room temperature
- 2 tablespoons olive oil
- 1 cup Five-Minute Amatrice-Style Sauce

Instructions

- Form the dough, and Traeger Grill the initial facet of this crust each the master directions for charcoal. Use tongs to move into some peel or rimless sheet. Twist the crust to show the Traeger Grill side.
- Distribute the whole surface with all the sauce. Sprinkle with the garlic, olives, and capers, then together with the cheeses. Artfully put the anchovies on top. End Traeger Grill the pizza each the master directions. Eliminate from the Traeger Grill and garnish with all the infused oil to flavor.

Double Treat Corn Pizza

Ingredients

- 2 ears corn, husks removed
- 12 asparagus spears, woody bottoms
- cut into ¼-inch-thick strips, then cut into
- 1-inch squares
- ¼ teaspoon red pepper flakes, to taste
- 4 tablespoons olive oil, divided
- Kosher salt to taste
- 1 cup Basil Pesto or store-bought
- 12 oil-packed sun-dried tomatoes, cut into
- 4 strips each
- 6 ounces Brie, rind removed if preferred,
- Freshly ground black pepper to taste

Instructions

- Instructions for gasoline. Brush the corn and simmer with two tbsp of the oil and season with salt, then set them onto the cook grate directly over the heat and Traeger Grill, flip occasionally, till they start to brown, about 5 minutes. Let cool.
- To eliminate the kernels, stand the corn vertical. Grip the cover of the cob and slip your sharpest knife down between the cob and kernels. Cut the asparagus tips off, then cut on the stay stalks into 1⁄4-inch bits. Reserve both for best. Roll out and form the dough, then Traeger Grill the initial facet of this crust each the master directions. Use tongs to move it in the Traeger Grill into some peel or rimless straight sheet. Twist the crust to show the Traeger Grill side. Distribute the whole surface with the pesto. Sprinkle with all the corn, asparagus, and tomatoes. End Traeger Grill the pizza each the master

directions. Eliminate from the Traeger Grill, scatter with the red pepper, and season with salt and black pepper.

Grilled Crabmeat Pizza
Ingredients

- 1 cup Artichoke Spread or store-bought
- 1 cup crabmeat, picked over for shells and cartilage
- 12 Fire-Roasted Cherry Tomatoes
- ¼ cup freshly grated pecorino Romano cheese
- Leaves from 2 sprigs fresh tarragon
- ¼ cup uncooked grits or polenta, for roll the dough
- 1 ball prepared pizza dough, at room temperature
- 2 tablespoons olive oil
- Kosher salt and freshly ground black pepper to taste

Instructions

- Form the dough, and Traeger Grill the initial facet of this crust each the master directions for charcoal. Use tongs to move into some peel or rimless sheet. Twist the crust to show the Traeger Grill side. Distribute the whole surface with all the artichoke spread.
- Top with the crabmeat and tomatoes and scatter the cheese. End Traeger Grill the pizza each the master directions. Eliminate from the Traeger Grill, scatter with the tarragon, and season with pepper and salt.

Traeger Grilled Pineapple and Onion Pizza
Ingredients

- 3 tablespoons olive oil, divided
- Kosher salt to taste; more to taste
- ¼ cup uncooked grits or polenta, for roll the dough
- 1 ball prepared pizza dough, at room temperature
- ½ cup Onion Marmalade
- 6 ounces Camembert cheese, sliced
- 4 ounces pancetta, sliced ¼ inch thick, or slab bacon, diced
- 1 ripe, fresh pineapple, peeled, cored, and cut into ½-inch-thick r s
- 1 tablespoon nut oil or vegetable oil
- 2 tablespoons sugar
- 6 scallions, root ends trimmed
- 2 tablespoons flaked sweetened coconut, toasted
- Red pepper flakes to taste

Instructions

- Cook the pancetta or bacon in a little Skillet medium-high heat until crispy, and drain on a paper towel. Reserve for best. Preheat the Traeger Grill per the master directions. Brush the lemon r s using all the nut oil, then sprinkle both sides with all the sugar and let sit 5 minutes. Brush the scallions using some of the olive oil and then sprinkle with salt. Set the lemon and scallions onto the cook grate directly over the heat and Traeger Grill until the lemon is nicely researched along with the scallions are limp and simmer in spots, 3 to 5 minutes each side. Eliminate from the Traeger Grill. Reserve for best.

- Roll out and form the dough, then Traeger Grill the initial facet of this crust each the master directions. Use tongs to move it in the Traeger Grill into some peel or rimless straight sheet. Twist the crust to show the Traeger Grill side. Distribute the whole surface with all the marmalade. End Traeger Grill the pizza each the master directions. Eliminate from the Traeger Grill, sprinkle with the toasted coconut, and season with salt and red pepper.

Shrimp Pizza with Tabasco sauce
Ingredients

- 1-pound colossal shrimp, thawed if necessary, shelled, and deveined
- 1 cup pepper vodka, or 1 cup vodka plus
- 1 cup Five-Minute Amatrice-Style Sauce or other cooked tomato sauce
- 10 black olives, such as Niçoise or Kalamata, pitted
- Zest of 1 lemon, finely grated with a
- Microplate or a zester
- Freshly ground black pepper to taste
- 1 teaspoon Tabasco sauce
- 4 cloves garlic, minced
- 6 tablespoons olive oil, divided
- Kosher salt to taste
- ¼ cup uncooked grits or polenta, for roll the dough
- 1 ball prepared pizza dough, at room temperature

Instructions

- Pat the fish dry. Combine the vodka, Garlic, along with 4 tbsp of the oil in a large nonreactive glass or metal bowl. Add the fish, cover with plastic wrap, and let marinate in the Refrigerator for half an hour. Preheat the Traeger Grill per the master Instructions for gasoline. Remove the fish from the marinade and season with salt. Put Them on the cook directly on the heat and Traeger Grill Until no more translucent, 2-3 minutes each side. Reserve for best. Roll out and form the dough, then Traeger Grill the initial facet of this crust each the Master directions. Use tongs to move it in the Traeger Grill into a peel or rimless sheet.
- Flip the crust to show the Traeger Grill side. Distribute the whole surface with all the sauce. Artfully arrange the Mozzarella pieces, then the beans and olives on top. Finish Traeger Grill that the Pizza each the master directions. Eliminate from the Traeger Grill, scatter with the lemon zest, and season with pepper and salt. Slice and serve immediately.